US Carrier War

US Carrier
War

Kev Darling

Pen & Sword
AVIATION

First published in Great Britain in 2011 by
Pen & Sword Aviation
an imprint of
Pen & Sword Books Ltd
47 Church Street
Barnsley
South Yorkshire
S70 2AS

ISBN 978 1 84884 185 7

A CIP catalogue record for this book is
available from the British Library

Typeset in Palatino by
Phoenix Typesetting, Auldgirth, Dumfriesshire

Printed and bound by
CPI Group (UK) Ltd, Croydon, CR0 4YY

Pen & Sword Books Ltd incorporates the Imprints of
Pen & Sword Aviation, Pen & Sword Family History, Pen & Sword Maritime,
Pen & Sword Military, Pen & Sword Discovery, Wharncliffe Local History,
Wharncliffe True Crime, Wharncliffe Transport, Pen & Sword Select,
Pen & Sword Military Classics, Leo Cooper, The Praetorian Press,
Remember When, Seaforth Publishing and Frontline Publishing.

For a complete list of Pen & Sword titles please contact
PEN & SWORD BOOKS LIMITED
47 Church Street, Barnsley, South Yorkshire, S70 2AS, England
E-mail: enquiries@pen-and-sword.co.uk
Website: www.pen-and-sword.co.uk

Contents

Preface

W hen you look at the progress of US Navy aircraft carrier design
over the past eighty years, the development is nothing short of
amazing. Allied to the development of the vessels themselves are
the aircraft that flew from them. The first US Navy carrier was a converted
collier that would become the USS *Langley*, featuring a flight deck of 524 feet.
Within five years the next carriers were beginning to show a consistent trait:
that of larger hulls and flight decks that were capable of operating a reasonable number of aircraft. After the Lexingtons, built on the hulls of cancelled
battlecruisers, came the Yorktowns, of a similar size but built as carriers from
the outset. By 1941 the service achieved consistency in carrier design when the
Essex class was commissioned. Eventually a total of twenty-four ships would
enter the Navy List and would serve through the Pacific campaign, the
Korean war and on to the Vietnam war.

While the Essex class as built had a flight deck of 860 feet, it would come
as no surprise to find that the Midways were even longer, at 932 feet, in order
to cater for any increase in aircraft size and capability. Just after the end of the
Second World War, the plan to build carriers of an even greater size were
derailed slightly when the USAF opposed their construction. These vessels
would have been the United States class, and their cancellation caused a rift
between the Navy and Air Force. The latter was determined to be the service
to carry the nation's nuclear weapons, and it managed to gain the funding for
the Convair B-36s to carry them, even though the Navy managed to prove
eventually that the carrier was a more flexible and viable platform.

Although the United States class had been cancelled, the design work that
had gone into it would have a profound effect on the ships that followed. The
first to benefit would be the Forrestal class, whose flight deck had grown to
over 1,000 feet. The extra length plus an angled deck and deck extensions
meant that this new breed of carrier could operate more than eighty modern
aircraft. It would be the launch of the USS *Enterprise* in 1960 that would

1

introduce another new and important feature to the carrier fleet – that of nuclear power. From that point on the US Navy would invest in nuclear-powered carriers only, with their conventional cousins going out of service throughout the 1990s. Over the next few years the US Navy will be introducing carriers that border on science fiction in their use of technology.

It should also be remembered that the US Navy would invest in the smaller escort, or jeep, carriers as there was a desperate need for flight decks to support the war in the Pacific. The quickest way to produce such a vessel was to take a standard merchant hull and add aviation capabilities. The resultant ships were gainfully employed in both the Atlantic and the Pacific, although they were quickly disposed of at the end of the Second World War, except for a handful that remained in service as transports.

Matching the progress of carrier development was that of the aircraft that operated from them. Like the rest of the world's navies that operated aircraft carriers, the initial aircraft types operated were biplanes, although the monoplane was just starting to appear. When the United States entered the war after Pearl Harbor, the manufacturers rose to the occasion by providing a range of fighters and attack aircraft that were big, powerful, well armed and capable of delivering and taking great punishment. At the pinnacle of this effort was the Grumman Corporation, which would create most of the carriers' fighters, the line ending with the F-14 Tomcat. The current fighter attack aircraft is the Boeing Super Hornet, although this will soon be joined by the Lockheed Martin F-35C.

Given the history of the US Navy aircraft carriers, it should come as no surprise to find that this book is very much a primer for the history of this service. Even so, it could not have been assembled without the help of my good friend Dennis R. Jenkins, who assisted with the US Navy, the Library of Congress and the National Archive and Records Agency. I would also like to thank Rick Harding, Trevor Jones and John Ryan for their help in tracking down those elusive photographs.

CHAPTER ONE

Origins and Development

On 25 November 1917 the four vessels of Battleship Division Nine, accompanied by the destroyer USS *Manley* as escort, departed from Lynnhaven Roads, Virginia, bound for the anchorage of the Grand Fleet at Scapa Flow in the Orkney Islands. Regarded as an uneventful transit, it was complicated by storms that increased in ferocity as the voyage continued. After battling through the weather, Battleship Division Nine arrived at Scapa Flow on 7 December.

Having survived their introduction to the Atlantic, the four battleships were assigned to the Sixth Battle Squadron of the Grand Fleet. While their role would be one of blockade, one thing did impinge itself thoroughly upon the US Navy officers, was the number of aircraft being carried aboard the ships of the Royal Navy. Not only were the battleships and battlecruisers complete with a range of aircraft, the fleet's cruisers also carried aircraft, and even the destroyers were capable of launching aircraft, although these smaller vessels towed their aircraft for launching on lighters.

The irony is that the US Navy was the pioneer in launching aircraft from naval vessels. The first attempt was courtesy of Samuel P. Langley, whose model of the 'Aerodrome' was undertaking successful flight trials in 1896. Such was their success that the US Government would issue a contract in 1898 for a full-scale version of the 'Aerodrome'. While Langley was building his aerial machine, the US Army and the Navy convened a joint board to study the future of flight in both services. Unfortunately for both, the Langley 'Aerodrome' failed its flight trials from the Potomac river at the end of 1903. It would be another five years before the US Navy took an interest in flying machines again. Two officers would be present when the Wright Model 'A' undertook its flight demonstrations at Fort Myer in September 1908. Other officers would observe flight demonstrations at home and abroad, and all would report enthusiastically upon the benefits to the US Navy of aircraft that could operate from ships. While the views within the US Navy concerning

3

aviation were diverse, an important step was taken on 26 September 1910 when Captain W.I. Chambers was designated as the officer in charge of naval aviation, a position he would hold for the next three years. As for Langley, while his aircraft was a failure, he would be commemorated by the naming of Langley Field in Virginia to celebrate his efforts.

The pioneer of US naval aviation was Eugene Burton Ely. Between 22 and 30 October 1910 Captain Washington I. Chambers, who was responsible for aviation matters at the Navy Department, would travel to Belmont Park, New York, to inspect the participating aircraft and meet pioneer aviators at the International Air Meet. While discussing the prospects for taking aircraft to sea, he was impressed by the technical abilities of Eugene Ely, a test and demonstration pilot working with the aircraft constructor Glenn Curtiss. From New York the captain would visit another air show near Baltimore, Maryland, where again he saw Ely undertaking flight demonstrations. After discussions between the pilot and Captain Chambers concerning the possibility of flying an aircraft from a ship, Ely volunteered for the task.

It took less than two weeks to start the process with financial help from a wealthy aviation enthusiast, John Barry Ryan, official backing from the Assistant Secretary of the Navy, Beekman Winthrop, and the drive of Eugene Ely for Chambers to achieve the event that marked the beginning of flying by the US Navy. At the Norfolk Navy Yard, Virginia, an 83 ft wooden platform was rapidly constructed over the foredeck of the cruiser USS *Birmingham*. Designed by the naval constructor William McEntree and paid for by John Barry Ryan, this structure sloped down five degrees from the cruiser's bridge to the bow to provide a gravity-assisted 57 ft take-off run for the Curtiss pusher aeroplane supplied for the trials.

The aircraft was lifted aboard the cruiser on the morning of 14 November 1910, and after it had been secured to the deck the engine was installed by Ely and the accompanying mechanics as the ship prepared to leave port. Shortly

A most important photograph, the Eugene B. Ely taking off from the cruiser USS Pennsylvania in January 1911. (Library of Congress/ Dennis R. Jenkins)

before noon USS *Birmingham* steamed down the Elizabeth river toward Hampton Roads where the flight was to take place. However, the weather deteriorated rapidly, with squalls rolling by, thus threatening to put a stop to the trials. Unable to carry out the trials, the USS *Birmingham* anchored to await an improvement in conditions. By mid-afternoon, with conditions showing signs of improvement, the vessel began to raise the anchor chain. Eugene Ely was occupied in warming up the aircraft's engine and checking its controls, waiting for the weather to clear. Noticing that visibility was again deteriorating, he concluded that the flight had to be made as soon as possible, even though the ship was still stationary. At 3.16 p.m. the pilot opened the engine throttle to full power, gave the release signal, rolled down the ramp and was airborne. Getting airborne was a bit of a struggle, as the Curtiss briefly touched the water, throwing up enough spray to damage its propeller, which caused heavy vibration through propeller imbalance as it climbed to height. Eugene Ely, a non-swimmer, realised that a quick landing on dry land was a priority, especially as his goggles were covered with spray. Fortunately Ely was able to land on nearby Willoughby Spit after some five minutes in the air. This two-and-a-half-mile flight, the first time an aircraft had taken off from a warship, was seen as something of a stunt, although it would receive wide publicity. After this flight Ely was made a lieutenant in the California National Guard to qualify for a $500 prize offered to the first reservist to make such a flight. On 18 January 1911, in San Francisco Bay, Eugene Ely would again operate from a ship, landing and taking off from the armoured cruiser USS *Pennsylvania*. During the landing the Curtiss pusher touched down on a platform on the *Pennsylvania*, which was anchored in San Francisco Bay, using the first-ever tail hook system to arrest the landing. This innovative item had been designed and built by circus performer and pioneer aviator Hugh Robinson.

Having successfully shown the US Navy that aviation from ships was possible, Ely contacted the US Navy for a job. However, the service was not organised for such a role yet, and he was informed that his application would be kept in mind. Unfortunately this would never happen, as on 19 October 1911 while flying at an exhibition in Macon, Georgia, his aircraft was late pulling out of a dive and crashed. Ely managed to jump clear of the wrecked aircraft, but his neck was broken and he died a few minutes later. In 1933, in recognition of his contribution to naval aviation, he was awarded the Distinguished Flying Cross posthumously by President Franklin D. Roosevelt.

On the day following Ely's landing aboard the *Pennsylvania*, Lieutenant Theodore G. Ellyson began the flight training that would make him the first aviator in the US Navy. Ellyson had been ordered to the Curtiss aviation camp at North Island, San Diego, California, to undergo flight training. He would qualify for his Aero Club of America licence on 6 July 1911, using the Curtiss A-1 Triad, this being the first aircraft purchased by the Navy. He subsequently became Naval Aviator No. 1 on 4 March 1913. The Curtiss A-1

Triad was also utilised in the Navy's first attempt to launch an aircraft using a compressed air catapult developed from a naval torpedo launcher, at Annapolis in 1912. The launching from a purpose-built deck failed due to a crosswind gust that blew the A-1 into the water. Also contributing to the launch failure was the inadequate restraining of the aircraft during engine run-up, so that the A-1 was airborne before the control surfaces became effective. A further attempt on 12 November was successful when a Curtiss A-3 piloted by Ellyson was launched at the Washington Navy Yard. The A-1, as the only naval aircraft at the time, would set numerous records, including flying from Annapolis, Maryland, to Milford Haven, Virginia, in 122 minutes, with Ellyson as pilot and Lieutenant John H. Towers as passenger. The A-1 would also be the first naval aircraft to carry a radio, although this was not very successful. More successful was the setting of a seaplane record of 900 feet on 21 June 1912.

That same year, the US Marine Corps entered the world of aviation, and from that time Marine aviation would develop in parallel with its naval counterpart. To celebrate this, Lieutenant Alfred A. Cunningham USMC reported to the aviation camp at Annapolis for duty in connection with aviation, arriving on 22 May 1912. He undertook his flight training at the Burgess aircraft factory in Marblehead, Massachusetts, being awarded his certificate as Naval Aviator No. 5.

Deployment of a small group of flyers, the entire aviation complement of the Navy, took place during January 1913, to cover fleet manoeuvres at Guantanamo Bay, Cuba. These demonstrated the operational capabilities of the available aircraft and stimulated further interest in aviation within the Navy. The first test of naval aviation at sea revealed some deficiencies in existing aircraft when two aviation detachments took their aircraft to Veracruz in the spring of 1914 to bolster US forces during the Mexican crisis.

The Glenn L. Curtiss Aircraft Company would be the first manufacturer to supply the US Navy with aircraft. This is one of the early hydroplanes. (Library of Congress/ Dennis R. Jenkins)

During one reconnaissance flight Lieutenant P.N.L. Bellinger returned to base with holes from hostile bullets through the skin of his aircraft, this being the first combat damage received by a Navy aircraft.

When the Great War began in Europe in July 1914, naval aviators were sent there as observers to report on aviation developments from bases in London, Paris and Berlin. The importance of aviation in the future of the US Navy was officially recognised in November 1914 with the creation of a Director of Naval Aeronautics. This appointment was followed during 1915 and 1916 by advances in technology, experimentation and new administrative procedures, all of which pointed to an increased role for aviation in the US Navy. During this period of change the first contract was awarded for the provision of a lighter-than-air craft, while the Aeronautical Engine Laboratory was set up at the Washington Navy Yard. This was followed by a Naval Appropriations Act that provided for a Naval Flying Corps that would be reinforced by a Naval Reserve Flying Corps.

During the nineteen-month period that the Naval Flying Corps was involved in the Great War the service saw a rapid expansion in its size. In April 1917 the corps had fifty-four aircraft on strength, manned by forty-eight qualified and student pilots, all at one base. By the end of the war the Navy had twelve air bases in America, plus a further twenty-seven in Europe from which the Naval Flying Corps had attacked twenty-five U-boats, sinking or damaging at least half of them. Operating from these bases were 6,716 officers and 30,693 enlisted men, and attached to them were 282 officers and 2,180 enlisted men from the USMC. This manpower operated 2,107 aircraft and fifteen dirigibles.

As with all services, the Naval Flying Corps underwent serious contraction at the cessation of hostilities, although the Bureau of Aeronautics did pursue the development of emerging technologies with vigour, including both aircraft and their carriers. This was not without its problems, as the US Army was determined to be the only aerial operator in America. However, the Navy managed to outflank the Army as its mission requirements were always different from those of land-based air forces. Eventually a legal termination to the various wrangles was needed, and the MacArthur-Pratt agreement of January 1931 defined the naval air force as an element of the fleet that was designed to move with it and assist it in carrying out its primary task.

To promote the aerial side of the Navy, the Bureau of Aeronautics was formed in August 1921 to assume responsibility for all matters concerning aircraft, personnel and their usage. The BuAer became the aviation department of the Secretary of the Navy's office, and would remain so until 1959. While the USN and the Marine Corps operated a similar range of aircraft, their aircraft needs were dealt with by the Director of Aviation at Headquarters, Marine Corps. During the period of inter-war contraction, the aircraft strength of the Navy fell to 1,000 machines in the 1920s, although it slowly climbed to 2,000 aircraft by 1938. Meanwhile rumblings of discord in Europe were becoming more perceptible, and there were signs of the Japanese thinking about spreading their influence over the whole of the Pacific, all of which was increasing global tension. The American answer to that was the Naval Expansion Act, which authorised the number of usable aircraft to increase to at least 3,000. This had risen to 4,500 by June 1940, although this was quickly added to by increases in the following months, which saw the level reaching 15,000 aircraft.

The third service with an interest in sea-going affairs was the US Coast Guard, this organisation being seen as an extension of the US Navy in periods of war. In more peaceful times, however, the USCG regarded the aircraft as a possible search and rescue tool, and in 1915 three Coast Guard officers based at Hampton Roads, Virginia, developed the concept of air patrols to search for disabled vessels along the Atlantic seaboard. To that end Captain R.M. Chiswell, commander of the Coast Guard cutter *Onondaga*, enlisted the support of two junior officers, Lieutenants Norman B. Hall and Elmer F. Stone, to test this theory. Their experiments with a Curtiss plane were so successful that the two junior officers obtained permission to pursue their interest in flying. Lieutenant Hall was assigned to the Curtiss plant at Hammondsport, New York, where he learned the art of aircraft construction. In contrast Lieutenant Stone was sent to the Naval Training School at Pensacola, Florida, in company with other Coast Guard personnel to undertake flight training. Lieutenant Hall would earn his Gold Navy Wings later, becoming Coast Guard Aviator No. 1.

Having provided the Navy with its first aircraft, the A-1, in 1911, Curtiss would follow this with the A-2, which was delivered to the Navy on 13 July 1911 configured as a land plane. The A-2 would be converted to seaplane configuration in mid-1912 by adding a superstructure to house the crew. In this form the aircraft set an endurance record of six hours and ten minutes on 6 October 1912. A further modification saw the installation of a retractable tricycle undercarriage, which saw the machine redesignated as the E-1. It was also known as the OWL (Over Water and Land), and for a short period the

The Curtiss Company would supply a range of patrol flying-boats to the US Navy during the First World War. This is an H5L, some of which were supplied to Britain. (US Navy/NARA via Dennis R. Jenkins)

Having supplied flying-boats to the Navy, Curtiss would then supply the ubiquitous JN-4, or Jenny, to the American services. (US Navy/NARA via Dennis R. Jenkins)

AX-1. Following the A-1 and the A-2 came the A-3 and the A-4, both being Curtiss pushers. The former would achieve a small degree of fame when, on 13 June 1913, it established an American altitude record of 6,200 feet. Soon after the A-3 and A-4 were delivered, the Navy changed the designation of its aircraft to reflect their usage, and so the Curtiss aircraft joined the AH series (Airplane Hydro), which reflected their role. Curtiss would continue to deliver further aircraft in this series, and the AH-8 to AH-13 models were delivered to the US Navy in varying quantities.

Curtiss would continue to deliver flying-boats to the Navy, each model being more reliable and substantial than the last. The first was the Model F, which featured a proper fuselage with a planing hull, although it still retained its pusher engine. The company would deliver some of its tractor-engined aircraft to the Navy, all being from the JN series of biplanes. Better known as the Jenny, the JN series gave the US Navy its first taste of a series aircraft built to a fixed design, and this aircraft remained in service from 1916 to 1922. Curtiss continued to build flying-boats for the US Navy, and it was close to the war's end in March 1918 that the service ordered its first wheeled fighter – the 18-T. Only two of these two-seat triplanes were ordered, but what they brought to the table was an advance in airframe construction to which was matched an engine specifically designed for its airframe. The 18-T managed

9

The Curtiss SBU Helldiver was designed as a dive-bomber for the Navy. This aircraft was on the strength of VS-3 aboard the USS Ranger when photographed. (US Navy/NARA via Dennis R. Jenkins)

to establish a world record of 163 mph on 19 August 1918, this being followed by the setting of an altitude record of 30,100 feet on 25 July 1919, which was increased to 34,610 feet on 19 November.

Curtiss would continue to develop and deliver various biplane fighters and racing-type aircraft to the Navy for development purposes, and they were therefore well placed to manufacture the F6C Hawk series of aircraft when the contract was placed. The first batch consisted of nine airframes, of which seven were delivered without arrester gear, while the final pair, designated F6C2, were fitted with arrester hooks and strengthened undercarriage for trial operations by VF-2 from the USS *Langley*. Having got off to a good start with the F6C Hawk, Curtiss had high hopes for the F11C Goshawk series, of which twenty-eight were delivered. Unlike its earlier fighters, Curtiss added a fighter-bomber capability to this design, all loads being carried on an under-fuselage station. Deliveries of this new type began in February 1933 to VF-1B for operations from the carrier USS *Saratoga*, while a further batch of twenty-seven were delivered under the new designation of BF2C-1 to VB-5 for service aboard the USS *Ranger*. The use of this type by the US Navy was short lived, as the type suffered from insurmountable undercarriage problems. These aircraft were destined to be the last fighters delivered by Curtiss to the US Navy.

The company would reap greater benefits from its fighter-bomber types, the first being the F8C-4 Helldiver, twenty-five of which were delivered to VF-1B aboard the USS *Saratoga* during 1931. A further sixty-three were delivered as O2C-1, although they primarily served with the USMC. Curtiss would have a second bite at the Helldiver cherry with the SBC Helldiver. Originally intended as a monoplane, this would be the last combat biplane produced for the US Navy. The contract for the final version was issued in August 1936 and covered the delivery of eighty-three production machines. The first deliveries were made in July 1937, the recipient being VS-5. The initial batch was followed by 174 further machines, of which fifty were diverted to France. Deliveries of this modified version began in March 1939, although by this time the type was obsolescent. When the Japanese attacked Pearl Harbor in December 1941 the US Navy had 186 Helldiver biplanes in service, mainly with VB-8 and VS-8 aboard the carrier USS *Hornet* and with the USMC, although most had already been passed to second-line units.

Competing with Curtiss would be the Lewis and Vought Corporation, later the Chance Vought Corporation, who produced a range of successful aircraft that served with the US Navy throughout the Great War. The corporation's first step towards producing carrier-compatible aircraft was the Vought O2U Corsair that was delivered to the Navy for use in the observation role. Designed as a two-seat aircraft, the Corsair featured a fuselage built round a steel-tube framework and the first examples of the Pratt & Whitney Wasp as its powerplant. The Navy began to accept the first of its 130 production machines in 1927, by which time it had been named the Corsair. So that the maximum use could be gained from the type it was capable of being fitted with floats, this allowing it to operate from battleships and large cruisers. The carrier complement was allocated to VS-1B aboard the USS *Langley*. After three years in front-line service these Corsairs were superseded by the improved O3U versions that served aboard the carriers USS *Saratoga* and *Lexington*, the operating units being VS-14M and VS-15M respectively – the only two USMC units to serve aboard aircraft carriers prior to the Second World War.

Boeing would be the third major manufacturer to enter the US Navy aircraft market, a sharp contrast to later years when the corporation would be

The Vought O2U-1 Corsair would be supplied to the Navy for observation purposes. (US Navy/NARA via Dennis R. Jenkins)

The Boeing Stearman NS-1 replaced the Curtiss Jenny as the Navy's primary trainer, a role that it undertook for the USAAC as well. (US Navy/NARA via Dennis R. Jenkins)

The Boeing FB2-1 was one of a range of biplane fighters supplied to the Navy in the inter-war period. (US Navy/NARA via Dennis R. Jenkins)

The XF-11C Goshawk was one of a series of Hawk fighters built by Curtiss for the US Navy. (US Navy/NARA via Dennis R. Jenkins)

better known for its strategic bombers and long-range airliners. Boeing's initial contribution to the ranks of the Navy was the 'C' series, although these were not very successful due to the poor performance of the Hall-Scott engine, and many were disposed of after the war, still in their original packing crates. While the C series was not successful, the FB fighter was a far greater success. This was a biplane fighter that was ordered by the Navy in 1925, the initial contract calling for sixteen machines. While these were not equipped for carrier use, a pair of FB-2s, complete with strengthened fuselage and under-carriage, were ordered for trials purposes. These were followed by a production order of twenty-seven aircraft designated the FB-5. After initial company flight testing the aircraft were loaded aboard barges at Seattle and transferred by water to the carrier USS *Langley*, where they equipped VF-1B and VF-6B, while VF-3B would fly the type from the USS *Saratoga*. These initial aircraft were followed by the F2B and F3B, these being ordered in March 1927. Deliveries of the F2B-1 began in January 1928, the first recipients being VF-1B and VB-2B, both based aboard the USS *Saratoga*. Even as the F2Bs were being delivered to the Navy, the F3B was already in production, with deliveries beginning in 1928. A total of seventy-four were ordered, the first examples being accepted by VF-2B aboard the *Langley*, while VF-2B would accept its aircraft aboard the *Saratoga*. It would be the *Lexington* that would receive the greater share, as both VF-3B and VB-1B would equip. Both of these

The Grumman F3F-2 was delivered to both the US Navy and the USMC
between 1937 and 1938, although its period in service was short as
technology overtook it. (US Navy/NARA via Dennis R. Jenkins)

aircraft had been passed to second-line units by 1932, where they were used
in the communications role.

Following on from the F2B and F3B series of aircraft came the famous F4B
fighter, which became the primary Navy biplane fighter prior to 1939. Initially
twenty-seven production aircraft were ordered, to which were added the two
prototypes after their conversion to production standard. Deliveries of these
aircraft, which featured separate undercarriage legs and a P&W Wasp engine,
were undertaken between June and August 1939, the first units to equip being
VB-1B and VF-2B aboard the *Lexington* and *Langley* respectively. The initial
model was followed by the F4B-2, this version featuring a ring cowling, Frise
ailerons, a tailwheel and a spreader-bar axle between the main wheels.
Deliveries were undertaken between January and May 1931, the first batch
consisting of forty-six machines. Initial deliveries were made to VF-6B aboard
the *Saratoga*, being followed by VF-5B aboard the *Lexington*. The appearance
of the dash 3, of which twenty-one were ordered in April 1923, saw the introduction of the semi-monocoque fuselage and other improvements. Deliveries
were undertaken between December 1931 and January 1932, the receiving
unit being VF-1B aboard the USS *Saratoga*. This small batch was followed by
a larger order for ninety-four aircraft designated the F4B-4, which had larger
fins and rudders. Deliveries began in July 1932 and were completed by
February 1933. F4B-4s were first delivered to VF-3B aboard the *Langley*,

The Grumman SF-1 was the first of these famous barrel-shaped fighters delivered to the US Navy. It was intended that the thirty-three production machines would act as command aircraft for the similar F1F-1 fighters. (US Navy/NARA via Dennis R. Jenkins)

followed by VF-6B on the *Saratoga*, while some were delivered to the USMC. The Boeing fighters remained in service aboard the carriers until 1937, when the first deliveries of Grumman's faster and more portly fighters entered service. The replacement of the Boeings was completed by 1938, after which they were relegated to secondary duties, including some as drones. The final examples were withdrawn in 1941, having lain unused at various naval shore bases for several years. These would be the final fighters that Boeing would build, as they would soon turn to other aviation avenues.

One of the biggest hitters for the US Navy was the Grumman Aircraft Engineering Corporation, which would win its first contract to build naval aircraft on 2 April 1931, thus beginning a relationship that would last for more than forty years. Its first offering would be the FF-1, or Fifi, which boasted a retractable undercarriage and full-length canopy that covered both cockpits. First deliveries were made to VF-5B, which was operating from the USS *Lexington*. The FF-1 was also delivered in another version, the SF-1, which also operated from the *Lexington* from March 1934 with VS-3B. The next in line from Grumman continued the dumpy fuselage that would feature for quite a period in the company's products, these being the F2F and F3F models. These

The Martin BM-1 dive-bomber served with the US Navy during the 1930s before it and other similar types were replaced by the more modern Douglas Dauntless. (US Navy/NARA via Dennis R. Jenkins)

were intended to be single-seat fighters, and so the new aircraft's dimensions were reduced accordingly. In common with the FF-1 the new fighters featured a retractable undercarriage, metal skin covering on the fuselage and a canopy for the pilot. A total of fifty-four F2F-1s were ordered by the Navy, with deliveries beginning in 1935. The F2F-1s were delivered to VF-3B aboard the *Lexington*, while VF-3B aboard the USS *Ranger* would receive the remainder. VF-5B would retain its 'flying barrels' until 1940, while VF-3B would later become VF-7B aboard the *Lexington*, this being followed by a move to the USS *Wasp*, where the unit was redesignated VF-5.

Grumman would offer the Navy an updated version of the F2F, which as the F3F featured a longer fuselage and a slightly increased wingspan. Fifty-four aircraft were ordered, with deliveries being undertaken during 1936. These machines equipped VF-5B aboard the *Ranger* and VF-6B aboard the USS *Saratoga*, these units later being redesignated VF-4 and VF-3 respectively in 1939, both units retaining the F3F until 1940. One final model of this aircraft was produced, which was the F3F-2. The major change between this and the original version was the installation of the bigger Wright R-1820-22 engine, which, although larger, improved the aircraft's performance. Eventually eighty-one were ordered by the Navy in March 1937, and they were delivered to VF-6 aboard the USS *Enterprise* and the USS *Yorktown* with VF-5. The remainder of this batch were delivered to the USMC serving with VMF-1 and VMF-2, but by the end of 1941 all of these units had dispensed with their Grumman biplane fighters, although some did remain in use later as station hacks.

One of the lesser suppliers of aircraft to the US Navy was the Glenn L. Martin Company, which was better known for providing aircraft for the US Army Air Corps. Having gained experience building the SC-1 torpedo scouts for the Navy, the company was able to offer an improved version when requested by the Bureau of Aeronautics. The contract for this aircraft, designated the T3M-1, was placed in October 1925. In a similar manner to its contemporaries the T3M-1 could operate on wheels or floats as required. Only twenty-four aircraft were ordered, these being followed by the T3M-2, which was fitted with a more powerful engine. In response the Navy ordered a hundred of this type for service with VT-1S aboard the *Lexington* and VT-2B aboard the carrier *Langley*. Martin would take a T3M-2 and fit it with a P&W Hornet as the XT3M-1, which improved the type's performance. This aircraft was passed on to the Naval Aircraft Factory for the installation of a Wright Cyclone, which also showed an improvement in performance. As a result of these experiments the Navy ordered 102 aircraft as the T4M-1, the contract being placed in June 1927. Although these aircraft could operate using both floats and wheels, it was the latter that came to prominence as the aircraft carrier became more important. Deliveries were made to VT-2B aboard the *Saratoga* in 1928, these being followed later by VT-1B aboard the *Lexington*. The T4M-1s were to remain in use until 1937, although they had left front-line service five years earlier.

Following on from the T-series aircraft, Martin developed a dive-bomber, designated the BM. A contract for a single prototype was issued to Martin as the XT5M-1, while another was issued to the Naval Aircraft Factory to construct a competitor designated the XT2N-1. Both were designed as two-seat torpedo-bombers, both being metal-framed biplanes with fabric-covered wings. The XT5M-1 passed its trials with aplomb, and so a contract was issued for twelve aircraft in April 1931. The production machines were designated BM-1, with deliveries beginning in September 1931. The first unit to accept the type was VT-1S, Navy Torpedo Squadron One, serving aboard the USS *Lexington*. A slightly modified version was known as the BM-2, deliveries of which began in October 1931, with a further four BM-1s being ordered soon afterwards. VT-1S would be the recipient, although this unit was redesignated as VB-1B, Bombing Squadron One. A second unit, VB-3B, was formed in 1934 to operate a mix of both types aboard the USS *Langley*. Both units would dispense with their Martin machines in 1937, although some would remain in use for test and utility duties until 1940, when the final one was scrapped.

Unlike most other services, the US Navy would have its own manufacturing facility, known as the Naval Aircraft Factory. Normally employed in manufacturing designs from other manufacturers, the NAF also managed to

Pictured at anchor in Pearl Harbor is the USS Langley, which had been converted from the fleet collier Jupiter. (US Navy/NARA via Dennis R. Jenkins)

design and manufacture aircraft for the Navy. Its first effort was the Model TS, designed by the Bureau of Aeronautics, which would issue a contract for thirty-four machines to Curtiss Aircraft. A further order for five aircraft was awarded to the NAF to act as a manufacturing and cost check. The first machine was rolled out in May 1922, just after the commissioning of the USS *Langley*. In common with other aircraft of the period, the TS-1 was capable of operating with a land undercarriage or floats as required. The first Curtiss TS-1 was delivered to the *Langley* in December 1922, equipping VF-1. The NAF machines were modified after construction for trials and evaluation purposes, being mainly involved in engine development. Curtiss would deliver two more TS-1s, although these were of metal construction. These were designated F4C-1 in the new naval nomenclature after delivery. This would be the last design built under the aegis of the Bu.Aer and the NAF, as the latter would henceforth build aircraft designed by other manufacturers.

Although a minor player in naval affairs, the Northrop Corporation would deliver one significant aircraft to that service. Headed by John K. Northrop, designer of the Lockheed Vega, the Northrop Corporation was founded in 1929, where he could continue developing designs for an all-metal aircraft. The only design delivered to the US Navy was the XBT-1, which featured a semi-retractable undercarriage and split trailing-edge flaps. Accepted by the Navy, fifty-four production machines were ordered as the BT-1, with deliveries beginning to VB-5 in April 1938. One airframe underwent rebuilding to create the XBT-2. This was a seemingly insignificant designation. However, by this time the Northrop Corporation had become the El Segundo division of Douglas Aircraft, and so the XBT-2 would finally appear as a Douglas product better known as the SBD Dauntless.

18

When the USS Langley had been superseded by larger aircraft carriers, the forward part of the flight deck was removed, while the remainder was used to support flying-boats and space for aircraft transport. (US Navy/NARA via Dennis R. Jenkins)

While the US Navy concentrated upon developing aircraft for the service, it was very cautious about developing aircraft carriers, even though it had observed the Royal Navy vessels in Scapa Flow during the Great War. The seeds of the first Navy carrier were sown by Congress in July 1919 when funding was approved to convert the naval collier *Jupiter* into a vessel that could carry, launch and recover aircraft while at sea. The decision to use an existing vessel meant that the creation of the first naval carrier could be expedited at a greater speed, thus allowing the service to catch up with the Royal Navy. The decision to use the *Jupiter* was that it had the cubic capacity to house aircraft below deck and that there was sufficient room to house the required stores, including fuel. The *Jupiter* also featured boiler uptakes that vented to both port and starboard, instead of centrally, as in most other vessels. Also pushing forward the conversion was the introduction of oil-fired boilers into the ships of the fleet, and so the life of the colliers was limited. The *Jupiter* was seven years old when it was taken in hand at the Norfolk Navy Yard in March 1920. Four of the vessel's six holds were adapted to hold thirty-four complete aircraft, or fifty-five if they were dismantled. One of the unused holds was modified as a lift well, while the remaining one was utilised as the fuel store. Much of the rear superstructure was removed and replaced by a steel framework that acted as the support for the wood-planked flight deck, which ran almost the full length of the ship. To navigate the ship the forward bridge was retained, while to handle the aircraft a pair of 35 ft gooseneck cranes were installed, one each being fitted port and starboard. These served the lift and also allowed the aircraft to lift any assigned float-planes in and out of the water.

The revamped *Jupiter* was reclassified as AV-1 and renamed USS *Langley*, being recommissioned in March 1922. The standard complement of aircraft assigned to this first carrier consisted of twelve pursuit fighter aircraft, twelve scouts and ten torpedo-bombers, of which six would be mounted on floats. The given complement actually varied during the five-year period when the *Langley* was the only fleet carrier, as it was utilised for numerous trials during this time. Launching and recovery of aircraft required two 60 ft catapults to launch float-planes using trolleys. Recovery of aircraft used either the longitudinal wire system, an idea borrowed from the Royal Navy, or transverse wires that were basic in the extreme, as they used weights on the end of the cables to slow the aircraft down. During its time as a carrier the *Langley* underwent some modifications that saw the longitudinal wires deleted and the original transverse wires replaced with more modern equipment. The *Langley* would remain basically unaltered until 1937, when the larger, more modern carriers were established in the fleet, and it was decided to convert the vessel into a seaplane tender. To that end 250 feet of the forward deck was removed to cater for the larger seaplanes then entering service. The ship's life in this new guise was brief, as on 27 February 1942 it was attacked by Japanese bombers when it was ferrying Curtis P-40s to Java. Hit by five bombs, the *Langley* began to list rapidly, and so after the crew were removed the ship was sunk by gunfire by the escorting destroyer USS *Whipple*.

The next round of aircraft carriers owe their existence to two sets of circumstances: the first was the accelerated Dreadnought building programme started near the end of the First World War, while the second was the Washington Naval Disarmament Treaty of 1922. The second would also help lay the seeds of the Second World War, even though the treaty was delivered in good faith, as all of the nations that had fought in the Great War were suffering financial hardship, and plans were made to restrict the number and size of capital ships. While this would pose no real problems to America and Great Britain, it was other nations, especially Japan, which saw this as an attempt to restrict their naval development. From the point of the US Navy it meant that the six 43,000 ton battlecruisers already on the stocks could be better used as aircraft carriers, although in the event only two of the hulls were advanced enough for consideration, the rest being scrapped on the stocks. Helping the US Navy was Stanley Goodall, on secondment from the Royal Navy Directorate of Naval Constructors to the Bureau of Construction and Repair in the United States. The irony is, of course, that a few years earlier the US Navy still regarded the Royal Navy as a definite rival and a possible enemy. Designated the Lexington class, the vessels' hulls remained virtually unaltered when orders were given to convert them for carrier use. The *Saratoga* was slated for conversion in October 1922, while the *Lexington*'s orders came through in November. Above the hull's main deck a 450 ft long main hangar, 70 ft wide and 21 ft high, was installed. Aft of the hangar was a 105 ft maintenance area, while underneath both was a 120 ft long storage area that was large enough to house dismantled aircraft, as well as spares. This meant that eighty aircraft could be carried, a capacity that would prove invaluable in the Second World War.

Unlike later carriers, the Lexington class had full armour plating up to

The Saratoga would serve the Navy well, not leaving service until after the war. In 1946 the carrier performed one more service for its country as a target for the Bikini atom bomb tests. (US Navy/NARA via Dennis R. Jenkins)

flight-deck level, pierced for boat stowage, while the bridge superstructure was connected to the large funnel structure via a lightly built walkway. The flight deck itself was teak planked and was pierced by two lifts, the larger of the two, at 30 x 60 ft, was located close to the bridge, while the smaller, at 30 x 36 ft, was located opposite the funnel. To assist in launching heavily loaded aircraft, a 155 ft long catapult was mounted at the bow of the deck. The armament, as allowed by the Washington Treaty, consisted of eight 8-inch guns, whose purpose was to fight off attacking vessels up to cruiser size and motor torpedo boats. The turret-mounted weapons were all concentrated fore and aft of the island, funnel and structures and were of limited value. Further armament consisted of 5-inch guns that were disposed to both port and starboard and could be used against both aircraft and torpedo boats. Initially the Lexington-class vessels were unaltered, although by 1936 some modification had been undertaken, the first being the fitting of sixteen 0.5-inch machineguns that were mounted in sponsons below flight-deck level. Further machine-guns were disposed onto the turret roofs and a platform fitted to the funnel. As technology advanced, the need for the 8-inch gun turrets was questioned, and so it was decided in early 1940 to remove them and replace them with 5-inch dual-purpose mountings instead. Those of the *Saratoga* were replaced almost immediately, but the *Lexington* never received the new weapons. The machine-guns were also replaced with heavier weapons, these being 20 mm initially, although these were replaced by guns of 40 mm calibre as the war progressed.

Structural changes involved widening the forward sections of the flight decks of both vessels, although the *Saratoga* would undergo remodelling when its flight deck was extended to 900 feet in 1942. Also altered was the height of the funnel, which was reduced by 14 feet; the bridge was also

21

With its flight deck covered with biplanes, the USS Lexington prepares to launch its fighters and attack aircraft for another aerial exercise. (US Navy/NARA via Dennis R. Jenkins)

radically altered, while a pole mast was fitted so that radar dishes could be mounted. The hull also received a major modification, this being a large bulge that was fitted to the starboard side, which allowed the 1,100 tons of fuel normally used as ballast to be used to increase the vessel's range. In 1941 both carriers were fitted with the CXAM-1 search radar, which was the only system carried by the *Lexington*. The *Saratoga* would receive the SK unit, augmented by the SC-1 air search in 1942. Further systems fitted as the war progressed included the SG-1 surface search and an FD fire-control radar. The SC-1 unit was replaced by an SC-3 radar, although the SC-1 was reinstated later in the war. By the war's end the *Saratoga* sported a Mk 22 fire-control auxiliary radar, SM, height-finding radar, IFF systems and YE/YG radio beacons. Other changes made to both included fitting arrester wires on the forward flight deck and the removal of the catapults. In 1944 the *Saratoga* had new catapults installed that allowed the carrier to launch heavily loaded Grumman Avengers, while a new forward lift of 45 x 45 ft was installed and the aft one was plated over. As the carriers underwent modifications it allowed the carriers to operate every aircraft type as they became available, so that by the end of the war the *Saratoga* could carry seventy aircraft, these being a mixture of Grumman Avengers and Hellcats.

Both of the Lexingtons were the largest aircraft carriers in US Navy service until the launching of the Midway class. During their early years both carriers were involved in formulating tactics for air operations, which would be put to serious use later after some modification. The *Lexington* also undertook a very special mission when the ship's generators were used to provide electrical power to the city of Tacoma, Washington, during the winter of 1929/30. This had been required after the preceding summer's drought, which caused the hydroelectric systems to fail. After the Japanese attack on Pearl Harbor in 1941 both carriers were involved with patrols out of Hawaii, during which they were involved in skirmishes with Japanese forces near Rabaul and New Guinea. The *Lexington* returned to Hawaii in March 1942 for rest and replenishment. The carrier departed in April to the same combat zone, and it was during this patrol that on 8 May the vessel was hit by two torpedoes and two bombs dropped by aircraft from the carriers *Shokaku* and *Zuikaka*. The impacts caused fires throughout the carrier, while the near-misses had strained the hull. Although the crew struggled manfully to quench the fires and contain the damage, their efforts were in vain as fresh fires started in other parts of the ship and could not be controlled. Again the crew tried to save their vessel, but the extent of the damage and the spread of the fire meant that the only course of action was evacuation; and so the crew were rescued and the stricken carrier was sunk by torpedoes fired by the destroyer USS *Phelps*.

The *Saratoga* was also subject to much attention by the Japanese, although in this case it was submarines that would do the most damage. During a patrol outbound from Hawaii the carrier was hit by a torpedo in January 1942,

The foredeck of the USS Saratoga is covered by Martin T4M aircraft waiting to be pushed back to the rear section of the deck so that flying can commence. (US Navy/NARA via Dennis R. Jenkins)

23

The USS Ranger, CV-4, was designed within the limits of the Washington Treaty. However, its shortcomings made it a less than useful vessel. (US Navy/NARA via Dennis R. Jenkins)

which caused minor damage that was later permanently repaired at the Puget Sound Naval Yard, Bremerton. A further submarine-fired torpedo would hit the *Saratoga* in August, and this caused greater damage, which flooded three boiler rooms and immobilised the vessel due to the shock of impact. Taken in tow to Tonga, the carrier was given emergency repairs that allowed it to return to Pearl Harbor for repairs. The *Saratoga* would spend much of 1943 launching air strikes on land targets and Japanese shipping, all in the south-west Pacific. After adventures in the Pacific the carrier was transferred to the Indian Ocean where she assisted the British fleet. After these operations the *Saratoga* underwent a three-month refit at Bremerton, being used for pilot training until the end of the year. By February 1945 the carrier had returned to fleet carrier operations. However, the ship was seriously damaged by bombs and kamikaze strikes during the assault on Iwo Jima. Obviously the carrier was leading a charmed life, as she managed to reach Bremerton for repairs. With these completed the *Saratoga* was utilised for carrier pilot training duties, although after VJ Day the ship was employed in bringing home US troops from the Pacific combat zones. Given the age of the *Saratoga*, the strains due to war damage and the increasing size and weights of the new aircraft types entering service, it came as no surprise that the vessel was to be retired from service. But the USS *Saratoga* had one more service to perform for the United States: it was expended as a target during the atomic bomb test at Bikini Atoll in July 1946.

The Vought SBU-1 was designed and built as a dive-bomber, and was the first such aircraft to exceed 200 mph in level flight. This aircraft was assigned to VS-1B aboard the USS Ranger. (US Navy/NARA via Dennis R. Jenkins)

The next aircraft carrier to join the US fleet pre-war was the USS *Ranger*, CV4. Conceived within the confines of the Washington Treaty the *Ranger* was limited to 14,000 tons. Unlike the earlier carriers, the *Ranger* was designed purely for the carrying and launching of the maximum number of aircraft, and so armour protection, fixed defensive batteries, speed and even sea-keeping capabilities were sacrificed for this capability. Experience with the earlier carriers also meant that there were significant design changes to the hull of the carrier. Therefore the boiler rooms were grouped close together and placed as far aft as possible, while the trunking uptakes were kept as short as possible and discharged to port and starboard as close to the boiler rooms as possible instead of being grouped together as in the Lexington class. This layout increased the volume available for aviation needs. However, these changes, plus the reduced protection, did make the vessel vulnerable to a direct hit in the wrong zone, which could either disable or sink the ship. Access to the hangar was via a pair of lifts, these being offset to starboard, which allowed landed aircraft to be moved to the forward part of the flight deck quickly. In the original design the *Ranger* lacked a superstructure. However, this was added during construction as it was needed for command and control purposes. In order to reduce the impact on the flight deck the superstructure was kept as small as possible. The *Ranger* was lightly armed as it sported four 5-inch guns, while the offensive air group consisted of thirty-six pursuit, thirty-six dive-bomber and four utility aircraft. While on paper

25

the *Ranger* may have appeared to be an effective weapon, in reality the trimming of the equipment fits meant the ship was too small to operate aircraft effectively. The *Ranger* was also deemed too small to keep up with the larger fleet carriers, as the lack of available power restricted her speed, while her small size also resulted in poor sea keeping. It was so bad, in fact, that in a moderate swell the *Ranger* was unable to launch its aircraft.

Due to her deficiencies the USS *Ranger* was confined to duties in the Atlantic, undertaking a mix of strike and transport duties. In 1943 the carrier was assigned to the British Home Fleet for strike duties against German shipping off the Norwegian coast. In 1944 the carrier returned to American waters, where she was used mainly as a training carrier, although this was interspersed with periods as a transport. The *Ranger* was decommissioned in October 1946, being scrapped in 1947. During her service the carrier underwent modifications that mainly concerned improving the weapons fit, but the radar systems were also updated and upgraded. In 1942 a CXAM-1 aircraft detection radar was installed, this being followed in 1943 by an SK, replacing the earlier SC-2, search radar, while the fire-control radar was upgraded to the Mk 4 in 1942. As the weight of aircraft was growing as the war progressed, the flight deck underwent strengthening, while a hydraulic catapult was installed.

After the USS *Ranger* the US Navy would receive the Yorktown class of carriers, which were designed from the outset to counter the deficiencies of the *Ranger*. Three vessels were constructed at Newport News Yard, these being the *Yorktown* (CV5), *Enterprise* (CV6) and the *Hornet* (CV8). The name ship was commissioned in September 1937, being followed by the *Enterprise* in May 1938 and the *Hornet* in October 1941. These three vessels were a quantum leap over the earlier carriers as they were designed from the outset as aircraft carriers, unlike the *Langley* (a converted coaler), the *Lexington* and *Yorktown* (battlecruiser hulls modified) and the *Ranger* (an attempt to force a quart into a pint pot). The resultant vessels were also an answer to the burgeoning disquiet that was being shown by other nations – in particular the Japanese, who were in the process of creating a fleet that exceeded the Washington Treaty limitations. The Yorktown class featured a combined superstructure and uptakes. The decks were 6-inch wood planks with arrester wires mounted fore and aft, and the launching of aircraft was undertaken using two bow-mounted hydraulic catapults plus a further unit mounted athwartships that was fitted in the forward hangar deck. Inset into the flight deck were three lifts, the centre lift requiring that the flight deck be widened to accommodate the island. The intended complement of ninety-eight aircraft was rarely achieved as the space restrictions limited it to eighty machines, a far more comfortable arrangement. Defensive armament was initially eight 0.5-inch guns. USS *Hornet* was a late order in response to events in other parts of the world, Congress authorising the funds in 1937 for the construction of this vessel. Ironically, had the *Essex* design been firmed up the *Hornet* would not have been built. As a later-built ship the *Hornet* featured a slight increase in dimensions and an increase in defensive armament.

The first modern attack aircraft delivered to the US Navy was the Douglas Dauntless. This aircraft was assigned to VT-5 aboard the USS Yorktown in the pre-war period, hence the colourful markings. (US Navy/NARA via Dennis R. Jenkins)

Modifications applied to all three carriers included fitting CXAM search radar, these being installed during 1941 to 1942, and these would be the only sets fitted to the *Yorktown* and *Hornet* before they were lost. In contrast, the *Enterprise* would have the CXAM-1 and SC-2 sets fitted in 1943, these later being replaced by the SK, SC-2 and the SP, plus the Mk 4 fire-control units.

The USS *Yorktown* was deployed to the east coast of America and was docked in the Norfolk Naval Yard when Pearl Harbor was attacked. Once the dust had settled, the *Yorktown* was transferred to the Pacific and was operating out of New Guinea attacking Japanese shipping and shore installations, during which period the *Lexington* assisted in the sinking of the Japanese carrier *Shoho* and the damaging of the *Shokaku*. Unfortunately during this engagement the *Yorktown* suffered damage that required repairs at Pearl Harbor. After repair she joined up with the *Enterprise* and *Hornet* to deploy to Midway. In concert with the other carriers, the *Yorktown* launched a combined attack against the Japanese fleet during which the carrier *Soryu* was left blazing furiously. In response the Japanese mounted a counter-attack during which the *Yorktown* was hit by both bombs and torpedoes. With her engines out of action, the carrier was taken in tow. However, this made the *Yorktown* an easy target, and a Japanese submarine managed to hit the carrier with more torpedoes. After much struggle to save their ailing ship, the crew finally abandoned the *Yorktown*, which sank soon afterwards.

The *Hornet* had a very short naval career, as it lasted barely more than a year. The carrier's most famous moment in her short life was to launch the North American B-25 Mitchells of the Doolittle Raiders in April 1942. To accomplish this the *Hornet*'s air group was stowed below while the eighteen Mitchells were carried on deck. While the attack on the Japanese mainland achieved little in the way of material damage, the propaganda value was tremendous and bore little in common to the ferocity that would assail the Japanese mainland later in the war. After the Doolittle Raid the *Hornet* participated in the Battle of Midway, later being sunk off Santa Cruz on 27 October 1942 after being hit by both bombs and torpedoes.

In contrast to her sister ships, the USS *Enterprise* would lead a charmed life. Operating alongside both her sisters ships at Midway, the air wing suffered heavy losses, with many of the Douglas TBD Dauntless torpedo-bombers being shot down. In contrast, the SBD Dauntless units managed to assist in the sinking of the *Akagi*, the *Kaga* and the *Hiryu*. During the battle off Guadalcanal the *Enterprise* suffered bomb damage that prompted a return to Pearl Harbor for repairs. After repair the carrier resumed her sea duties, undertaking air strikes off Santa Cruz during which further bomb damage was incurred. Further repairs were carried out, allowing the carrier to resume operations during which she assisted in the sinking of the battleship *Hiei*. After these initial exertions the *Enterprise* underwent a major refit during 1943. Post-refit the carrier was involved in strikes against Japanese targets that included sinking the battleships *Fuso* and *Musashi*. During May 1945 the carrier was hit by a kamikaze that blew out the forward aircraft lift, which meant that the carrier was still in dock undergoing repairs when the war ended. Although the *Enterprise* was repaired, she was placed straight into the reserve and decommissioned in February 1947. While held in reserve the ship was re-designated as an anti-submarine warfare (ASW) carrier in July 1953. The carrier never entered service again, and despite great efforts to bring her into preservation the vessel was sold as scrap in July 1958.

Between the building of the *Yorktown*, *Enterprise* and *Hornet* enough tonnage was found to construct another smaller carrier, this being the USS *Wasp*, CV7. This carrier was definitely a product of the Washington Treaty, and had it not been in existence it is likely that such a small carrier would not have been built. The resultant vessel was built within the 15,000 tons limit and incorporated as many of the innovations from the Yorktown class as possible, although this did not result in a successful ship. Not helping was the desire to fit as many aircraft as possible into the hull. To achieve this, low-power propulsive machinery was installed, and the armour initially proposed at the design stage was not fitted. Not only was the armour protection omitted, but the torpedo protection was also omitted, both omissions later proving fatal.

At the design stage the designers had looked at installing lower flight decks to augment the main flight deck, but in the event extra catapults were installed in the hangar in a similar manner to that of the *Yorktown*. One saving grace was the bulging of the fuselage to compensate for the island, which in turn increased the amount of space for fuel bunkerage. Internally the boiler rooms were situated between the machinery rooms, the theory being that one hit would not stop the ship. As with the other carriers, arrester wires were fitted at both the fore and aft of the flight deck, which allowed landings to be made from either direction. The *Wasp* also featured three lifts, although the third was based around a movable girder mounted on the deck edge. The deckside lift allowed entry directly into the hangar, and this could be closed off using reinforced shutters. The assigned air wing included a squadron of fighters, two squadrons of scout bombers, but no torpedo-bombers. These would finally be added in August 1942 when space was found to house the torpedoes. Defensive armament of light weapons was dispersed around the edge of the flight deck.

During her short life the USS *Wasp* underwent few modifications, most of which centred around improving the defensive armament, improving the shell splinter protection and adding radar. Further weaponry was fitted in 1941, while the radar installation was upgraded to CXAM-1 search radar plus the Mk 4 fire-control radar. Given the small size of the carrier and her slow speed, the *Wasp* was assigned to duties in the Atlantic in 1941, after which the ship was involved in the relief of Malta between March and May 1942. During this period the carrier successfully delivered a hundred Spitfires to the beleaguered island. After its adventures in the Mediterranean the USS *Wasp* entered the Norfolk Navy Yard, after which it departed in June 1942 for the Pacific theatre. In its new theatre the *Wasp* was engaged in attacks against Japanese positions around Guadalcanal. However, on 15 September 1942 the carrier was hit by three torpedoes fired by a Japanese submarine, which caused serious fires and explosions throughout the hull. The fire was exacerbated by the leaks caused by ruptured aircraft fuel lines, which hastened the carrier's end. With no chance of saving the stricken vessel, the crew abandoned the *Wasp*, and she was later sunk by the destroyer USS *Lansdowne*.

Having started its adventure in naval aviation, the US Navy would proceed quickly to develop both its carrier fleet and the aircraft. The service was therefore well placed to begin the fight back against the Japanese in the Pacific and to assist the British in the Atlantic and the Mediterranean.

CHAPTER TWO

Neutrality and Atlantic Crossings

On 1 September 1939 the forces of a renewed Germany invaded Poland and France and began offensive operations against Britain. On the other side of the Atlantic the United States was publicly trumpeting its isolationist policies, these being espoused by the more jingoistic politicians with the support of the popular press. While such a policy, more concerned with protecting their own territory and interests, made sense to many Americans, the more astute thinkers realised that the world had changed significantly. This had been brought home with some force during the Wall Street Crash of 1929, whose effects were felt around the world. While the financial chaos would last until the mid-1950s, the United States was becoming drawn into the affairs of the world whether it wished to or not. In 1928 the country was invited to join the newly emerged League of Nations. However, wary of having her foreign policy mandated by others, it took the signing of the Kellogg-Briand Pact to draw America towards the rest of the world. This pact allowed the League signatories to defend their interests, while another section of the Pact allowed the signatories to group together should one country decide to undertake some military adventurism against the other members.

The Kellogg-Briand Pact, while laudable, would soon be overwritten as America viewed with concern the growing war clouds over Europe. With that in mind the US Congress passed the Neutrality Acts during 1936 and 1937 that required the country to stay clear of any such conflict. This seriously dismayed President Roosevelt, who was very pro-British in his stance. It also created two strong factions within the country – the isolationists and the interventionists –, the latter seeing that the outbreak of war would eventually affect everyone and that trying to ignore the fact would endanger the country. While Roosevelt continued to reassure the American people about remaining

30

uninvolved, he also warned that should it be needed America would have little option but to become entangled in any global conflict.

Not on the radar of the American people, the press and many politicians were the actions and ambitions of the Japanese. Having defeated the Russians thoroughly earlier in the century, the Japanese had embarked on a programme of naval ship building that had been stunted by the Washington Treaty, and this was seen as an insult to both the nation and the Emperor. As Japan was located a world away from America and Europe, the Japanese felt able to ignore the various treaties and protocols, and they would therefore start to build major combat vessels outside the agreed tonnage limits. It would be the successful invasion of China in 1937 that would flag up the Japanese as a nation that required the use of increased intelligence assets by America. The possibility of conflict with Japan would be exacerbated by the attack on the US Navy gunboat *Panay* while it was anchored in the Yangtze river outside Nanjing on 12 December 1937. This, coupled with the Nanking Massacre, would swing both public and political opinion against the Japanese. But even more worrying was the possibility of the Japanese undertaking an expansionist campaign in the Pacific, which was of even more concern to both America and Britain, who had extensive interests in the area.

President Roosevelt was a very able and astute politician who quickly realised that should Germany, Japan and to a lesser extent Italy succeed in their conquest plans, America would in reality be completely isolated. Obviously such an outcome was not acceptable. Therefore the President requested that plans be laid to assist Britain in its fight against all three aggressor nations, while quietly arming the United States to enter the war. The first signs of American preparedness was the organisation of the Neutrality Patrols off the coasts of America, which utilised destroyer patrols backed up by the battleships USS *New York*, *Texas*, *Arkansas* and *Wyoming*, and the aircraft carrier USS *Ranger*. These patrols remained in operation until America entered the war formally in 1941. Aware that America was moving slowly towards war, President Roosevelt signed the Two-Ocean Navy Expansion Act, which allowed for the construction of 1,325,000 warship tonnage plus a further 100,000 tons for auxiliaries. Added to this were 15,000 aircraft for naval purposes.

Further moves by the Japanese would take place on 22 September 1940 when the Vichy French government signed an agreement that allowed Japanese forces unrestricted access to French bases in Indo-China. In response to this move and others by Axis forces, representatives of America and Britain met in Washington, where secret talks thrashed out how America would enter the war. After these talks there was a change in the stance of US Navy operations, since while the Neutrality Patrols continued as before, there was an alteration in attitude towards the British war effort. On 1 March 1941 a support force for the Atlantic Fleet was formed under the command of Rear Admiral Bristol Jnr USN, which consisted of three destroyer flotillas and some flying-boat squadrons, their purpose being to provide convoy protection in

Seen in pre-war years is the USS Wasp, CV-7,. After its service in the Atlantic the carrier was transferred to the Pacific, where it was sunk by the Japanese in September 1942. (US Navy/NARA via Dennis R. Jenkins)

the north Atlantic. Further increases in Atlantic strength saw the establishment of the US Navy base in Bermuda on 7 April 1941. The following day, Task Group TG.7.3 would take up residence, ostensibly to increase Neutrality patrols, although its task was more concerned with detecting and destroying enemy submarines and escorting convoys safely to harbour. Within TG.7.3 was the carrier USS *Ranger*, which was complemented by four cruisers and ten destroyers. A few days later the carrier USS *Wasp* would join the task group, and this would later be augmented by the arrival of the carrier *Yorktown* plus numerous escort vessels that had been transferred from the Pacific to the Atlantic to further strengthen the forces in the Atlantic. These forces would pass through the Panama Canal during early June. By this time American destroyers were operating freely in the Atlantic, and on 11 April, while *en route* to Iceland with a convoy, the destroyer USS *Noblack* stopped to pick up survivors from the Dutch freighter *Saleier*, soon afterwards detecting a possible submarine contact that was attacked, although the contact later proved to be false.

Further changes to the South Atlantic Neutrality Patrol saw the carrier USS *Wasp* plus escorts operate from Hampton Roads from 26 April 1941 to extend the patrol area even further south, and the task group would return to Bermuda some two weeks later. While the US Navy was concentrating its efforts in the Atlantic, the country's diplomats were endeavouring to find ways to shore up the defences in the Far East without actually becoming involved in a conflict for which America was not ready. To that end a conference was held in Singapore on 27 April, attended by delegates from Britain, Australia and the Netherlands, while the Americans were there as observers, although their input was gratefully received.

As a show of strength a further powerful force was dispatched from Bermuda on 9 May consisting of the carrier USS *Ranger* plus the heavy cruiser USS *Vincennes* with the destroyers *Sampson* and *Eberle*. The purpose of TG.1

was to further reinforce the Neutrality Patrol and to hunt for any submarines in the vicinity After fourteen days TG.1 returned to Bermuda to await further tasking. Even as the *Ranger* was heading back towards Bermuda, another patrol was readying to leave. Designated TG.2, the carrier was the USS *Wasp*, escorted by the cruiser USS *Quincy* and the destroyers *Livermore* and *Kearny*. After an uneventful fortnight in the central Atlantic, the task force returned to Bermuda, arriving on 3 June 1941. TG.3 was the next patrol for the *Ranger* group, although this time the escorts were the USS *Tuscaloosa*, plus the destroyers *McDougal* and the *Eberle*, and it departed on 29 May for the central Atlantic, returning to base on 8 June. Two days after TG.3 had left, the USS *Yorktown* plus the cruiser USS *Vincennes* with the destroyers *Sampson* and *Gwin* in company, departed from Bermuda as TG.1 for patrol duties around the Canaries, returning to Hampton Roads on 12 June. The *Yorktown* was later joined at Hampton Roads by the USS *Wasp*. On 20 June 1941 the carrier, in company with the cruiser *Tuscaloosa* and the destroyers *Anderson* and *Rowan*, set sail for the central Atlantic as TG.2.6. At the conclusion of the patrol the task group returned to Bermuda on 4 July. The USS *Yorktown* had remained at Hampton Roads and was made ready for another patrol. Designated as TG 2.8, the carrier was joined by the cruisers *Vincennes* and *Quincy* plus the destroyers *Wainwright*, *Hammann*, *Mustin* and *Stack*, departing on 29 June for the central Atlantic. The *Yorktown* plus the *Wainwright* and *Stack* returned to Hampton Roads on 12 July, while the remainder spent another three days at sea *en route* to Bermuda.

The north Atlantic from 19 July would be the next venue for the USS *Wasp*, which was the carrier assigned to TF.1. The escort vessels were the cruisers *Quincy* and *Vincennes* plus the destroyers *O'Brien* and *Walke*, their initial task being to transport Curtiss P-40 Warhawk fighters for the defence of Iceland, after which the task group was expected to provide protection for convoys arriving at and departing from the island. To speed up the process of offloading the fighter cargo it was decided to fly the P-40s off the carrier, and all the fighters arrived safely without loss. As Iceland was seen as pivotal to American operations once the war overtook them, it was decided to provide a permanent force to escort the expected convoys, and so a protection force of twenty-four destroyers was deployed, as were a pair of seaplane patrol squadrons.

The USS *Yorktown*, in port at Hampton Roads, was warned for another patrol as TG.2.5. The carrier departed on 30 July in company with the cruiser *Brooklyn* and the destroyers *Roe*, *Grayson* and *Eberle* for the central Atlantic. However, instead of returning to Hampton Roads the group sailed on to Bermuda, arriving there on 10 August. The USS *Wasp*, still in the north Atlantic, formed the core of a new Task Group, TG 16, under the command of Rear Admiral Monroe USN. The purpose of the force that included the battleship *Mississippi*, the cruisers *Quincy* and the *Wichita* plus five destroyers was to escort convoys to and from Reykjavik, their first customers being the transports *American Legion*, *Mizar* and the *Almaack*. In contrast to the *Wasp* the

Yorktown was still involved in Neutrality patrols and would form the core of TG 2.5. Departing on 15 August 1941 the carrier was escorted by the cruiser *Brooklyn* plus the destroyers *Roe*, *Grayson* and *Eberle*, the group returning to Bermuda on 27 August.

On 1 September 1941 the US Navy Atlantic Fleet assumed responsibility for the escort of the fast north Atlantic convoys from a point off Argentia near Newfoundland to a meridian point south of Iceland. The C-in-C of the Atlantic Fleet, Admiral King, ordered the vessels assigned to the Denmark Strait patrol to operate between Iceland and Greenland. On 23 September, even though America was still not officially engaged in the war, the carrier *Yorktown* plus the cruisers *Brooklyn* and *Savannah* and a destroyer group were transferred from Bermuda to Argentia in response to a cracked Ultra code message that indicated that the *Tirpitz* might undertake a break-out from the Baltic. On that same day a task group that comprised the battleship USS *Mississippi* and the carrier USS *Wasp*, in company with the cruiser *Wichita* and the destroyers *Gwin*, *Meredith*, *Grayson* and *Monssen*, with the repair and support vessel *Vulcan*, were transferred from Argentia to Hvalfjord. After a five-day voyage the force was used to strengthen the White Patrol covering the Denmark Strait, although the USS *Wasp* would depart for Argentia on 6 October, as conditions for flying in the strait were poor, and she arrived there five days later.

On 2 October 1941 the Japanese Prime Minister, Prince Konoye, proposed a meeting with President Roosevelt to discuss the cultural and political differences between America and Japan. President Roosevelt would reject the proposal as the State Department thought that such a summit was a complete waste of time.

Argentia saw the departure of the USS *Yorktown* on 10 October for Casco Bay for patrol duties. Accompanying the carrier was the battleship USS *New Mexico*, the cruisers *Quincy* and *Savannah* plus eight destroyers. However, some of the latter were damaged when the group was hit by a severe storm. At the other end of the continent, Brazil would grant the US Navy access rights to ports in the north of the country. Brazil would eventually wade in to support the Allied cause, sending an air combat group equipped with Republic P-47 Thunderbolts to Europe. At the completion of its operations off Argentia, the *Yorktown* task force would head towards Casco Bay. However, *en route* the group was hit by another heavy storm, and so it was a very bedraggled flotilla that limped into port on 13 October 1941. As ever, it would be the smaller vessels that would suffer the most damage. After two weeks in port the USS *Yorktown* would form the core of TF.14 in company with the battleship *New Mexico*, the cruisers *Philadelphia* and *Savannah* plus the destroyer group, Desron 2, their task to escort six American cargo vessels to Britain to replace tonnage already lost due to U-boat activity. As these vessels were capable of running at high speed, they and their escorts would attempt a high-speed transit across the Atlantic. Having avoided the known U-boat-covered zones, the US Navy-escorted ships would meet the British convoy

The USS Wasp would assist the Royal Navy by delivering Supermarine Spitfires to that beleaguered island. Here a much-needed fighter departs on its journey across the Mediterranean. (John Ryan Collection)

CT.5, complete with its troops, coming the other way. The British escort vessels turned round and escorted the new freighters back to Britain while the American escort group took over the troop convoy. The task force and its vital cargo would reach Halifax by 7 November, with the troops being transferred to the American convoy WS.124.

On 10 November the US Navy would also start to provide escort for ships transiting from the Atlantic to the Indian Ocean. The first such convoy was designated WS.24, and comprised American troop transports that were carrying 20,000 British troops and their equipment to the Middle East. The escort was TG.14.4 commanded by Admiral Wood USN, the vessels being the carrier USS *Ranger* supported by the cruisers USS *Vincennes* and *Quincy* plus eight destroyers. The USS *Ranger* would later return to Trinidad, while the convoy itself was ordered to Bombay instead of Basra in Iraq. However, the convoy would stop over at Cape Town, departing on 27 December for Bombay.

During the attack on Pearl Harbor on 7 December 1941, the Japanese Navy would mount a strike against the US Navy base, causing massive destruction to the vessels located there. While the carriers were safely at sea, the destruction caused a hiatus in American operations globally. The first change in Atlantic operations would take place on 1 January 1942, when Admiral

Ingersoll replaced Admiral King as Commander-in-Chief Atlantic Fleet. Initially the Atlantic Fleet was not able to provide aircraft carriers for escort duties, as the US Navy was gearing up to drive the Japanese forces from the territories they had already captured in the Pacific. Due to this change in focus, convoy escorts would be provided by a mix of destroyers and cutters from the US Coast Guard. Also adding to Admiral Ingersoll's woes was the transfer of the battleships USS *Idaho, Mississippi* and *New Mexico*, in company with seven destroyers, these being redeployed to the Pacific to increase the forces there. The entry of America into the war would also signal another change when the destroyers of TG.4.1.2 entered British waters while escorting a convoy, instead of handing over to British escorts in the open sea. The United States would continue running convoys across the Atlantic throughout February and March, although the lack of aircraft carriers still worried the US Navy's senior commanders. Fleet carriers would finally reappear on 15 March 1942 when the USS *Wasp*, in company with the newly commissioned battleship USS *Washington*, plus the cruisers *Tuscaloosa* and *Wichita* with six escort destroyers, was transferred from Casco Bay to the Royal Navy base at Scapa Flow to provide convoy cover in support of British operations. The *Wasp* would depart from Scapa Flow for Norfolk naval base soon after arrival, but the carrier would be damaged after colliding with the destroyer USS *Stock*, both vessels requiring repair upon arrival.

The damage to the USS *Wasp* was quickly repaired, as the entire escort group TF.39 departed Casco Bay bound for Scapa Flow, where they would replace the Royal Navy Force H that was required to undertake duties in support of Operation Ironclad against Japanese forces based on Madagascar. The British convoy departed on 23 March, while the US Navy arrived at Scapa Flow on 5 April. The USS *Wasp* would set sail again on 14 April to take part in Operation Calendar as part of the Anglo-American Force W under the command of Commodore Daniell RN. The purpose of this operation was to fly off forty-seven much-needed Supermarine Spitfires desperately needed for the defence of Malta. All were launched from the carrier on 20 April, and all but one of the fighters arrived safely on the island. Having delivered its vital cargo, the task force departed the Mediterranean and headed back to Scapa Flow, where it arrived on 26 April.

While the *Wasp* was undertaking its delivery mission, the USS *Ranger* was also operating in the south Atlantic as part of Task Force TF.36. The carrier and its escorts had arrived at NAS Quonset Point to collect the aircraft of the 33rd Pursuit Group, plus extra replacement airframes, departing on 22 April. The destination of the carrier and her escorts was Accra on Africa's Gold Coast. As the task force neared the African coast on 10 May, the carrier launched its cargo of sixty-eight Curtiss P-40 Warhawk fighters for use by the USAAF in Africa and the Middle East. At the completion of this mission TF.36 would return to the United States, with the carrier continuing to Argentia, where it would undertake an anti-submarine patrol. The USS *Ranger* would join up with the battleship USS *North Carolina*, later replaced by the *South*

The USS Ranger was also assigned to the Atlantic, although its primary task was to deliver Curtiss P-40 fighters to USAAC units operating in the Middle East. (US Navy/NARA via Dennis R. Jenkins)

Dakota, while the USS *Wasp* plus some cruisers and destroyers were soon added. Their purpose was to stand by for a possible break-out of the German battleship *Tirpitz*. The USS *Wasp* would soon depart from the *Tirpitz* watch to rejoin the Anglo-American Force W arriving at Scapa Flow on 3 May. The *Wasp* would yet again be loaded with Spitfires. Forty-seven would be loaded aboard the American carrier, while a further seventeen would be carried aboard the Royal Navy carrier HMS *Eagle*. Known as Operation Bowery, the combined force would launch its Spitfires on 9 May, all but three arriving at their new base safely. After launching their aircraft, the USS *Wasp* plus escorts would return to Scapa Flow, arriving on 16 May, while *Eagle* returned to Gibraltar. The delivery of these Spitfires to Malta was vital, as on 4 May the German High Command had issued its directive that would signal the launch Operation Herkules, the capture of Malta. The USS *Ranger* also returned to the aircraft-delivery role on 10 May, when a further forty Curtiss P-40s were launched off the Gold Coast, having collected the aircraft from NAS Quonset Point as before. After arrival in Africa the fighters were transferred to India via the bases in the Middle East. This would be the last time that the USS *Wasp* would undertake Atlantic duties, as in mid-1942 the carrier would depart to Norfolk Navy yard for modifications and repairs prior to joining the war in the Pacific. This move was seen as essential as the Navy had only two carriers available for combat duty in the region.

The USS *Ranger* would undertake another Argentia patrol before returning to Quonset Point to collect another load of P-40s on 1 July. A total of seventy-two aircraft were loaded, and as before they were flown off close to the Gold Coast. This batch of aircraft was also destined for the China–Burma–India (C–B–I) theatre, routeing via the Middle East before joining up with the American Volunteer Group in China. At the conclusion of this delivery run,

These Douglas SBDs overfly their carrier home during Operation Torch. Of note are the markings applied for this operation, the most obvious being the surrounds for the national markings. (US Navy/NARA via Dennis R. Jenkins)

Pictured in happier times are these Douglas SBD Dauntless dive-bombers assigned to VT-2, practising their peacetime formation flying. (US Navy/NARA via Dennis R. Jenkins)

Captured at dusk is the crowded flight deck of the USS Ranger as the ground crews prepare the carrier's aircraft for their part in Operation Torch. (US Navy/NARA via Dennis R. Jenkins)

the USS *Ranger* returned to the Norfolk Navy Yard for refitting, after which the carrier undertook some combat training covering anti-submarine duties, air defence and exercising the air wing. After the completion of these exercises the carrier returned to Norfolk for a quick refit. This completed, the *Ranger*, plus the escort carriers *Sangamon*, *Chenango* and *Suwanee*, with the *Santee* and escorts, departed the United States to take part in Operation Torch, the Allied invasion of French North Africa. This was a large force, with the Americans providing the Western Task Force. This was commanded by Rear Admiral Hewitt, and its target was Casablanca. Under his command was TG.34.1, consisting of the battleship USS *Massachusetts*, the cruisers *Wichita* and *Tuscaloosa*, four destroyers and an oiler. The Northern Attack Group TG.34.8 comprised the battleship *Texas*, the cruiser *Savannah*, a group of troop transports and five destroyers. The escort carriers USS *Sangamon* and *Chenango*, with their own destroyer escort and oiler, were provided for air-cover duties. The Central Attack Group, TG.34.9, consisting of the cruisers *Augusta* and *Brooklyn*, with ten destroyers and fifteen troop transports, were covered by the carrier *Ranger* for air support, and the escort carrier *Suwanee*. Attached to this group was the cruiser *Cleveland*, plus two submarines and an oiler. The Southern Attack Group TG.34.10 was assembled around the battleship USS *New York* and the cruiser *Philadelphia*. Supporting the larger vessels were eight destroyers, while standing further off were the ships of the air group, these being the USS *Santee* and the usual range of escort destroyers. As this was a combined force, the Royal Navy also provided a sizeable force that consisted of seven carriers, covering battleships plus hordes of cruisers and destroyers and a large flotilla of auxiliaries.

The gambit was played by the destroyer USS *Dallas*, which tried on 8 and 10 November to land a raider battalion near Fedhala. However, on both

The Ranger is seen here in its wartime camouflage, by which time the carrier had increased defensive armament. The Ranger would survive the war, being decommissioned in 1946. (US Navy/NARA via Dennis R. Jenkins)

occasions the ship was driven back out to sea by gunfire from the French shore batteries. Further resistance was put up by the defenders of Casablanca under the command of Vice-Admiral Michelier, although the incomplete battleship *Jean Bart* was badly damaged by shelling and air attacks by the Allied forces. A further French naval sortie was launched under the command of Rear Admiral de Lafond against the ships of the Western Task Force. While this was a reasonable force consisting of a cruiser and eight destroyers, it was outgunned by the Allied fleet, with four of the destroyers being badly damaged by gunfire and forced to run aground while the remainder were sunk departing the harbour; a similar fate befell three of the eleven submarines present. Two others suffered minor damage while the remainder managed to depart in the confusion. The six that had escaped attempted to attack the Allied shipping, but their attempts failed. This was not the end for these six vessels, as one was sunk by a mine, another by a Vought OS2U Kingfisher spotter patrol aircraft from the USS *Philadelphia*, another was sunk by aircraft from the escort carrier USS *Suwanee*, and another, making for Dakar, was sunk by a US Navy Consolidated Catalina. The Allies, having sunk the smaller vessels, made strenuous efforts to stop the French Navy from scuttling the battleships at Oran, but in this they were unsuccessful. Operation Torch was deemed a success, and would be followed by attacks upon other French and German-held territory. During its period of combat, the USS *Ranger* launched 496 sorties during the three days the carrier was involved. On 12 November 1942 the *Ranger* departed the Torch combat zone, arriving at Norfolk Naval Yard on 23 November.

It was also in 1942 that the escort, or 'jeep', carriers began to enter service. It had become obvious to the US Navy that more deck space was needed to

A Grumman F4F Wildcat prepares to launch from the USS Ranger during Operation Torch. This aircraft also sports the yellow surrounds applied to the national markings. (US Navy/NARA via Dennis R. Jenkins)

launch aircraft for various roles and that construction of major aircraft carriers would take more time than developing a design based on an already available hull. After two initial forays with the USS *Long Island* and *Charger*, the US Navy ordered the conversion of four vessels based on the hull of the merchant T-3 type, which became the Sangamon class. Not only could these ships carry and launch aircraft, they could also double as fleet oilers. However, it was becoming obvious that even escort carriers would need a credible number of aircraft to make a difference. The answer to these concerns were the Bogue, Casablanca and Commencement classes. These classes were similar in size, with a length between 490 and 525 feet, while the maximum beam was around the 80 ft mark. As each vessel had a hangar under the deck, this allowed an operational complement of twenty-eight aircraft to be carried, although this could multiplied massively if used in the transport role. The Sangamon class would later undergo conversion to full carrier status, re-entering service during 1943. While many of these vessels entered service with the Royal Navy, a goodly number would serve with the US Navy and would stay on the Navy List until struck off, being finally sold for scrap in the 1960s.

While the *Ranger* returned to the United States, the escort carriers were

41

One of the first vessels converted for escort carrier purposes was the USS Sangamon. It would survive the war, being decommissioned just afterwards. (US Navy/NARA via Dennis R. Jenkins)

utilised in supporting convoys running between America and Casablanca. The USS *Sangamon* covered convoy TG.34.8, while the USS *Chenango* covered TG.34.9. At the conclusion of these convoys both escort carriers were ordered to return to the United States, but both would be badly damaged by heavy seas while in transit. The USS *Ranger* would return to the Atlantic in January 1943 when it departed Quonset Point with seventy-five Curtiss P-40s aboard. As before, the aircraft were flown off-shore of Accra, the final destination being North Africa. At the completion of this delivery run the *Ranger* returned to America, where it was employed in training pilots prior to their deploying aboard other carriers. Having completed its period as a pilot trainer, the USS *Ranger* would yet again be employed as an aircraft transport. As before, the load was Curtiss P-40 Warhawks, seventy-five in this group, but on this trip they would be delivered to Casablanca for onward deployment in North Africa. The *Ranger* would depart the United States on 7 February, arriving in Casablanca on 24 February. Returning to America, the carrier undertook a series of patrols along the Atlantic coast, frequently reaching Halifax, Nova Scotia.

Although the USS *Ranger* featured in many of the Atlantic operations, it would soon be joined by the first of the escort carriers that were beginning to make their presence felt. The first of these was the USS *Bogue*, which had been commissioned in September 1942, with Captain G.E. Short USN in command. It would take four months of shake-down cruising, modifications and repair before the carrier was considered fit for combat duties. The *Bogue* would form the nucleus of the first American anti-submarine group, Support Group 6, being deployed on convoy escort duties in the Atlantic. The vessel and its escorts, consisting of the destroyers *Belknap*, *Greene*, *Osmond Ingram* and

George E. Badger, undertook three uneventful escort voyages during March and April 1943 without attacking a single submarine. It would be on its fourth voyage, which started on 22 April, that the *Bogue* group would score its first success on 21 May, when the carrier's Grumman Avengers damaged the German submarine *U 231*. The *Bogue* group would sink its first submarine of 22 May, when the *U 569* was sunk by the Avengers of VC-9. These concentrations of U-boats were successfully passed without loss to the vital convoy.

While the USS *Bogue* was defending its charges in the north Atlantic, another escort carrier was carrying out a similar task in the south Atlantic and the Mediterranean. The USS *Card*, another member of the Bogue class, had been commissioned in November 1942 with Captain J.B. Sykes USN as commander, and undertook its first voyage as a troop transport and aircraft supply vessel during Operation Torch. At the completion of this first voyage

These Grumman Avengers are wearing the scheme applied to aircraft serving in the Atlantic. As the flight deck is full, the Avenger buzzing this escort carrier is probably from another vessel. (US Navy/NARA via Dennis R. Jenkins)

With Grumman Avengers on the flight deck, the USS Card proceeds across the Atlantic. The Card was a member of the Bogue class, being finally decommissioned in 1970. (US Navy/NARA via Dennis R. Jenkins)

the *Card* became the focus of an anti-submarine group, TG.21.14, undertaking its first trip in its new role during July 1943. The USS *Card* joined convoy UGS.13 and ran straight into a swarm of U-boats lying in wait south of the Azores. The Avengers from the USS *Card* had their first success on 6 August when *U 66* was badly damaged, while the air group managed its first sinking the following day when *U 117* was destroyed. The Avengers of VC-1 also sank *U 664* on 9 August. The same group also sank *U 525* and *U 847* within two days. This would be one of the pivotal days of the war as the German submarines had taken a pasting, and this led to a reduction in German long-range U-boat operations.

While much of the US 8th Fleet, assigned to operations in the Atlantic and Pacific, was undertaking support for Operation Husky, the invasion of Sicily, the carrier escort groups were continuing their vital duties escorting convoys across the Atlantic. One new route opened in September 1943 was that from America to Gibraltar. The carrier assigned to GUS.13 was the USS *Croatan*, which was part of TG.21.15, while the primary escort was provided by the destroyers of TF.65. The *Croatan* was a member of the Bogue class of escort carriers and had been commissioned in April 1943. After use as an aircraft transport, the *Croatan* was redeployed as an ASW hunter-killer carrier. The following convoy was GUS.14, this being escorted by TF.61, while the carrier support group was TG.21.11 with the USS *Santee* at its core. Also sailing in company with the convoy was a further escort group, this being TG.21.14, whose carrier was the USS *Card*. Convoy UGS.17 was a return trip that was

Travelling at speed is the USS Core, undertaking its share of convoy escort duties across the Atlantic. The Core would also survive the war, being retired soon afterwards. (US Navy/NARA via Dennis R. Jenkins)

escorted by TF.62, while the support group was provided by TG.21.12 with the USS *Bogue* as the escort carrier. The penultimate convoy to work between Gibraltar and America in September 1943 was GUS.14, which was undertaking the return trip, having ended its delivery journey at Casablanca. The carrier support group was TG.21.15 centred around the USS *Croatan*. The final convoy to undertake the journey back to the United States was GUS.13, which had TG.68 with the battleship USS *Texas* at its core, while the escort group was TG.21.11 with the USS *Santee* as its assigned escort carrier.

After a short period to restore and repair and to give the crews a break, the convoys from the United States to Gibraltar would resume on 15 September. The first would be GUS.15 escorted by TF.61, with the escort carrier USS *Santee* and TG.21.11 in support. Once the convoy reached Gibraltar the merchant vessels would come under the protection of the Royal Navy, which would escort them to their final destination, normally Casablanca. Going the other way was convoy UGS.19 escorted by TF.64 with TG.21.14 in support. TG.21.14,which included the escort carrier USS *Card*, was detached *en route* to investigate information gained from cracking the Ultra code. Their target was a group of four U-boats refuelling away from the known shipping lanes. During the attack launched from the USS *Card*, the Grumman Avengers and Wildcats managed to sink two of the refuelling submarines, one escaped, and the tanker was lost during its escape dive. The Avengers from the USS *Card* would strike lucky again on 13 October 1943 when they managed to sink *U 402*. GUS.16 would be the next convoy to head for America, escorted by TF.62 with the USS *Bogue* and TG.21.11 acting as the ASW escort. GUS.16 would arrive in New York on 15 October. Coming the other way was UGS.20, which was covered by TF.65, while TG.21.5 with the USS *Core* was the escort group. The aircrew from the USS *Core* would manage to sink *U 378* on 1 November.

TG.21.14 with the USS *Card* as the assigned escort carrier was crossing the Atlantic with convoy UGS.19 when one of the carrier's aircraft spotted three U-boats being refuelled by a submarine tanker on 4 October. The spotter aircraft called the carrier for reinforcements, which arrived in three waves and promptly sank *U 422* and *U 264* successfully. The USS *Core* was also involved with sinking further U-boats while escorting convoy UGS.20. On 27 October two aircraft from VC-13 sank *U 378* and damaged *U 271*. The following day the carrier's aircraft would successfully deal with *U 220* in a similar manner. Aircraft from another escort carrier, the USS *Block Island*, would sink *U 256* while in transit across the Atlantic. The USS *Card* ASW group would score another success on 31 October when their aircraft sank *U 584*.

After a period of rest and restoring, the carrier support groups were ready to restart their escort duties. The first convoy they escorted was GUS.23 with the USS *Bogue* as the escort carrier. During the transit across the Atlantic the escorts encountered a U-boat tanker refuelling an attack submarine, *U 172*. Avengers of VC-19 were launched from the *Bogue* to attack the submarines. The tanker managed to escape, but *U 172* was not so lucky and was sunk. VC-19 and its Avengers would score a further success on 20 December when *U 850* was sunk while in transit to the Indian Ocean. The GUS.23 carrier support group was not so lucky further on in the voyage when the German blockade runner *Osorno* slipped through the wake of the convoy and headed towards Germany. Not only did TG 21.12 miss the blockade runner, the escort group supporting the return convoy UGS.23 that was being covered by TG.21.16, the core of which was the USS *Block Island*, missed it also. The *Osorno* also managed to evade the escort group covering UGS.27, this being TG.21.15 with the USS *Core* as its aircraft carrier. Having evaded the various carrier groups, the blockade runner entered the Bay of Biscay and prepared to make its final run to home.

The USS *Card* would head for choppier climes on 20 December 1943, as intelligence had revealed that some U-boats from the Coronel pack had been detached south as the Borkum pack to intercept convoy MKS.33/SL.142. In support of the U-boats the *Luftwaffe* launched FW 200 Condors in an effort to track the convoy. The USS *Card* was escorted by extra destroyers detached from the GUS.24 escort force. The premise behind the Borkum deployment was to give the *Orsono* a greater chance of reaching Germany without inter-ference. However, this was not to be, as a Grumman Wildcat from the *Card* spotted the ship on 23 December while patrolling in bad weather. The fighter's radio call had been intercepted, and so the U-boats attempted some retaliation when *U 415* fired three torpedoes at the carrier. However, the weapons missed their target. A further attack was made by *U 645*, but it, too, missed its target and was sunk by the escorting destroyer USS *Schenk*. After these engagements the USS *Card* and its escorts were forced to withdraw as

Given the extent of its orders, Grumman sub-contracted production of the F4F Wildcat to General Motors, whose product was designated FM-2. (US Navy/NARA via Dennis R. Jenkins)

fuel was running low. The *Orsono* would eventually reach Germany, although it was damaged *en route*, and this would be the last blockade run of the war.

As the Borkum pack was still active, the Commander US 8th Fleet decided to deploy the *Block Island* escort group to provide extra cover for MK.34/SL.143. On 11 January 1944, *U 305* attempted to attack the convoy, and had some success in keeping the *Block Island* aircraft away using the submarine's anti-aircraft guns. *U 758* and *U 953* were the next submarines to attempt an attack. Both were unsuccessful, as were the aircraft from the USS *Block Island* that tried to sink *U 758* with rockets as the submarine put up a spirited anti-aircraft barrage. Running short of weapons and fuel, the submarines decided to withdraw, although even this was not without loss, as aircraft from the *Block Island* vectored a Vickers Wellington of No.172 Squadron towards *U 231*, which was promptly destroyed in the bomber's attack.

The next group of U-boats to appear in the Atlantic was the Rugen pack, to which was added the ragged remainder of the Borkum boats. Its target would be convoy SL.144/MKS.35 with the support group TG.21.12, whose carrier was the USS *Guadalcanal*. The *Guadalcanal*, a member of the Casablanca class, had entered service with the Atlantic Fleet in late 1943. The carrier's aircraft would score their first success on this voyage when they surprised a group of U-boats on the surface. During the attack an Avenger of VC-13 sank *U 544*. The USS *Block Island* and its attendant destroyers would have some success against the U-boats during the middle of March 1944. Operating south of the Azores, TG.21.16 was hunting submarines that had been reported in the area. In this the group was successful as it managed to sink *U 801* and *U 1059*. Running low on fuel, TG.21.16 was relieved by TG.21.12, whose carrier was the USS *Guadalcanal*. During this group's patrol it managed to sink the U-boats *U 515* and *U 68*.

Although the German U-boats were starting to suffer significant losses, they were still capable of causing significant damage to convoys, especially if their protection was less than normal. In February 1944 the Preussen pack would assume new positions to the south of Ireland, their first intended victims being the convoys ON 225 and HX 279. In order to protect both sets of vessels, TG.21.16 was deployed to the area to begin submarine hunting. Both escorts and the aircraft assigned to the *Block Island* undertook this task with some success, as *U 91*, *U 709* and *U 603* were dealt with swiftly. Task Group 21.11 was also employed in this task, the carrier as before being the USS *Bogue*. While the Avengers of *Bogue* were unsuccessful in sinking any submarines, their efforts did drive them towards a Royal Navy anti-submarine group that was successful. These losses would persuade the Commander U-boats that the practice of operating in packs was no longer viable, and the concept was therefore scrapped, each boat being ordered to operate individually.

In April 1944 another escort carrier would join the war in the Atlantic. This was the USS *Tripoli*, a member of the Casablanca class. This carrier and its air group, VC-13, would form the core of TG.21.15 in company with the *Croatan*. This group managed to sink the *U 66* and *U 488*. Task Group 22.2 with the USS *Bogue* would manage to sink a most unusual submarine, this being a Japanese vessel, *Ro-501*, which was sunk on 13 May 1944. The south Atlantic would gain another task group, unnumbered, that was based at Recife, being constructed around the Casablanca-class escort carrier, the USS *Solomon*. Throughout May to October 1944 the US Navy task groups would be tasked with hunting down any notified U-boat packs. Their first area of operations was off the Azores where the *Block Island* group, TG.22.1, would attempt to sink the *U 549*. However the submarine was the eventual victor when, on 29 May, it hit the carrier with three torpedoes, causing it to sink. The submarine in turn would be sunk by the escorting destroyers, many of whom returned to pick up survivors from the carrier.

To replace the lost *Block Island*, TG.22.3 with the *Guadalcanal* as its escort carrier was deployed. Its first success was against *U 505*, which was forced to the surface by naval and aerial action. The result was that the submarine was taken over by a prize crew and sailed to Bermuda. The USS *Tripoli*, a member of the Casablanca class, would be deployed to Brazil after commissioning to operate from Recifie in the hunt for Axis submarines. After the carrier's first deployment to Recife it returned to the United States, putting into Norfolk for rest and restoring, arriving there on 29 April 1944. After a period of pilot training the *Tripoli* was prepared for combat operations. Embarking the composite squadron VC-6, the vessel departed for Brazil on 1 August. During the transit south, one of the escorts detected a submarine trace on its sonar. In support of the destroyer escorts the aircraft from the *Tripoli* dropped sonar buoys and flares, and the escorts closed in and thoroughly depth-charged the area. The result was some wreckage and a reasonable quantity of diesel oil.

The task group would claim this as a sinking, though examination of the German records showed that no vessel had been lost that day. Had this been a case of a decoy move correctly and successfully executed? We shall probably never know.

After this mild diversion the *Tripoli* finally reached Recife on 13 August, where the carrier was designated as the core of TG.47.7. After restoring and mission briefing, the task group put to sea on 22 August. The group's first task was to hunt a U-boat that was reported to be transiting through the area. The *Tripoli* group spent a fruitless fourteen days chasing sonar contacts before returning to Recife on 11 September. The period in port was short, as TG.47.7 departed two days later in order to join up with the USS *Mission Bay* (another Casablanca-class vessel) task group in order to intercept two U-boats known to be passing through the zone. One was a prize target, being the tanker submarine *U 1062 en route* to Penang, Malaysia, with much-needed aviation fuel, while the other was a standard boat *U 219*. In order to improve the chances of detecting either vessel, radar-equipped Grumman Avengers were launched from both carriers. In this the air groups were successful, as *U 219* was detected just eleven miles in front of the *Tripoli* group. Grumman Avengers were launched armed with rockets and depth charges, but the U-boat was not going to go down without a fight. As the first Avenger attacked, it was met by a hail of anti-aircraft fire that caused its destruction. A second Avenger attacked the submarine, which continued to twist and turn while throwing up a curtain of anti-aircraft fire. Eventually *U 219* managed to slip the attackers, although it would be attacked again a few days later by

The USS Croatan has a mix of Grumman Avengers and Wildcats on the flight deck. The Croatan was finally decommissioned in 1970. (US Navy/NARA via Dennis R. Jenkins)

Preparing to depart the flight deck of the USS Bogue is this Grumman Avenger of composite squadron VC-9. The Bogue was retired in 1946. (US Navy/NARA via Dennis R. Jenkins)

aircraft from both carrier groups. This time the aircrew were insistent that this time they had sunk the German vessel. Unfortunately for them, the submarine had escaped again, finally resurfacing in Batavia, Java. *U 1062* was not so lucky, as it was detected by the *Mission Bay* escorts and sunk.

After this excitement the *Tripoli* group returned to Recife to refuel and restore, arriving on 12 October. The carrier and its escorts departed Recife to undertake their final Atlantic patrol, departing port on 26 October. This patrol was quiet, and ended on 12 November, after which the carrier departed for a much-needed refit at the Norfolk Navy Yard. At the conclusion of this refit the carrier transited through the Panama Canal to join the Pacific Fleet, arriving at Hawaii in January 1945.

The two other carriers in the area, the *Card* and *Guadalcanal*, plus their supports, tried to sink *U 539* without success. TG.22.3 was more successful when the escorts and aircraft from *Croatan* managed to sink the remaining U-boat tanker, *U 490*, in the Atlantic on 11 June. The *Croatan* and its escorts departed the area to refuel, being replaced by TG.22.2 with *Bogue* at its core. Their target was *U 530*, although the group did manage to sink the Japanese supply submarine *I-52* on 23 June. On 2 July TG.22.4 with the carrier *Wake Island* successfully detected and sank *U 543* to the east of the Azores, even though the submarine put up a strong anti-aircraft resistance. Close to the Canadian coast, near Halifax, the USS *Card* group, TG.22.10, successfully sank *U 233* on 5 July. Further success was had off the Azores when the USS

Solomon's group, by now designated TG.41.6, intercepted and sank the submarine *U 860* using Avengers and Wildcats from VC-9. The USS *Solomon* and its escorts would then head towards Brazil in order to intercept *U 861*, which was hunting a convoy bound for Italy from Brazil. The submarine managed to evade TG.41.6, sinking a vessel that was part of convoy JT.39 as a consolation.

In late June 1944 TG.22.6 with *Wake Island* as its carrier was sent to hunt down a group of all-weather U-boats operating in the north Atlantic. The first submarine found was *U 804*, which managed to evade the destroyers and sink the escort USS *Fiske*. The *Wake Island* group was replaced by the *Bogue* group, TG.22.2, which scored a success when aircraft from VC-42 sank *U 1229*.

On 6 June 1944 the Allies launched Operation Overlord, better known as D-Day. Its purpose was the invasion of Europe, and one of the side effects was to force the U-boats away from their established bases in France. Most of the boats, whether seaworthy or not, were transferred to Norway in order to further prosecute the war, although in reality the menace of the U-boats had been greatly reduced. However, the German submarine service would have a final fling, which began on 26 September 1944. Operating mainly off the Canadian coast, the submarines began to sink convoy vessels almost with

Operating in fairly calm seas, the USS Core launches a Grumman Avenger assigned to VGS-13 for another anti-submarine patrol. (US Navy/NARA via Dennis R. Jenkins)

The weather in the Atlantic could be very rough at times, as this view of the USS Croatan shows. To protect the aircraft from damage they are securely lashed down. (US Navy/NARA via Dennis R. Jenkins)

impunity. To answer these attacks the escort carrier *Mission Bay* and *Card* task groups were sent to the region in an effort to curb their success. While none of the German submarines were detected or sunk, the presence of the two carrier groups did drive the submarines away. Throughout the remainder of 1944 the carrier escort groups continued to ply their trade in the Atlantic, although anti-submarine trade had started to fall off as the Allies took a firmer grip on Europe.

While 1945 saw the U-boat menace severely curtailed, there was still some use for the carrier group, although by this time many of the escort groups had been dispatched to the Pacific to prosecute the war against the Japanese. One of the major sorties carried out by the Atlantic group began on 5 April, being codenamed Operation Teardrop. The escort carriers involved were the USS *Croatan*, TG.22.5, and *Mission Bay*, TG.22.2. Surrounded by the usual pack of escorting destroyers, the carriers began their operations just north of the Azores. From the start their endeavours bore fruit, as submarines *U 1235* and *U 880* were sunk on 15 and 16 April respectively. The groups were not quite so lucky on 22 April when, after extensive searching, neither managed to snare *U 805*, which evaded the searchers. However, later that day *U 518* was not quite so lucky, as it was detected and sunk by escorts from the *Croatan* group. Over the next twenty-four hours the two original carrier groups were replaced by two fresh groups. The replacement groups were TG.22.3, whose carrier was the USS *Bogue*, and TG.22.4 with the USS *Core*. TG.22.3 would start the ball rolling by detecting *U 546*, although the submarine did manage to score some success by sinking one of the escorts. After a six-hour hunt the submarine was forced to the surface, where it launched a final torpedo before sinking. The remaining U-boats, *U 858*, *U 805*, *U 853*, *U 530*, *U 899* and *U 881*, managed to reach the east coast of America. Unfortunately for *U 881* it ran straight into the *Mission Bay* group, which promptly sank it. *U 853* would manage to sink a collier before being sunk itself on 5 May 1945, and this would be the final U-boat sinking before the war against Germany finally ended.

CHAPTER THREE

War in the Pacific:
Attack and Fightback

On the morning of 7 December 1941 the peace was shattered by the roar of piston aero engines. Personnel at Pearl Harbor were nonplussed as no flying from the island was scheduled for that day. As the roar grew louder it soon became apparent that the aircraft were not American, and the next thought was that they were under attack. Out of the sky swept a strong force of Japanese Navy dive-bombers, torpedo aircraft and supporting fighters. Battleship Row was the intended target, with wave after wave of attackers heading towards the steel behemoths safely tied up at their anchorages. Some of the battleship crews were more alert than others and began to mount a spirited defence to the fleet-wide order, 'Air raid Pearl Harbor. This is not a drill', against the aerial intruders, even though most of the ammunition lockers were secured. After ninety minutes the air over Hawaii grew quiet as the Japanese aircraft departed for their carriers. Behind them they left a scene of utter devastation: four battleships were sunk at their mooring, four more were damaged and another seven vessels were sunk or damaged. Personnel losses were grievous, with 2,402 being killed and another 1,282 suffering wounds. As well as the loss to the fleet, much of the island's infrastructure was also damaged and destroyed, including the power station, the shipyard and other maintenance facilities. But while all this was a major blow to the US Navy, the Japanese missed the most vital naval vessels, the aircraft carriers.

The attack on Pearl Harbor had its roots in many areas. At the conclusion of the Great War in 1918 there was a veritable pause in warship construction, all the participants realising that the building of capital ships would place a great strain on their already shaky economies. However, such a situation would not remain static for long, as Britain, Japan and the United States were close to bringing new battleship construction planning to fruition in 1920.

54

A fire vessel assists the crew of the USS Nevada, BB-36, as the crew battles with the fire caused by the Japanese attack on Pearl Harbor in December 1941. The crew eventually grounded their damaged battleship, their actions allowing the vessel to be rebuilt quickly and to rejoin the war effort. (US Navy/NARA via Dennis R. Jenkins)

The USS California was also hit by the Japanese attack aircraft on 7 December 1941. This battleship was also rebuilt and served through the remainder of the war. (US Navy/NARA via Dennis R. Jenkins)

This fine portrait of a Vought SB2U Vindicator shows the markings applied to pre-war aircraft of the US Navy. This aircraft was assigned to VS-72 aboard the USS Wasp. (US Navy/NARA via Dennis R. Jenkins)

Having seen one arms race that ran from 1909 to 1918, it was obvious to all the major powers that starting another arms race was not a good idea. The result would be the Washington Treaty, or Five Nations Treaty, that was designed to limit the amount of naval tonnage constructed by the signatories. The five nations that signed the treaty were Britain, France, Italy, Japan and the United States. All met in Washington in December 1921 to negotiate the tonnages allowable for each class of vessel. The various wrangles were finally cleared by late January 1922, the treaty being signed on 6 February. Following the Washington Treaty came the London Treaty signed in 1930, which modified the terms of the treaty. A second London Treaty was signed in 1936, although by this time Japan was completely ignoring the amounts and tonnages for each vessel class, as they regarded the treaties as limiting their sovereign rights and their plans for the future. Adding to the Japanese sense of grievance was the global economic collapse that started in 1926 and from which Japan emerged in the mid-1930s. Allied to this was the fact that the touted free trade around the world was being totally ignored by the major powers. In fact the practice was to protect their special economic rights within their own areas of influence while taxing imports from other areas heavily.

By this time Japan had increased her sphere of influence to encompass Korea, Taiwan and Manchuria, from where she exported goods to America and Europe at greatly reduced prices while charging extortionate tariffs on incoming goods. While much of the civilian raw materials were readily available within the Japanese sphere of influence, two vital materials, oil and rubber, were not easily obtainable, as the former came from America and the

When Pearl Harbor was attacked, the USS Wasp was operating in the Atlantic, although it would be quickly transferred to the Pacific to bolster the carrier force operating there. (US Navy/NARA via Dennis R. Jenkins)

latter from the British colonies in the Far East. Fearing Japanese expansion, both of these nations sought to restrict Japanese military growth by controlling the export of both of these materials. In order to further control any possible Japanese plans, President Franklin D. Roosevelt placed an embargo on exporting oil to Japan. Helping to increase the Japanese oil and rubber deficiencies were the military adventures being undertaken in China, where Russian resistance to the Japanese expansion was strong. It was at this point that the military-controlled government decided that a naval request to invade the Dutch East Indies and British Malaya was formulated, as the capture of both would give Japan easy access to both vital raw materials. The first move made by Japan outside her earlier territory conquests was the invasion of French Indo-China in 1940. This was the final straw for President Roosevelt, who completely banned the export of oil and steel to Japan in an effort to stop any further territorial gains.

While President Roosevelt and his senior advisers were rightly concerned about the Japanese adventurism in the Far East and the Pacific, it would be difficult for the Federal Government to sell a possible war against an enemy half a world away to the American people. In order to keep the vital assets of the US Navy safe, the President ordered the Pacific Fleet to abandon its exercises off Hawaii and return to port in Pearl Harbor on 7 May 1940 and to stay there until further notice. While the fleet was in port the President ordered the US Navy to undertake an evaluation of its available ships and to report on any deficiencies. The report was studied during August 1940, the result being the issue of contracts at the beginning of September for the construction of new vessels. The orders covered a total of 210 ships, which included two Iowa-class battleships, five Montana battleships, twelve Essex-class aircraft carriers, six Alaska-class battlecruisers, four Baltimore-class heavy cruisers, nineteen Cleveland-class light cruisers and four Atlanta-class light cruisers, while the remainder were various classes of destroyer.

Although the battleships were ordered to remain in Pearl Harbor, the remainder of the US Navy was ordered to resume normal patrols and visits. The first of these was undertaken in April 1941 when the heavy cruisers *Chicago* and *Portland*, plus a selection of destroyers and an oiler, departed Hawaii for Samoa as TG.9.1. From Samoa the task group headed for Sydney, Australia, this being followed by Brisbane, Tahiti and Auckland before it headed to Hawaii at the end of the month. A further US Navy visit was undertaken in August, taking in ports in Australia, plus Port Moresby and Rabaul.

While the Americans were busy supporting the convoys in the Atlantic, and patrolling that ocean, the Japanese and the Germans were busy in the Pacific. Although Japan had not formerly declared war in support of Germany, she was providing vital supplies to that nation. Instead of German blockade runners entering a Japanese friendly port where they could be spotted, the plan was for both parties to meet out at sea where exchanges could be made with greater privacy. While many of these were undertaken without any interference, some of the blockade runners were intercepted *en route* by Royal Navy patrols, and their valuable cargoes were impounded.

In October 1941 the President finally rescinded his 'stay in port' order to allow the battleships to gain some sea time. However, this was not without incident as the battleships *Arizona* and *Oklahoma* managed to collide, forcing an early return to port. A further move saw the submarines *Narwhal* and *Dolphin* arrive off Wake Island to undertake a simulated war patrol. During this 'not at war' period it was obvious that the Federal Government and the armed forces were gearing up for a potential conflict. To that end the American Neutrality Law was altered on 13 November to allow merchant ships to enter all zones and to provide for the arming of same. Twelve days later the US Navy introduced compulsory convoys for merchant shipping operating in the Pacific. On 25 November President Roosevelt, in negotiation with a Japanese delegation concerning their future plans, was forced to break off negotiations as the Japanese were proving intractable. The following day the American government through Secretary of State Hull handed the Japanese Ambassador in Washington a ten-point note that requested their compliance. The Japanese refused to accept these conditions and threatened to break off diplomatic relations. In response the Americans increased their intelligence gathering in the Pacific.

The inevitable breakdown in relations between America and Japan began to accelerate as a large carrier-based striking force assembled at Hitokapou Bay set out towards Pearl Harbor on 26 November. In this fleet were the aircraft carriers *Akagi*, *Kaga*, *Hiryu*, *Soryu*, *Shokaku* and *Zuikaku* with a total complement of 423 aircraft. Escorting the carriers were eight destroyers and a light cruiser. The support group consisted of the two battleships *Hiei* and *Kirishima*, plus two heavy cruisers. A smaller cruiser and destroyer force would also depart, although their target was Midway. Although the strike target had not been confirmed, the Federal Government issued a War Warning to all overseas commanders. The warning had been issued in response to signal analysis and gathered intelligence that revealed unusual concentrations of Imperial Japanese Navy vessels. The information only covered the IJN forces under the command of the Commander-in-Chief of the 2nd Fleet, Vice-Admiral Kindo, which were taking up positions around Formosa, Hainan, Indo-China and Palua. Missing from this intelligence-gathering effort were the vessels gathered together for the Pearl Harbor strike, Operation *Kido Butai*. While some signals traffic was intercepted from this force, these were not decoded due to lack of source material and the small number of Japanese-speaking translators available. In fact this scarce resource was concentrating upon the telegrams and other signals traffic being generated by the various Japanese diplomatic embassies around the world, and the war would have ended before the remaining signals traffic was finally decoded. To make matters even more difficult for the Americans, the Japanese changed all the callsigns for their warships and task forces. In response to the IJN movements the US Navy stationed the submarines *Tambour* and *Triton* off Wake Island, while the *Argonaut* and *Trout* were stationed off Midway for reconnaissance purposes. On 4 December the Japanese caused even more consternation among the American intelligence community by changing the super-cypher codebook for its naval units and task groups.

As the Pearl Harbor task force continued towards its target, a further task force assigned for the capture of Malaya departed Hainan on 4 December. Also departing was the task force escorts plus the Southern Expeditionary Force, which departed from Saigon. Their intended targets were Prachuab, Jimbhorn, Bandon and Nakhorn to block off the Kra isthmus. A larger force attacked Signora and Patani, while a further, smaller group headed for Khota Bharu and Kurita. Two days later another assault force departed on 6 December from Palau and set sail for the Philippines with the aircraft carrier *Ryujo*. The carrier launched thirteen bombers and nine fighters to attack Davao, while the support group held a position off Mindanoa. Operating in conjunction with the air strike, other naval forces entered the Gulf of Davao to undertake bombardment duties. A further assault group also departed Palau on 8 December and headed towards Legaspi. *En route* the escort force laid mines in the San Bernadino Strait and the Surigo Strait in order to frustrate any possible American reprisals.

The Japanese battle group assigned to attack Pearl Harbor reached its launch point just north of Oaha, and the first wave of aircraft, led by Commander Fuchida, departed the carriers at 06.00 hrs. This wave of aircraft consisted of fifty high-level bombers, forty torpedo-bombers, fifty-one dive-bombers and forty-three escorting fighters. Not long afterwards the second wave was launched, consisting of fifty-four high-level bombers, eighty-one dive-bombers and thirty-six fighters. As the Japanese air armada headed towards Pearl Harbor the intention had been for the Japanese Ambassador to deliver a formal note declaring that a state of war existed between America and Japan. Timed to coincide with the first bombs being dropped, problems with translation meant that the declaration of war was delivered late.

While the United States intelligence services were aware of the movements of the various Japanese forces heading to other parts of the Pacific, they had also been monitoring the communications of the Japanese Consul, Kita. However, those that had been deciphered had given no strong indications that any such attack was forthcoming. As the Pearl Harbor strike force sailed towards Hawaii some of the escorting submarines had been detected by the destroyer USS *Ward*, while the incoming aerial strike force had been detected on long-range radar. Adding to the marginal intelligence was a warning telegram from General George Marshall, US Army Chief of Staff, that highlighted the possibility of an attack on Pearl Harbor and the other major military establishments on Hawaii. The warning signals were not regarded as significant by Washington, and the telegram from General Marshall was misdirected, so that it reached the President after the bombs had begun falling. While some post-war critics would claim a conspiracy was in place to allow the attack to take place and force the United States into the war, it was more the lack of positive intelligence that allowed the strike to take place, as in truth America was only one short step from hostilities. To add to the American woes, Germany and Italy formally declared war on 11 December.

Fortunately the two aircraft carriers assigned to the Pacific fleet were already at sea. The USS *Lexington* was the core of Task Force 11 under the

Fortunately for the US Navy, the aircraft carriers were away from Pearl Harbor. One of them was the USS Lexington, seen here. (US Navy/NARA via Dennis R. Jenkins)

With its protective destroyer in the background, the deck crews of VT-6 prepare their charges aboard the USS Enterprise prior to the Battle of Midway. (US Navy/NARA via Dennis R. Jenkins)

command of Rear Admiral Newton, and was heading at full speed towards Midway with a full load of US Marine Corps aircraft to defend the island. As the US Navy was already on a war footing the carrier was provided with a full flotilla of escorting destroyers, while the submarine USS *Trout* was still stationed close to Midway. The other Pacific carrier, USS *Enterprise*, was assigned to Task Force 8 under the command of Admiral Halsey, and was returning to Hawaii after delivering aircraft for the defence of Wake Island. However, these were attacked by the Japanese as they passed near Ford Island. As the *Enterprise* headed towards Hawaii the Japanese submarines strung out along various patrol lines attempted to intercept the carrier and its escorts. Fortunately the carrier's aircraft and the escorts were fully alert and managed to drive off the intruding submarines.

While the Japanese were devastating Pearl Harbor, another Japanese combat group was beginning its assault upon the Philippines. The North Philippines Force began its attack on Luzon on 8 December when a force of 192 aircraft under the command of Vice-Admiral Tsukahara struck against the aircraft based at Clark and Ida Fields, while other aircraft from Formosa attacked the bases at Tuguegaro and Baguio. While the aircraft were keeping the Americans occupied, a further task force landed on Bataan, catching the defenders totally by surprise. Following the first Luzon assault came the second wave of vessels, carrying more troops, who were landed north of Luzon on 10 December, although by this time the defenders were more organised and were able to launch a force of Boeing B-17 Flying Fortress bombers and Curtiss P-40 Warhawk fighters to attack the assault fleet. While the attack was mainly unsuccessful, the USAAC aircraft did manage to badly damage one of the escort vessels. A third force commanded by Rear Admiral

Nishimura attempted to land another assault force at Padan near Luzon, but bad weather stopped the landing taking place. While standing off from shore the ships were attacked by USAAC aircraft, during which one of the escorts was sunk and two transports were damaged. A successful landing took place twenty-four hours later at Vingan. With the beachheads secured the naval aircraft undertook a devastating attack on the USAAC bases at Luzon on 12 December which destroyed the bulk of the Far East Air Force, the survivors managing to make their way to Mindanao and Australia.

With the Philippines under Japanese control, their next target was Guam. As the task force advanced they sank the minesweeper USS *Penguin,* after which the way was clear to take the island. After a period of token resistance the American garrison surrendered on 10 December. During that same period another assault group hit the Gilbert Islands, which after some resistance also fell into Japanese hands.

As the Japanese assault forces spread across the Pacific, another large assault group was heading towards their main prize, Malaya. The assault started on 7 December on the Thai coast, the Japanese meeting little opposition until they reached Kota Bharu. Here the Royal Air Force attempted to intervene, attacking targets on land and at sea. However, the British defence would soon crumble, as the Japanese aircraft would attack and sink the battleship HMS *Prince of Wales* and the battlecruiser HMS *Repulse* on the afternoon of 8 December, with great loss of life on both vessels. This victory seemed to spur the invaders on as they raced down Malaya sweeping all before them. Even the Royal Air Force would fail to make much of an impact, as its obsolescent aircraft were outflown and outgunned by their Japanese counterparts. A second landing by the Japanese Malaya Force would take place on the night of 16/17 December near Kuantan. While Dutch naval submarines attempted to stop the attack, their efforts, while praiseworthy, only caused minimal delay, as only one transport was sunk. Borneo would also be the subject of Japanese attention as another assault convoy attacked on 16 December. Again the Allied forces attempted to stem the attacks without much success.

The first setback for the Japanese forces took place over the night of 10/11 December, when the assault force under the command of Rear Admiral Kajioka was repulsed by the defenders based on Wake Island. As the attack began, the 450 US Marines under the command of Major Devereaux, with the support of the island's coastal batteries, drove the invaders back into the sea. Also on the island were sixty-eight US Navy personnel and 1,200 civilian workers who were finishing off the recently completed military works on the island. The USMC force was armed with six guns for coastal defence, and twelve M3 guns. Further defensive weaponry included thirty machine-guns of various manufacture and serviceability. On 28 November 1941 Commander Winfield S. Cunningham USN arrived on Wake to assume overall command of the forces on the island. During the following two weeks he examined the available defences and increased the training of his men before hostilities began. On 8 December 1941 thirty-six Mitsubishi G3M

A Grumman F4F Wildcat assigned to VF-71 aboard the USS Wasp taxies out to undertake a training sortie before returning to its carrier home. (US Navy/NARA via Dennis R. Jenkins)

bombers flown from bases on the Marshall Islands attacked Wake Island, destroying eight of the twelve Grumman F4F-3 Wildcat fighter aircraft belonging to USMC fighter squadron VMF-211 on the ground. All of the Marine garrison's defensive emplacements were untouched during the raid, although twenty-three Marines were killed and a further eleven were wounded. Ten civilian employees of Pan American Airways based on the island were also killed.

In the early hours of the morning of 11 December, the garrison, with the support of the four remaining Wildcats, successfully repulsed the first Japanese landing attempt, the force consisting of the light cruisers *Yubari*, *Tenry* and *Tatsuta*, eight destroyers and two troop transport ships containing 450 Special Naval Landing Force troops. The US Marines fired at the invasion fleet with the coastal artillery guns, although Major Devereux had ordered the gunners to hold their fire until the enemy moved within effective range of the guns. Battery L under the command of Sergeant Henry Bedell on Peale islet succeeded in sinking the Hayate at a distance of 4,000 yards with direct hits to the magazines, which caused the ship to explode and sink within two minutes. The four remaining Wildcats also succeeded in sinking another destroyer by dropping a bomb on the stern, where the depth charges were stored. Both Japanese destroyers were lost with all hands, with the *Hayate* becoming the first Japanese surface warship to be sunk during the Second World War. The severity of the defence caused the Japanese force to withdraw before landing. This was also the first Japanese defeat of the war. After the initial raid was beaten off the United States news media reported that, when asked about the need for reinforcement and resupply, Cunningham retorted, 'Send us more Japs!'

Commander Cunningham had sent a long list of critical equipment requirements, which included gunsights for the defensive guns and

The Brewster Buffalo was already outdated when hostilities began. Even so, in some distant outposts their pilots fought well against overwhelming odds. (John Ryan Collection)

fire-control radar, to his immediate superior, Commandant, 14th Naval District. The siege of the island continued, punctuated by frequent air attacks on the Wake garrison. The strong resistance offered by the garrison prompted the Japanese Navy to detach the two aircraft carriers *Soryu* and *Hiryu* from the force that had attacked Pearl Harbor to support the second landing attempt. The projected American relief attempt by Task Force 11 commanded by Admiral Frank Fletcher, and supported by Task Force 14 commanded by Admiral Wilson Brown, consisted of the fleet carrier *Saratoga*, the fleet oiler USNS *Neches*, the seaplane tender *Tangier*, the cruisers *Astoria*, *Minneapolis* and *San Francisco* plus ten destroyers. The convoy carried the 4th Marine Defence Battalion, VMF-221 fighter squadron equipped with Brewster F2A Buffalo fighters. Also carried by the force were 9,000 5-inch rounds, 12,000 3-inch rounds, and three million machine-gun rounds, as well as ammunition for mortars and other small arms. Task Force 14, consisting of the fleet carrier *Lexington*, three heavy cruisers, eight destroyers and one oiler, was ordered to undertake a diversionary raid on the Marshall Islands to distract the Japanese. On 22 December, after receiving intelligence that indicated the presence of two Japanese carriers plus two fast battleships near Wake Island, Vice-Admiral William S. Pye, the Acting Commander-in-Chief of the US Pacific Fleet, ordered TF.14 to return to Pearl Harbor as he feared for its safety. Also, problems with refuelling at sea had delayed the arrival of the task force, and this hastened its recall.

The second Japanese invasion force, under the command of Rear Admiral Kajioka, departing from Kwajalein on 20 December and arriving on station by 23 December, was composed mostly of the same ships from the first attempt

A mix of Wildcat fighters and Dauntless dive-bombers run up their engines to full power prior to launching from the USS Saratoga. (US Navy/NARA via Dennis R. Jenkins)

with extra additions plus 1,500 Japanese marines. The landings began in the early hours of the morning, the opening gambit being a preliminary bombardment. During the initial landings Patrol Boat No. 32 and Patrol Boat No. 33 were beached and burned in their attempts to land the invasion force. After a full night and morning of fighting, the Wake garrison surrendered to the Japanese during the afternoon. The USMC lost forty-seven killed during the entire fifteen-day siege, with three Navy personnel and at least seventy civilians killed, while a further twelve civilians were wounded. Japanese losses were recorded at between 700 and 900 killed, while a further 300 were wounded. During the assault the Japanese lost two destroyers in the first invasion attempt, plus twenty-eight land-based and carrier aircraft either shot down or damaged. The Japanese captured all men remaining on the island, the majority being civilian contractors employed by the Morrison-Knudsen Company. Captain Henry T. Elrod, one of the pilots from VMF-211, was later awarded the Medal of Honor posthumously for his actions defending the island during the second landing attempt, having shot down two Japanese A6M Zero fighters and sunk the Japanese destroyer *Kisaragi*. A special

Ranged on the foredeck of the USS Lexington are these Douglas Dauntlesses of VB-16 being prepared for a mission. (US Navy/NARA via Dennis R. Jenkins)

military decoration, the Wake Island Device, was also created to recognise those who had fought in the defence of the island.

On 17 December 1941 there was a change of command for the Pacific fleet when Admiral Chester W. Nimitz replaced Admiral Husband E. Kimmel, although during the intervening period Admiral Pye had assumed temporary command. The Japanese forces, having undertaken their initial conquests, would start to consolidate their hold on their new territories. The first to experience reinforcement were the Philippines, when further forces were landed on 17 December. The following day the final battle for Hong Kong took place, the British forces finally surrendering as they were faced by overwhelming odds. At the year's end further Japanese forces were landed throughout Malaya, with others invading Sarawak, Labuan, Brunei Bay and North Borneo. The next year, 1942, would open with a United Nations meeting in Washington, where twenty-six nations agreed that they would not conclude a separate peace with either Germany or Japan.

Meanwhile, in the Pacific the American war to repulse the Japanese was passed to the submarine service, which set about sinking as many ships as possible. Surface activity resumed on 6 January when a convoy departed San Francisco, consisting of five troop transports escorted by Task Force 17 with the fleet carrier USS *Yorktown*, recently transferred from Atlantic duties. Their destination was Pago Pago on Samoa, and this force was also escorted by another task force, TF.8, with the USS *Enterprise* as its aircraft carrier. On 9

Like all the available carriers, the USS Saratoga had its air wing updated as new types came into service. Here a Grumman F6F prepares to launch to undertake another sortie. (US Navy/NARA via Dennis R. Jenkins)

January, TF.14 with the carrier USS *Saratoga* was ordered to join these task groups. However, *en route* the carrier was torpedoed by a Japanese submarine, one of a patrol line stationed off Hawaii. Luckily personnel losses were kept to six men, while structural damage was limited to three compartments. Fortunately the *Saratoga* had undergone major modifications at Bremerton Naval Yard, which included the fitment of external bulges that helped limit the damage. Even so the carrier had to return to Hawaii for more extensive repair work. While the United States was continuing to build up her war machine, the Japanese forces were undertaking further assaults throughout South-East Asia. One of the first reinforcement attacks took place on 14 January against Rabaul and Kavieng. As the Japanese High Command had anticipated great resistance, at least four aircraft carriers and escorts were assigned to the mission. Their assault was successful, and the covering forces, carriers and battleships departed the area and returned to the main naval base that had been established at Truk Atoll.

Pearl Harbor would be the scene of much activity on 22 January when Task Force 11 under the command of Rear Admiral Brown set out to mount an attack on Wake Island. At the core of TF.11 was the carrier USS *Lexington*, plus an array of escorting cruisers and destroyers. It would be the Japanese who would spoil the progress of the mission, as one of their submarines managed to sink the oiler USS *Neches*. With no mobile fuel supply, the task force had to return to Pearl Harbor, as the destroyers needed the oiler for refuelling. Another attack would be mounted on 25 January, although this time the

Everywhere was a tight fit aboard, the early carrier reveals. Here ground crews prepare their charges, Douglas Dauntlesses of VT-6, aboard the USS Enterprise. (US Navy/NARA via Dennis R. Jenkins)

target was the Marshall and Gilbert Islands. Two carrier groups would be involved in this raid, these being TF.8 under the command of Vice-Admiral Halsey and TF.17 with Vice-Admiral Fletcher commanding. Their assigned carriers were the *Enterprise* and *Yorktown* respectively. Operations began on 1 February when aircraft from the *Enterprise* were launched, including eighteen torpedo and forty-six dive-bombing aircraft against the islands of Wotje, Maloelap and Kwajalien. During the attack seven IJN vessels, including a cruiser, were damaged, while one vessel was sunk for the loss of six aircraft. The Japanese would launch an aerial counter-attack during which the *Enterprise* suffered minor damage. The *Yorktown* group undertook an attack on the islands of Jaluit, Mili and Makin for the loss of six aircraft. At the completion of the raids the US Navy forces withdrew. However, the IJN decided to send a carrier group in pursuit, although this was recalled three days later on 4 February, as the High Command was worried about raids on the Japanese home islands.

Having returned to Hawaii after the loss of the group's oiler, Task Force 11 would depart from Pearl Harbor on 31 January. Its mission was to provide protection for two convoys that had passed through the Panama Canal and were heading to the south Pacific. The first convoy consisted of six vessels packed with troops heading for Bora Bora, while the second consisted of eight ships, with 20,000 troops aboard, destined for New Caledonia. The journey was completed with little incident, and so the carrier group was assigned to ANZAC under the overall command of Vice-Admiral Leary USN. The first mission for TF.11 was to undertake an attack on Rabaul, departing from the New Hebrides on 17 February. *En route* the task force was spotted by Japanese Emily flying-boats, of which two were shot down by the carrier's air cover. At this point the task force was some 300 miles short of its target, and would come under attack from Japanese aircraft based on Rabaul. During the defensive effort Lieutenant O'Hare, one of the fighter pilots from the USS *Enterprise*, managed to shoot down five enemy aircraft. Having been discovered, the task force commander decided to cancel the attack and return to harbour. Instead of pressing on towards Rabaul, TF.11 would undertake a patrol of the Coral Sea before joining up with TF.17 on 6 March, just off the New Hebrides. Both carrier groups then returned to Pearl Harbor for repairs and restoring. On 14 February Task Force 8 departed from Pearl Harbor to undertake raids on Marcus and Wake Islands. The first raid was undertaken on 24 February, thirty-six bombers being launched, with six fighters as escort. During the raid one aircraft was lost. The aircraft from USS *Enterprise* undertook a further raid this time against Marcus on 4 March during which one aircraft was lost. Following on from the *Enterprise* raid, Task Group 17 would depart from Hawaii on 16 February to undertake a raid on Eniwetok Atoll in the Carolines. However, this raid was called off as the task force was desperately needed to provide cover for a convoy heading to the south-west Pacific. At the completion of the escort run the carrier group headed for the Phoenix Islands on 17 February, arriving off the New Hebrides on 6 March, where the group joined up with TF.11.

On 24 February 1942 the renumbered TF.8, now known as TF.16, under the command of Vice-Admiral Halsey, departed from Hawaii to undertake a raid on Wake Island. The carrier's air group bombed the Japanese positions on the island while the escorts shelled other installations. All of the aircraft returned to the carrier safely. While the Americans were making some progress and honing their battle skills, the Japanese were making further inroads into the Dutch East Indies. These began on 25 February, with Java being the main target, the invasion being completed by 9 March. Although the *Enterprise* task force had been unable to attack Wake Island, the group was reassigned to attack Marcus Island, setting out on 4 March. While the *Enterprise* group was *en route* to Marcus the *Lexington*, at the core of TF.11 under the command of Vice-Admiral Brown, joined up with TF.17 under the command of Rear Admiral Fletcher to undertake a combined raid on the Japanese landing-points on the south of the Papuan Peninsula. On 10 March the carriers launched a total of 104 aircraft to attack the harbours on the other side of the Owen Stanley Mountains. During the attack three vessels were sunk, and a further seven naval vessels were damaged. A further transport was so damaged that it had to be beached. At the conclusion of these raids the carrier task forces would withdraw and return to Pearl Harbor.

On 30 March 1942 the United States Joint Chiefs of Staff decided to divide the Pacific Ocean into two separate commands. The first was the Pacific Ocean Area under the command of Admiral Nimitz, while the other, the South-West Pacific Area, would be under the command of Lieutenant-General MacArthur. One of the first tasks of the rehashed naval command was to undertake the Doolittle Raid. This mission, undertaken on 18 April 1942, was the first air raid by American forces to strike at the Japanese home island of Honsu. It demonstrated to the Japanese that they were vulnerable to Allied air attack, and provided some reparation for Japan's attack on Pearl Harbor. The raid was conceived, planned and led by Lieutenant-Colonel James 'Jimmy' Doolittle. Sixteen North American B-25B Mitchell bombers were launched from the aircraft carrier USS *Hornet* deep within enemy waters. The plan called for them to bomb military targets in Japan and then land in China. All of the aircraft involved in the bombing were lost and eleven of the crewmen were either killed or captured. One of the B-25s landed in Soviet territory, where its crew remained interned for over a year. The complete crews from thirteen of the sixteen aircraft, and all but one of a fourteenth, returned to America or other Allied forces The raid itself caused little material damage to Japan, but it did succeed in its goal of lifting American morale. It also resulted in the Japanese High Command withdrawing a carrier group from the Indian Ocean to defend the home islands.

The raid had its roots in a desire by President Franklin D. Roosevelt, expressed to the Joint Chiefs of Staff in a meeting at the White House on 21 December 1941, for Japan to be bombed as soon as possible to boost public morale after the disaster at Pearl Harbor. The idea for the attack came from Captain Francis Low USN, Assistant Chief of Staff for anti-submarine warfare, whose report to Admiral Ernest J. King on 10 January 1942 stated that it would be possible for twin-engined USAAF bombers to be successfully launched from an aircraft carrier. Requirements for the aircraft included a cruising range of 2,400 miles with a 2,000 lb bomb load, and this resulted in the selection of the North American B-25B Mitchell to carry out the mission. Subsequent flight trials with a B-25 indicated they would be able fulfil the mission requirements. Doolittle's first report suggested that the bombers could land in Vladivostok, Russia, thus shortening the outbound flight by 600 miles, after which they would be turned over as Lend-Lease supplies. When planning indicated that the B-25 was the aircraft that best met all specifications of the mission, two were loaded aboard the aircraft carrier USS *Hornet* at Norfolk, Virginia, and subsequently flown off the deck without difficulty on 3 February 1942. The raid was immediately approved, and the 17th Bomb Group (Medium) was chosen to provide the pool of crews from which volunteers would be recruited. The 17th BG had been the first group to receive B-25s, with all four of its squadrons equipped with the bomber by September 1941. The 17th BG was originally flying anti-submarine patrols from

Pendleton, Oregon, and was ordered to move to Lexington County Army Air Base, South Carolina, to prepare for the mission against Japan. The group officially transferred to Columbia on 9 February, where its combat crews were offered the opportunity to volunteer for an extremely hazardous, but unspecified, mission.

Initial planning called for twenty aircraft to fly the mission. Therefore twenty-four of the group's B-25B Mitchell bombers were diverted to the Mid-Continent Airlines modification centre in Minneapolis for alterations that included removal of the lower gun turret, installation of de-icers and anti-icers, steel blast plates fitted on the fuselage around the upper turret, installation of three additional fuel tanks and support mounts in the bomb bay, crawl way and lower turret area to increase fuel capacity, and mock gun barrels installed in the tail position. Two bombers also had cameras mounted to record the results of bombing. The crews selected for the mission collected the modified bombers from Minneapolis and flew them to Eglin Field, Florida, during March 1942. There the crews received intensive training for three weeks in simulated carrier-deck take-offs, low-level and night flying,

A Douglas Dauntless angles onto the deck of the USS Hornet, while the control batsman prepares to dive clear of the slightly off-centre dive-bomber. (US Navy/NARA via Dennis R. Jenkins)

With their restraining struts still in position, this pair of Grumman Wildcats come up on the elevator from the hangar aboard the USS Enterprise. (US Navy/NARA via Dennis R. Jenkins)

low-altitude bombing, and over-water navigation. On 25 March the B-25s took off from Eglin for McClellan Field, California. They arrived on 27 March for final modifications by the Sacramento Air Depot. A total of sixteen B-25s were subsequently flown to Alameda, California, on 31 March.

Fifteen raiders would be assigned to the mission, while a sixteenth aircraft would be carried on the deck to be flown off shortly after departure from San Francisco to provide feedback to the Army pilots about take-off characteristics. On 1 April 1942 the sixteen modified bombers were loaded onto the USS *Hornet* at Alameda, with each aircraft carrying four specially constructed 500 lb bombs. Three of these were high-explosive munitions, while the other was a bundle of incendiaries. After loading aboard the carrier, the aircraft were tied down on the carrier's flight deck in the order of their expected launch. The *Hornet* and Task Force 18 left the port of Alameda on 2 April, and a few days later rendezvoused with Task Force 16, which included the USS *Enterprise*, commanded by Vice-Admiral Halsey, in the mid-Pacific Ocean north of Hawaii. The *Enterprise* fighters and scout planes would provide protection for the entire task force in the event of a Japanese air attack, since the *Hornet*'s fighters were stowed below decks to allow the B-25s to use the

A B-25 Mitchell departs from USS Hornet, en route to bomb Japan. While the raid caused little physical damage, the lift to American morale was tremendous. (US Navy/NARA via Dennis R. Jenkins)

With throttles wide open, the first of the Doolittle Raiders lifts off from the deck of the USS Hornet. Unlike normal operational B-25s, these aircraft had fake tail guns and increased fuel tankage in the fuselage, among other modifications. (US Navy/NARA via Dennis R. Jenkins)

flight deck. Early in the morning of 18 April the task force was sighted by a Japanese picket boat, which radioed a warning to Japan. Although the boat was fatally damaged by gunfire from the cruiser USS *Nashville*, Doolittle and the *Hornet* commander, Captain Mitscher, decided to launch the bombers immediately, at least ten hours early and 170 miles farther from Japan than originally planned. After respotting to allow for engine starts and run-ups, all sixteen aircraft departed safely. This would be the only time that USAAF bombers were launched from an aircraft carrier on a combat mission.

Safely airborne, the B-25s then flew towards Japan in groups of two to four aircraft before changing to single file at wave-top level to avoid detection. The aircraft then arrived over Japan and bombed ten military and industrial targets in Tokyo, two in Yokohama, and one each in Yokosuka, Nagoya, Kobe and Osaka. Although some B-25s encountered light anti-aircraft fire and a few enemy fighters over Japan, no aircraft was shot down. Only the B-25 of Lieutenant Joyce received any battle damage – minor hits from anti-aircraft fire. Aircraft No. 4, piloted by Lieutenant Everett W. Holstrom, jettisoned its bombs before reaching its target when it came under attack by fighters after its gun turret malfunctioned. Fifteen of the sixteen aircraft then proceeded south-west along the southern coast of Japan and out across the East China Sea towards eastern China, where several airfields in Chekiang Province were supposed to be ready to guide them in, using homing beacons for refuelling. The raiders faced several unforeseen challenges during their flight to China,

Grumman F6F Hellcats of VF-20 are prepared for flight aboard the USS Lexington. Note the widespread use of helmets for head protection among the deck crews. (US Navy/NARA via Dennis R. Jenkins)

as night was approaching, the aircraft were running low on fuel and the weather was rapidly deteriorating. As a result of these problems, the crews realised they would probably not be able to reach the intended bases in China, leaving them the option of either baling out over eastern China or crash-landing along the Chinese coast. Following the Doolittle Raid, the crews that came down in China eventually made it to safety with the help of Chinese civilians and soldiers. While the raid created little material damage, unlike the B-29 raids later in the war, the psychological effects were more widespread. The attack revealed that the Japanese homelands were vulnerable to further raids, even as their forces were pushing through south-east Asia towards Australia.

After launching the Mitchells, the USS *Hornet* group steamed at full speed towards Pearl Harbor, while the carrier *Enterprise* as part of TF.11 was heading in the other direction towards Palmyra Island, where it offloaded a much-needed cargo of USMC fighters on 18 April. The *Yorktown* group, TF.17, under the command of Admiral Fletcher, would strike the next blow against the Japanese in early May. The Japanese High Command had decided that their next move would be to invade Port Moresby on New Guinea, while another force was headed towards to Tulagi on the Solomons. To ensure success the IJN provided a large number of cruisers and destroyers to escort the transports for both missions. The first strike from the *Yorktown* involved ninety-nine aircraft directed against the Tulagi assault force. The attack took place on 4 May, during which four naval vessels were sunk and a further four were badly damaged. Having realised that the Americans had a pair of carriers in the area, the Japanese High Command decided to undertake a decisive strike against the American carriers. On 7 May the carrier forces from the both navies exchanged air strikes that continued over the next two days.

On the following day the Japanese fleet carrier *Shokaku* was heavily damaged, while the main fleet carrier USS *Lexington* was scuttled as a result of major structural damage, and the *Yorktown* was damaged. With both sides having suffered heavy losses in aircraft and carriers damaged or sunk, the two fleets disengaged and retired from the battle area. Due to the loss of vital carrier air cover, Admiral Inoue recalled the Port Moresby invasion fleet with the intention of trying again later. While the Battle of the Coral Sea was a tactical victory for the Japanese in terms of vessels sunk, the battle would prove to be a strategic victory for the Allies, for several reasons. The first was that the Japanese expansion in the Pacific, seemingly unstoppable till then, had been repulsed for the first time. Of greater importance was the reduction of the Japanese fleet carriers, with the *Shoho* being sunk and the *Shokaku* damaged, while the *Zuikaku* had a severely depleted aircraft complement. They were therefore unable to participate in the Battle of Midway that took place the following month. However, the Japanese Port Moresby Invasion Force, commanded by Rear Admiral Koso Abe, which included eleven transport ships carrying approximately 5,000 soldiers from the IJA South Seas Detachment, plus approximately 500 troops from the 3rd Kure Special Naval

Landing Force, was dispatched towards the intended target. Escorting the transports was the Port Moresby Attack Force with one light cruiser and six destroyers under the command of Rear Admiral Kajioka. Abe's ships departed Rabaul for the voyage to Port Moresby on 4 May, being joined by the Kajioka force the next day. Leading the attack on Tulagi was the Tulagi Invasion Force, commanded by Rear Admiral Shima, consisting of two minelayers, two destroyers, six minesweepers, two submarine chasers, and a transport ship carrying approximately 400 troops from the 3rd Kure SNLF.

Supporting the Tulagi force was the Covering Group with the light carrier *Shoho*, four heavy cruisers and one destroyer, commanded by Rear Admiral Goto. A separate Cover Force, commanded by Rear Admiral Marumo, and consisting of two light cruisers, a seaplane tender and three gunboats, joined the Covering Group in providing distant protection for the Tulagi invasion. Once Tulagi had been secured, the Covering Group and Cover Force were to reposition to help screen the Port Moresby invasion. The Goto force departed the main naval base at Truk on 28 April, passing through the Solomons between Bougainville and Choiseul, and took station near New Georgia Island, while the Marumo support group left New Ireland on 29 April and headed for Thousand Ships Bay, Santa Isabel Island, to establish a seaplane base, and the Shima invasion force departed Rabaul on 30 April.

The Carrier Strike Force, with the carriers *Zuikaku* and *Shokaku*, two heavy cruisers, and six destroyers, left Truk on 1 May. The strike force was commanded by Vice-Admiral Takagi, with Rear Admiral Hara in tactical command of the carrier air forces. The Carrier Strike Force was to proceed down the eastern side of the Solomon Islands and enter the Coral Sea south of Guadalcanal. Once in the Coral Sea the carriers would provide air cover for the invasion forces, eliminate Allied air power at Port Moresby and intercept and destroy any Allied naval forces that entered the Coral Sea in response to the attacks. To give advance warning of the approach of any Allied naval forces, the Japanese had dispatched submarines *I-22*, *I-24*, *I-28* and *I-29* to form a scouting line in the ocean about 450 nautical miles south-west of Guadalcanal. The forces under the command of Admiral Fletcher had already entered the Coral Sea prior to the submarines taking station, and so the Japanese were unaware of the Allies' presence. On the morning of 1 May 1942 TF17 and TF11 came together approximately 300 nautical miles north-west of New Caledonia. Admiral Fletcher immediately sent TF.11 to refuel from the oiler *Tippecanoe*, while TF.17 refuelled from the oiler *Neosho*. TF.17 was ready to proceed the next day, but TF.11 reported that it would take until 4 May before all its ships were fully replenished.

Not wishing to wait for TF.11, Fletcher elected to take TF.17 north-west towards the Louisiades, ordering TF.11 to join up with Task Force 44, which was *en route* from Sydney and Nouma, once refuelling was complete. TF.44 was a joint Australian-American warship force under the command of General MacArthur, being led by Rear Admiral John Crace RAN. This force consisted of the cruisers HMAS *Australia*, HMAS *Hobart* and USS *Chicago*, plus three destroyers. In the early hours of 3 May the Shima force arrived off Tulagi and began disembarking the naval troops to occupy the island. Tulagi was undefended, as the small garrison of Australian commandos and an RAAF reconnaissance unit had been withdrawn just before the Japanese arrival. After landing, the Japanese forces immediately began construction of a seaplane and communications base. On the evening of 3 May Admiral Fletcher was notified that the Japanese Tulagi invasion force had been sighted the day before approaching the Solomons. However, Fletcher was unaware that TF.11 had completed refuelling that morning, earlier than expected, and was only sixty nautical miles east of TF.17, but was unable to communicate its status because of standing orders to maintain radio silence. TF.17 changed course and proceeded at speed towards Guadalcanal to launch air strikes against the Japanese forces at Tulagi the next morning.

On 4 May some one hundred nautical miles south of Guadalcanal, a total of sixty aircraft from TF.17 were launched in three consecutive waves against the Shima force off Tulagi. The *Yorktown*'s aircraft surprised Shima's ships and sank the destroyer *Kikuzuki* and three of the minesweepers, while four other ships were damaged. Also destroyed were four seaplanes that had been supporting the landings. In return the US Navy lost one dive-bomber and two fighters in the strikes, although all of the aircrews were eventually rescued. After recovering its aircraft late in the evening, the *Yorktown* and TF.17 departed to the south. In spite of the damage suffered during the carrier attacks, the Japanese continued construction of the seaplane base and began flying reconnaissance missions from Tulagi on 6 May. The Takagi Carrier Force had been refuelling 350 nautical miles north of Tulagi when word of the US Navy strike on 4 May was received. Takagi ceased refuelling and headed south-east, sending scout aircraft to search east of the Solomons, as they believed that the American carriers were in that area. On 5 May TF.17 rendezvoused with TF.11 and TF.44 at a predetermined point 320 nautical miles south of Guadalcanal. During this period four Grumman F4F Wildcats from *Yorktown* intercepted a Kawanishi Type 97 reconnaissance aircraft from the Yokohama Air Group of the 25th Air Flotilla based at the Shortland Islands, and shot it down eleven nautical miles from TF.11. The aircraft had been unable to send a report before it crashed, but when it failed to return to base the Japanese correctly reasoned that it had been shot down by carrier aircraft.

A coded message from Pearl Harbor notified Admiral Fletcher that radio intelligence gathering had deduced that the Japanese planned to land their troops at Port Moresby on 10 May, with their fleet carriers operating close to the invasion convoy. With this information, Fletcher directed TF.17 to refuel from the oiler *Neosho*. Refuelling was completed on 6 May, after which he planned to take his forces north towards the Louisiades and to engage the enemy on 7 May. While the Americans were repositioning, the Takagi carrier force steamed down the east side of the Solomons throughout 5 May before turning west to pass south of San Cristobal and entering the Coral Sea in the early morning hours of 6 May. Takagi commenced refuelling his ships 180 nautical miles west of Tulagi in preparation for the carrier battle he expected would take place the next day. On 6 May Admiral Fletcher combined TF.11 and TF.44 into TF.17 to create a larger strike group. During mid-morning a Kawanishi reconnaissance flying-boat from Tulagi sighted TF.17, and notified its headquarters by radio of the force's position. When this information was received by the Takagi force it was approximately 300 nautical miles north of Fletcher, close to the maximum effective range for his carrier aircraft. Takagi concluded, based on the sighting report, that TF.17 was heading south, away from the Japanese. As well as the aircraft range problem, the American vessels were under a large, low-hanging overcast that the IJN senior officers felt would make it difficult for their aircraft to detect the American carriers. Takagi detached two carriers with two destroyers to intercept TF.17 at 20 knots in order to attack the Americans at first light the next day.

USAAF Boeing B-17 bombers based in Australia that were staged through Port Moresby attacked the approaching IJN Port Moresby invasion forces several times during the day on 6 May without any success. General MacArthur's headquarters then radioed Fletcher with reports of the B-17 attacks and the locations of the Japanese invasion forces. TF.17 then turned to head north-west towards Rossel Island in the Louisiades. By this time both sets of carriers were only seventy nautical miles apart. Overnight on 6/7 May the seaplane tender *Kamikawa Maru* set up a seaplane base in the Deboyne Group in order to help provide air support for the invasion forces as they approached Port Moresby. The rest of the Cover Force then took up station near the D'Entrecasteaux Islands to help screen the incoming convoy. In the early hours of 7 May TF.17 was 115 nautical miles due south of Rossel Island. Admiral Fletcher then detached a cruiser and destroyer force, designated Task Group 17.3, to block the Jomard Passage. The detachment of TG 17.3 reduced the anti-aircraft defences available to defend the carriers. However, Fletcher decided that the risk was necessary in order to ensure that the Japanese invasion forces could not slip through to Port Moresby while he was engaged with the Japanese carriers. Believing that the Takagi carrier force was somewhere north of his location, Fletcher directed the USS *Yorktown* to send ten Douglas SBD dive-bombers as scouts to search that area.

In the meantime the Takagi force launched twelve Type 97 carrier bombers to scout for TF.17. The senior officers believed that the US Navy carriers were located to the south, and advised Takagi to send the aircraft to search that area. Around the same time the cruisers *Kinugasa* and *Furutaka* launched four Kawanishi E7K2 Type 94 floatplanes to search south-east of the Louisiades. Augmenting their search were several float-planes from Deboyne, four Kawanishi Type 97s from Tulagi, and three Mitsubishi Type 1 bombers from Rabaul. Soon after the IJN patrols had launched, one of the Takagi carrier scouts, from *Shokaku*, reported that it had located American ships 163 nautical miles from the Takagi force. This was later confirmed that at least one carrier, one cruiser, and three destroyers had been located. Believing that the

With Grumman Avengers flying past, the IJN carrier Shoho is wracked by fire and explosions prior to sinking. (US Navy/NARA via Dennis R. Jenkins)

American carriers had been spotted, the Takagi force immediately launched all available aircraft. A total of seventy-eight aircraft – eighteen Zero fighters, thirty-six Type 99 dive-bombers and twenty-four torpedo-aircraft – began launching from the *Shokaku* and *Zuikaku*, heading towards the reported sighting. Not long after the Takagi carriers had launched, one of the *Furutaka* aircraft found the American carriers and immediately reported their location to Inoue's headquarters at Rabaul, from where the report was then passed on to Takagi. Confused by the conflicting sighting reports that were arriving, Takagi decided to continue with the strike on the ships to their south, although the carriers were turned towards the north-west to reduce the distance from the *Furutaka's* reported contact.

While the Japanese were spotting the Americans, a *Yorktown* Douglas SBD sighted the Goto force screening the invasion convoy. After receiving the report Fletcher concluded that the Japanese main carrier force had been located, and ordered the launch of all available carrier aircraft to attack. By mid-morning the American strike of ninety-three aircraft – eighteen Wildcat fighters, fifty-three SBD dive-bombers and twenty-two TBD Devastator torpedo-bombers – was airborne. As the American carriers were between him and the invasion convoy, thus placing the Japanese invasion forces in extreme danger, Takagi ordered all aircraft to be prepared for an immediate attack. The American strike aircraft sighted the carrier *Shoho* a short distance north-east of Misima Island and turned to attack. The Japanese carrier was protected by six Zeros and two Type 96 fighters flying combat air patrol, as the remainder of the carrier's aircraft were being prepared below decks for a strike against the American carriers. Attacking first, the *Lexington* air group struck *Shoho* with two 1,000 lb bombs and five torpedoes, causing severe damage. This attack was followed by one from the *Yorktown* air group that attacked the burning and now almost stationary carrier, scoring hits with at least eleven more 1,000 lb bombs and at least two torpedoes. Torn apart by massive explosions, the *Shoho* sank in late morning.

Fearing more air attacks, Admiral Goto withdrew the remainder of the group to the north, although the destroyer *Sazanami* returned in mid-afternoon to rescue survivors. Only 203 of the carrier's 834 man crew were recovered. Three American aircraft were lost in the attack, comprising two SBD Dauntlesses from *Lexington* and one from *Yorktown*. Of *Shoho*'s aircraft complement of eighteen aircraft, one was lost, while three of the defending fighter pilots were able to ditch at Deboyne and survived. The American aircraft returned and landed on their carriers just after lunch, the aircraft being quickly rearmed and prepared for launch against the Port Moresby Invasion Force or the IJN cruiser group. Admiral Fletcher's main concern was that the whereabouts of the rest of the Japanese fleet carriers was still unknown, as he had been informed that Allied intelligence sources believed that up to four Japanese carriers might be supporting the Port Moresby operation. The Admiral then concluded that by the time his scout aircraft located the remaining Japanese carriers it would be too late to mount a strike. Therefore it was decided to hold off on another strike and remain concealed under the thick cloud overcast. Having been informed of the loss of the carrier *Shoho*, Admiral Inoue ordered the invasion convoy to withdraw to the north and, ordered Takagi to mount a major attack against the American carrier forces. After the invasion convoy had reversed course it was bombed by eight USAAF B-17s although none of the ships were damaged.

Just after lunchtime a Deboyne-based patrol seaplane sighted and reported the Crace cruiser force seventy-eight nautical miles from Deboyne. This was followed by a report from a Rabaul-based aircraft that sighted the force. However, the report was in error, as it stated that the force contained two carriers and was located some 115 nautical miles from Deboyne. Using these reports, Takagi, who was still awaiting the return of all of his aircraft from attacking the American oiler *Neosho*, turned his carriers due west and advised Inoue that the American carriers were at least 430 nautical miles to the west of his location and that he would therefore be unable to attack them as they were too far away. The senior IJN staff ordered that two groups of attack aircraft from Rabaul, already airborne, turn towards the Crace cruiser group's reported position. The first group consisted of twelve torpedo-armed Type 1 bombers, while the second group comprised nineteen Mitsubishi Type 96 land-attack aircraft armed with bombs. Both groups would find and attack the American ships in mid-afternoon, and claim to have sunk a battleship and damaged another battleship and cruiser. In reality the US Navy ships were undamaged and shot down four Type 1s. Crace then radioed Admiral

Fletcher that he could not complete his mission without air support, and so he was ordered to retire southwards to a position about 220 nautical miles southeast of Port Moresby to increase the range from the Japanese carriers or land-based aircraft while remaining close enough to intercept any Japanese naval forces advancing beyond the Louisiades through either the Jomard Passage or the China Strait.

To try to confirm the location of the American carriers, Admiral Hara sent a flight of eight torpedo-bombers as scouts to sweep an area 200 nautical miles westward. In the late afternoon TF.17, still operating under the thick overcast some 200 nautical miles west of Takagi, detected the Japanese strike force on radar, heading in its direction, and the USS *Yorktown* was turned south-east into the wind to launch defensive fighters. The eleven Grumman Wildcats were vectored towards the incoming aircraft. Catching the Japanese formation completely by surprise, the Wildcats shot down seven torpedo-bombers and one dive-bomber, besides heavily damaging another torpedo-bomber, which later crashed, all for the loss of three Wildcats. As nightfall had ended aircraft operations, Fletcher ordered TF.17 to head west and prepare to launch a full search at first light. While the Americans were positioning themselves for the next day's operations, Admiral Inoue would direct Takagi to make sure he destroyed the US Navy carriers the next day. To that end the Port Moresby landings proposed for 12 May were postponed in order that the maximum number of naval vessels would be available for the coming battle.

Takagi elected to take his carriers 120 nautical miles north during the night so that he could concentrate his morning search to the west and south and ensure that his carriers could provide better protection for the invasion convoy. Having suffered heavy losses in the attack that also scattered their formations, the Japanese strike leaders cancelled the mission after conferring by radio. After confirming this course of action, the Japanese aircraft jettisoned their bombs and reversed course in order to return to their carriers. Both naval forces expected to find each other early the next day, and so they spent the night period preparing their strike aircraft for the anticipated engagement. In the early hours of 8 May, from a position a hundred miles south-east of Rossel Island, Hara launched seven torpedo-bombers to search an area between 140 and 230 degrees south and up to 250 nautical miles from the Japanese carriers. Assisting in the search were three Kawanishi Type 97s from Tulagi and four Type 1 bombers from Rabaul. Soon after the launch the carrier striking force turned to the south-west being joined by two of the Goto cruisers, *Kinugasa* and *Furutaka*, for screen support. During the night the warm frontal zone with low-hanging clouds that had hidden the US Navy carriers during 7 May had moved north and east, and now covered the Japanese carriers, thus limiting visibility to between two and fifteen miles.

As the Japanese carriers were launching their scouts, TF.17, operating under Admiral Fitch's tactical control and positioned 180 nautical miles south-east of the Louisiades, launched eighteen Dauntlesses to conduct a full 360-degree search up to a range of 200 nautical miles. By this time the skies

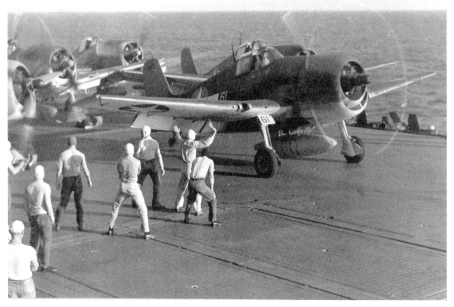

With a vast spread of vessels heading towards the horizon, the USS Santee heads towards its next target, while the deck crews prepare their charges for their next missions. (US Navy/NARA via Dennis R. Jenkins)

over the American carriers were mostly clear, with visibility of seventeen nautical miles. Just over two hours later a Dauntless from the USS *Lexington* spotted the Japanese carriers through a hole in the clouds, and signalled TF.17. At the same time a *Shokaku* search aircraft sighted TF.17, notifying the IJN command. The two forces were approximately 210 nautical miles away from each other when spotted, and both sides raced to launch their strike aircraft. The Japanese carriers would launch a combined strike force consisting of eighteen fighters, thirty-three dive-bombers, and eighteen torpedo-planes, while the American carriers each launched a separate strike group. The *Yorktown* force of consisted of six fighters, twenty-four dive-bombers and nine torpedo-aircraft, both nations' air strikes departing at the same time. The *Lexington* group of nine fighters, fifteen dive-bombers and twelve torpedo-planes departed a few minutes later. The American and Japanese carrier forces turned to head directly towards each other's location at high speed in order to shorten the distance their aircraft would have to fly upon their return. The *Yorktown* dive-bombers reached the Japanese carriers just over an hour after launch, slowing slightly to allow the slower torpedo squadron to catch up so that they could conduct a simultaneous attack.

At this time the IJN carriers *Shokaku* and *Zuikaku* were about 10,000 yards apart, with the *Zuikaku* hidden under a rain squall of low-hanging cloud, both carriers being protected by Zero fighters. The *Yorktown* dive-bombers commenced their attacks on the *Shokaku* and hit the violently manoeuvring carrier with two 1,000 lb bombs, blowing open the forecastle and causing heavy damage to the carrier's flight and hangar decks. The *Yorktown* torpedo-planes missed with all of their weapons. During the attack two American dive-bombers and two IJN Zeros were shot down. The *Lexington* aircraft arrived and attacked soon afterwards. Two dive-bombers attacked the *Shokaku*, hitting the carrier with one 1,000 lb bomb and causing further extensive damage. Two other dive-bombers attacked the *Zuikaku*, although they missed with their bombs. The rest of the *Lexington* dive-bombers were unable to find the Japanese carriers in the heavy clouds, while the *Lexington* TBDs missed the *Shokaku* with all of their torpedoes. The defending Zeros shot down three Wildcats. With its flight deck and other primary zones heavily damaged, and 223 of her crew killed or wounded, the *Shokaku* was unable to conduct further aircraft operations. Given the state of the vessel, the captain requested permission from Takagi to withdraw from the battle. This was agreed, and the *Shokaku*, accompanied by two destroyers, departed to the north-east.

In the late morning the *Lexington* air defence radar detected the inbound Japanese strike force at a range of sixty-eight nautical miles, vectoring nine Wildcats to intercept. Expecting the Japanese torpedo-bombers to be approaching at a much lower altitude than they actually were, six of the Wildcats were flying too low and so missed the Japanese aircraft as they passed by overhead. Due to the heavy aircraft losses suffered previously, the Japanese were unable to execute a full torpedo attack on both carriers. The attack commander ordered fourteen aircraft to attack the *Lexington*, while the other four were ordered to attack the *Yorktown*. A Wildcat shot down one, while some Dauntlesses from the *Yorktown* destroyed three more as the Japanese torpedo-aircraft descended to take up their attack position. In retaliation four Dauntlesses were shot down by the Zeros escorting the torpedo-aircraft. The Japanese attack began on the carriers, which were cruising 3,000 yards apart, and as the Japanese attacked the carrier escort vessels opened fire with their anti-aircraft guns. The four torpedo-bombers that attacked the *Yorktown* all missed, while the remaining aircraft successfully employed a pincer attack on the *Lexington*, which had a greater turning radius than the *Yorktown*, and the carrier was hit by two Type 91 torpedoes. The first torpedo buckled the port aviation fuel stowage tanks, which caused gasoline vapour to spread into surrounding compartments. The second torpedo ruptured the port water main, which reduced the water pressure to the forward firerooms, thus forcing the associated boilers to be shut down, although the carrier was still able to make 24 knots with its remaining boilers.

Four of the Japanese torpedo-aircraft were shot down by the defensive anti-aircraft fire. The Japanese dive-bombers were circling to attack from upwind, and so they did not begin their dives from 14,000 feet until a few minutes after the torpedo-bombers had begun their attacks. Some of the dive-bombers lined up on the *Lexington*, while the remainder targeted the *Yorktown*. The escorting Zeros protected the dive-bombers from the four Grumman Wildcats defending the *Lexington* as they attempted to intercept. However, a further two Wildcats circling above the *Yorktown* were able to

As the crew abandons ship, the USS Lexington burns after a bomb hit. Although the crew fought valiantly to save their ship, it would sink on 8 May 1942. (US Navy/NARA via Dennis R. Jenkins)

disrupt the bomber formation. The bombers damaged the *Lexington* with two bomb hits plus several near-misses, causing fires that were successfully contained. The *Yorktown* was hit in the centre of the flight deck by a single 551 lb semi-armour-piercing bomb that penetrated four decks before exploding. This caused severe structural damage to an aviation storage room and killed or seriously wounded sixty-six men. A further dozen near-misses damaged the carrier's hull below the waterline. As the Japanese aircraft completed their attacks and began to withdraw they ran a gauntlet of defending Grumman Wildcats and Douglas Dauntlesses. In the ensuing aerial battle three SBDs and three Wildcats, plus three torpedo-bombers, one dive-bomber, and one Zero, were shot down. By midday the respective strike groups were on their way back to their carriers. During their return journey aircraft from the two groups passed each other in the air, which resulted in more air battles. The remaining strike aircraft reached and landed on their respective carriers in the early afternoon. In spite of the damage the *Yorktown* was able to recover its aircraft and those from the *Lexington*. The *Yorktown* limped back to Pearl Harbor, where the vessel was turned over to the dockyard for repairs. However, the *Lexington* was engulfed in flames again, even though the crew had fought valiantly to contain the conflagration. Eventually it became obvious that the *Lexington* was beyond saving, and so the crew were taken off and the badly damaged carrier was sunk by the destroyer USS *Phelps*.

CHAPTER FOUR

War in the Pacific:
Turning Point to Victory

While the Battle of the Coral Sea had some positive results for both combatants, it would be the Americans who would take the greater benefit from the engagement. While the loss of a fleet carrier was a serious blow, the United States production base was running at full tilt, and the US Navy, having learnt valuable lessons, had put in place an extensive training programme to produce combat-ready airmen ready to join the variety of aircraft carriers as they became available. From the Japanese point of view the eventual loss of the USS *Lexington* was seen as a positive step. However, the Japanese High Command was well aware that the US Navy carrier groups were the linchpin of the American fight-back in the Pacific. This had been reinforced by the bombing of the home islands by B-25 Mitchell bombers launched from the USS *Hornet*.

To reduce the risk of further American attacks, Admiral Yamamoto, the IJN commander, saw his primary strategic objective as the elimination of the American carriers, which were seen as the main obstacle to the success of the overall Pacific campaign. Therefore the destruction of the American aircraft carriers and the seizure of Midway was seen as the only way of nullifying this threat. Yamamoto initially reasoned that an operation against the main naval base at Pearl Harbor would induce the US Navy to come out and fight. However, upon reflection, and given the strength of the land-based air power on Hawaii, it soon became obvious that the base could not be attacked directly. Avoiding Hawaii completely, Admiral Yamamoto selected Midway, located at the extreme north-west end of the Hawaiian island chain. Midway Island was not over-important in the Japanese scheme of things, but the Japanese felt that the Americans would consider Midway a vital outpost for Pearl Harbor and would therefore strongly defend it.

Typical of Japanese naval planning during the Pacific conflict, the

Late evening, and the deck crews aboard the carrier USS Lexington prepare the Douglas SBD Dauntless of VB-16 for the next day's missions. (US Navy/NARA via Dennis R. Jenkins)

Yamamoto battle plan was very complex and was based on optimistic intelligence suggesting that the USS *Enterprise* and USS *Hornet*, forming the core of Task Force 16, were the only carriers available to the US Navy Pacific Fleet at the time, as the *Lexington* had been sunk and the *Yorktown* had been severely damaged during the Battle of the Coral Sea a month earlier. Japanese intelligence were also aware that the USS *Saratoga* was undergoing repairs on the west coast after suffering torpedo damage. Also reinforcing the Japanese point of view was Yamamoto's belief that the Americans had been demoralised by their frequent defeats during the preceding six months, although he misread the situation, as the Doolittle Raid and events in the Coral Sea had strengthened the nation's morale.

Admiral Yamamoto also felt deception would be needed to lure the American fleet into a decisive confrontation. To that end, he dispersed his forces so that their full extent would not be discovered by the Americans prior to battle. The theory behind this plan was that supporting battleships and cruisers would follow the carrier striking force, commanded by Vice-Admiral Chuichi, by several hundred miles, and so the heavy surface units would be able to destroy whatever part of the American fleet might come to Midway's relief, once Nagumo's carriers had weakened them sufficiently for a daylight gun duel. However, Yamamoto was unaware that the United States had

86

broken the main Japanese naval code, known as JN-25 by the Americans. The Admiral's emphasis on spreading his forces also meant that none of his groups could provide support for each other. This resulted in the only warships larger than Nagumo's destroyer screen fleet being two battleships and three cruisers, even though the carriers were expected to carry out the strikes and bear the brunt of American counter-attacks.

In contrast, the flotillas of Yamamoto and Kondo had between them two light carriers, five battleships and six cruisers, none of which would see any combat at Midway. Their distance from Nagumo's carriers would also have further implications during the battle, as the larger warships in Yamamoto and Kondo's forces carried scout planes, an invaluable reconnaissance capability denied to Nagumo.

To fight an enemy that was reported to have four or five carriers, Admiral Nimitz, Commander in Chief, Pacific Ocean Areas, called in every available flight deck. To hand were Vice-Admiral Halsey's carriers, the *Enterprise* and *Hornet,* although Halsey was taken ill and was temporarily replaced by Rear Admiral Spruance, normally Halsey's escort commander. Nimitz also called back Rear Admiral Fletcher's task force, which included the carrier *Yorktown,* although this had been severely damaged during the Battle of the Coral Sea. Original engineering estimates stated that the *Yorktown* would require several months of repairs at Puget Sound Naval Shipyard. However, the elevators were intact, while much of the flight deck was undamaged. The Pearl Harbor Naval Shipyard worked flat out round the clock, so that in seventy-two hours the carrier was declared to be battle ready, and was judged good enough for two to three weeks of operations. The effected repairs included patching the flight deck, while complete sections of the internal frames were cut out and replaced. To bring the carrier finally up to speed several new squadrons were drawn from the *Saratoga,* although the pilots would need to undertake training *en route.* After one of the quickest turnarounds, the *Yorktown* was declared ready to depart even though repairs were continuing as the carrier sailed, with work crews being based aboard the repair ship USS *Vestal.*

On Midway Island the USAAF increased the island's strength by stationing four squadrons of Boeing B-17 Flying Fortresses there, along with several B-26 Marauders for target towing. The Marine Corps had nineteen Douglas SBD Dauntless dive-bombers, seven Grumman F4F-3 Wildcats, seventeen Vought SBU-3 Vindicators, twenty-one Brewster F2A-3s and six Grumman TBF-1 Avenger torpedo-bombers, although the latter were a detachment of VT-8 from the *Hornet.*

After the Battle of the Coral Sea, the Japanese carrier *Zuikaku* was berthed at Kure, awaiting a replacement air group. However, none was immediately available due to a failure of the IJN crew training programme, which was unable to cope with replacing combat losses. In an attempt to provide enough pilots, instructors from the Yokosuka Air Corps were deployed to make up the shortfall. Meanwhile the heavily damaged *Shokaku* was undergoing repair in dry dock after suffering three bomb hits during the Battle of the Coral Sea, and so the aircraft of both vessels were combined to re-equip the *Zuikaku* with a composite air group, although the Japanese made no serious attempt to prepare the ship for the forthcoming battle. Therefore Admiral Nagumo would only have four fleet carriers: the *Kaga* and *Akagi* would form Carrier Division 1, while the *Hiryu* and *Soryu* would form Carrier Division 2. The primary Japanese strike aircraft were the Aichi D3A1 dive-bomber and the Nakajima B5N2, which was capable of being used either as a torpedo-bomber or as a level attack bomber, while the main carrier fighter was the Mitsubishi A6M2 Zero. However, the Japanese carriers were suffering from a shortage of front-line aircraft as production of the D3A had been drastically reduced and that of the B5N had been stopped completely. As a consequence, there were no spare aircraft available to replace the outstanding losses. This also meant that many of the aircraft being used during this period had been operational since late November 1941, and as a consequence, while having been well maintained, they were fatigued and had become increasingly unreliable. These factors meant that the carriers were operating with fewer than their designed aircraft complement.

Making the task more difficult was the Japanese strategic scouting arrangements, which were in disarray, as the picket line of Japanese submarines was late moving to their operational positions, and this allowed the American carriers to reach their assembly point north-east of Midway, Point Luck, undetected. A second attempt at reconnaissance, using four-engine Kawanishi H8K flying-boats to overfly Pearl Harbor prior to the battle to

The scourge of the American carrier fleet was the Kawanishi H6K Mavis flying-boats that were used by the Japanese to track the task forces. Unfortunately for the Japanese shadowers, their missions frequently ended like this – in flames. (US Navy/NARA via Dennis R. Jenkins)

check on the location of the American carriers, Operation K, also failed, as Japanese submarines assigned to refuel the search aircraft discovered that the intended refuelling point near French Frigate Shoals was patrolled by American warships. As a consequence Japan was deprived of any intelligence concerning the movements of the American carriers immediately prior to the battle. Japanese radio intercepts of US Navy traffic did reveal an increase in both American submarine activity and messages. This information was passed to Yamamoto prior to the battle. However, Yamamoto, at sea on the battleship *Yamato*, could not inform Nagumo for fear of exposing his position, and assumed that Nagumo had received the same signal from Tokyo. However, Nagumo's radio antennae were unable to receive such long-wave transmissions, and so he was left unaware of the American ship movements.

In complete contrast, Admiral Nimitz had one priceless asset: the US Navy crypto-analysts had broken the JN-25 code, and so they were able to confirm Midway as the target of the impending Japanese strike and to determine that the date of the attack was either 4 or 5 June. They were then able to provide Nimitz with a complete IJN order of battle. The Japanese intention to intro-duce a new code-book had been delayed, and this gave the analysts several extra days to decrypt the signals and pass on garnered intelligence. As a result the Americans, when they entered the battle, had a very good picture of where, when, and in what strength the Japanese would appear. Nimitz was aware that the vast Japanese numerical superiority had been diluted by its division into no fewer than four task forces, while the escort for the Carrier Striking Force was limited to just a few fast ships. With this knowledge Nimitz could calculate that his three carriers, plus Midway Island, gave the US Navy parity, as the American carrier air groups were larger than those of the enemy. In contrast, the Japanese remained almost totally unaware of the Americans' true strength and dispositions, even after the battle began. The first air attack took off just after midday on 3 June, and consisted of nine Boeing B-17s operating from Midway. After four hours' flying they found the Japanese transport group 570 miles to the west. The vessels put up heavy anti-aircraft fire, but even so they dropped their bombs. While hits were reported, none of the bombs actually landed on target, and so no significant damage was inflicted. Early the following morning the Japanese oil tanker *Akebono Maru* sustained the first hit when a torpedo from an attacking PBY Catalina flying-boat struck just after midnight.

In the early hours of 4 June, Nagumo launched his initial attack on Midway itself, consisting of thirty-six Aichi D3A dive-bombers and thirty-six Nakajima B5N torpedo-bombers, escorted by thirty-six Zero fighters. At the same time a combat air patrol was launched, plus eight search and rescue aircraft. Japanese reconnaissance arrangements for this operation were paltry, with too few aircraft assigned to cover the assigned search areas adequately. They were also beset by poor weather conditions to the north-east and east of the task force, while Yamamoto's faulty fleet dispositions had now become a serious liability.

American radar picked up the enemy at a distance of several miles, and fighters were soon scrambled to intercept, while unescorted bombers headed off to attack the Japanese carrier fleet, their fighter escorts remaining behind to defend Midway. Two hours after launching, the Japanese carrier aircraft bombed and heavily damaged the American base on the island. The Midway-based Marine fighter pilots who were flying obsolescent Grumman F4F-3 Wildcats and outdated Brewster F2A-3s intercepted the Japanese and suffered heavy losses, although they managed to shoot down four bombers and at least three Zeros. The majority of the defending aircraft were downed in the first few minutes, while several were damaged, so that only two remained flyable. In all, three F4Fs and thirteen F2As were shot down, but American anti-aircraft fire was accurate and intense, damaging many Japanese aircraft and claiming a third of the Japanese aircraft destroyed. While the Japanese had launched an extensive strike force they did not succeed in neutralising Midway, and so another attack would be necessary if troops were to go ashore on 7 June as planned. Until Midway was neutralised, American bombers could still use the airbase to refuel and attack the Japanese invasion force.

Having departed from Midway prior to the Japanese attack, American bombers from the base made several attacks on the Japanese carrier fleet. The strike force included six TBF Avengers from the USS *Hornet*'s VT-8, the crews undertaking their first combat operation and being supplemented by four USAAF B-26 Marauders armed with torpedoes – the first and last time that the B-26 was used in this role. The Japanese managed to avoid these attacks with minimal losses, only two fighters being lost. In return the Japanese shot down five of the six Avengers and two of the B-26s. One B-26, badly damaged by anti-aircraft fire from the *Akagi*, narrowly missed crashing directly into the carrier's bridge. This attack would see Nagumo launching another air strike on Midway Island in order to suppress the possibility of further American attacks, though this was in direct contravention of Yamamoto's order to keep the reserve strike force armed for anti-ship operations. Admiral Nagumo, in accordance with Japanese carrier doctrine of the time, had retained half of his aircraft in reserve. These comprised two squadrons each of dive-bombers and torpedo-bombers, should any American warships be located. As a result of the attacks mounted by the Midway forces, Nagumo ordered that the reserve planes be rearmed with contact-fused general-purpose bombs for use against land targets. However, Nagumo received contradictory intelligence that an American carrier task force was close, and so he quickly reversed his order and requested that the scout plane confirm the composition of the American force. After forty minutes' wait the scout finally confirmed the presence of a single carrier in the American force, TF.16.

Admiral Nagumo was stuck in a dichotomy. Should the strike be mounted against Midway or were the American carriers the primary threat? Rear Admiral Tamon, commanding Carrier Division 2, the *Hiryu* and *Soryu*, recommended that Nagumo strike immediately with the forces at hand, these consisting of eighteen Aichi D3A2 dive-bombers on the *Soryu* and *Hiryu*, plus

This side view is of a Douglas SBD Dauntless of VT-6 from the USS Hornet. This unit took part in the battle of Midway. (US Navy/NARA via Dennis R. Jenkins)

half the ready-cover patrol aircraft. However, for Nagumo the opportunity to attack the American ships was now limited, as the Midway strike force was *en route* to the carriers and would need to land promptly or be lost. Due to the constant flight deck activity required for the launching and recovery of the defensive fighter screen, the Japanese were unable to spot their reserve for launch. The few aircraft arrayed on the Japanese flight decks at the time of the attack were defensive fighters or fighters being prepared to augment the task force defences. To realign the carrier decks to rearm and launch strike aircraft would have required at least thirty to forty-five minutes. However, by rehashing the available aircraft and launching immediately, Admiral Nagumo would be committing a percentage of his reserve to an attack without proper anti-ship munitions. Japanese carrier doctrine stated that only fully constituted strikes would be launched, and without confirmation of whether the American force included carriers, the Admiral was inclined to follow established doctrine reaction. Also adding to the Admiral's confusion was the arrival of another American air strike, which gave impetus to attacking the island again. In response Nagumo decided to wait for the first strike force to land, clear the decks and then launch the reserve, which would by then be properly armed and ready.

While the Japanese were deciding which target to attack, the Americans had already launched their carrier aircraft against the Japanese. Admiral Fletcher, aboard the USS *Yorktown*, and benefiting from Catalina patrol sighting reports delivered in the early morning, ordered Spruance to launch against the Japanese carrier groups as soon as was practical. Spruance ordered the attack launch close to dawn, the first aircraft departing nearly an hour later from the carriers *Enterprise* and *Hornet.* Admiral Fletcher would launch the *Yorktown* air group an hour later. Even as the Spruance force was departing, the Admiral ordered the task force to head towards the enemy warships, having decided that the need to attack the Japanese as soon as possible was more important than the need for a co-ordinated attack among the different types of aircraft. The American squadrons were therefore launched piecemeal, and proceeded to the target in separate groups. This would reduce the overall effectiveness of the American attacks and greatly increase their casualties. However, it also reduced the Japanese ability to counterstrike, and left Nagumo with his decks at their most vulnerable.

The American carrier aircraft initially had difficulty locating the target, but VT-8 from the USS *Hornet* finally sighted the enemy carriers and began its attack, followed by the aircraft of VT-6 from the USS *Enterprise*. Without the much-needed fighter escort, every TBD Devastator of VT-8 was shot down without hitting any targets. The aircraft of VT-6 nearly met the same fate, also having no hits to show for their effort. During these attacks the abysmal performance of the American Mark 13 aircraft torpedoes was revealed in full. The Japanese defensive fighters flying Mitsubishi A6M2 Zeros made short work of the unescorted, slow, under-armed TBDs.

An unidentified Douglas SBD Dauntless releases a bomb while dive-bombing its target. While not the quickest of aircraft, the SBD played a vital part in the opening rounds of the war in the Pacific. (US Navy/NARA via Dennis R. Jenkins)

Having suffered grievous losses, the American torpedo attacks indirectly achieved three important results. Firstly, the attacks unsettled the routine of the Japanese carriers so that they had no ability to prepare and launch their own counterstrike. Secondly, the attacks pulled the Japanese defensive fighters out of position. The third point was that many of the Zeros were running low on ammunition and fuel. The appearance of a third torpedo attack wave from the south-east by VT-3 would draw the majority of the Japanese fighters to the south-east quadrant of the fleet. At the same time as VT-3 was sighted by the Japanese, two separate formations of American SBD Dauntless dive-bombers were approaching the Japanese fleet from the north-east and south-west. While the aircraft were running low on fuel because of the time spent looking for the enemy, the squadron commander decided to continue the search, after spotting the wake of the Japanese destroyer *Arashi*. The destroyer was steaming at full speed to rejoin Nagumo's carrier force after having attempted to depth-charge the submarine *Nautilus*, which had unsuccessfully attacked the battleship *Kirishima*.

The decision by the strike commander to continue the search was credited by Admiral Nimitz as deciding the fate of the carrier task force and the forces at Midway. The American dive-bombers arrived at the perfect time to attack, as the flight decks were packed with armed Japanese strike aircraft being refuelled: fuel hoses snaked across the decks while the repeated change of weapon loads meant bombs and torpedoes were stacked around the hangars rather than being stowed safely in the magazines. All these circumstances made the Japanese carriers extraordinarily vulnerable to attack.

The *Enterprise* air group began its attacks, during which it scored multiple hits on the carrier *Kaga*, while to the north the *Akagi* was struck minutes later by three of the *Enterprise* bombers. The *Yorktown*'s aircraft headed for the *Soryu*, and the VT-3 aircraft targeted *Hiryu*, which was sailing between the *Soryu*, *Kaga* and *Akagi*, although they failed to score any hits. In contrast the dive-bombers had, within six minutes, left the *Soryu*, *Kaga* and *Akagi* blazing merrily. The *Akagi* was hit by just one bomb that penetrated the upper hangar deck, where it exploded among the armed and fuelled aircraft. One bomb exploded underwater very close astern, the resulting blast and water pressure distorting the flight deck upwards and causing damage to the rudder. The *Soryu* received three bombs in the hangar deck, while the *Kaga* was hit by at least four. All three carriers were so badly damaged that they were put out of action and were deemed beyond repair; therefore they were abandoned and scuttled.

The *Hiryu*, as the sole surviving Japanese aircraft carrier, would waste little time in mounting a counter-attack. The first wave of Japanese dive-bombers badly damaged the *Yorktown* with three bomb hits that shut down the boilers. This immobilised the carrier initially. However, the damage-control teams repaired the damage quickly, so that when the second wave of torpedo-bombers arrived the carrier was mistaken for an undamaged vessel. Despite Japanese intentions to even the odds by sinking two carriers with two strikes, the *Yorktown* absorbed both Japanese attacks, as the second wave believed that she had already been sunk and they were attacking the USS *Enterprise*. After two torpedo strikes the *Yorktown* lost power and developed a 26-degree list to port, which put the carrier out of action. It also forced Admiral Fletcher to move his command staff to the heavy cruiser *Astoria*. In contrast, both carriers of Spruance's Task Force 16 were undamaged.

News of the two carrier attacks, coupled with the reports that each wave had sunk an American carrier, greatly improved morale among the IJN command staff. The few surviving aircraft were all recovered aboard the *Hiryu*, where they were prepared for a further strike against what was believed to be the only remaining American carrier. However, late in the afternoon a *Yorktown* scout aircraft located the *Hiryu*, prompting the *Enterprise* to launch a final strike of dive-bombers, including ten aircraft from the *Yorktown* that had landed on the alternative carrier. This attack delivered a fatal blow that left the *Hiryu* burning fiercely despite being defended by a strong fighter cover of more than a dozen Zero fighters. Vice-Admiral Yamaguchi chose to go down with his ship, which cost Japan her best carrier commander. The *Hornet* strike was launched late due to a communications error. This wave concentrated on the remaining escort ships, although they failed to score any hits.

As the light faded, both sides took stock and made plans for continuing the battle. Admiral Fletcher, having abandoned the derelict *Yorktown*, felt he could not adequately command the fight from a cruiser, and so he ceded operational command to Admiral Spruance. Spruance was already aware that America had won a great victory, but he was still unsure of the strength of the remaining Japanese forces, and was determined to safeguard both Midway

Listing to port after being struck by three torpedoes, the USS Yorktown was not far from sinking. No power was available to rescue the ship as the escorting destroyer had been sunk. (US Navy/NARA via Dennis R. Jenkins)

This view shows a flight of Douglas SBD Dauntlesses of VS-6 from the USS Enterprise heading towards Santa Isobel. (US Navy/NARA via Dennis R. Jenkins)

and the carriers. To assist the aircraft crews, who had launched at extreme range, the carriers had continued to close with Nagumo during the day, persisting as night fell. Fearing a possible night encounter with Japanese surface forces, Spruance changed course and withdrew to the east, later turning back west towards the enemy at midnight.

In contrast Yamamoto was determined to continue the engagement, and sent his remaining surface forces searching eastwards for the American carriers. At the same time a cruiser raiding force was detached to bombard Midway Island. The Japanese cruiser force failed to make contact with the American carriers due to Spruance's decision to briefly withdraw eastwards, and so Yamamoto ordered a general retirement to the west. American search aircraft failed to detect the departing Japanese task forces on 5 June, while an afternoon strike narrowly missed finding the Yamamoto main force. They also failed to score hits on a straggling Japanese destroyer. The strike aircraft returned to the carriers after dark, which prompted Spruance to order the *Enterprise* and *Hornet* to turn on searchlights in order to assist their landings.

In the early hours of 5/6 June the submarine USS *Tambor*, stationed some ninety nautical miles west of Midway, made the second of the Submarine Force's two major contributions to the outcome of the battle. Cruising the patrol line, they sighted several ships that could not be identified. However, they reported their presence to Admiral Robert English, Commander, Submarine Force, Pacific Fleet. Unaware of the exact location of the Yamamoto main force, Admiral Spruance assumed that this was the invasion force. Therefore he moved to block it, taking station some one hundred nautical miles north-east of Midway. This resulted in Yamamoto's efforts being frustrated, and the night passed without any contact between the opposing forces. The naval units that had been spotted by the American submarine were Yamamoto's bombardment group of four cruisers and two destroyers, which were then ordered to withdraw to the west with the rest of his forces. The *Tambor* was sighted at around the same time by the escort destroyers, but when the force turned to avoid the submarine the cruisers *Mogami* and *Mikuma* collided, the result being serious damage to the *Mogami's* bow. In the early hours of the morning the sky brightened enough for Murphy to be certain that the ships were Japanese, although by this time staying on the surface was hazardous. Therefore the submarine dived to approach for an attack. Over the next two days, first the base at Midway and then Spruance's carriers launched several successive strikes against the stragglers, which resulted in the *Mikuma* being sunk by Dauntlesses, while the *Mogami* survived severe damage to return home for repairs.

While the active part of the American task force was still engaging the Japanese, the salvage efforts on the *Yorktown* were encouraging, the carrier being taken in tow by the USS *Vireo*. This was continuing successfully until late afternoon on 6 June when the *Yorktown* was struck by two torpedoes from the Japanese submarine *I-168*. There were very few casualties aboard the *Yorktown* as most of the crew had already been evacuated. However, a third torpedo from this salvo also struck and sank the destroyer USS *Hammann*, which had been providing auxiliary power to the *Yorktown*. The *Hammann* broke in two, with the loss of eighty lives, while the *Yorktown* remained afloat until the early hours of 7 June, when the list increased rapidly and the carrier went down with its battle flags still flying. An exploration by Robert Ballard in May 1998 would find the *Yorktown* resting the right way up and looking almost pristine after its time under the sea.

At the conclusion of the Coral Sea and Midway actions, not only did the US Navy undergo some much-needed reinforcement, but the entire Pacific Fleet was restructured to fit it for the forthcoming campaign. The reinforcements included the carrier USS *Wasp*, returned from its duties with the Royal Navy Home Fleet. The *Wasp* passed through the Panama Canal on 10 June 1942 in company with the cruiser USS *Quincy*, a protective destroyer screen plus some new vessels that included the battleship USS *North Carolina*, the escort carrier USS *Long Island* and another five escort destroyers. The reorganisation of the US Navy Pacific Fleet began on 15 June and resulted in the creation of TF.1 commanded by Vice-Admiral Pye, and including the battleships *Pennsylvania, Colorado, Maryland, Tennessee, Idaho, Mississippi* and *New Mexico*, plus ten destroyers; TF.8 under the command of Rear Admiral Theobald, consisting of five cruisers and five destroyers; TF.11 commanded by Rear Admiral Flitch, including the carrier USS *Saratoga*, three cruisers and seven destroyers; TF.16 with the carrier USS *Enterprise*, escorted by three cruisers and seven destroyers; TF.17 with the carrier USS *Wasp*, plus four cruisers and seven destroyers, commanded by Rear Admiral Mitscher; TF.18 commanded by Rear Admiral Noyes with the carrier USS *Wasp* supported by the battleship

Coming home, a flight of Curtiss Helldivers assigned to VB-86 head towards their home, the USS Wasp, CV-18. (US Navy/NARA via Dennis R. Jenkins)

USS *North Carolina*, four cruisers and four destroyers; and the final unit, TF.44, which was commanded by Rear Admiral Crutchley RN and was a mixed force consisting of three RAN cruisers, *Australia*, *Canberra* and *Hobart*, plus the USS *Chicago* with an escort of nine destroyers.

Once these machinations had been completed, the US Navy in the Pacific began preparations for its next major operation, the capturing of Guadalcanal, part of the Solomon Islands Group. The Americans, with British permission, chose the Solomon Islands as their first target, specifically the southern Solomon Islands of Guadalcanal, Tulagi, and Florida. The Imperial Japanese Navy, IJN, had occupied Tulagi in May 1942, and then constructed a seaplane base there. Allied concern increased in early July 1942 when the IJN began constructing a large airfield at Lunga Point on nearby Guadalcanal. By August 1942 the Japanese had about 900 naval troops on Tulagi and nearby islands, plus 2,800 personnel on Guadalcanal. These bases upon completion would protect the Japanese major base at Rabaul and threaten the Allied supply and communication lines in the Pacific. The base would also establish a staging area for a planned offensive against Fiji, New Caledonia, and Samoa, designated Operation FS. The Japanese planned to deploy forty-five fighters and sixty bombers to Guadalcanal, once the airfield was complete, these aircraft being required to provide air cover for Japanese naval forces advancing farther into the South Pacific.

The American plan to invade the southern Solomons was conceived by Admiral Ernest King USN, Commander-in-Chief, United States Fleet. He proposed the offensive in order to deny the use of the islands to the Japanese as bases to harass the vital supply routes between the United States and Australia, and after their capture to use them as starting points for a series of counter-invasions. With the tacit support of President Roosevelt, Admiral

King also advocated the invasion of Guadalcanal, although General George C. Marshall USA would resist this course of action, as well as who would command the operation. Given the opposition of the Army, King stated that the Navy and Marines would carry out the operation using their own resources, and instructed Admiral Nimitz to undertake the preliminary planning. Admiral King eventually won his argument, and the invasion would proceed with the backing of the Joint Chiefs.

The invasion of Guadalcanal would be carried out in conjunction with an Allied offensive in New Guinea under General Douglas MacArthur, who was ordered to capture the Admiralty Islands and the Bismarck Archipelago, which included the major Japanese base at Rabaul. The intention was that this would lead eventually to the American retaking of the Philippines. The Joint Chiefs of Staff created the South Pacific theatre, with Vice-Admiral Ghormley USN taking overall command in June 1942, his mandate being to direct the offensive in the Solomons. Admiral Chester Nimitz, based at Pearl Harbor, was then designated as the overall Allied commander-in-chief for Pacific forces. In preparation for the future offensive in the Pacific in May 1942, Major-General Alexander Vandegrift USMC was ordered to move his 1st Marine Division from America to New Zealand, while other Allied land, naval, and air force units were sent to establish bases in Fiji, Samoa, the New Hebrides, and New Caledonia. Espiritu Santo, New Hebrides, was selected as the headquarters and main base for the offensive, which was codenamed

The USS Saratoga fought its way across the Pacific and took part in most of the major engagements, all of which would lead to the carrier's retirement soon after the end of the war due to general fatigue. (US Navy/NARA via Dennis R. Jenkins)

Operation Watchtower, the commencement date being set for the invasion being 7 August 1942. In the beginning the Allied offensive was planned to cover just Tulagi and the Santa Cruz Islands, omitting Guadalcanal. However, Allied reconnaissance would discover the Japanese airfield construction efforts on Guadalcanal, and so its capture was added to the plan while the Santa Cruz operation was later cancelled. The Japanese were aware, courtesy of signals intelligence, of the large-scale movement of Allied assets in the South Pacific area, although they concluded that the Allies were reinforcing Australia and Port Moresby in New Guinea.

The Watchtower force would consist of seventy-five warships and transports, and the fleet, including vessels from both America and Australia, would assemble near Fiji in July 1942, undertaking a single rehearsal landing prior to leaving for Guadalcanal on 31 July. The tactical commander of the Allied expeditionary force was Vice-Admiral Frank Fletcher USN flying his flag aboard the aircraft carrier USS *Saratoga*. Commanding the amphibious forces was Rear Admiral Richmond Turner USN. Major-General Vandegrift commanded the 16,000 Allied infantry earmarked for the landings, most of these being USMC personnel. Inclement weather allowed the Allied expeditionary force to arrive off Guadalcanal undetected by the Japanese on the morning of 7 August, after which the landing force split into two groups, one group to assault Guadalcanal, and the other to attack Tulagi, Florida and nearby islands. As preparation for the landings, Allied warships bombarded the invasion beaches, while US Navy carrier aircraft bombed Japanese positions on the target islands, successfully destroying Japanese seaplanes at their base near Tulagi. Two nearby small islands, Gavutu and Tanambogo, were attacked by 3,000 US Marines, although the IJN personnel manning the naval and seaplane bases on the three islands fiercely resisted the Marine attacks. Eventually the Marines secured all three islands after overcoming stiff resistance; Tulagi fell on 8 August, while Gavutu and Tanambogo were under Allied control by 9 August.

The Japanese defenders were killed almost to the last man, while the USMC lost 122 Marines. In contrast to the fierce resistance experienced on Tulagi, Gavutu and Tanambogo, the landings on Guadalcanal encountered less opposition. On 7 August Major-General Vandegrift and 11,000 US Marines came ashore on Guadalcanal between Koli Point and Lunga Point. Advancing towards Lunga Point, they encountered no resistance except from forces in the rain forest, and so they halted for the night close to the Lunga Point airfield. The next day the Marines advanced all the way to the Lunga river and secured the airfield in the afternoon of 8 August. The Japanese naval construction units and combat troops had panicked after the warship bombardment and aerial bombing, and had abandoned the airfield area and fled west to the Matanikau river and Point Cruz area, leaving behind them food, supplies, intact construction equipment and vehicles, plus thirteen dead. During these landing operations over 7/8 August Japanese naval aircraft based at Rabaul attacked the Allied amphibious forces several times, setting fire to the American transport *George F. Elliot*, which would sink two days later. Also hit and badly damaged was the destroyer USS *Jarvis*. During the air attacks over the following two days the Japanese lost thirty-six aircraft and the Americans lost nineteen, including fourteen carrier-borne fighters.

After these opening engagements, Admiral Fletcher was concerned about the losses to his carrier fighter aircraft strength, and this in turn made him worried about the threat to his carriers from further Japanese air attacks. Coupled to this was the worry that his ship's fuel levels were low, and so Fletcher withdrew from the Solomon Islands area during the evening of 8 August. As a result of the loss of the much-needed carrier-based air cover, Turner decided to withdraw his ships from Guadalcanal even though less than fifty per cent of the supplies and heavy equipment needed by the troops ashore had been offloaded. However, Turner planned to offload as many supplies as possible on Guadalcanal and Tulagi throughout the night of 8 August, departing with his ships in the early hours of 9 August. As the transports were unloaded, two groups of screening Allied warships under the command of Rear Admiral Crutchley RN were surprised and defeated by a Japanese force of seven cruisers and one destroyer from the 8th Fleet, based at Rabaul. One Australian and three American cruisers were sunk, while one American cruiser and two destroyers were damaged in the Battle of Savo Island. The Japanese suffered moderate damage to one cruiser. Admiral Mikawa, who was unaware that Fletcher had withdrawn with the American carriers, immediately withdrew to Rabaul without attempting to attack the now unprotected transports. Mikawa was rightly concerned about daylight carrier air attacks had he remained in the area. Turner would withdraw all remaining Allied naval forces by the evening of 9 August, leaving the Marines ashore without much of their heavy equipment and provisions, while some troops were still aboard the transports. Therefore Mikawa's decision not to attack the Allied transport ships when he had the chance would prove to be a crucial strategic mistake.

The 11,000 Marines on Guadalcanal initially concentrated on forming a loose defensive perimeter around Lunga Point and the airfield while moving the landed supplies within the defensive perimeter. Once these tasks had been completed they concentrated upon finishing the airfield. While the required heavy earth-moving equipment was still aboard the transports, work began on the airfield using captured Japanese equipment. On 12 August the nearly completed airfield was named Henderson Field, after a Marine aviator, Lofton R. Henderson, who was killed during the Battle of Midway. The completed airfield was ready for operations on 18 August. To increase the available air strength, the escort carrier USS *Long Island* delivered two squadrons of Marine aircraft to Henderson Field on 20 August. One was a squadron of nineteen Grumman F4F Wildcats, the other a squadron of twelve Douglas SBD Dauntlesses. The aircraft at Henderson would became known as the 'Cactus Air Force' (CAF), after the Allied codename for Guadalcanal. The Marine fighters were in action the next day, attacking one of the almost daily

Japanese bomber air raids. To reinforce the air strength, five US Army P-400 Airacobras and their pilots arrived at Henderson Field on 22 August. In response to the Allied landings on Guadalcanal the Japanese Imperial General Headquarters assigned the Imperial Japanese Army's 17th Army the task of retaking Guadalcanal. The army would be supported by Japanese naval units, including the Combined Fleet under the command of Yamamoto, which had its headquarters at Truk.

The 17th Army was heavily involved in the Japanese campaign in New Guinea, and so only a few units were available. Of these the 35th Infantry Brigade under Major-General Kawaguchi was at Palau, the 4th Infantry Regiment was in the Philippines and the 28th Infantry Regiment was on board transport ships near Guam. The different units began to converge upon Guadalcanal via Truk and Rabaul immediately. However, Ichiki's regiment, being the nearest, would arrive in the area first. The first element of Ichiki's unit landed from destroyers at Taivu Point, east of the Lunga perimeter, on 19 August.

The Japanese had underestimated the strength of Allied forces on Guadalcanal, and so Ichiki's unit conducted a night frontal assault on Marine positions at Alligator Creek, also known as the Ilu river on USMC maps, on the east side of the Lunga perimeter in the early hours of 21 August. Ichiki's assault was defeated with heavy losses in what was later known as the Battle of Tenaru. At daybreak the Marine units counter-attacked Ichiki's surviving troops, killing more, including the commander Ichiki. In total, only 128 of the original 917 members of the Regiment's First Element were killed in the battle, and those who survived escaped to Taivu Point, where they notified 17th Army Headquarters of their defeat. Even as the Tenaru battle was ending, further Japanese reinforcements had already been dispatched. Leaving Truk on 16 August were three slow transports carrying the remaining 1,400 soldiers from the 28th Infantry Regiment, plus 500 naval marines from the 5th Yokosuka Special Naval Landing Force. Escorting the transports were thirteen warships commanded by Rear Admiral Raizo Tanaka, who planned to land the troops on Guadalcanal on 24 August. To support the landing of these troops and provide support for the operation to retake Henderson Field from Allied forces, Admiral Yamamoto directed Nagumo to depart from Truk with a carrier group on 21 August and proceed towards the southern Solomon Islands. The Japanese force included three carriers and thirty other warships.

Having received intelligence concerning the disposition of the Japanese forces, three American carrier task forces under Fletcher approached Guadalcanal to counter the Japanese offensive. On 24/25 August the two carrier forces became engaged in the Battle of the Eastern Solomons, which resulted in both fleets retreating from the area after suffering damage, although the Japanese would lose a light aircraft carrier, the *Ryujo*, this being sunk by Douglas SBDs from the USS *Saratoga*. Tanaka's convoy, after suffering heavy damage and the loss of a transport during the battle after an air attack by CAF aircraft operating from Henderson Field, was forced to divert to the Shortland Islands in the northern Solomons in order to transfer the remaining troops to destroyers for later delivery to Guadalcanal.

Throughout August small groups of American aircraft and their crews continued to arrive at Guadalcanal, and so by the end of August sixty-four aircraft of various types were stationed at Henderson Field. On 3 September the commander of the 1st Marine Aircraft Wing, Brigadier-General Geiger USMC, arrived with his staff and took command of all air operations at Henderson Field. Air battles between the Allied aircraft from Henderson and Japanese bombers and fighters from Rabaul continued almost daily. Between 26 August and 5 September the American forces lost about fifteen aircraft, while the Japanese lost approximately nineteen aircraft. More than half of the downed US aircrews were rescued, while most of the Japanese aircrews were never recovered. The eight-hour flight to and from Rabaul to Guadalcanal would seriously hamper the Japanese efforts to establish air superiority over Henderson Field.

Assisting the American defenders were Australian coast watchers based on Bougainville and New Georgia islands, who were often able to provide the Allied forces on Guadalcanal with advance notice of inbound Japanese air strikes, which allowed the US fighters time to take off and position themselves to attack the Japanese aircraft as they approached the island. As the result of these early warnings the Japanese air forces were slowly losing a war of attrition in the skies above Guadalcanal. During this time Vandegrift continued to direct efforts to strengthen and improve the defences of the Lunga perimeter. Between 21 August and 3 September he relocated three Marine battalions from Tulagi and Gavutu to Guadalcanal. These units added about 1,500 troops to the original 11,000 men defending Henderson Field.

Small Allied naval convoys arrived at Guadalcanal on 23 August, 29 August, 1 September and 8 September, supplying the Marines at Lunga with more food, ammunition, aircraft fuel and much-needed aircraft technicians. The 1 September convoy also brought 392 construction engineers to maintain and improve Henderson Field. On 23 August the 35th Infantry Brigade reached Truk and was embarked onto slow transport ships for the rest of the voyage to Guadalcanal. The damage done to the earlier convoy during the Battle of the Eastern Solomons caused the Japanese to reconsider trying to deliver more troops to Guadalcanal by this method, and so the ships carrying the soldiers were sent to Rabaul, from where the Japanese planned to deliver the troops to Guadalcanal by destroyers that would stage through the Japanese naval base on the Shortland Islands.

The Japanese destroyers were usually able to make round trips via the New Georgia Sound to Guadalcanal and back in a single night throughout the campaign, so minimising their exposure to Allied air attack. These trips became known as the 'Tokyo Express' to the Allies, and were labelled 'Rat Transportation' by the Japanese. Delivering the troops in this manner prevented the majority of the heavy equipment and supplies, which included heavy artillery, vehicles, food and ammunition, from being carried to

Deck crews push torpedoes towards a Curtiss Helldiver from VT-2 aboard the USS Hornet. (US Navy/NARA via Dennis R. Jenkins)

Guadalcanal with them. In addition these activities tied up destroyers that the IJN desperately needed for convoy protection. During the period 29 August to 4 September Japanese light cruisers, destroyers, and patrol boats were able to land almost 5,000 troops at Taivu Point, including most of the 35th Infantry Brigade, the majority of the 4th Regiment and the remainder of Ichiki's regiment. General Kawaguchi, who landed at Taivu Point on the 31 August Express run, was placed in command of all Japanese forces on Guadalcanal. On 7 September Kawaguchi released his attack plan, which called for his forces to rout and annihilate the enemy in the vicinity of the Guadalcanal Island airfield.

On 15 September the Japanese command at Rabaul learned of the defeat on Guadalcanal, and forwarded the news to Imperial General Headquarters in Japan. In an emergency meeting the Japanese IJA and IJN command staffs concluded that Guadalcanal might develop into the most decisive battle of the war. The results of the battle to date began to have a telling strategic impact on Japanese operations in other areas of the Pacific. Hyakutake realised that in order to send sufficient troops and matériel to defeat the Allied forces on Guadalcanal he would not be able at the same time to continue to support the major ongoing Japanese offensive on the Kokoda Track in New Guinea. After consultation with General Headquarters, he ordered his troops on New Guinea, who were within thirty miles of Port Moresby, to withdraw until the Battle for Guadalcanal was resolved. Hyakutake then prepared to send more troops to Guadalcanal for another attempt to recapture Henderson Field.

While the Japanese regrouped west of the Matanikau, the American forces concentrated on reinforcing the Lunga defences, and to that end on 14 September a US Marine battalion was moved from Tulagi to Guadalcanal, while on 18 September an Allied convoy delivered 4,157 men from the 3rd Provisional Marine Brigade plus 137 vehicles, tents, aviation fuel, ammunition, rations and engineering equipment to Guadalcanal. These crucial reinforcements allowed Vandegrift, beginning on 19 September, to establish an unbroken line of defence around the Lunga perimeter. During the convoy's transit the aircraft carrier USS *Wasp* was sunk by the Japanese submarine *I-19* south-east of Guadalcanal. The three torpedoes from the submarine ruptured aircraft fuel lines, causing serious fires and explosions throughout the ship. Eventually the *Wasp* was abandoned, the hulk being torpedoed by the destroyer USS *Lansdowne*. The loss of the *Wasp* left only one aircraft carrier, the USS *Hornet*, for operations in the South Pacific area.

After such a period of frantic activity a lull occurred in the air war over Guadalcanal, with no Japanese air raids taking place between 14 and 27 September due to bad weather. During this period both sides increased the strength of their respective air units. The Japanese delivered eighty-five fighters and bombers to Rabaul, while the Americans delivered twenty-three fighters and attack aircraft to Henderson Field. Thus, by 20 September, the Japanese strength was 117 aircraft at Rabaul, and the Allies had seventy-one aircraft at Henderson Field. The air war resumed with a Japanese air raid on Guadalcanal on 27 September, which was contested by Navy and Marine fighters based at Henderson Field. The Japanese had also begun to prepare for their next attempt to recapture Henderson Field, and to that end the 3rd Battalion, 4th Infantry Regiment, had landed at Kamimbo Bay on the western end of Guadalcanal on 11 September, although it was too late to join Kawaguchi's attack. Joining the 3rd Battalion were the Japanese 2nd and 38th Infantry Divisions that were transported from the Dutch East Indies to Rabaul from 13 September. Major-General Vandegrift and his staff were aware that Kawaguchi's troops had retreated to the area west of the Matanikau and that numerous groups of Japanese stragglers were scattered throughout the area between the Lunga perimeter and the Matanikau river. Vandegrift decided to conduct another series of small-unit operations around the Matanikau valley, the purpose of these operations being to clean up the various groups of Japanese troops east of the Matanikau and to keep the main group of Japanese soldiers unbalanced, so preventing them from consolidating their positions so close to the main Marine defensive perimeter at Lunga Point.

The Japanese 8th Fleet staff scheduled a large and important Tokyo Express for the night of 11 October. This consisted of two seaplane tenders and six destroyers that were to deliver 728 soldiers plus artillery and ammunition to Guadalcanal. In parallel a separate operation involving three heavy cruisers and two destroyers under the command of Rear Admiral Goto bombarded Henderson Field with special explosive shells, with the object of destroying the CAF and the airfield's facilities. As the US Navy warships had not attempted to intercept any Tokyo Express missions to Guadalcanal, the Japanese were not expecting any opposition from Allied naval surface forces that night. But just before midnight American warships detected the Goto force on radar near the entrance to the strait between Savo Island and Guadalcanal. The Allies were in a position to cross the 'T' of the Japanese ships. Opening fire, the Allied warships sank one of the Japanese cruisers and one of the destroyers, while heavily damaging another cruiser, and this mortally wounded the Goto force overall, forcing the rest of the Japanese warships to abandon the bombardment mission and retreat. During the exchange of gunfire one of the Allied destroyers was sunk and one cruiser and another destroyer were heavily damaged. In the meantime the Japanese supply convoy successfully completed the unloading at Guadalcanal, beginning its return journey without being discovered by the defenders. On the morning of 12 October four Japanese destroyers from the supply convoy turned back to assist retreating, damaged Japanese warships. Air attacks by CAF aircraft from Henderson Field sank two of these destroyers later that day. The American supply convoy reached Guadalcanal as scheduled the next day, and successfully delivered their cargo and passengers to the island. In spite of the American victory off Cape Esperance, the Japanese continued with their plans and preparations for their large offensive scheduled for later in October.

On 13 October a convoy comprising six cargo ships with eight screening destroyers departed the Shortland Islands for Guadalcanal. The convoy carried troops from the 16th and 230th Infantry Regiments plus some naval marines, two batteries of heavy artillery and one company of tanks. To protect the convoy from attack by CAF aircraft, Admiral Yamamoto sent two battleships from Truk to bombard Henderson Field. In the early hours of 14 October the Japanese battleships *Kongo* and *Haruna*, escorted by one light cruiser and nine destroyers, reached Guadalcanal and opened fire on Henderson Field from a distance of 17,500 yards. Over the next hour and twenty-three minutes, the two battleships fired 973 14-inch shells into the Lunga perimeter, most of which fell in and around the airfield. Many of the shells were fragmentation shells that were specifically designed to destroy land targets. The bombardment heavily damaged both runways, burned most of the available aviation fuel, destroyed forty-eight of the CAF's ninety aircraft, and killed forty-one men, including six CAF pilots. At the conclusion of the bombardment the battleship force immediately returned to Truk.

While the airfield had suffered heavy damage, Henderson personnel quickly restored one of the runways to operational condition within a few hours. Seventeen Douglas SBDs and twenty Grumman Wildcats based at Espiritu Santo were flown to Henderson Field, while USAAF and USMC transport aircraft began to shuttle aircraft fuel from Espiritu Santo to Guadalcanal. Aware of the approach of the Japanese reinforcement convoy, the Americans sought some way to attack the convoy before it could reach Guadalcanal. The answer was to use fuel drained from damaged aircraft plus that held in a cache in the nearby jungle, and the CAF attacked the convoy twice on the 14th, but caused no damage; however, a Japanese cargo ship was destroyed at Tassafaronga the following day.

The main Japanese convoy reached Tassafaronga on Guadalcanal at midnight on 14 October, and immediately began unloading, continuing throughout the following day. However, a wave of CAF aircraft from Henderson bombed and strafed the unloading vessels, destroying three of the cargo ships. The remaining ships departed that night, having unloaded all of the troops and most of the supplies and equipment. While the freighters were being unloaded, Japanese heavy cruisers bombarded Henderson on the nights of 14/15 October,t destroying a few CAF aircraft, although they failed to cause significant further damage to the airfield or its facilities. The first phase of the Japanese attack took place at dusk on 23 October when two battalions of the 4th Infantry Regiment and the nine tanks of the 1st Independent Tank Company launched an attack on the USMC defences at the mouth of the Matanikau. Marine artillery, cannon, and small-arms fire repulsed the attacks, destroying all the tanks and killing many of the Japanese soldiers while suffering only light casualties. A few small groups of Japanese managed to break through the American defences, but were all hunted down and killed over the next several days. Over 1,500 of Maruyama's troops were killed in the attacks, while the American defenders lost sixty killed. During the fighting, aircraft from Henderson Field defended against attacks by Japanese aircraft and ships, destroying fourteen aircraft and sinking a light cruiser in the process.

While the Japanese ground forces were trying to defeat their American counterparts, Japanese aircraft carriers and other large warships under the overall command of Admiral Yamamoto moved into a position near the

Under a stormy sky the USS Hornet steams towards the Battle of Santa Cruz, where it will be sunk by a mixture of bombs and torpedoes on 27 October 1942. (US Navy/NARA via Dennis R. Jenkins)

southern Solomon Islands, from where they hoped to engage and decisively defeat any Allied naval forces, especially the US Navy carrier forces. Allied naval carrier forces in the area, now under the overall command of Admiral William Halsey Jr, who had replaced Ghormley on 18 October, were also hoping to confront the Japanese naval forces in battle. Nimitz had replaced Ghormley with Halsey after concluding that Ghormley had become too conservative to continue leading the Allied forces in the South Pacific area effectively. The two opposing carrier forces confronted each other on the morning of 26 October in what became known as the Battle of the Santa Cruz Islands. After an exchange of carrier air attacks the Allied surface ships were forced to retreat from the battle area with the loss of one carrier sunk, this being the USS *Hornet*. The ship suffered four bomb hits and sixteen torpedo hits, some of the latter having been administered by US Navy destroyers after they had failed to take the stricken carrier in tow.

Another carrier, the USS *Enterprise*, was also heavily damaged and would require repair work at Pearl Harbor. The participating Japanese carrier forces were also forced to retire due to high aircraft and aircrew losses, as well as significant damage to two of their carriers. Although an apparent tactical victory for the Japanese in terms of ships sunk and damaged, the loss by the Japanese of many veteran aircrews would provide a long-term strategic advantage for the Allies, whose aircrew losses in the battle were relatively low. The damaged Japanese aircraft carriers would play no further role in the campaign, reducing the available cover for the ground forces. In order to exploit the victory in the Battle for Henderson Field, General Vandegrift sent six Marine battalions, joined later by one US Army battalion, on an offensive

Caught at the moment of touchdown is this Grumman F6F Hellcat of VF-25, landing on the USS Cowpens, an Independence-class light aircraft carrier. (US Navy/NARA via Dennis R. Jenkins)

A Douglas Dauntless from the USS Yorktown overflies the USS Enterprise while both carriers are en route to Midway to face down the Japanese fleet in combat. (US Navy/NARA via Dennis R. Jenkins)

west of the Matanikau. The American offensive began on 1 November and succeeded in destroying the Japanese forces defending the Point Cruz area two days later, including the rear-echelon troops sent to reinforce Nakaguma's battered forces. The Americans were on the verge of breaking through the Japanese defences and capturing Kokumbona, while other American forces discovered and attacked newly landed Japanese troops near Koli Point on the eastern side of the Lunga perimeter. To counter this new threat Vandegrift temporarily halted the Matanikau offensive on 4 November. At Koli Point early in the morning of 8 November five Japanese destroyers delivered 300 troops to support Shoji and his troops, who were *en route* to Koli Point after the Battle for Henderson Field. Having learned of the planned landing, General Vandegrift sent a battalion of Marines to intercept the Japanese at Koli. Soon after landing, the Japanese troops encountered and drove the USMC battalion back towards the Lunga perimeter.

The Tokyo Express runs on 5, 7 and 9 November delivered additional troops from the Japanese 38th Infantry Division to Guadalcanal to replace those so far lost. These fresh troops were quickly emplaced in the Point Cruz and Matanikau area, and helped to successfully resist further attacks by American forces on 10 and 18 November. The Americans and Japanese remained facing each other along a line just west of Point Cruz for the next six weeks. After the defeat in the Battle for Henderson Field the IJA would again plan to try to retake the airfield during November 1942; however, further reinforcements were needed before the operation could proceed. The IJA requested assistance from Admiral Yamamoto to deliver the needed reinforcements to the island and to support the next offensive. Yamamoto provided eleven large transport ships to carry the remaining troops from the 38th Infantry Division plus their equipment from Rabaul to Guadalcanal. He

108

was also asked to provide a warship support force that included two battle-ships – the *Hiei* and the *Kirishima*. Loaded with special fragmentation shells, they were to bombard Henderson Field on the night of 12/13 November, and destroy it and the aircraft stationed there in order to allow the slow, heavy transports to reach Guadalcanal and unload safely the next day. The support force was commanded from the IJN *Hiei* by the recently promoted Vice-Admiral Abe.

In early November Allied intelligence learned that the Japanese were again preparing to try to retake Henderson Field, and so the Americans sent Task Force 67, plus a large reinforcement and resupply convoy carrying troops, to Guadalcanal on 11 November. The ships were attacked several times on 11 and 12 November by Japanese aircraft from Rabaul staging through the air base at Buin, Bougainville, although most were unloaded without serious damage. American reconnaissance aircraft spotted the approach of Abe's warships and passed a warning to the Allied command. Now warned, Turner detached all available combat ships under Callaghan to protect the troops ashore from the expected Japanese naval attack and troop landing, and ordered the supply ships at Guadalcanal to depart by 12 November. Callaghan's force comprised two heavy cruisers, three light cruisers, and eight destroyers, and he intercepted Abe's warships between Guadalcanal and Savo Island. In addition to the two battleships, Abe's force included a light cruiser and eleven destroyers. In the darkness the two groups of warships intermingled before opening fire at unusually short range. In the resulting mêlée, Abe's warships sank or severely damaged all but one cruiser and one destroyer in Callaghan's force, and both Callaghan and Scott were killed. Two Japanese destroyers were sunk, and another destroyer and the *Hiei* were heavily damaged. In spite of his victory over Callaghan's force, Abe ordered his warships to depart without bombarding Henderson Field. The *Hiei* sank later that day after repeated air attacks by CAF aircraft and aircraft from the carrier *Enterprise*. Because Abe's force had failed to neutralise Henderson Field, Yamamoto ordered the troop convoy to wait an additional day before heading towards Guadalcanal. He also ordered Kondo to assemble another bombardment force using warships from Truk and Abe's force to attack Henderson Field again on 15 November.

Prior to this, on 14 November, a cruiser and destroyer force under Mikawa, which was based at Rabaul, conducted an unopposed bombardment of Henderson Field, causing some damage, although it failed to put the airfield out of operation. As the bombardment vessels retired towards Rabaul, Tanaka's transport convoy, under the impression that Henderson Field was now inoperable, began its move towards Guadalcanal. Throughout 14 November aircraft from Henderson Field and the USS *Enterprise* attacked both groups of Japanese ships, sinking one heavy cruiser and seven of the trans-ports. Most of the troops were rescued from the transports by Tanaka's escorting destroyers and returned to the Shortland Islands. After night had fallen Tanaka with the remaining four transports continued towards

The rear section of the Enterprise flight deck is covered with armed Douglas SBDs and handling parties, as another strike wave prepares for departure. In the background is BB-56 USS Washington. (US Navy/NARA via Dennis R. Jenkins)

Guadalcanal as Kondo's force approached the area to bombard Henderson Field. In order to stop Kondo's force, Admiral Halsey detached two battleships, the USS *Washington* and *South Dakota*, plus four destroyers, from the *Enterprise* task force. The American force under the command of Rear Admiral Lee aboard the *Washington* reached Guadalcanal and Savo Island just before midnight on 14 November, just before Kondo's force arrived. The Japanese force consisted of the *Kirishima*, plus two heavy cruisers, two light cruisers, and nine destroyers. After the two forces made contact, Kondo's force quickly sank three of the US Navy destroyers and heavily damaged the fourth. The Japanese warships then opened fire on and damaged the *South Dakota*. However, as Kondo's warships concentrated on the *South Dakota*, the *Washington* approached the Japanese ships unobserved and opened fire on the *Kirishima*, hitting the Japanese battleship repeatedly and causing extensive damage. After pursuing the departing *Washington* towards the Russell Islands, Kondo ordered his warships to retire without bombarding Henderson Field. As Kondo's warships departed, the four Japanese transports beached themselves near Tassafaronga on Guadalcanal in the early hours of the morning and quickly began unloading. Two hours after they had first beached, American aircraft and artillery began attacking the transports, destroying all four, plus most of the supplies that they carried. As fewer troops than needed for the assault had been landed, the Japanese were forced to cancel their planned November offensive on Henderson Field.

On 26 November Lieutenant-General Imamura took command of the newly formed Eighth Area Army at Rabaul, encompassing Hyakutake's 17th Army and the 18th Army in New Guinea. One of Imamura's first priorities upon assuming command was the continuation of the attempts to retake Henderson Field and Guadalcanal. However, the Allied offensive at Buna in New Guinea changed the General's priorities. Because the Allied attempt to take Buna was considered a more serious threat to Rabaul, Imamura postponed the provision of further major reinforcement efforts to Guadalcanal, and decided to concentrate on the situation in New Guinea.

Due to the deteriorating condition of the troops fighting to retake Guadalcanal, the Eighth Fleet's Guadalcanal Reinforcement Unit, better known as the Tokyo Express, was tasked with making the first of five scheduled runs to Tassafaronga on Guadalcanal on the night of 30 November. This unit consisted of eight destroyers plus a further six destroyers assigned for this run to carry between 200 and 240 drums of supplies apiece. However, the US Navy had received intelligence concerning the Japanese supply attempt. In response Admiral Halsey ordered the newly constituted Task Force 67, comprising four cruisers and four destroyers under the command of Rear Admiral Wright USN, to intercept Tanaka's force off Guadalcanal. Late on the evening of 30 November Tanaka's force arrived off Guadalcanal and prepared to unload the supply barrels. The TF.67 destroyers detected Tanaka's force on radar, and the destroyer commander requested permission to attack with torpedoes. However, they were forced to wait for a few minutes, thereby allowing the Japanese force to escape from an optimum firing setup. All of the American torpedoes missed their targets, although the cruisers opened fire, hitting and destroying one of the Japanese escort destroyers. The remaining Japanese warships abandoned the supply mission, increased speed and launched a total of forty-four torpedoes in the direction of the American cruisers. The Japanese torpedoes hit and sank the USS *Northampton*,while others badly damaged the cruisers *Minneapolis, New Orleans* and *Pensacola*. The remainder of the destroyers escaped without damage, although they had failed to deliver any of the much-needed provisions to Guadalcanal.

By 7 December 1942 the Japanese Army was losing approximately fifty men each day from malnutrition, disease, and Allied ground or air attacks. Further attempts by Tanaka's force to deliver provisions on 3, 7 and 11 December failed to alleviate the crisis, and one of Tanaka's destroyers was sunk by a US Navy PT boat torpedo. Given the critical situation, the Japanese Navy proposed on 12 December that attempts to capture Guadalcanal be abandoned. At the same time several senior army staff officers at the Imperial General Headquarters also suggested that further efforts to retake Guadalcanal would be excessive in both manpower and materials. By 19

December the Japanese had decided to abandon the Guadalcanal campaign and to establish a new defence line in the central Solomons, plus a change of priorities and resources to the campaign in New Guinea. On 28 December General Sugiyama and Admiral Nagano informed Emperor Hirohito of the decision to withdraw from Guadalcanal, this being formally endorsed on 31 December. The Japanese immediately began preparations for the evacuation, called Operation Ke, which was scheduled to begin during the latter part of January 1943.

On 18 December Allied forces began attacking the Japanese positions on Mount Austen, although a strong Japanese fortified position, called the Gifu, confounded the attacks, and the Americans were forced to temporarily halt their offensive on 4 January. The offensive resumed on 10 January, reattacking the Japanese on Mount Austen as well as on the two nearby ridges, known as Seahorse and Galloping Horse, and the Allies had captured all three by 23 January. The Americans suffered 250 killed in the operation, while the Japanese suffered approximately 3,000 casualties. On 14 January a Tokyo Express run delivered a battalion of troops to act as a rearguard for the Ke evacuation. At the same time Japanese warships and aircraft moved into position around Rabaul and Bougainville in preparation to execute the withdrawal operation. Allied intelligence had detected the Japanese movements, although they had misinterpreted them as preparations for another attempt to retake Henderson Field and Guadalcanal. As part of the evacuation plan the Japanese 17th Army withdrew to the west coast of Guadalcanal, while rearguard units countered the American offensive. On the night of 1 February twenty destroyers from the 8th Fleet successfully collected nearly 5,000 soldiers from the island. On the nights of 4 and 7 February the Japanese destroyers completed the evacuation of most of the remaining Japanese forces from Guadalcanal.

Altogether the Japanese successfully evacuated 10,652 men from Guadalcanal. Two days later the Americans realised that the Japanese were gone and declared Guadalcanal secure for Allied forces, and this officially ended the campaign. After the Japanese withdrawal, Guadalcanal and Tulagi were developed into major bases supporting the Allied advance further up the Solomon Islands chain.

In addition to Henderson Field, two additional fighter runways were constructed at Lunga Point, while a bomber airfield was built at Koli Point. Extensive naval port and logistics facilities were established at Guadalcanal, Tulagi, and Florida. The anchorage at Tulagi would become an important advanced base for Allied ships supporting the Solomon Islands campaign. After their failure to keep Guadalcanal, the Japanese were clearly on the defensive in the Pacific. The constant need to reinforce Guadalcanal had weakened Japanese efforts in other areas, which contributed to a successful Australian and American counter-offensive in New Guinea that culminated in the capture of the key bases of Buna and Gona in early 1943.

CHAPTER FIVE

War in the Pacific:
Battles and Defeats

At the beginning of 1943 the US Navy was in a very strong position. Although it had lost the carriers *Lexington, Yorktown, Hornet* and *Wasp*, it still had the *Saratoga, Ranger* and *Enterprise* in service, while the first of the Essex class had entered service, with another twenty-three scheduled to slide down the slips until 1946. Supporting the major fleet carriers were the escort or jeep carriers, which included the USS *Charger*, four ships of

This Grumman F6F Hellcat of VF-2 has run off the flight deck of the escort carrier USS Charger. Recovery requires the deck crew to counterbalance the weight of the aircraft so that it can be rolled back on deck. Although this particular vessel was not deployed on operations, its primary task was to train pilots for the Pacific campaign. (US Navy/NARA via Dennis R. Jenkins)

the Sangamon class, eleven Bogue, fifty Casablanca, nineteen of the Commencement Bay class and the nine vessels of the Independence light carrier class.

In contrast, the Imperial Japanese Navy was in very bad shape, having lost the *Akagi, Kaga, Ryujo, Soryu, Hiryu* and *Shoho*. These losses left the Japanese with the *Hosho, Chitose, Chiyoda, Zuiho, Shokaku, Zuikaka, Taiyo, Unyo, Chuyo, Hiyo, Junyo, Ryuho, Taiho, Ibuki, Unryu, Amagi* and *Shinano*, although many of these would never be deployed due to the lack of aircraft, crews and fuel. While on paper this seemed a strong force, the IJN was suffering from a lack of trained crews, as many had been lost during the carrier battles of 1942, while the training regime was not robust enough to provide replacements quickly enough and in large enough quantities. Not helping the Japanese with their expansion plans was the need to withdraw from the Guadalcanal campaign, as it was consuming vast resources and had become unwinnable.

After sustained operations through the Coral Sea, Midway and Guadalcanal, the US Navy aircraft carriers spent a short period in repair and re-equipment, as they were desperately in need of them for the next major operation. This would be Operation Cartwheel, which was intended to be a multi-pronged attack on Japanese forces throughout the Pacific theatre. The gambit of this operation took place on 29 June 1943 when the Americans managed to land troops on New Georgia in the central Solomon Islands, and this was followed by further landings early the next morning on Rendova. Supporting these first landings was Task Force 36.3, whose carriers were the USS *Saratoga* and HMS *Victorious*, these in turn being supported by numerous cruisers and destroyers plus a large contingent of battleships. The second carrier group was designated TF.36.5, which had the escort carriers *Sangamon, Suwanee* and *Chenango*, plus the usual destroyer escort. During these landings the carrier-based aircraft were more concerned with supporting the ground forces, and so the major naval battles took place between the surface vessels and submarines, with losses being experienced by both sides. The carrier groups continued to provide air support for various attacks on Japanese-held Islands in the Pacific. Between 15 and 26 August support was provided for the US III Amphibious Force during their landing upon Vella Lavella in the central Solomon Islands, and this was followed by landings upon Nekufetau in the Ellice Islands, which in turn was followed by a further landing in the Solomon Islands, when Arandul Island was captured. As each of these territories was captured, various construction units were landed, their primary purpose being to construct air bases and harbourage as needed.

As the year progressed, a further reshuffle took place in the carrier task force. On 31 August 1943 the newly formed US Fast Carrier Task Force came into being, designated TF.15, under the command of Rear Admiral Pownell. TF.15 went straight into action on 31 August, the force consisting of the carriers *Yorktown, Essex* and *Independence*, whose support was led by the battleship USS *Indiana*, plus the cruisers *Nashville* and *Mobile* with eleven destroyers and a fleet oiler. By this time the battleships of the US Navy were

VB-1 was one of the Curtiss Helldiver units assigned to the USS Yorktown, an Essex-class carrier that replaced the carrier of the same name lost in 1942. (US Navy/NARA via Dennis R. Jenkins)

covering two vital roles – the first was to use their main armament for bombardment, while the second was that of air defence, for which they started to sprout masses of anti-aircraft guns. The first target for TF.15 was Marcus Island, a Japanese stronghold. Although 257 sorties were flown against the Japanese installations during six attacks, very little damage was inflicted for the loss of four aircraft. While TF.15 was trying to unseat the Japanese on Marcus Island, TF.11, under the command of Rear Admiral Lee, was supporting the 804th Aviation Battalion of the US Army to land on Baker Island on 1 September so that an airstrip could be constructed. The carriers assigned to TF.11 were the USS *Princeton* and *Belleau Wood.*

Having learned from the Marcus Island adventure, TF.15 was back in action on 17 September, when it attacked Tarawa in the Gilbert Islands. The carriers assigned to this task force were the *Lexington, Princeton* and *Belleau Wood*, plus the usual selection of cruisers and destroyers. The carriers launched 190 sorties as part of the softening-up process, during which four aircraft were lost. After these attacks the task force retired, although Tarawa was attacked on 19 September by USAAF B-24 Liberators that pounded the island, destroying twelve Japanese aircraft and two torpedo boats, and damaging installations around the island. The assault on these various islands had the desired effect, as the Japanese tried to evacuate first Kolombangara and then Vella Lavella. The former was mostly successful, while the latter was headed off by a US Navy destroyer force. Having started the evacuation of Kolombangara on 25 September, the Japanese finally recovered their remaining personnel on 3 October.

Wake Island would be the next target for the American carriers. On 5 October, TF.14, under the command of Rear Admiral Montgomery, carried out attacks on the Japanese forces using aircraft from the carriers *Essex*, *Yorktown*, *Lexington*, *Cowpens*, *Independence* and *Belleau Wood*. Given the number of aircraft carriers, there was an extensive escort force, composed of seven cruisers and twenty-four destroyers. Over a twenty-four-hour period the aircraft carriers launched 738 sorties, during which twelve aircraft were lost due to enemy action, while a further fourteen were lost to accidents. After this action the task force withdrew toward Hawaii, during which transit the carrier USS *Cowpens* was damaged after colliding with the destroyer USS *Abbot*.

The Allied plan to drive the Japanese from the South-West Pacific Area, Operation Cartwheel, aimed to isolate Rabaul and reduce its importance by air raids, a complete change from its more peaceful existence earlier in 1943. When the attacks on Rabaul began, Japanese ground forces were already retreating from New Guinea and the Solomon Islands, abandoning Guadalcanal, Kolombangara, New Georgia and Vella Lavella. Rabaul, on the island of New Britain, was one of two major ports in the Australian Territory of New Guinea, and had become the main Japanese naval base for the Solomon Islands and New Guinea campaigns. Simpson Harbour, captured in February 1942, held a similar position for Japan as Pearl Harbor did to America, and was well defended by an extensive array of anti-aircraft guns and five airfields. Lakunai and Vunakanau airfields were pre-war Australian constructions. Lakunai had an all-weather runway of sand and volcanic ash, while Vunakanau was surfaced with concrete. Another airfield, Rapopo, which was fourteen miles to the south-east, had became operational in December 1942, complete with concrete runways and extensive support and maintenance facilities. Tobera, halfway between Vunakanau and Rapopo, had been completed in August 1943, and also featured concrete runways. The four airfields had 166 protected revetments for bombers and 265 for fighters, all having additional unprotected dispersal parking areas. The fifth airfield, protecting Rabaul, was Borpop airfield, located across the St George's Channel on New Ireland, which had been completed in December 1942.

The anti-aircraft defences were well co-ordinated by army and naval units, as the IJA manned 192 of the 367 anti-aircraft guns, while the IJN manned the remainder. The naval anti-aircraft guns protected Simpson Harbour and its shipping, plus the three airfields of Tobera, Lakunai, and Vunakanau. The army units were charged with defending Rapopo airfield, supply dumps and army installations. An effective early-warning radar system provided ninety-mile coverage from Rabaul, being backed up by extended coverage with additional radars on New Britain, New Ireland, and at Buka. These radar outposts provided between thirty and sixty minutes' early warning of an air attack.

On 12 October 1943, as part of Operation Cartwheel, the USAAF 5th Air Force, in company with the Royal Australian Air Force and the Royal New Zealand Air Force, launched a sustained campaign of bombing against the airfields and port of Rabaul. After the first raid of 349 aircraft, bad weather reduced the options to bomb Rabaul, and only a single raid by fifty B-25s was mounted on 18 October. Once the weather cleared, sustained attacks resumed on 23 October and continued over the next six days, before culminating in the large raid of 2 November. Nine squadrons of B-25 Mitchells, totalling seventy-two bombers, and six squadrons of P-38 Lightning escorts attacked the anti-aircraft defences and Simpson Harbour with low-altitude strafing and bombing attacks.

Putting even greater pressure on the Japanese forces was the invasion of Bougainville on 1 November 1943, which placed Rabaul under increased threat from another direction. A hurried attempt to drive Allied forces off Bougainville had been defeated in the Battle of Empress Augusta Bay. Admiral Koga, the commander-in-chief of the Japanese Fleet after the death of Admiral Yamamoto, then planned to reinforce Rabaul and overwhelm the limited Allied forces around Bougainville while most of the American Navy was involved in preparations for the invasion of Tarawa. Rear Admiral Sherman planned to counteract this threat by a carrier raid from Task Force 38, and so the carriers *Saratoga* and *Princeton* were ordered to head for New Britain, using a weather front for cover. Upon their arrival on 5 November, the carriers launched ninety-seven aircraft against Rabaul. Although no ships were sunk in the raid, six cruisers were hit, of which four were badly damaged. The *Atago* suffered three near-misses by 500 lb bombs that caused extensive underwater shock damage, while shrapnel shards killed twenty-two crewmen, including the captain. The *Maya* was hit by one bomb above one of the engine rooms, which caused extensive damage and killed seventy of the crew. The *Mogami* was struck by a single 500 lb bomb that set the vessel afire, as well as causing heavy damage and killing nineteen crewmen. The *Takao* was hit by two 500 lb bombs that caused heavy damage and killed twenty-three crewmen, while the *Chikuma* was slightly damaged by several near-misses. The *Agano* suffered a near-miss from one bomb, which damaged one anti-aircraft gun and killed one crewman. Three destroyers also suffered damage, although this was light in nature. Most of the Japanese warships departed for Truk the next day for repairs and to escape further Allied airstrikes. The 5th Air Force followed up the Navy strikes an hour after the American carrier attacks had ceased with a raid by twenty-seven B-24 Liberator heavy bombers escorted by P-38 Lightnings.

An additional carrier task group from the American Fifth Fleet reached Halsey on 7 November, commanded by Rear Admiral Montgomery, consisting of the carriers *Bunker Hill*, *Essex* and *Independence*. Halsey used these ships as part of Task Force 38 to undertake a double carrier strike against Rabaul on 11 November. The cruiser *Agano*, which had remained at Rabaul after the 5 November strike, was torpedoed during these attacks and suffered further extensive damage. The Japanese launched a series of counter-attacks, which involved 120 aircraft against the American carriers, but this force was intercepted *en route*, losing thirty-five aircraft without inflicting damage on the task force.

Even as Rabaul was being attacked, TF.38 under the command of Rear Admiral Sherman was approaching the Solomon Islands from the west. The carriers in this group, *Saratoga* and *Princeton*, would launch air strikes against the Japanese airfields at Buna and Buka over 1 and 2 November. On 3 November the Japanese 2nd Fleet under the command of Vice-Admiral Kurita, with elements of the 3rd Fleet, was dispatched from Rabaul to intercept TF.38. However, the Japanese vessels were spotted by a reconnaissance aircraft, and in response B-24 Liberators of the 5th AAF attacked as the ships neared Bismark Archipelago, being backed up by a strike force launched by the carriers. This comprised twenty-two dive-bombers, twenty-three torpedo-bombers and fifty-two escorting fighters. During this attack ten aircraft were shot down, while the Japanese had six cruisers and a destroyer badly damaged. During this period the Japanese counter-attacks saw the loss of 121 carrier aircraft of the 173 available, which rendered the carrier forces non-operational, while those pilots who survived claimed the destruction of five battleships, ten aircraft carriers, nineteen cruisers, seven destroyers, nine transports and twenty-four other vessels.

The next major battle for the US Navy carriers would be Operation Galvanic, whose preparations began on 10 November 1943.

After the success at Midway and the positive conclusion of the Guadalcanal campaign it was becoming obvious to the American Joint Chiefs that the Japanese dominance in the Pacific was on the wane. To keep the pressure on the Japanese High Command, the Joint Chiefs determined that it was important to set up forward air bases capable of supporting operations across the mid-Pacific, this in turn leading to retaking the Philippines and thence on to Japan. To that end it was decided that the American forces would need to take the Marianas Islands. The downside was that the Marianas were heavily defended, and so in order for attacks against them to succeed, land-based bombers provided by the USAAF would be needed to soften up the defences. The nearest islands capable of supporting long-range bombers were the Marshall Islands, located north-east of Guadalcanal. Capturing these islands would provide the base needed to launch such an offensive on the Marianas. But the Marshall Islands were cut off from direct communications with Hawaii by a Japanese garrison on the small island of Betio, located on the western side of Tarawa Atoll in the Gilbert Islands. Therefore it was determined that to launch an invasion of the Marianas the battle had to start at Tarawa.

The Japanese High Command in Tokyo was well aware of the Gilberts' strategic location, and had invested considerable time and effort in fortifying the island. The 7th Sasebo Special Naval Landing Force under the command of Commander Sugai, the 111th Pioneers and personnel of the Fourth Fleet's construction battalion were deployed, although many of the men in these groups were Korean forced labourers. Peripheral coastal defence guns were located around the island, being placed in concrete bunkers for protection. Further defences involved 500 pillboxes built from logs and a further forty

Ship's personnel swarm round a battle-damaged Grumman Avenger assigned to VT-84 aboard the Essex-class carrier USS Bunker Hill. (US Navy/NARA via Dennis R. Jenkins)

artillery pieces placed around the island at strategic points. To provide for possible aircraft support, an airfield was cut into the bush along the high point of the island, while trenches connected all points of the island, allowing troops to move where needed under cover.

The island of Betio is shaped like a long, thin, curved triangle with the point to the east and the base on the west. Any attack would almost certainly have to approach from the lagoon, as the deeper waters to the south presented no really usable landing areas. Therefore, in order to prevent this happening, a huge wall was constructed across the lagoon just above the high-water mark. Behind the wall was a series of machine-gun posts and pillboxes that could fire on any invaders trying to climb over the wall. The American invasion force was the largest yet assembled for a single operation in the Pacific, consisting of seventeen aircraft carriers, six fleet carriers, five light carriers and six escort carriers. The carriers were supported by twelve battleships, eight heavy and four light cruisers, plus sixty-six destroyers and thirty-six transports. This force carried the 2nd Marine Division and a part of the Army's 27th Infantry Division, giving a total of about 35,000 soldiers and Marines. These forces were divided into two separate groups: the Northern Attack Force, TF.52, would depart from Pearl Harbor on 10 November, while the Southern Attack Force, designated TF.53, would leave the New Hebrides on 13 November. Refuelling of the TF.52 vessels would take place between Baker and Canton Islands, while TF.53 would do the same off Funafuti, both groups undertaking this on 15 November. Two days later both groups would join up at a point halfway between Baker and Nanomea Islands. The carrier groups were designated TF.50.1 and TF.50.2, these having sailed from Pearl Harbor while TF.50.3 and TF.50.4 had sailed from Espiritu Santo. Task Force 50.1, under the command of Rear Admiral Pownall, had the carriers *Yorktown*, *Lexington* and *Cowpens* available, plus the battleships USS *South Dakota* and *Washington* for bombardments and air defence duties, while anti-submarine duties were covered by six destroyers. Task Force 50.2, under the command of Rear Admiral Radford, utilised the carriers *Enterprise*, *Belleau Wood* and *Monterey*, these being protected by the battleships USS *Massachusetts*, *North Carolina* and *Indiana*, together with a screen escort of another six destroyers. Task Force 50.3, with Rear Admiral Montgomery in command, had the carriers *Essex*, *Bunker Hill* and *Independence* at its core, while defence duties were provided by four cruisers and a similar number of destroyers. The final group, TF.50.4, was smaller, as only two carriers were assigned, these being the USS *Saratoga* and *Princeton*, plus two cruisers and four destroyers, all under the command of Rear Admiral Sherman.

The other task forces were concerned with supplying the land forces with close air support, and to that end TG.52.3, under the command of Rear Admiral Mullinex, launched air attacks from the escort carriers *Luscombe Bay*, *Coral Sea* and *Corregidor* against the Japanese. For the landings at Betio, Tarawa air support was provided by TF.53.6, whose carriers were *Suwanee*, *Chenango*, *Barnes* and *Nassau*, under the command of Rear Admiral Ragsdale.

The heavy units of the naval forces opened fire on the Japanese positions on 20 November, shelling continuing for over ninety minutes, being briefly interrupted to allow dive-bombers from the carrier groups to bomb various fixed positions on the island. The aircraft were launched from the carriers of TF.50.1, their primary target being Mili, while the aircraft from TF.50.2 concentrated their efforts upon the Japanese positions at Makin. The carriers of Task Force 50.3 launched their aircraft against Tarawa, while those of TF.50.4 attacked the enemy positions at Nauru. The majority of the larger-calibre Japanese guns were destroyed during this initial attack. The island was at some points only a few hundred yards wide, and the bombardment turned much of it into rubble. Given the level of destruction it was thought that by the time of the landings no one would remain to defend the tiny island.

The American assault plan centred around landings on three beaches, designated Red 1 to Red 3, located along the northern coast of the island. Red 1 was on the extreme west of the island, while Red 3 was to the east, close to the pier, with Red 2 in the centre. The airstrip was located east to west and divided the island into north and south sectors. The US Marines started their attack on the lagoon somewhat later than expected, and promptly found themselves stuck on the reef some 500 yards off shore. The campaign planners had allowed for Betio's neap tide and therefore expected the normal rising tide to provide a water depth of five feet over the reef, allowing the larger landing craft, whose draughts were at least four feet, to pass over with room to spare. However, on that day and the next there was little tidal movement, which left a mean depth of three feet over the reef. When the supporting naval bombardment stopped to allow the troops to land, the Japanese emerged from the deep shelters where they had sheltered from the shell-fire, and manned their protected gun positions. The landing craft launched by Task Force 52 caught on the reef were soon hit, and were set on fire by the defenders' artillery and mortar fire, even though air support was being supplied by the carriers of TF.52.3. The Marines abandoned the boats and started making their way ashore, being assailed by machine-gun fire the entire time. Initial early attempts to land tanks and break through the wall failed when the landing craft were hit by shellfire on the way in and either sank or had to withdraw while taking on water.

By 21 November the Marines were holding a defensive line on the island, and the American forces concentrated upon dividing the Japanese forces in two by expanding the bulge near the airfield until it reached the southern shore. Other forces on Red 1 were then instructed to secure Green beach, which encompassed the entire western end of the island. Operations along Red 2 and Red 3, in contrast, were considerably more difficult, as the defenders had set up several new machine-gun posts between the closest approach of the forces from the two beaches, and so fire from these machine-gun nests split the American forces from each other for a period. By the end of the day, however, the entire western end of the island was under American control, as was much of the area around the airfield. During the American assault the Japanese commander, Rear Admiral Shibasakit, was killed in his concrete command post, and this disrupted the Japanese command structure.

On 22 November, the third day of the battle, the American forces consolidated their position, while bringing ashore additional heavy equipment and tanks needed to complete the operation. By that afternoon the Marines began the task of clearing out the remaining Japanese forces. As evening approached, the remaining forces were either contained within a pocket of land to the east of the airstrip or in other smaller areas near the eastern edge of the airstrip. During the final day of the battle, 23 November, the Japanese launched a counter-assault in the early hours of the morning. When the fighting ended, 200 of the estimated 300 attackers were found dead in front of the American defensive positions, the vast majority having been killed by artillery fire. At the conclusion of the fighting only one Japanese officer, sixteen enlisted men and 129 Koreans were captured. The total Japanese and Korean casualties were approximately 4,713 dead. In contrast, the Marine Corps losses were 990 killed, with a further 2,296 wounded, while 687 USN personnel also lost their lives during the landing. While the losses at Tarawa were much higher than expected, the lessons learned at Tarawa would be applied to the Battle of Iwo Jima that would follow.

Meanwhile, beginning on 20 November, the Japanese launched air attacks against the American naval forces, during which the USS *Independence* was hit by a torpedo, the carrier being put out of commission for the next six months

The deck crews unhook a Grumman Avenger of VT-20 as it stops on the deck of the USS Enterprise. (US Navy/NARA via Dennis R. Jenkins)

while repairs were carried out. A further grievous loss occurred on 24 November when the Casablanca-class escort carrier USS *Liscombe Bay* was sunk by torpedoes launched by the Japanese submarine *I-175* off the Gilbert Islands. The torpedoes struck the ammunition and fuel areas and set off a massive explosion that tore the vessel apart; of the crew, 644 were killed, including the vessel's commander, Captain Wiltsie USN, and the task group commander, Rear Admiral Mullinex. Such was the strength of the explosion that wreckage landed on the battleship USS *New Mexico*, which was cruising a distance away. Surprisingly, 272 survivors were rescued by the destroyers *Morris* and *Hughes.* Now aware that there was a strong Japanese submarine group working in the Tarawa area, the Americans increased their anti-submarine patrols, and this paid off when among other successes the carrier USS *Chenango* sank the *I-21* on 29 November. From Tarawa the US Fast Carrier Task Force set out for Kwajalein to attack the Japanese fortifications there. The carrier component was designated TG.50.1, under the command of Rear Admiral Pownall, and included the *Yorktown, Lexington* and *Cowpens*, while the support consisted of four cruisers and six destroyers. A second carrier group, TG.50.3, consisted of the carriers *Essex, Enterprise* and *Belleau Wood*, under the command of Rear Admiral Montgomery, with five cruisers and five destroyers in support. During the carrier-launched air attacks 386 sorties were dispatched. The attacks saw six transports and three other vessels sunk, while a pair of Japanese cruisers were damaged. During the air battles fifty-five Japanese aircraft were shot down for a total of five American aircraft lost.

In a retaliatory attack on 4 December, the USS *Lexington*, an Essex-class carrier, was struck by a torpedo launched by a Japanese torpedo-bomber. The crew managed to control the flooding, so that the injured carrier was able to reach Puget Sound Navy Yard for much-needed repairs. On 8 December TG.50.8, with the carriers *Bunker Hill* and *Monterey* to provide air cover, mounted an attack on Nauru. The main attack was a bombardment undertaken by the battleships USS *South Dakota, Washington* and *Massachusetts*, which fired 810 rounds of 16-inch ammunition, while the escort vessels fired 3,400 5-inch rounds. The next attack undertaken by the US Navy took place on Christmas Day 1943, when TG.50.3, commanded by Rear Admiral Sherman, with the carriers *Bunker Hill* and *Monterey*, mounted an attack on Kavieng, the capital of New Ireland. The carriers were accompanied by six destroyers. This attack was in response to Japanese reinforcements being moved from Truk to Rabaul and Kavieng, these troops being moved by four IJN cruisers and escorting destroyers. It had been planned to deploy the battleship *Yamato*, although this had been stopped by a torpedo launched from the submarine USS *Skate*. Although damaged, the *Yamato* would be quickly repaired for further service. During the air assault three ships were sunk and another was damaged. On New Year's Day the carrier group had a further success when two Japanese cruisers dispatched from Truk with reinforcements, and a destroyer, were damaged. Three days later TG.50.8 returned to Kavieng to undertake further air strikes, during which another Japanese destroyer was damaged.

All of the foregoing were part of the preparations for the attack and invasion of Kwajalein in the Marshall Islands. These early movements were not without incident, as the escort carrier *Sangamon* was damaged when one of its aircraft crash-landed into the barrier. To add insult to injury, the *Sangamon* and *Suwanee* collided the following day, 25 January 1944. While the two Sangamon-class carriers were trying to put themselves out of action, TF.58, under the command of Vice-Admiral Mitscher, began attacks on targets in the Marshall Islands on 29 January as part of Operation Flintlock. The carrier group TG.58.1, commanded by Rear Admiral Reeves, had the carriers *Enterprise, Yorktown* and *Belleau Wood* assigned, while the main support came from the battleships *Massachusetts, Indiana* and *Washington* and the cruiser *Oakland*. Further support was given by nine destroyers. The first aerial attacks were undertaken on 29 January against Maloelap, while further attacks were launched the following day against Kwajalein.

A second carrier group, TG.58.2, was also assigned to this enterprise, this group being commanded by Rear Admiral Montgomery, whose carriers included the USS *Essex, Intrepid* and *Cabot*, while the supporting battleships were the *South Dakota, Alabama* and *North Carolina*, plus the cruiser USS *San Diego* with nine destroyers. This group attacked Roi over the period 29–31 January and again on 1–3 February. The third task group, TG.58.3, commanded by Rear Admiral Sherman, had the carriers *Bunker Hill, Monterey* and *Cowpens* assigned, while the battleships included the *Iowa* and *New Jersey*, assisted by the cruiser *Wichita* and nine destroyers, which undertook attacks upon Eniwetok from 30 January to 2 February. The final carrier group was TG.58.4, commanded by Rear Admiral Ginder, whose carriers were the *Saratoga, Princeton* and *Langley,* plus three cruisers and eight destroyers, whose task was to initially attack Wotje on 29 January, followed by aerial attacks on Maloelap on 30/31 January. After the group had refuelled on 1 February, it returned to the fray by attacking Eniwetok between 3 and 6 February. Overall a total of 6,232 sorties were flown, during which twenty-two aircraft were lost to the Japanese defences and a further twenty-seven to accidents. While the carriers were attacking from the air, the battleship contingent was also getting in on the act. On 30 January the USS *Washington, North Carolina, Indiana* and *Massachusetts,* plus a destroyer escort, laid down a heavy bombardment on Kwajalein during which three Japanese ships were sunk.

On 31 January the main phase of Operation Flintlock began. The primary force was the US 5th Fleet under the command of Admiral Spruance USN. The Southern Attack Force was designated TF.52, under the command of Rear Admiral Turner, whose land forces were the 7th Infantry Division under the command of Major-General Corlet USA. The air support group was designated TF.52.9, the carriers assigned being the *Manila Bay, Coral Sea* and *Corriegidor,* under the command of Rear Admiral Davison. Fire support was covered by four battleships, the USS *Idaho, Pennsylvania, New Mexico* and *Mississippi,* these in turn being escorted by three cruisers and eleven destroyers, all being designated TF.52.8, with Rear Admiral Giffin in command. Another ten destroyers were allocated to supporting the landings directly.

The Northern Attack Force commanded by Rear Admiral Connolly was known as TF.53, and the assigned ground force was the 4th Marine Division commanded by Major-General Smith USMC. The Air Support Group was designated TF.53.6, and had the carriers *Sangamon, Suwanee* and *Chenango,* under the command of Rear Admiral Ragsdale. Fire support was courtesy of the battleships *Tennessee, Colorado* and *Maryland,* commanded by Rear Admiral Oldendorf, being designated TF.53.3. Supporting the capital units were six cruisers and twenty destroyers. Initial landings began on 31 January, with the Army division targeting Kwajalein while the Marines were due to land on Roi. Within seven days over 21,000 troops had been landed by the Southern Attack Force, while the northern group had landed over 20,000 troops. Total losses during these attacks were 372 killed and a further 1,582 listed as wounded. The Japanese force, commanded by Rear Admiral Akiyama, had over 8,000 men. While being a small force, the Japanese put up a stout resistance that would see no more than 256 surviving to be taken prisoner. Kwajalein and Roi were completely in American hands by 7 February 1944. A slightly easier target was Majuro Atoll, which was completely in American hands by 2 February. The task force was designated TG.51.2, under the command of Rear Admiral Hill, while the assigned carriers were the USS *Nassau* and *Natoma Bay.* The ground force was the 27th Infantry Division, which landed without meeting any resistance on 31 January. After occupa-

During the assault on the main Japanese naval base at Truk, the air fleets hurled everything they had at the attacking carriers. Here a Japanese torpedo-bomber heads towards the USS Yorktown. (US Navy/NARA via Dennis R. Jenkins)

tion, this atoll would become an important base for future American operations in the Pacific.

Having captured the atolls the Americans turned their attentions to the next target on the list, Eniwetok. Designated Operation Catchpole, the primary group was TF.51.11, commanded by Rear Admiral Hill, whose troop-carrying vessels had the troops of the 22nd Marine RCT and two battalions of the 106th Regiment/27th US Infantry Division aboard, some 8,000 men in total. The carrier group, commanded by Rear Admiral Ragsdale, had the carriers *Sangamon*, *Suwanee* and *Chenango* assigned. The heavy units were the battleships *Pennsylvania*, *Colorado* and *Tennessee*, with Rear Admiral Oldendorf in command. The lighter support vessels included three cruisers and nineteen destroyers. Further aerial support was provided by TG.58.4, which had completed its task of supporting the Wotje landings earlier.

Running at the same time was Operation Hailstone, under the overall command of Vice-Admiral Mitscher, whose task was to attack the main Japanese naval base at Truk. The air support was provided by TG.58.1, under the command of Rear Admiral Reeves, the carriers assigned being the USS *Enterprise*, *Yorktown* and *Belleau Wood*, and TG.58.2, whose carriers were the USS *Essex*, *Intrepid* and *Cabot*, commanded by Rear Admiral Montgomery. The third group, TF.58.3, was commanded by Rear Admiral Sherman, the assigned carriers being the *Bunker Hill*, *Monterey* and *Cowpens*. The battleships in the force comprised the USS *North Carolina*, *Massachusetts*, *South Dakota* and *Alabama*, and the supporting vessels consisted of six cruisers and at least fifteen destroyers. A further addition was Task Force 50.9, whose commander was Vice-Admiral Spruance, this group having the battleships USS *Iowa* and *New Jersey*, plus the usual range of cruisers and destroyers in support.

The opening move by the Americans began early in the morning of 17 February, when a fighter strike launched by the five fleet carriers attacked the 365 Japanese aircraft based on Truk, while the lighter carriers launched their aircraft against shipping in and around Truk. In response to these attacks the Japanese launched a retaliatory air strike using seven Kate torpedo-bombers, whose persistence paid off when one of their torpedoes hit the carrier USS *Intrepid*. Escorted by the *Cabot* and a cruiser and a destroyer screen, the *Intrepid* was escorted to Majuro for repair work. On the following day strike forces were launched by the four remaining fleet carriers against shipping in and around Truk. Overall 1,250 sorties were flown, during which 400 tons of bombs were dropped. Unfortunately for the US Navy, the Japanese Combined Fleet, which included the capital vessels such as carriers and battleships, had already been withdrawn from Truk to Singapore. However, the aerial armada made the most of the available targets by sinking the small number of warships present and many of the numerous auxiliaries anchored at Truk. As well as the twenty-six ships sunk, the strikes had also destroyed 250 of the resident aircraft. The withdrawal of the Japanese heavy units indicated to the Americans that their foe was beginning to realise that his war was lost, so that Truk became a less important base of operations.

While the main groups were concentrating on attacking Truk, TF.50.9 had steamed to the other side of Truk in order to intercept any ships fleeing the Japanese base. During this phase of the operation the ships of TF.50.9 inter-

Caught at the moment of touchdown is this Grumman F6F Hellcat of VF-25, landing on the USS Cowpens, an Independence-class light aircraft carrier. (US Navy/NARA via Dennis R. Jenkins)

With engines turning, the first flight of Curtiss Helldivers from VB-5 aboard the USS Yorktown are prepared for departure. (US Navy/NARA via Dennis R. Jenkins)

cepted and sank two cruisers, five destroyers, a submarine chaser, two submarines and two support vessels. Only one IJN vessel escaped, this being the destroyer *Nowake*. Further Japanese losses were inflicted by submarines stationed in the exit channels, which managed to sink eight escaping ships. Moving on from Truk, the carriers of TG.58.1 launched their aircraft to attack Jasluit on 20 February, this being followed three days later by bombardments of Tinian and Rota by TG.58.3, while TG.58.2 bombarded Saipan and Tinian. A further bombardment took place against one of the alternative targets between 18 and 20 March. The target was Kavieng, and the deployed ships included the battleships *New Mexico*, *Tennessee*, *Idaho* and *Mississippi*, under the command of Rear Admiral Griffin. Air support was provided by the carriers *Manila Bay* and *Natoma*, while a screen of fifteen destroyers protected against submarines. During the bombardment over 13,000 rounds of 14-inch and 5-inch ammunition was expended. While Kavieng was under fire another task group was heading towards Emirau in the Bismark Archipelago. Commanded by Commodore Reifsnider, TG.31.2 landed the 4th Marine Division under the command of Brigadier-General Noble from nineteen destroyers. Support for the operation was provided by seven USN cruisers plus the fleet carriers *Enterprise* and *Belleau Wood*, and the escort carriers *Coral Sea* and *Corregidor*. No Japanese resistance was encountered, and so the establishment of an airfield and harbour facilities was quickly achieved. In a further encounter on Bougainville, the defending Japanese forces, under the command of Lieutenant-General Hyakutake, committed 12,000 troops to attack the American bridgehead near Cape Torokina as Operation TA. At the end of the battle, which lasted from 9 to 24 March, over 5,000 Japanese troops had been killed, for the loss of 263 Americans.

After the minor diversions earlier, the Americans launched Operation Desecrate on 23 March. The overall commander was Admiral Spruance, while the commander of TF.58 was Vice-Admiral Mitscher. The targets for this group were the islands of Palau, Yap and Woleai, all of which were Japanese bases. As these were to be carrier-based raids, TG.58.1, under the command of Rear Admiral Reeves, took the carriers *Enterprise*, *Belleau Wood* and *Cowpens* from Espiritu Santo on 23 March, while TG.58.2, under the command of Rear Admiral Montgomery, was also dispatched, taking the carriers *Bunker Hill*, *Hornet*, *Cabot* and *Monterey*. A third task group, TG.58.3, commanded by Rear Admiral Ginder, took the carriers *Yorktown*, *Lexington*, *Princeton* and *Langley*, departing from Majuro accompanied by the usual selection of battleships, cruisers and destroyers. *En route* to their targets the forces were spotted by a Japanese reconnaissance aircraft from Truk on 25 March. The combined force was spotted again the following day. As a result of the American force in the vicinity of Truk, the Japanese naval vessels based at Palau departed and headed off to join the remainder of the fleet at Tawi-Tawi. The Japanese suffered further losses when the C-in-C of the IJN, Admiral Koga, was killed when his Emily flying-boat crashed *en route* to Mindanao on 31 March. Adding to the woes of the Japanese, another Emily flying-boat, carrying the IJN Chief of Staff, Vice-Admiral Fukudome, made a forced landing. The Admiral was captured by Filipino guerrillas at Cebu, together with the important documents the aircraft was carrying. The loss of these senior officers resulted in the appointment of Vice-Admiral Takasu as interim commander, although he would be replaced on 5 May by Admiral Toyoda. As TF.58 proceeded towards its targets it was attacked by a force of Japanese aircraft on 28 March, but with little success. By 30 March all three carrier groups were in a position to launch the first wave of attacks against Palau. The aircraft from the *Lexington*, *Bunker Hill* and *Hornet* would specifically be tasked to lay mines across the access channels. During the air attacks thirty-five vessels of various sizes were sunk. Further Japanese vessels were sunk outside Palau. Having pounded Palau, the task force moved on to Yap on 31 March, and on 1 April all three carrier groups unleashed their wrath upon the Japanese positions on Woleai.

Following the completion of Operation Desecrate, TF.58 moved on to attack Hollandia after refuelling and replenishment of stores. The task force departed from Majuro on 13 April and undertook a further refuel just off the

With its arrester hook deployed and its weapons racks empty, this Douglas Dauntless of VB-10 prepares to enter the landing pattern of the USS Enterprise. (US Navy/NARA via Dennis R. Jenkins)

Admiralty Islands on 19 April, finally moving into its attack position two days later. The air support group, TG.58.1, under the command of Rear Admiral Clark, launched aircraft from the carriers USS *Hornet, Belleau Wood, Cowpens* and *Bataan* that attacked Japanese positions on Wakde and Sarmi during the day, while the support vessels shelled the same areas at night. The same carrier group undertook another raid on 22 April, while over the following two days a second carrier group, TF.58.2, under the command of Rear Admiral Montgomery, whose carriers *Bunker Hill, Yorktown, Monterey* and *Cabot* carried out strikes on Hollandia. The third task group, TG.58.3, had already launched attacks on Hollandia on 21 April with aircraft launched from the *Enterprise, Lexington, Princeton* and *Langley*. After these attacks TG.58.3 supported the landings on Tanahmerah Bay during 22–24 April. During these operations twenty-one aircraft were lost, although by now a very efficient rescue operation recovered most of these crews. The entire task force launched an aerial attack on Truk over 29 and 30 April. During this assault fifty-nine Japanese aircraft were destroyed in aerial combat, while a further thirty-four were destroyed on the ground. This assault badly depleted the 104 aircraft that had originally been based on the atoll. The cost to the United States was twenty-six aircraft shot down and a further nine lost through accident. In a secondary action near Truk, aircraft from VT-30 from the USS *Monterey* sank the Japanese submarine *I-174*. A further mission on 1 May saw a battleship group, the *Iowa, New Jersey, North Carolina, Indiana,*

Massachusetts, South Dakota and *Alabama,* under the command of Vice-Admiral Lee, plus a screen of protective destroyers, bombard the Japanese positions on the island of Ponape. Air support was provided by TG.58.1. After completion, this group returned to Eniwetok on 4 May, and on the same day TG.58.2 and 58.3 anchored in Majuro.

While the carriers of TG.58 were preparing for their next mission, Task Force 77 was being prepared for Operations Reckless and Persecution, the landings on Hollandia and Aitape. Overall commander for both operations was General MacArthur, while the naval commander was Vice-Admiral Kinkaid. Air support was provided by TG.78.1 under the command of Rear Admiral Ragsdale, the carriers assigned being the escort carriers *Sangamon, Suwanee, Chenango* and *Santee.* A second air support force was also assigned, this being TG.78.2, whose commander was Rear Admiral Davison. The assigned escort carriers were the USS *Natoma Bay, Coral Sea, Corregidor* and *Manila Bay.* The troops came from US I Corps, commanded by Major-General Eichelberger, and personnel from the 41st Infantry Division. Support vessels consisted of fifty destroyers and five cruisers, plus the landing ships carrying the troops. The landings at both locations were undertaken against little Japanese resistance, all being secured by 28 April. After their successes against Hollandia and Aitape, the US Navy again turned its attention to Ponape when TG.58.1 bombarded the defences once more on 1 May. At the conclusion of the operations the battle groups arrived at Eniwetok, while the carrier groups anchored at Majuro.

After the success of the American operations it was becoming obvious to the Japanese High Command that the next target for US forces would be the Marianas. Its response was Operation A-Go, which would see large groups of troops being transported over 11 and 12 May, these being joined by groups dispatched from Tawi-Tawi and Lingga Bay. Most of the Japanese battleships, supported by the 1st and 2nd Carrier Squadrons and a vast array of cruisers and destroyers, all headed towards the Marianas group. During the transit the US Navy submarines would sink at least ten vessels, three of which were very vital tankers.

Having noted the Japanese movements towards the Marianas, the US Navy sent TG.58.2, commanded by Rear Admiral Montgomery, with the carriers *Essex, Wasp* and *San Jacinto,* plus five cruisers and twelve destroyers, from Majuro on 14 May, heading for Marcus Island, a location *en route* to the Marianas. Aerial attacks and bombardments were carried out on 19 and 20 May before the same force moved on to Wake Island to carry out the same task on 23 May. TF.58.6 was also in action when the force's carrier aircraft carried out an aerial attack on Marcus Island on 20 May. Rear Admiral Montgomery's task force would carry out another attack on 23 May, this time the target being Wake Island. After these raids the carrier groups would return to their forward operating bases to prepare for the next operation.

During the period after the various nuisance raids undertaken in May, the escort carriers were used for escort duties and to hunt down Japanese

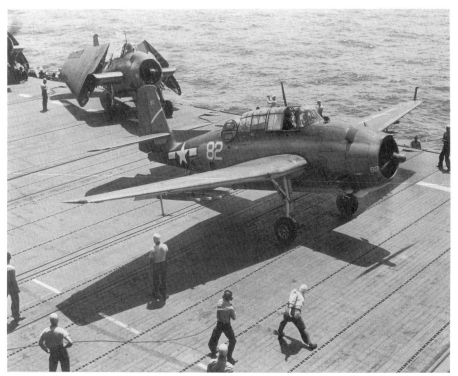

A Grumman Avenger of VT-1 aboard the USS Yorktown prepares to depart on an Operation Forager on Saipan. (US Navy/NARA via Dennis R. Jenkins)

submarines. One of these sinkings involved a Grumman Avenger from VT-60 aboard the USS *Suwanee* that depth-charged and destroyed the *I-158* on 21 June south of Guam. While the *Suwanee* was operating off Guam, the majority of vessels in TF.58 were beginning the movements that would be designated Operation Forager. Beginning on 11 June, the targets were the Marianas and the Vulcan Islands. TF.58.1, under the command of Rear Admiral Clark, had the carriers *Hornet, Yorktown, Belleau Wood* and *Bataan* assigned, accompanied by four cruisers plus nine destroyers as escorts. The second carrier group was TF.58.2, with the carriers *Bunker Hill, Wasp, Monterey* and *Cabot*, under the command of Rear Admiral Montgomery, with four cruisers and nine destroyers as escorts. The third carrier group was designated TF.58.3, and had the carriers *Enterprise, Lexington, San Jacinto* and *Princeton* under the command of Rear Admiral Reeves, these being accompanied by five cruisers, the extra being used as a command ship by Admiral Spruance, plus thirteen destroyers. The final carrier group was TF.58.4 commanded by Rear Admiral Harrill, the assigned carriers being the *Essex, Langley* and *Cowpens*, with four cruisers and fourteen destroyers as escorts. Accompanying the carrier groups was TG.58.7,

131

whose vessels included the battleships USS *Washington, North Carolina, Iowa, New Jersey, Indiana, South Dakota* and *Alabama*, with four cruisers and fourteen destroyers, all under the command of Vice-Admiral Lee.

The first attack carried out by this force was the shelling of Saipan before all four carrier groups launched a massive air strike against the Marianas Island group, during which thirty-six Japanese aircraft were destroyed. At the conclusion of this action TF.58.4 launched an air strike towards Saipan, which intercepted a convoy that had just left the island. During the attack ten merchant vessels and four warships were sunk. Two days later TG.58.1 launched an attack against Guam, while the other three carrier groups launched their aircraft against Saipan and Tinian. Over 14 and 15 June carrier activity was reduced to patrol sorties as the carriers and escorts refuelled. Once ready to resume operations, TG.58.1 and 58.4, under the combined command of Rear Admiral Clark, undertook attacks on Iwo Jima, Chichi Jima and Hahajima over 15 and 16 June. Further attacks were undertaken by TG.58.4 on the island of Pagan while *en route* to join Task Force 58. The main part of Operation Forager started when the vessels of TF.52, commanded by Vice-Admiral Turner, began to land the V Amphibious Corps commanded by Lieutenant-General Smith on Saipan. Prior to the landings the battleships and cruisers undertook a heavy bombardment of the Japanese positions on the island. Joining the main task groups was TG.52.14 commanded by Rear Admiral Bogan, with the escort carriers *Fanshaw Bay, Midway, White Plains* and *Kalinin Bay*, plus an escort of destroyers, providing aerial support. Also supporting the landings was TG.52.11, commanded by Rear Admiral Sallada, with the escort carriers *Kitkun Bay, Gambier Bay, Corregidor* and *Coral Sea*, and a destroyer escort. Further landings took place on 15 June, by which time some 67,000 troops had reached the beachheads. Facing them was the re-inforced 43rd Infantry Division commanded by Lieutenant-General Saito. After heavy fighting between the two opposing forces, the island was finally captured on 9 July. Japanese casualties at the conclusion of the fighting included nearly 24,000 dead and 13,000 wounded, while the American casualties totalled nearly 3,500 killed and 13,000 wounded.

Having completed the Saipan operation, TF.58 prepared to provide support for the capture of the Philippines. Before that, the Battle of the Philippine Sea took place. On 13 June the Japanese fleet departed from Tawi-Tawi to undertake Operation A-Go, the attempt to trap the US fleet in the Marianas. Unfortunately for the Japanese, the US Navy had spread a line of submarines across the potential routes of transit, and so by 18 July Admiral Spruance was already aware of the Japanese approach. Heading towards the Americans was the Japanese fleet commanded by Vice-Admiral Kurita, whose light carriers were the *Chitose, Chiyoda and Zutho*, with the battleships *Yamato, Musahi* and *Kongo*. Supporting this force were four cruisers and eight destroyers. Two further groups also set sail with the primary group. Group A was under the command of Vice-Admiral Ozawa, with the carriers *Taiho, Shokaku* and *Zuikaku*, plus three cruisers and six destroyers in support, while

132

The escort carriers not only carried aircraft for the fleet, they were not averse to launching aircraft for the USAAF. Here a Republic P-47 Thunderbolt is launched for the forces based on Saipan in the Marianas Islands. (US Navy/NARA via Dennis R. Jenkins)

Carrier Group B, commanded by Rear Admiral Joshima, had the carriers *Junyo*, *Hiyo* and *Ryuho* assigned, plus the battleship *Nagato*, and a single cruiser and nine destroyers as escorts. Supporting the battleships, carriers and other vessels were six tankers and six escorting destroyers.

Japanese reconnaissance aircraft spotted some of the TF.58 vessels in the evening of 18 June, while further flights early the next morning detected others. With the ships of TF.58 detected, the Japanese decided to fly off 372 aircraft in four waves to attack the Americans. The incoming attack was detected by radar some 200 miles away, and so the US Navy carriers were able to launch 300 fighters to intercept the raid. Of the 372 Japanese aircraft airborne that day, ships' anti-aircraft fire and the fighters shot down 242, and this later became known as the Great Marianas Turkey Shoot. Of the attackers only two got through, one managing to dive-bomb the *South Dakota*, while a kamikaze struck the USS *Indiana*. The *Bunker Hill*, *Wasp*, *Minneapolis* and the destroyer *Hudson* were damaged by near-misses, but were still able to function. During this engagement only twenty-nine American fighters were lost in action. The landings on Guam continued, during which the US Navy fighters shot down thirty Japanese aircraft and a further nineteen that attempted to land on Guam were destroyed. The Japanese carriers were also in trouble, as the *Taiho*, part of Carrier Group A, was torpedoed by the submarine USS *Albacore*, the carrier sinking after the torpedo hit set off a massive explosion. Another carrier from the same group, the *Shokaku*, was also hit by torpedoes from the USS *Cavalla*, these strikes sinking the vessel. The remainder of Carrier Group A refuelled from the tankers on 20 June. However, they had been spotted, and so Admiral Mitscher launched an aerial attack from the carriers *Hornet, Belleau Wood, Lexington, Monterey* and *San Jacinto* at maximum range. A total of 216 aircraft were launched by the American carriers, encountering no more than thirty-five Japanese defending fighters, which were easily dealt with. The dive-bombers and torpedo-bombers from the USS *Belleau Wood* sank the remaining Japanese carrier, *Hiyo*, while aircraft from the USS *Wasp* badly damaged two of the tankers, which were later sunk by the Japanese escort destroyers. During the attack twenty US Navy aircraft were shot down, while a further seventy-two were lost in crash landings as they attempted to make night landings, even though the carrier decks were floodlit. Over the night of 20/21 June the commander-in-chief of the IJN, Admiral Toyoda, ordered the remaining Japanese vessels to withdraw. Admiral Mitscher was keen to pursue the fleeing Japanese ships with the fast battleships and carriers, but he was overruled by Admiral Spruance. After the carrier groups had completed refuelling over 22/23 June, they return to Eniwetok, although Admiral Clark with the carriers *Hornet, Yorktown, Bataan* and *Belleau Wood* carried out an attack on Iwo Jima and Chichi Jima on 24 June, during which a further sixty-six Japanese aircraft were destroyed.

The landings on Guam began on 21 July when III Amphibious Corps commanded by Major-General Geiger was landed by vessels of TF.53 under the command of Rear Admiral Connolly. Providing the destructive firepower for this assault were the battleships of TG.53.5, while the air support component was supplied by TG.53.7 under the command of Rear Admiral Ragsdale. The carriers assigned to this group included the USS *Sangamon, Suwanee, Chenango, Corregidor* and the *Coral Sea*. During the landing phase over 54,000 troops were put ashore, annihilating the defending Japanese forces under the overall command of Lieutenant-General Obata. Of the approximately 11,000 Japanese troops on Guam, over 10,500 were killed and ninety-eight were taken prisoner. In response the American forces lost 1,200 dead, 145 missing and more than 5,500 wounded. Some of the Japanese troops escaped into the jungle and would continue to provide a nuisance value till the end of the war, and one soldier would finally be convinced that the war had ended when discovered in 1972. The seaborne support was reduced when the majority of the fleet departed Guam on 23 July and headed west to undertake attacks on Palau, Yap, Ulithi, Tais, Ngulu and Sorol. All three carrier groups, TG.58.1, 58.2 and 58.3 undertook these attacks, suffering minimal losses in the process. At the completion of this engagement TG.58.1 and 58.3 were refuelled and headed off to carry out raids on Iwo Jima and Chichi Jima. During these attacks, carried out over 4 and 5 August, a number of Japanese transports were sunk, and a destroyer was sunk by three of its US Navy counterparts.

The invasion of Tinian began on 24 July 1944, with TF.52, commanded by Rear Admiral Hill, landing the V Amphibious Group, commanded by Major-General Schmidt. Fire support for the landing was supplied by TG.52.17 and TG.52.10, while air support was courtesy of TG.52.14 under the command of Rear Admiral Bogan and TG.52.11 commanded by Rear Admiral Sallada.

While the Japanese defenders, under the command of Vice-Admiral Kakuta, mounted a stiff resistance, the might of the American forces inflicted grievous losses on the defenders. Overall, 6,000 Japanese were killed, with 252 being taken prisoner. The American forces lost 389 killed and 1,800 wounded. In response to these latest American successes, the Japanese C-in-C Combined Fleet Admiral Toyoda would implement Operation Sho-Go-1, which would result in a redeployment of all forces in the Pacific in order to create a defensive ring. To that end the land-based forces were concentrated upon the Philippines and Formosa, the main fleet was redeployed to Brunei Bay to protect the oil field, and the remaining aircraft carriers moved to the Inland Sea within the bounds of the Japanese home islands.

Rear Admiral Montgomery, in command of TG.58.3, carried out aerial attacks against Iwo Jima, Chichi Jima and Haha Jima, while TG.58.3, commanded by Rear Admiral Clark, with the carriers USS *Bunker Hill*, *Lexington* and *Cabot*, plus four cruisers and seven destroyers, undertook an attack on Japanese convoy 4804 near Muko Jima, sinking an escort destroyer and five transports, while two corvettes and another transport were damaged.

On 28 August, TF.38 with Vice-Admiral Mitscher departed from Eniwetok, its purpose being to undertake attacks in support of the Palau and Morotai operations. TG.38.1, with the carriers *Wasp*, *Hornet*, *Cowpens* and *Belleau Wood*, was commanded by Rear Admiral McCain, while TG.38.1 was commanded by Rear Admiral Bogan, and included the carriers *Bunker Hill*, *Intrepid*, *Hancock* and *Cabot*, plus the *Independence*, specially modified for night operations. The third carrier group was designated TG.38.3, and was commanded by Rear Admiral Sherman, with the carriers *Lexington*, *Essex*, *Princeton* and *Langley* assigned. TG.38.4 was the fourth assigned carrier group, which included the *Franklin*, *Enterprise*, *Monterey* and *San Jacinto*, being commanded by Rear Admiral Davison. The battleships in the force included the *Iowa*, *New Jersey*, *Washington*, *Indiana*, *Massachusetts* and *Alabama*. Escorting these vessels were twelve cruisers and sixty-four destroyers. TG.38.4 launched its aircraft against targets on Iwo Jima and Chichi Jiman, during which a transport was badly damaged. The USS *Monterey* was detached to cover the bombardment of Wake Island being undertaken by the cruiser group TG.12.5. This was followed up over the period 6–8 September when all four carrier groups launched attacks on Mindanao, this being followed by attacks on Visayas in the Philippines. During these raids twenty-one enemy ships were sunk and many others were damaged. Following on from Visayas, the carrier groups received intelligence information that revealed that the Japanese forces defending Leyte were smaller than expected. Admiral Halsey therefore proposed to bring forward the invasion date from 20 December to 20 October. This change was confirmed on 16 September at the 2nd Quebec Conference.

The carrier task groups undertook a further attack on Mindanao on 14 September, when another transport was sunk. Up to this point over 2,400 sorties had been flown, during which 200 enemy aircraft were destroyed. A few days off the line saw the carrier groups being replenished before they began their attacks on Luzon on 21 and 22 September, concentrating upon Manila and Visayas, these areas being attacked again on 24 September. During the first raids a destroyer, a corvette, five tankers and sixteen freighters were sunk, while on the second raid four naval ships, two tankers and seven freighters were destroyed. Overall 1,000 Japanese aircraft were destroyed, while the shipping losses were 150 vessels of various types and sizes, all for the loss of fifty-four US Navy aircraft, plus eighteen damaged.

Morotai would be the next target for the Americans, and so TF.77, the VII Amphibious Force, departed from its bases at Aitape, Wakde and Hollandia on 15 September. The task force was split into two groups – 'White' commanded by Rear Admiral Barbey, and 'Red' commanded by Rear Admiral Fechteler. Air support was provided by TG.77.1, commanded by Rear Admiral Sprague, which included the escort carriers *Sangamon*, *Suwanee*, *Chenango*, *Santee*, *Saginaw Bay* and *Petrof Bay*, with an eight-destroyer escort force. Over the period 16 September to 3 October over 26,000 troops were landed, meeting little opposition from the defending Japanese forces. While TF.77 was landing on Morotai, Operation Stalemate II was also beginning, being the invasion of Palau. Overall command of TF.31 was vested in Rear Admiral Wilkinson, while the commander of III Amphibious Corps was Major-General Geiger. Initally the operation concentrated upon shelling the islands of Paella and Anger, which were scheduled to be invaded first. The main firepower was provided by the battleships *Pennsylvania*, *Tennessee*, *Maryland*, *Mississippi* and *West Virginia*, with nine cruisers and fourteen destroyers escorting. Air support was provided by between seven and eleven carriers as the operation continued. During the first day of the assault, 13 September, over 380 sorties were flown against enemy installations. While the Palau landings were meeting moderate resistance, those on Paella were met with much stronger efforts. So well entrenched were the Japanese forces that it took until 25 December for the final troops to be winkled out. Anger was landed on by the Americans on 17 September, and again the Japanese put up a stout resistance, their defence being broken only on 23 October. Of the 5,300 Japanese troops on the islands, only 301 survived to be captured, while the Americans suffered 1,200 dead with 6,500 wounded.

On 6 October 1944 Admiral Halsey, Commander of the 3rd Fleet, joined TF.38 as it moved to a position off Formosa in order to destroy the remaining Japanese aircraft based there and at Luzon. TF.38 had departed from Ultithi with Vice-Admiral Mitscher in command. Within the fleet were three of the available carrier task groups, these being TG.38.1, 38.2 and 38.3. The final carrier group, TG.38.4, joined the remainder of the fleet on 7 October, having arrived from a position off Palau. Even as the main fleet was heading towards the Philippines, a diversionary mission centring around TG.30.2, under the command of Rear Admiral Smith, headed towards Marcus Island to heavily bombard the Japanese based there. As the battleships were part of the main force, TG.30.2 consisted of three cruisers and six destroyers.

The TF.38 carrier groups consisted of TG.38.1 commanded by Vice-

Captured in flight are these Douglas Dauntless dive-bombers of VC-21 from the Bogue-class escort carrier USS Nassau. Of note are the bombs on the centre-line crutches. (US Navy/NARA via Dennis R. Jenkins)

Admiral McCain with the carriers *Wasp*, *Hornet*, *Monterey* and *Cowpens*, plus an escort of four cruisers and fifteen destroyers. TG.38.2 had the carriers *Intrepid*, *Hancock*, *Bunker Hill*, *Cabot* and *Independence*, commanded by Rear Admiral Bogan. Escorting the carriers were the battleships *Iowa* and *New Jersey*, with Admiral Halsey aboard, plus four cruisers and nineteen destroyers. Rear Admiral Sherman was in command of TG.38.3 with the carriers *Essex*, *Lexington*, *Princeton* and *Langley* assigned, while the escorts included the battleships *Washington*, *Massachusetts*, *South Dakota* and *Alabama*, with four cruisers and fourteen destroyers. TG.38.4, which had joined the main force on 7 October, had the carriers *Franklin*, *Enterprise*, *San Jacinto* and *Belleau Wood*, and was under the command of Rear Admiral Davison. Two cruisers and eleven destroyers provided escort cover. The carrier groups were in position on 10 October, all four launching strikes. One air group was directed to attack Amani-o-Shima, two attacked Okinawa and the fourth group attacked Sakishima Gunto. These raids involved nearly 2,000 sorties, during which twenty-one American aircraft were lost. During these attacks the Japanese lost forty-two vessels of varying sizes and thirty aircraft. After the US Navy had hit its targets, the Japanese forces attempted to launch a retaliatory attack, as TF.38 had been detected by aerial reconnaissance, but poor navigation resulted in the attack formations not finding their targets. On the following day TG.38.1 and 38.4 flew off sixty-one missions against the Japanese airfield at Aparri, while the other two task groups undertook essential refuelling from TG.30.8. This vital cog in the naval logistics chain comprised thirty-four tankers with forty-three escorts. Also in this formation were the escort carriers *Altamaha, Barnes, Silkoh Bay, Cape Esperance, Nassau, Kwajalein, Shipley Bay, Steamer Bay, Nehenta Bay, Sargent Bay* and *Rudyerd Bay*, which were acting as replenishment decks and as such would send sixty-one aircraft from their on-board stocks to the front-line carriers.

On 12 October all four carrier groups launched a continuous series of strike waves against the Japanese airfield and installations on Formosa. During the first day over 1,300 sorties were flown, while on the following day just under 1,000 missions were launched. During these sorties forty-eight American aircraft were lost, although most of the crews were recovered, but these losses were nothing compared to those suffered by the Japanese, as uncountable numbers of aircraft were destroyed in the air and on the ground. The Japanese attempted to launch raids in retaliation, 'T' Force dispatching fifty-six aircraft from Kyushu on 12 October, while on the following day fifty-two sorties were launched from Okinawa. During these attacks the carrier USS *Franklin* was narrowly missed by torpedoes and a kamikaze, although one of the Japanese torpedo-bombers crashed on the carrier's deck, causing light damage that was quickly dealt with. On 14 October TG.38.1 launched a further 246 aircraft against targets on Formosa, during which twenty-three aircraft were lost.

While TG.38.1 was pounding Formosa, TG.38.4 was undertaking a similar exercise against Aparri. As the US Navy aircraft withdrew from the skies over Formosa, Boeing B-29s launched from bases in China continued the attacks, although they also added Okinawa to the list of targets. The Japanese again tried to turn back the increasingly large American forces forcing their way towards the home islands. The Japanese 2nd Air Force launched 419 sorties from bases on Formosa, Okinawa and Kyushu against the ships of TF.38. Of these aircraft 225 aircraft would not find their designated targets, although those that did did manage to inflict some damage. The carrier *Hancock* suffered some injury, as did two cruisers and a destroyer. While the damaged ships were towed out of the combat zone, their removal and that of the required escorts, including the USS *Cowpens*, barely dented the strength of TF.38.

On 15 October units of the Japanese 2nd Fleet dispatched 199 aircraft to attack the American fleet, although only the cruiser USS *Houston* was damaged by a torpedo strike. In retaliation TG.38.4 undertook attacks on the airfields north of Manila, during which there were fierce air battles over the islands. The Japanese 1st Air Fleet launched fifty fighters and 130 dive-bombers and torpedo-bombers to attack the incoming raids and the TF.38 carriers. During this fighting the USS *Franklin* was again damaged, although in response the US Navy shot down thirty-two enemy aircraft. During the period 12–15 October the US Navy launched 881 missions against the various

A pair of Grumman Avengers from VT-7 aboard the USS Hancock pose for the camera. Of note is the horseshoe emblem on the fin, denoting the Hancock. (US Navy/NARA via Dennis R. Jenkins)

Japanese installations for the loss of 321 aircraft, although as before many of the downed aircrew were rescued. Japanese claims during this period included the sinking of eleven aircraft carriers, two battleships, one cruiser and thirteen other vessels. On 16 and 17 October the Japanese 1st and 2nd Air Fleets undertook 107 sorties against TF.38, although again they failed to find their targets and in the process lost twenty-four aircraft. While the Japanese aircraft were searching in vain for the American forces, they in turn were launching further attacks against Luzon. At the completion of these attacks the majority of the carrier groups returned to Ultithi to prepare for the Leyte operation.

The Battle of Leyte would begin with air attacks that took place over 16 and 17 October utilising B-24 Liberators, with P-38 Lightnings as escort, these being provided by the 5th and 13th Air Forces. The USAAF bombing raids were supported by carriers from TG.77.4 commanded by Rear Admiral T.L. Sprague. These aircraft attacked targets on Leyte, Cebu and North Mindenao. The carriers assigned to this task included the *Sangamon, Suwanee, Chenango, Santee, Saginaw Bay* and *Petrof Bay*, escorted by eight destroyers. A second carrier group, commanded by Rear Admiral Stump, included the *Natoma Bay, Manila Bay, Maces Island, Kadashan Bay, Savo Island* and *Ommaney Bay*, with an escort of eight destroyers. Another Rear Admiral Sprague would be in command of a third carrier force, comprising the carriers *Fanshaw Bay, St. Lo, White Plains, Kalinin Bay, Kitkun Bay* and *Gambier Bay*. This group was escorted by seven destroyers.

The first carrier group entered Leyte Gulf early in the morning of 17

October and prepared to launch aerial strikes. The escort carriers were spotted as intended by Japanese coast watchers, who as expected informed Imperial Headquarters. In response the Japanese put Operation Sho-1 into force, this being the intended main fleet movements needed to counter the American movements. While the escort carrier group was entering the gulf the primary fleet carriers of TF.38 were preparing to launch a series of attack waves against the bases of the 1st and 4th Air Fleets on Luzon. The assigned carrier groups were TG.38.4, commanded by Rear Admiral Davison, whose carriers included the *Franklin, Enterprise, San Jacinto* and *Belleau Wood*. Support was provided by the battleships *Washington* and *Alabama*, with two cruisers and fifteen destroyers. On the following day two other groups, TG.38.2 and TG.38.3, also launched air strikes against Luzon. TG.38.2 consisted of the *Intrepid, Hancock, Bunker Hill, Cabot* and *Independence*, plus the battleships *Iowa* and *New Jersey*, with three cruisers and sixteen destroyers as escorts. TG.38.3 consisted of the carriers *Lexington, Essex, Princeton* and *Langley*, with the battleships *Massachusetts* and *Indiana*, plus four cruisers and twelve destroyers as escorts. The Japanese responded to the carrier attacks by launching a hundred-strong raid, none of which got through. Further attacks were made by both carrier and air force units against Luzon, during which twenty-three ships were sunk.

With massive air support in place, the United States 7th Fleet entered the Leyte Gulf with the 6th Army under the command of Lieutenant-General Krueger aboard. The troop landings began on 20 October, with fire support being provided by the battleships *Mississippi, Maryland* and *West Virginia*. Another fire support group consisting of the battleships *Tennessee, California* and *Pennsylvania* was stationed to the other side of the landing beachheads. Due to the strength of the US Navy bombardment, the Japanese defending forces were forced to move to prepared positions further inland. During these operations the escort carrier USS *Sangamon* was damaged by a Japanese bomber, while two of the escorting cruisers were damaged by a torpedo and a kamikaze, and required that both be towed away for repairs. On 21 October aircraft from TG.77.4 supported the troop landings, while those of TG.38.2 and 38.4 undertook attacks on the western Vizayan Islands, after which both groups withdrew for replenishment.

On 22 October the C-in-C of the Combined Fleet under the command of Admiral Toyoda set out to intercept TF.38, departing from Brunei with the battleships *Yamato, Musashi, Nagato, Kongo* and *Haruna*, plus twelve cruisers and fifteen destroyers as escorts. The second force, consisting of the battleships *Fuso* and *Yamashiro*, with three cruisers and seven destroyers, departed at the same time. A third force, consisting of fast transports and escorts, sailed soon afterwards. A separate force commanded by Vice-Admiral Ozawa set out to create a diversion, the intention of which was to draw TF.38 into the waiting guns and aircraft of the Japanese Navy. Included in this diversion force were the carriers *Zuikaku, Zuiho, Chiyoda* and *Chitose*, these being escorted by the battleships *Ise* and *Hyuga*. Escort was provided by three

140

Almost gutted by fire, the crew of the carrier USS Princeton fight the flames that threaten the ship. After much effort by the crew, the conflagration finally took over the ship, which finally exploded. (US Navy/NARA via Dennis R. Jenkins)

cruisers and eight destroyers. A support group comprising two tankers, a destroyer and six corvettes left at the same time as the main combat group.

Unfortunately for the Japanese force, it was spotted by an American submarine, which promptly reported it. Further submarines soon reached the Japanese position and mounted a combined attack that saw the sinking of two destroyers and the serious damaging of two more. Admiral Halsey decided to attack this force, and so TF.38 altered course towards the Japanese with the carriers of TG.38.3, 38.2 and 38.4 moving into position in preparation for these attacks. However, this was not without incident, as a bomber force from the Japanese base on Luzon reached the carrier groups, when a single attacker got through and hit the USS *Princeton*. The single attacker managed to release a single bomb that passed through the flight deck and entered the hangar before exploding. This caused a massive fire, which quickly spread and required assistance from other vessels to combat the flames. Further explosions ripped through the carrier, causing further extensive damage. At this point most of the surviving crew were evacuated, while the vessels alongside continued to fight the fires. By late afternoon it had become obvious that the fires aboard the *Princeton* were completely out of control, and the remaining crew were evacuated. There was an attempt to torpedo the hulk, but this was abandoned due to torpedo malfunctions. No further attempt was made to sink the stricken vessel as a bomb magazine eventually exploded, completely destroying the forward part of the ship and sending the debris high into the air. The rear hull section slid beneath the waves soon after. Only one other vessel was damaged, this being the cruiser USS *Birmingham*, which had been hit by flying debris when the *Princeton* exploded, and required towing clear for repairs.

On 24 October four waves of US Navy strike and fighter aircraft were launched to attack the Japanese main force in the Sibuyan Sea. The first wave

Resplendent in its new camouflage scheme, the USS Essex departs America to return to the fray in the Pacific. (US Navy/NARA via Dennis R. Jenkins)

was generated by the *Intrepid* and the *Cabot*, and consisted of twelve dive-bombers and twelve torpedo-bombers, escorted by twenty-one fighters, that attacked the *Myoko* and the *Musashi*, the sister vessel to the *Yamato*, causing serious torpedo damage on the first, and bomb and torpedo damage on the latter. The *Myoko* was so badly damaged that it was forced to withdraw from the conflict. A second wave from the same carriers, consisting of twelve dive-bombers and eleven torpedo-bombers, with an escort of nineteen fighters, also scored further hits on the *Musashi*. A third wave, launched by the *Essex* and the *Lexington*, consisted of twenty dive-bombers and thirty-two torpedo-bombers, plus a sixteen-strong fighter escort, also attacked the *Musashi*, scoring a further two torpedo and four bomb strikes on the battleship. The *Yamato* was also struck by a pair of bombs, although the vessel's armour resisted these bombs successfully. As all three attack waves had arrived almost simultaneously, the effect of the attacks had the desired effect on the *Musashi*, which then sank. The remaining battleships in this group had also suffered some damage, although all were able to continue. During these attacks on the battle fleet, the US Navy lost thirty aircraft.

While the two fleets were engaging in combat, Japanese reconnaissance aircraft had detected TG.38.3. This information was passed onto Admiral Ozawa, who ordered his carrier group to launch seventy-six attack aircraft towards the American carrier group. However, the Japanese aircraft crews failed to find their targets and were forced to fly on to Luzon. The departure of this large strike force left the Japanese carriers with twenty-five aircraft between them. The US Navy had detected the Japanese aerial force *en route* towards the American carriers and their subsequent turn away towards Luzon. As the Americans were aware that the Japanese aircraft carriers were low on aircraft, Admiral Halsey ordered all of the task groups of TF.38 to head towards the Japanese carrier group. To ensure that there was enough fire power to utterly destroy the Japanese carriers, he recalled TG.38.1, which was heading towards Ulithi.

While Halsey was heading towards the Japanese carriers, a detachment from TG.38.4 was heading south to intercept a Japanese force that was proceeding towards the American fleet. During the engagement aircraft from the USS *Franklin* sank the IJN destroyer *Wakana*. Meanwhile, in the approaches to the Surigoa Strait, the US Navy was using its smaller vessels to attack the Japanese fleet during which activity the IJN cruiser *Abukuma* was hit by a torpedo, which forced it to retire from the action. Further engagements saw three destroyers sunk and badly damaged, while hits were scored upon the battleship *Yamashiro*. Another battleship, the IJN *Fuso*, was struck by numerous torpedoes from the American destroyers; they struck a magazine, causing a massive explosion that destroyed the ship completely. Even as the smaller US Navy ships were scoring successes against their larger enemies, the main TF.38 battleships and cruisers were arriving from the north-east. When they sighted the Japanese battle fleet, the six battleships and five cruisers let loose with their main armaments while the American destroyers continued their pin-prick harrying attacks. During this confused situation the battleship *Yamashiro* was sunk by torpedoes, while the IJN cruiser *Mogami* limped away badly damaged, only to collide with the approaching cruiser *Nachi*. After suffering such damage, the remaining crew were evacuated and the ship was sunk by an escorting destroyer.

In the dark of 24 October the Japanese force commanded by Vice-Admiral

After a heavy landing this Douglas Dauntless of VB-16 had ripped its engine from its mounts after an undercarriage failed on touchdown aboard the USS Lexington. (US Navy/NARA via Dennis R. Jenkins)

Kurita managed to pass through the San Bernadino Strait unobserved by the American forces, and was to the east of Samar in the early hours of the morning. Unfortunately for the Kurita force, it then ran straight into TG.77.4.3, commanded by Rear Admiral C.A.F. Sprague, whose escort carriers promptly flew off a strike attack force. Knowing that it had been spotted, the Japanese force flew off its available aircraft, laid down a smoke screen and used local rain squalls to evade its American attackers, while still heading towards Leyte Gulf. Commendable those these efforts were, the overwhelming strength of the US Navy forces soon bore fruit, as the cruiser IJN *Kumano* was brought to a standstill. The aircraft of TG.77.4.2 had come into range and were soon attacking the Japanese vessels. But careful manoeuvring by the IJN force and the arrival of the battleships *Yamato* and *Nagato* brought the American escort carriers into range of the warships' big guns. In the ensuing carnage the escort carrier *Gambier Bay* was sunk. TG.77.4.2 had launched a strike against two Japanese cruisers, which were sunk, while the battleships *Kongo* and *Haruna* tried to get into a position to attack the task group. Although the Japanese forces were closing on the American force, Admiral Kurita decided to break off the engagement. As Kurita ordered his ships to break away, a kamikaze raid hit the carriers of TG.77.4.3. During this attack the carrier *St. Lo* was sunk, while the *Kalinin Bay*, *Kitkun Bay* and *White Plains* were damaged, and only *Fanshaw Bay* would escape injury. A further kamikaze formation attacked the escort carriers of TG.77.4.1 and damaged the *Sangamon*, *Suwanee* and *Santee*. In response to the Japanese attacks, the returning carriers of TG.38.1 launched retaliatory air strikes against the Kurita

Sitting on the catapult of the USS Kitkun Bay, a Casablanca-class escort carrier, is this Grumman Avenger assigned to composite squadron VC-63. Once the launch officer flags take-off clearance, the chockmen will pull the chocks clear and the aircraft will depart. (US Navy/NARA via Dennis R. Jenkins)

force. While no ships were sunk, the attacking aircraft did inflict some damage on the fleeing ships.

As the fighting in the Surigoa Strait was taking place, a further battle was taking place off Cape Engano, involving the remaining task groups of TF.38. These groups had headed north at high speed to intercept the Ozawa force. In the early hours of 25 October the American carriers flew off six attack waves, including 326 dive-bombers and torpedo-bombers, with 201 fighters as escorts. During these attacks the IJN carrier *Chitose* was badly damaged by aircraft from the *Lexington*, which later resulted in the carrier sinking. The next vessel to be sunk was the fleet carrier *Zuikaku*, which was hit repeatedly by aircraft from the *Intrepid*, *San Jacinto*, *Lexington* and *Cowpens*. The light carrier *Zuiho* was also sunk by aircraft from the *Essex* and the *Langley*, while the light carrier *Chiyoda* and its escorting destroyer were badly damaged. The American carrier aircraft also attacked the Japanese battleships, although the *Hyuga* escaped after thirty-four near-misses, while the *Ise* escaped completely unscathed. Although Admiral Halsey had sped towards the San Bernadino Strait at high speed in order to intercept the Kurita force, he arrived too late. However, Kurita and his ships ran into TG.38.1 and 38.4, with TG.77.4, which promptly sank two cruisers and three destroyers. A further cruiser and a destroyer were later sunk by B-24 Liberators from the 5th AAF. During this final act of the Battle of Leyte Gulf the escort carrier *Suwanee* was damaged by five kamikazes dispatched from Cebu.

In order to maintain American control over Leyte, General MacArthur requested aerial support from the US Navy, as the USAAF units in the area were unable to provide the close-in support needed. To comply with MacArthur's request, TF.38.3, under the command of Rear Admiral Sherman, was directed to provide fighter cover from the carriers *Lexington*, *Langley* and *Essex*. While most of fighters were providing the much-needed fighter cover, the remainder of the air wings were directed to attack any Japanese shipping in the area. Their efforts brought success, as aircraft from the *Essex* and *Enterprise* managed to attack a small convoy, sinking two destroyers and damaging some of the transports. Replacing TF.38.3 on support duties were TG.38.4 and 38.2, which arrived on station on 28 October. Included in the carrier groups were the vessels *Franklin*, *San Jacinto* and *Belleau Wood* with TG.38.3, while the other group included *Intrepid*, *Hancock*, *Cabot* and *Independence*. Soon after its arrival, TG.38.4 was attacked by forty-four Japanese aircraft, of which thirteen were shot down for the cost of four US Navy machines.

The following day saw the carriers of TG.38.2 launching a massive attack on the airfields around Manila, during which seventy-one Japanese aircraft were shot down and thirteen were destroyed on the ground for the cost of eleven American aircraft. The bombers and torpedo-aircraft attacked the shipping in the area, causing damage to a Japanese cruiser. While TG.38.2 was destroying the Japanese around Manila, TG.38.4 was covering Leyte Gulf, during which six kamikazes struck the carriers *Franklin* and *Belleau Wood*, so that both vessels had to retire towards Ulithi for repairs. The two damaged carriers were followed by the remainder of TF.38, TG.38.1 arrived on 29 October and TG.38.3 the following day, while the other two groups arrived on 2 November. Over 5 and 6 November TG.38.1, TG.38.2 and TG.38.3 departed from Ulithi anchorage to undertake attacks against Luzon. The first group comprised the carriers *Wasp, Hornet, Monterey* and *Cowpens,* the second comprised *Intrepid, Hancock, Cabot* and *Independence,* and the third consisted of the *Lexington, Langley* and the newly arrived *Ticonderoga.* During these attacks over 400 Japanese aircraft were destroyed for the loss of twenty-five aircraft. The strike waves also sank two cruisers and seven other vessels. The American forces were not completely immune, however, as twelve kamikazes attacked TG.38.3, badly damaging the *Enterprise* in the process.

Having attacked the Japanese fixed installations, TF.38 then turned its attention to attacking and destroying the reinforcement convoys. This mission began on 11 November and utilised aircraft from the *Hornet, Monterey, Cowpens* of 38.1, *Essex, Ticonderoga* and *Langley* of 38.3, and *Enterprise* and *San Jacinto* of 38.4. Although the carriers lost eleven aircraft, the attacking aircraft sank four destroyers and six other ships. As these were mainly troop transports, most of the 10,000 troops embarked failed to reach their destination. A period of replenishment followed on 12 November, after which the three carrier groups undertook further attacks on the Luzon area on 13 and 14 November. Two days later the carrier air groups attacked again, although by this time TG.38.3 had been replaced by TG.38.2. During this period the carriers had sunk eighteen Japanese ships and damaged nearly as many. A further period of replenishment saw the carrier groups resume their strikes against Luzon on 25 November. This strike force included four fleet carriers, three light carriers with six battleships, and a large escort of cruisers and destroyers. During these operations aircraft from the American carriers sank two IJN cruisers and six others, and damaged half a dozen more. In return the Japanese scored some success when a twenty-five-strong kamikaze force managed to cause severe damage to the *Intrepid* and *Cabot,* while the *Essex* and *Hancock* were slightly damaged. The USS *Independence* was also damaged, although this was caused when one of the carrier's aircraft crashed into the island on landing. Needing to undergo a period of repair and replenishment, TF.38 withdrew to Ulithi, arriving between 25 and 27 November.

Having undergone a much needed period of replenishment, TF.38 departed Ulithi on 11 December with Vice-Admiral McCain in command. The carrier groups assigned to this force included TG.38.1 with the carriers *Yorktown, Wasp, Cowpens* and *Monterey* commanded by Rear Admiral Montgomery, TG.38.2 commanded by Rear Admiral Bogan with the carriers *Lexington, Hancock, Hornet, Independence* and *Cabot,* and TG.38.3 comprising the *Essex, Ticonderoga, Langley* and *San Jacinto* with Rear Admiral Sherman in command. Also with TF.38 were the battleships *Massachusetts, Alabama, New Jersey, Iowa, Wisconsin, North Carolina, Washington* and *South Dakota,* with thirteen cruisers and fifty-six destroyers making up the remainder.

The war in the Pacific had another enemy – the weather. The USS Wasp had been damaged by a typhoon when photographed, and as a result of this damage the Essex class would later be rebuilt with hurricane bows that would lessen the effects of such violent weather. (US Navy/NARA via Dennis R. Jenkins)

Refuelling took place on 13 December, after which the carriers moved into range to continue their attacks on the airfields around Luzon in support of the Mindoro operation between 14 and 16 December. During these attacks other aircraft from the carriers sank Japanese shipping in the area, and aircraft from the *Hornet* sank a transport on 14 December, and another the following day when an IJN corvette was also badly damaged. During this period over 1,400 fighter and 244 bomber sorties were flown for the loss of twenty-seven aircraft in combat and thirty-eight from accidents. In return 170 Japanese aircraft were destroyed. At the completion of these operations TF.38 withdrew for re-fuelling, running into Typhoon Cobra on 18 December. This was a powerful storm, which caused the destroyer USS *Spence* to founder, while the carriers *Cowpens*, *Monterey*, *Cabot* and *San Jacinto* were damaged, as were the destroyers *Dyson*, *Hickox*, *Benham* and *Maddox*. The support and supply group suffered even worse, as the destroyers *Hull* and *Monaghan* were sunk, while the escort carriers *Altamaha*, *Nehenta Bay*, *Cape Esperance* and *Kwajalein*, together with the cruiser *Miami* and the destroyers *Aylwin*, *Dewey* and *Buchanan*, were damaged, as were the escorts *Waterman*, *Melvin R. Newman*, *Tabberer* and the oiler *Nantahala*. Also destroyed were 146 aircraft, whose lashing to the carrier decks was not enough to save them. As the priority was to search for survivors, the planned attack on Luzon set for 19–21 December was abandoned. Once the search mission had been completed, TF.38 returned to Ulithi for repairs.

Although the attack on Luzon had been postponed, other operations did continue. Therefore, on 15 December TG.78.3, under the command of Rear Admiral Struble, began the task of landing the troops commanded by Brigadier-General Dunckel on Western Vasayas. The landing force was escorted by three cruisers and twenty destroyers. Firepower support was provided by TF.77.12 under the command of Rear Admiral Ruddock, and comprised the battleships *West Virginia*, *Colorado* and *New Mexico*, plus three cruisers and eighteen destroyers. The escort carriers included in this task group were the USS *Natoma Bay*, *Manila Bay*, *Marcus Island*, *Kadashan Bay*, *Savo Bay* and *Ommaney Bay*. During the landings the kamikaze threat raised its head again, causing damage to the command cruiser USS *Nashville*, two landing ships, two destroyers and the escort carrier *Marcus Island*. There was some cheer for the Allies during this period when on 20 December the Japanese resistance on Leyte finally ended.

On 30 December 1944 the 3rd US Navy Fleet under the command of Admiral Halsey set sail to lend support to TF.38, whose next task was to invade Luzon in an operation that would last until 25 January. As before, TF.38 was under the command of Vice-Admiral McCain, while TG.38.1 was commanded by Rear Admiral Radford. The carriers in this group were the *Yorktown*, *Wasp*, *Cabot* and *Cowpens*, plus the battleships *South Dakota* and *Massachusetts*, together with four cruisers and seventeen destroyers as escorts. TG.38.2 also departed Ulithi at the same time, under the command of Rear Admiral Bogan, the assigned carriers being the *Lexington*, *Hancock* and *Hornet*, plus the battleships *New Jersey* and *Wisconsin*, with an escort of four cruisers

The Independence-class light carrier, the USS San Jacinto, played an important part in the Pacific war. Here a Grumman Avenger of VT-45 prepares to launch on another mission. (US Navy/NARA via Dennis R. Jenkins)

A flight of Vought F4U Corsair fighters from VF-86 aboard the USS Wasp patrol above the fleet, keeping a good lookout for incoming kamikazes. (US Navy/NARA via Dennis R. Jenkins)

and twenty destroyers. The third carrier group was TG.38.3, commanded by Rear Admiral Sherman, with the carriers *Essex*, *Ticonderoga*, *Langley* and *San Jacinto*, the battleships *Washington* and *North Carolina*, and five cruisers and eighteen destroyers as escorts. The fourth carrier group was TG.38.5, commanded by Rear Admiral Gardner, with the carriers *Enterprise* and *Independence*, and six destroyers for escort duties.

Refuelling of all ships took place on 2 January, after which TG.38.1 and 38.3 undertook raids on northern Formosa, while TG.38.2 and 38.5 attacked southern Formosa and the southern Ryukyu Islands. Although inclement weather caused some problems for the attacking forces, they still managed to destroy over a hundred Japanese aircraft in exchange for twenty-two US Navy machines. A refuelling break took place after this opening round before raids were mounted on the kamikaze airfields around Luzon in preparation for the landings on Lingayen. During these operations over eighty Japanese aircraft were destroyed in exchange for twenty-eight American machines. A further refuelling break followed this, after which on 8 January the carrier groups mounted further attacks on Formosa and Okinawa, part of the Ryukyu Islands. Although five American aircraft were lost, the attackers managed to sink eight Japanese ships and damage twelve more. Assisting the US Navy efforts were the Boeing B-29s based in China, which also bombed Formosa.

By 10 January TF.38 had entered the South China Sea, where the force re-fuelled prior to launching attacks against Can Ranh Bay, where it was

149

suspected that the major IJN warships were based. While no IJN battleships or carriers were found, the carrier groups did manage to sink fifty-one vessels and damage a further twenty or more for the loss of twenty-three aircraft. A further refuelling took place over 13/14 January, after which the carrier groups launched raids against Formosa, the Pescadores and the Chinese province of Fukien. During these attacks five IJN ships were sunk for the loss of twelve aircraft. A further raid on the Chinese coast on 16 January saw the loss of twenty-seven aircraft, although they did sink two ships and damaged a further five. Bad weather hampered operations until 21 January, when further attacks were mounted on Formosa. Some 1,100 sorties were flown, with 104 Japanese aircraft being destroyed and ten ships sunk, while a further five were damaged. During the Japanese attacks on the fleet, a bomb hit the *Langley*, while a kamikaze hit the *Ticonderoga*. A further raid by seven kamikazes was destroyed by fighters launched by the USS *Cowpens*, although another attack was more successful when the *Ticonderoga* was hit again. The US Navy were also responsible for some of its own damage when an Avenger landing on the USS *Hancock* lost a bomb, which exploded and caused some damage. During these attacks on the carriers, 205 sailors and airmen were killed and a further 351 were wounded. On 22 January the carrier groups launched 628 sorties against Okinawa, this operation being completed by 23 January. After withdrawing for refuelling, TF.38 proceeded to Ulithi, where it arrived on 25 January. During this operational period over 300,000 tons of shipping were sunk, while more than 600 aircraft were destroyed in exchange for 201 American aircraft and 167 pilots.

CHAPTER SIX

War in the Pacific: The Setting of the Rising Sun

After a successful 1944, the American forces continued their operations in a similar vein during 1945. On 2 January TF.38 began operations in support of the Lingayen landings on the island of Luzon. Combat operations began the following day, and eleven Japanese vessels were sunk and a similar number damaged. Engaged in these missions was TG.38.2, commanded by Rear Admiral Bogan, whose assigned carriers were the *Lexington, Hancock, Hornet* and *Cabot*, these being supported by the battleships *New Jersey, Wisconsin* and *Iowa*, with five cruisers and twenty destroyers, all of which were operating off Pescador and Formosa. Night flying was becoming a requirement for US Navy operations, and so TG.38.5 was deployed with the carriers *Enterprise* and *Independence* and an escort of six destroyers. Two further carrier groups were also deployed. The first was TG.38.3, commanded by Rear Admiral Sherman, which was operating off central Formosa, Okinawa and Sakishima Gunto; the carriers assigned to this group included the *Essex, Ticonderoga, Langley* and *San Jacinto*, supported by the battleships *Washington, North Carolina* and *South Dakota*, together with four cruisers and eighteen destroyers. The second carrier group, TG.38.1, was under the command of Rear Admiral Radford, and was operating off north Formosa, using the carriers *Yorktown, Wasp, Cowpens* and *Monterey*,with cover supplied by the battleships *Massachusetts* and *Alabama*, plus four cruisers and eighteen destroyers.

The US Navy landing fleets departed from the Leyte Gulf, passing through the Surigao Strait, the Sulu Sea and the Mindoro Strait *en route* to the Lingayen Gulf. To the fore of the landing fleets was a minesweeping group and a destroyer escort, followed by the fire support group, TG.77.2, commanded by Vice-Admiral Oldendorf. This in turn was divided into two separate forces, these being designated Unit 1 and Unit 2. Unit 1 was commanded by Rear

151

After repairs for its typhoon damage, the USS Wasp, the Mighty Stinger, would resume combat operations in the Pacific. (US Navy/NARA via Dennis R. Jenkins)

Admiral Weyler and was charged with supporting the landings off San Fabian. The battleships in this group included the *Mississippi, West Virginia* and *New Mexico*, plus three cruisers and eight destroyers. Unit 2 was commanded by Vice-Admiral Oldendorf and comprised the battleships *California, Pennsylvania* and *Colorado*, with an escort of three cruisers and eleven destroyers. Providing air support for the landings was carrier group TG.77.4 commanded by Rear Admiral Durgin, who also took charge of carrier Unit 1 and was charged with operating off Lingayen. The escort carriers in the group were the *Makin Island, Lunga Point, Bismarck Sea, Salamaua* and the *Hoggett Bay*, these being covered by a force of nine destroyers. A second escort carrier group, Unit 2, was commanded by Rear Admiral Stump and included the *Natoma Bay, Manila Bay, Wake Island, Steamer Bay, Savo Island* and *Ommmaney Bay,* their target being San Fabian. This group was escorted by seven destroyers. One final carrier group was also deployed, this being the Hunter Killer Group, whose role was anti-submarine warfare. Commanded by Captain Cronin USN, the carrier was the *Tulagi*, with five escort and support vessels.

As all the support groups were in position on 4 January, the San Fabian

Seen overflying the task force is this Curtiss Helldiver assigned to VB-3
aboard the USS Yorktown in 1945. (US Navy/NARA via Dennis R. Jenkins)

force began to depart from Leyte Gulf. The troops were commanded by
Major-General Swift, the land force being designated I Corps. Escorting the
troop ships were the carriers *Kadashan Bay* and *Marcus Island* and twelve
destroyers. The Lingayen force departed the following day with the troops of
XIV Corps aboard, being commanded by Major-General Grimshaw. The air
escort for this force was provided by the escort carriers *Kitkun Bay* and
Shamrock Bay, with nine destroyers. The Japanese forces had already detected
the American forces on the move, and set in motion an attack plan that
involved the IJN submarine force, this being followed by a kamikaze attack
launched from Luzon on 5 January. These aircraft managed to damage the
escort carrier *Manila Bay*, two cruisers and four other vessels. The following
day the Japanese launched a further twenty-nine kamikaze fighters, which
managed to sink the minesweeper USS *Long*, as well as causing damage to the
battleships *New Mexico* and *California*, three destroyers and two other ships.
At the end of these attacks the Americans had lost 156 killed and 452
wounded. Over the night of 6/7 January two other vessels were sunk by the
Japanese. A further attack by kamikaze aircraft took place on 8 January when
the escort cruisers *Kadashan Bay* and *Kitkun Bay*, and a cruiser, were damaged.
These attacks resulted in seventeen dead and thirty-six wounded.

On 9 January Operation Mike I began utilising TG.77.2 and 77.4 to land the
USA I Corps in Langayen Gulf, this force comprising 70,000 troops, who met
little resistance from the Japanese as the majority of the defending force had
withdrawn to the mountains. The major engagement would begin on 11
January as the American troops moved inshore. To support the landings and
to suppress as much of the Japanese sea and air opposition as possible, the
carrier groups of TF.38 launched missions against the airfields on Formosa

153

Pictured just before touchdown is this Grumman F6F Hellcat of VF-6 from the USS Hancock. (US Navy/NARA via Dennis R. Jenkins)

and the Ryukyus and Pescadore Islands. During these raids fifteen IJN vessels were sunk and a similar number damaged. In retaliation the Japanese launched nine kamikaze aircraft against the US Navy fleets, causing damage to the battleship *Mississippi*, two cruisers and a destroyer.

On 11 January Amphibious Group 3, commanded by Rear Admiral Conolly, arrived off Lingayen, the fleet consisting of more than fifty vessels. The air escort for this force was provided by the escort carriers *Saginaw Bay* and *Petrof Bay*, commanded by Rear Admiral Henderson. As before, the Japanese launched massive kamikaze attacks against the attacking naval forces, causing damage to the carrier *Hoggett Bay*, numerous other vessels also being damaged. Although the Japanese would put up a stout resistance, the US Army forces had made enough headway to allow the naval forces to withdraw and prepare for the next mission. During these landings the carriers had launched over 6,000 missions, of which 1,400 were close support sorties, during which only two American aircraft were shot down.

The landing on Luzon began on 27 January, when the 32nd Infantry Division and the 1st Cavalry Division were put ashore at Lingayen Gulf to support the US 6th Army. Two days later, Operation Mike VII saw Amphibious Group 9 under the command of Rear Admiral Struble landing the 38th Infantry Division near Subic Bay. During these operations approximately 30,000 troops were disembarked from fifty-five landing vessels. Air support was provided by the 5th AAF commanded by Lieutenant-General Kenney, while naval fire support was courtesy of TG.74.2, comprising a cruiser and fourteen destroyers. The next landings, Operation Mike VI, took

Captured on the point of touchdown is this Douglas SBD Dauntless of VB-4 landing on the deck of CV-4, USS *Ranger*.

US Navy/NARA via Dennis R Jenkins

Douglas AD-4NA Skyraider of VF-194 based aboard the Essex class carrier USS *Valley Forge* when operating off the Korea coast.

US Navy/NARA via Dennis R Jenkins

This Vought F4U Corsair was assigned to VC-3 aboard the USS *Bon Homme Richard*, an Essex class carrier that was involved in operations off the coast of Korea.

US Navy/NARA via Dennis R Jenkins

Departing the flight deck of the Independence class light carrier, USS *Monterey*, is this Grumman F6F Hellcat assigned to NAS Pensacola. The *Monterey* undertook pilot training during the Korean War.

US Navy/NARA via Dennis R Jenkins

The Grumman Avenger still had a role to play in the Korean war, this example was being operated by VR-24 in the on-board delivery role.

US Navy/NARA via Dennis R Jenkins

In the immediate post WW II period the attack squadrons of the US Navy were still flying the Curtiss SB2C Helldiver. This aircraft is assigned to VA-9 aboard the Essex class carrier, USS *Philippine Sea*.

US Navy/NARA via Dennis R Jenkins

The Martin AM Mauler was the main competitor to the Douglas Skyraider. Although it lost out to the Douglas aircraft the Mauler did achieve a small production run. These examples were assigned to VA-17A, an attack unit.

US Navy/NARA via Dennis R Jenkins

Being guided in by the deck handler is this Sikorsky HO3S assigned to helicopter squadron, HU-1, this unit provided rescue services aboard the various carriers operating off the Korean coast.

US Navy/NARA via Dennis R Jenkins

The primary jet aircraft utilised aboard the aircraft carriers taking part in the Korean War was the Grumman F9F Panther. VF-51 aboard the USS *Essex* was home for this particular example.

US Navy/NARA via Dennis R Jenkins

Seen being craned aboard the USS *Midway* is this North American Aviation AJ Savage, the first type assigned to carry nuclear weapons from aircraft carriers. It was later used as a tanker aircraft aboard those same vessels.

US Navy/NARA via Dennis R Jenkins

After the Sikorsky HO3S helicopter squadron HU-1 would receive the Piasecki HUP-1 helicopter. This aircraft from HU-1 is seen here touching down on the USS *Coral Sea*.

US Navy/NARA via Dennis R Jenkins

This McDonnell F3H Demon was assigned to VF-51 aboard the USS *Coral Sea*. The Demon had only one fault, its Westinghouse engine had a tendency to malfunction in flight.

US Navy/NARA via Dennis R Jenkins

This Douglas AD Skyraider of VA-176 based aboard the USS *Intrepid* sports the famous thunderbolt flash on the fin with the stinging hornet emblem superimposed.

US Navy/NARA via Dennis R Jenkins

At a later date the Skyraiders of VA-176 sported the thunderbolt on the mid fuselage as shown here.

US Navy/NARA via Dennis R Jenkins

Preparing to depart for another Pacific cruise is CV-43, USS *Coral Sea*. On the flight deck are Douglas A3D Skywarriors, Douglas A-4 Skyhawks and McDonnell F3H Demons, just visible to the rear is a Grummam E-1 Tracer AEW aircraft.

US Navy/NARA via Dennis R Jenkins

This head on view is of the USS Intrepid, CV-11, when it was operating in the anti submarine role as exemplified by the Grumman S-2 Trackers on the flight deck.
US Navy/NARA via Dennis R Jenkins

Photographed at anchor in Yokosuka harbour is CV-41 USS *Midway*. This was one of the last conventionally powered carriers in the US Navy, eventually it was replaced by a nuclear powered carrier in April 1992.

US Navy/NARA via Dennis R Jenkins

After its time as a front line carrier the USS *Lexington* was utilised as a training carrier, a task it ful-filled until 1991 when it finally retired into preservation.

US Navy/NARA via Dennis R Jenkins

The USS *Ranger* was a Forrestal class carrier, it is seen here preparing to launch another strike of Douglas Skyraiders off the coast of Vietnam while cruising on Yankee Station.

US Navy/NARA via Dennis R Jenkins

The USS *Constellation*, CVA-64, was a member of the Kitty Hawk or Improved Forrestal class. The deck has KA-3B Skywarrior tankers, A-7 Corsair II's F-4 Phantoms plus E-2 Hawkeyes and S-2 Viking on it waiting to launch.

US Navy/NARA via Dennis R Jenkins

Douglas A-4 Skyhawks taxi to the catapults aboard the carrier USS *Hancock*. All are toting bombs on the centreline pylons plus underwing tanks for raids over North Vietnam.

US Navy/NARA via Dennis R Jenkins

CVN-65 USS *Enterprise* was the first nuclear powered aircraft carrier commissioned into the US Navy. The solitary A-4 Skyhawk on the deck was used as a training aid.

US Navy/NARA via Dennis R Jenkins

Seen just before touchdown is this F-4B Phantom of VF-14 returning to the USS *John F Kennedy* after a mission over North Vietnam.

US Navy/NARA via Dennis R Jenkins

The flight deck of USS *Hancock* is a busy place as its complement of A-4F Skyhawks prepare to depart. The nearest aircraft is on the strength of VA-55 while others came from VA-212.

US Navy/NARA via Dennis R Jenkins

Carrying the titles of the USS *Franklin D Roosevelt* this Vought RF-8G of VFP-62 banks away from the camera. This version of the Crusader shared reconnaissance duties with RA-5C Vigilante.

US Navy/NARA via Dennis R Jenkins

The Improved Forrestal class carrier USS *Kitty Hawk* cruises towards Vietnam with its air wing on the flight deck.

US Navy/NARA via Dennis R Jenkins

VF-121 was the Pacific fleet replacement air group that was responsible for providing crews for the F-4 Phantom units of the Pacific air wings. Here a brace is prepared for launching from an unidentified carrier.

US Navy/NARA via Dennis R Jenkins

After its time as a bomber the Douglas A-3 Skywarrior was reworked for the tanker role being redesignated as a KA-3B in the process. This aircraft was assigned to VAH-4 aboard the USS *Hancock*.

US Navy/NARA via Dennis R Jenkins

place on 31 January, when Amphibious Group 8, commanded by Rear Admiral Fechteler, landed the 11th Airborne Division near Nasugbu, close to Manila Bay, using more than forty landing ships. Fire support was courtesy of a cruiser and six destroyers. During the fighting the Japanese resistance at Subic Bay was minimal, although it increased as the Americans forged inland. However, the deployment of tactical air power soon broke their opposition. A total of 175,000 men proceeded across the beachhead within a few days. With heavy air support the Army units pushed further inland, capturing Clark Field some forty miles north-west of Manila at the end of January. Two major landings followed, one to cut off the Bataan Peninsula, and the other including a parachute drop south of Manila. A pincer movement closed on the city, and so on 3 February 1945 elements of the 1st Cavalry Division entered the northern outskirts of Manila, and the 8th Cavalry passed through the suburbs. It took until 3 March to clear Manila of all Japanese troops, while Fort Drum, a fortified island in Manila Bay near Corregidor, resisted until 13 April. The Japanese forces based there were nullified when a team went ashore on the island and pumped 3,000 gallons of diesel fuel into the fort, and set charges that were then detonated. No Japanese survived the subsequent blast and fire. During the fighting over 13,000 Americans were killed, with more than 48,000 being wounded. Japanese losses were over 336,000 killed, with a further 12,000 being captured.

After the retaking of the Philippines, the Americans moved on to Iwo Jima. The opening gambit was a major carrier raid against Tokyo, using TF.58 under the command of Vice-Admiral Mitscher. On 10 February TF.58 departed from Ulithi, undertaking exercises off Tinian on 12 February, with a pre-strike refuel taking place two days later. The carrier groups

Flying over the Philippines is this Grumman Avenger of VT-89 from the USS Antietam, complete with a radar pod under the wing. (US Navy/NARA via Dennis R. Jenkins)

included TG.58.1, commanded by Rear Admiral Clark, the carriers comprising the *Hornet, Wasp, Bennington* and *Belleau Wood*, with the battleships *Massachusetts* and *Indiana*, plus three cruisers and fifteen destroyers assigned for escort and defensive duties. The second carrier group consisted of the *Lexington, Hancock* and *San Jacinto*, with the battleships *Wisconsin* and *Missouri* (the 'Mighty Mo'), plus two cruisers and nineteen destroyers, all commanded by Rear Admiral Davison. Rear Admiral Sherman was the commander of TG.58.3, whose carriers were the *Essex, Bunker Hill* and *Cowpens*, plus the battleships *South Dakota* and *New Jersey*, the battlecruiser *Alaska*, and four cruisers and fourteen destroyers. The fourth group was TG.58.4, commanded by Rear Admiral Radford. The carriers in this group were the *Yorktown, Randolph, Langley* and *Cabot*, with support being supplied by the battleships *Washington* and *North Carolina*, together with three cruisers and seventeen destroyers. TG.58.5, under the command of Rear Admiral Gardner, was deployed for night operations, and had the carriers *Enterprise* and *Saratoga*, with two cruisers and twelve destroyers for support purposes. A screen of destroyers proceeded the main fleet, their main task being to deter submarines and other IJN attack vessels. By 16 February the main fleet was 125 miles from Tokyo. The fighters were launched first by the carrier groups, their purpose being to eliminate any aerial resistance. They were followed by the bomber groups, whose designated targets were of an industrial nature, with aircraft manufacturing facilities being the highest priority. While some targets were destroyed, many of the attacks were unsuccessful as bad weather obscured the targets. A further attack took place against shipping off Yokohama, during which a freighter and two IJN vessels were sunk. Overall 2,761 sorties were flown during this period, with sixty aircraft being lost in combat and a further twenty-eight being lost to accidents.

After the completion of the combined carrier operations, TG.58.4 was diverted to undertake raids on Hahajima and Chichi Jima in order to neutralise the Japanese forces based there. On 16 February preparations began for the invasion of Iwo Jima. The opening move was by TF.54 under the command of Rear Admiral Rodgers. This task force consisted of the battleships *Tennessee, Idaho, Nevada, Texas, New York* and *Arkansas*, plus five cruisers and sixteen destroyers, which arrived off the island to undertake a bombardment of the designated landing areas. Following the battleship group came TG.52.2, commanded by Rear Admiral Durgin. This was a carrier group that included *Sargent Bay, Natoma Bay, Wake Island, Petrof Bay, Steamer Bay, Makin Island, Lunga Point, Bismark Sea, Saginaw Bay* and *Rudyerd Bay*. In position, the carriers launched their first missions, eventually completing 158 sorties in this initial phase. The following day the carriers flew another 226 sorties, followed by a further 612 missions on 18 February.

At 02.00 hrs on 19 February 1945 the powerful 16-inch guns of the battleships USS *North Carolina, Washington* and *West Virginia* let loose the first salvoes that signalled the commencement of the invasion of Iwo Jima. Operation Detachment, the actual landings, would follow soon after when

TF.51, commanded by Vice-Admiral Turner, disembarked V Amphibious Corps commanded by Lieutenant-General H.T. Smith. Overall, TF.51 consisted of 495 ships. Even as the guns fell silent, more than forty USAAF B-24 Liberators from the 7th AAF then attacked the island, this being followed by another intense volley from the naval guns. Interspersed with the USAAF bomber attacks and the naval bombardments, the pressure on the Japanese was increased by attacks from the carrier air groups. Overall the carrier groups flew more than 600 missions during this phase. While the bombing and shelling was mostly accurate, it did not greatly damage the Japanese defences, as the majority were well fortified and protected from shelling. Most were in the shelter of Mount Suribachi, as the Japanese defenders had spent the months prior to the invasion creating an elaborate system of tunnels and firing positions that ran throughout the entire mountain. Most of the Japanese heavy artillery was concealed behind reinforced steel doors in massive chambers built inside the mountain, and these were nearly impenetrable to bombs and shells from the American air and naval bombardment.

At 08.59 the first of 30,000 Marines of the 3rd, 4th, and 5th Marine Divisions landed on the beach. This initial wave was not subject to Japanese defensive fire, as the plan by the Japanese commander was to hold fire until the beach was full of Marines and their equipment. Supporting the Marines were the carrier groups TG.58.1 and 58.4, the other two having pulled back for a much-needed refuel. It was only when the first wave of Marines reached the first line of Japanese bunkers that they took hostile fire. Many of the Japanese bunkers and firing positions were well concealed, and so the first wave of Marines suffered devastating losses from the Japanese machine-guns. Allied to the Japanese defences situated close to the beaches the Marines also faced heavy fire from the positions around Mount Suribachi to the south of the island. The Japanese defensive positions made it extremely difficult for the Marines to advance because of the inhospitable terrain, which consisted of volcanic ash. Close air support for the Marines was initially provided by fighters flying from the carriers cruising off the coast.

With the landing areas secured, more troops and heavy equipment were landed, and the invasion force proceeded north to capture the airfields and the remainder of the island. During the closing stages of the battle there was a kamikaze air attack by thirty-two aircraft on the ships anchored at sea on 21 February, which resulted in the sinking of the escort carrier USS *Bismarck Sea*, with the loss of 218 men. Severe damage was also caused to the USS *Saratoga*, which caused 123 deaths with 192 wounded, while slight damage was caused to the escort carrier USS *Lunga Point*, an LST and a transport vessel. The island was officially declared secure on 16 March, twenty-five days after the landings had begun, although the 5th Marine Division still faced some strong Japanese opposition from small pockets of troops and various stragglers. Of the 22,785 Japanese soldiers defending the island, 21,570 died, with only 216 being captured. The American forces suffered 26,038 casualties: 6,821 were killed in action, with the remainder being wounded.

Even as the fighting on Iwo Jima continued, the Americans gained control of the passage through the San Bernadino Strait between Samar and Luzon, allowing the Marine Corps to land on Samar and the smaller islands of Dalupiri, Capul and Buri. The capture of these islands was followed by those of Ticoa and Burias, these operations being completed by 3 April. Task Force 58 then switched its attention to mounting carrier aircraft attacks on airfields and other facilities around Tokyo in conjunction with the XXth AAF, which sent waves of Boeing B-29 bombers to the same destination. After two days of attempting to mount further raids, Vice-Admiral Mitscher decided to call off the attacks planned for 26 February against Nagoya and Kobe due to heavy seas, which made launching and recovery of aircraft impossible. Also, on the same date, the USAAF suffered a grievous loss when the aircraft carrying Lieutenant-General Millard F. Harmon disappeared while in the vicinity of the Marshall Islands, *en route* from Hawaii. General Harmon had been appointed Commanding General USAAF Pacific in late 1943.

Although the raids on Nagoya and Kobe had been cancelled, TF.58 turned its attention to the shore installations, airfields and shipping in the vicinity of Okinawa. These raids on 1 March succeeded in sinking fourteen Japanese vessels, although the carrier USS *Biloxi* was damaged by shore gunfire. TF.58 set out from Ulithi to undertake further raids on Japan, although the force would be without the carrier USS *Randolph*, which had been damaged by a Japanese kamikaze air raid on 11 March. As before, the carrier groups were the core of this task force, and so TG.58.1 consisted of the carriers *Hornet*,

After the war had ended, the USS Cabot would still remain in the operational fleet and would be operating Grumman aircraft. (US Navy/NARA via Dennis R. Jenkins)

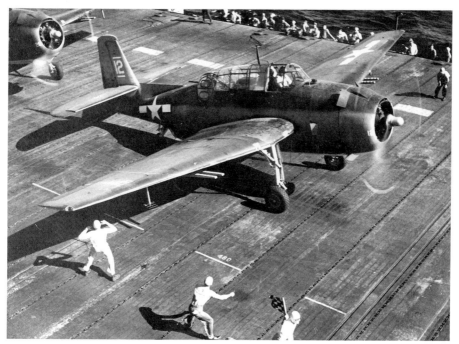

Surrounded by launch crew, a Grumman Avenger of VT-8 aboard the USS Bunker Hill prepares to depart on another sortie. Of note are the radar antennae under the outer wing panels. (US Navy/NARA via Dennis R. Jenkins)

Wasp, Bennington, Belleau Wood and *San Jacinto,* the battleships *Massachusetts,* and *Indiana,* and six cruisers and twenty destroyers, all under the command of Rear Admiral Clark. Accompanying TG.58.1 was TG.58.2, whose carriers included *Enterprise* and *Franklin,* plus a single cruiser and eight destroyers, all commanded by Rear Admiral Davison. The second full carrier group was TG.58.3, commanded by Rear Admiral Sherman. The carriers assigned to the group included the *Essex, Bunker Hill, Hancock, Cabot* and *Bataan,* with the battleships *Washington, North Carolina* and *South Dakota* and five cruisers and sixteen destroyers. The final full carrier group was TG.58.4, under the command of Rear Admiral Radford. Included in this group were the carriers *Yorktown, Intrepid, Langley* and *Independence,* plus the battleships *Wisconsin, Missouri* and *New Jersey,* the battlecruisers *Alaska* and *Guam,* and four cruisers and eighteen destroyers.

The fleet refuelled on 16 March, and as the US Navy had developed an excellent logistics supply train this process did not take unduly long. The American fleet train stretched all the way from the United States across the Pacific, and included oilers, repair ships, ammunition ships and escort carriers that carried a supply of spare aircraft to replenish the carriers of TF.58. Two days later, the carrier groups launched an all-out attack on Kyushu, concentrating on the airfields. However, some of the attackers did attack shipping in the area successfully, sinking six ships and damaging three more. In response the Japanese 5th Air Fleet, commanded by Vice-Admiral Ugaki, launched forty-eight kamikazes against the American carrier forces. While eighteen failed to find the targets, the remainder attacked the carriers of TG.58.4, during which the USS *Intrepid* was struck. While this caused a serious fire aboard the carrier, the crew managed to control and extinguish the blaze. The *Yorktown* and *Enterprise* suffered minor damage, although both were able to continue operations. On 19 March the TF.58 carrier groups concentrated on the Japanese bases in the Inland Sea, Kure being the primary target. In this harbour were the IJN carriers *Amagi, Katsuragi, Ryuho, Hosho, Kaiyo* and *Ikoma*. Also at Kure were the battleships *Yamato, Hyuga* and *Hurana*, two cruisers and three other naval vessels. All of the ships were damaged to some degree during these raids. The 5th Air Fleet launched another kamikaze counter-attack, during which the USS *Wasp* was struck and set on fire. Although the fire was quickly brought under control, 101 naval personnel were killed and a further 269 were wounded. Two kamikazes also hit the USS *Franklin*, nicknamed 'Big Ben', which was badly damaged by internal ammunition and bomb explosions that left 724 dead and 265 injured. Although the *Franklin* was badly damaged in the attack, the fires were soon quenched and the ship brought back under full control, and so Captain Gehres, with a

A flight of Curtiss Helldivers from VB-7 based on the USS Hancock begin their turn towards the carrier prior to landing. (US Navy/NARA via Dennis R. Jenkins)

With a few of its aircraft on the flight deck, the USS Natoma Bay heads towards the next target in the Pacific conflict. (US Navy/NARA via Dennis R. Jenkins)

destroyer escort, managed to sail the carrier to a dockyard for repairs. Initially the carrier was towed clear by the cruiser USS *Pittsburgh*, although the tow was cast off once the carrier was able to reach 14 knots under its own power. Temporary repairs were carried out at Ulithi, these being improved upon at Pearl Harbor. The USS *Franklin* finally docked at Brooklyn Navy Yard on 28 April for a full repair after a safe transit via the Panama Canal.

On 21 March the Japanese launched the greatest aerial attack to date when eighteen bombers carrying Ohkas – manned rocket-powered aircraft similar to the doodle bug – were dispatched. Also in this formation were fifty-five kamikazes with a fifteen-strong fighter escort. The radars aboard the task force quickly detected this incoming force, and launched 150 fighters to intercept them;, all bar one of the incoming aircraft were shot down. After this series of attacks, TF.58 withdrew for refuelling, and the carrier groups were redistributed to equalise each group for losses. The re-formed carrier groups were TG.58.1 with the *Hornet, Bennington, Belleau Wood* and *San Jacinto*, TG.58.3 with the *Essex, Bunker Hill, Hancock* (later replaced by the *Shangri La*) and *Bataan*, and TG.58.4 comprising the *Yorktown, Intrepid, Enterprise* and *Langley*. The damaged carriers, *Wasp* and *Franklin*, were accompanied to Ulithi by the carrier *Independence* and the battleships *Washington* and *North Carolina*, plus five cruisers.

On 23 March TF.58 began the preparatory phase for the invasion of Okinawa, when all three carrier groups undertook increased air attacks against the Japanese airfields and installations. These attacks continued over the next two days. Some of the carrier aircraft from TG.58.1 were diverted to attack a Japanese convoy, all of whose eight vessels were sunk in 112 sorties. TF.58 withdrew for refuelling over 27/28 March before returning to the

Although it looks in really bad shape, the USS Hancock, hit by a bomb on 19 March 1945, will later be repaired and rejoin the US Navy for further service. (US Navy/NARA via Dennis R. Jenkins)

combat zone, where the carriers launched further aerial attacks against Okinawa and the battleships resumed their bombardment duties against the same targets. These attacks continued relentlessly until the end of March. By this time Royal Navy carriers had joined the US Pacific Fleet as TF.57, their first task being to launch attacks against the Sakishima- Gunto group of islands at the southern end of the Ryukyus Islands.

Okinawa would again be the target when TG.52.1 arrived off the island to provide cover for TF.58 while it refuelled. Commanded by Rear Admiral Durgin, this task group was subdivided into three separate groups. Group 1 consisted of the escort carriers *Makin Island, Fanshaw Bay, Lunga Point, Sangamon, Natoma Bay, Savo Island* and *Anzio*, plus an escort of seventeen destroyers. Group 2 was commanded by Rear Admiral Stump, the escort carriers being *Saginaw Bay, Sargent Bay, Marcus Island, Petrof Bay, Tulagi* and *Wake Island*, plus an escort of ten destroyers. The third group, commanded by Rear Admiral Sample, included the *Suwanee, Chenango, Santee* and *Steamer Bay*, the escort comprising two destroyers. On 26 March, TF.54, the fire support group commanded by Rear Admiral Deyo, started to lay down a heavy barrage across Okinawa. The task force was divided into five groups. Group 1 comprised the battleships *Texas* and *Maryland*, plus a cruiser and four destroyers. Group 2 had the battleships *Arkansas* and *Colorado*, plus two cruisers and five destroyers. Group 3 had the battleships *Tennessee* and *Nevada* assigned, plus two cruisers and five destroyers. Group 4 comprised the battleships *Idaho* and *West Virginia*, with three cruisers and five destroyers. The final battleship group, No. 5, consisted of the battleships *New Mexico* and *New York*, plus two cruisers and five destroyers for escort purposes.

Seen from overhead is the IJN battleship Yamato, surrounded by the explosions of its defensive fire as carrier attack aircraft move in for the kill. The ship was sunk on 7 April 1945. (US Navy/NARA via Dennis R. Jenkins)

To counter the obvious goals of the Americans, the Japanese ordered the implementation of Operation Tengo – the defence of Okinawa and South Japan. Activated on 25 March, the air formations of the 3rd and 10th Naval Air Fleets were placed under the command of Vice-Admiral Ugaki, whose 5th Air Fleet was based on Kyushu. The first kamikaze attack was launched in the early hours of 25 March, during which four US Navy ships were damaged. The next attack took place in the evening of the following day, when eleven kamikazes managed to obtain hits on the battleships, a cruiser and three destroyers. Even with these interruptions, TF.54 continued to shell its assigned targets, although the fleet was subject to another kamikaze attack, during which two of the smaller US Navy vessels were damaged. In response to these attacks the Americans concentrated upon hitting the airfields and explosive boat bases. Further kamikazes were launched against the fleet on 30 March, during which the flagship of Admiral Spruance, the USS *Indianapolis*, was hit, which forced the Admiral to transfer his flag to the battleship USS *New Mexico*.

On 1 April 1945 Operation Iceberg began as 1,213 ships brought thousands of troops to begin the invasion of Okinawa. Even as this mighty armada approached, the battleship task forces continued to bombard the island. The landings went as planned, meeting little resistance, as the Japanese 2nd Army, commanded by Lieutenant-General Ushijama, had entrenched its forces in the southern mountain terrain. On the evening of the invasion the fleet was assaulted by kamikazes and rocket-powered Ohka powered bombs that damaged the battleship *West Virginia* and seven other vessels. The invasion of

163

Okinawa had political ramifications in Japan, as the Premier, General Koiso, was forced to resign, being replaced by Admiral Suzuki, the former having promised to recapture Iwo Jima. Over 6/7 April the Japanese launched a kamikaze attack known as Operation Kikusui 1 against the invasion and fire support fleets. Other groups of aircraft attacked the carrier groups TG.58.1 and 58.3 situated north-east of Okinawa, and TF.57 south of the island, although the escort carriers of TG.52 to the east were not affected. The Japanese attack, consisting of 198 aircraft, damaged twenty-seven ships to some degree, while three destroyers and three ammunition supply vessels were sunk. The defending American fighters shot down fifty-five aircraft, while a further thirty-five were downed by the anti-aircraft barrage from the fleet. Of the ammunition vessels, the *Logan Victory*, hit by a kamikaze, and carrying 7,000 tons of ammunition, exploded after the hit, while the *Hobbs Victory* was abandoned, later exploding, on 7 April.

The Japanese subsequently launched an even larger kamikaze force, consisting of fifty-four naval and 125 army pilots, that attacked the American fleet. Although the majority of the attacking aircraft were downed by the fighter cover and a curtain of anti-aircraft fire, a few managed to slip through. The battleship *Maryland* and a destroyer were damaged, as was the carrier *Hancock*, while other smaller vessels were damaged to some extent. The damage to the *Hancock* was limited, and so the carrier was able to resume operations almost immediately. The Japanese would make one further naval effort to drive the Americans away from their shores. This force consisted of the battleship *Yamato*, a cruiser and an extensive array of destroyers, all running on fuel scavenged from various sources. Unfortunately for the IJN, its

Surrounded by deck crews, these Grumman F6Fs of VF-45 are prepared for their next sorties aboard the USS San Jacinto. (US Navy/NARA via Dennis R. Jenkins)

The USS Chenango played a prominent part in the Pacific campaign, although it would be quickly retired at the end of the war. (US Navy/NARA via Dennis R. Jenkins)

ships movements were quickly spotted by US submarines and Boeing B-29s. Further confirmation of the IJN movements were made by Catalina flying-boats and aircraft dispatched from carrier groups TG.58.1 and 58.3 to shadow the ships. By mid-morning the carrier attack groups struck at the Japanese ships, with the *Yamato* being struck by two bombs and a torpedo, while two destroyers were sunk. A further attack took place in mid-afternoon, when the *Yamato* was hit by further bombs and torpedoes, which caused the vessel to sink, with the loss of 2,498 lives. The aerial attack force also sank three destroyers, while the few remaining destroyers limped away, some badly damaged.

TF.58 would return to the fray on 8 April, by now consisting of four carrier task groups, all under the command of Vice-Admiral Mitscher. TG.58.1, commanded by Rear Admiral Clark, consisted of the carriers *Hornet*, *Bennington*, *Belleau Wood* and *San Jacinto*, the battleships *Massachusetts* and *Indiana*, plus four cruisers and a dozen destroyers. TG.58.2 had the carriers *Randolph*, *Enterprise* and *Independence* assigned, plus the battleships *Washington* and *North Carolina*, while the escort was provided by four cruisers and a dozen or more destroyers, all commanded by Vice-Admiral Bogan. TG.58.3, commanded by Rear Admiral Sherman, had the carriers *Essex*, *Bunker Hill* and *Bataan*, with the battleships *New Jersey* and *South Dakota*, plus four cruisers and a large force of destroyers. The last task group, TG.58.4, consisted of the carriers *Yorktown*, *Intrepid* and *Langley*, with the battleships *Wisconsin* and *Missouri* and the battlecruisers *Alaska* and *Guam*, while the escort included a single cruiser and a large number of destroyers. In order to

Fire crews fight the flames aboard the USS Intrepid after the carrier has been hit by a kamikaze. Once the fire had been dealt with the carrier was quickly made ready for operations again. (US Navy/NARA via Dennis R. Jenkins)

apply continuous pressure on the Japanese defenders, two carrier groups remained on station while another was refuelling and another was in transit. On 8 and 9 April an American carrier group, TG.52.1, under the command of Rear Admiral Sample and comprising the carriers *Suwanee*, *Chenango*, *Santee* and *Rudyerd Bay*, stood in for the Royal Navy Task Force 57, to continue its task of suppressing the Japanese on the Sakishima-Gunto Islands. TF.57 returned to station on 11 April, being replaced by TG.52.1 on 14 April. During much of May 1945, TF.57, commanded by Vice-Admiral Vian RN, alternated with TG.52.1.3 and its carriers *Sangamon*, *Suwanee*, *Chenango* and *Santee*, in mounting aerial attacks against the Sakishima-Gunto Islands. During this period the carrier USS *Sangamon* was badly damaged by a kamikaze hit. As the *Sangamon* was unable to continue in action, the escort carrier limped away from the combat zone, becoming one of the earliest strikes from the Navy List, as it was deemed too expensive to repair.

On 11 April sixty-four kamikazes were dispatched to attack TF.58, and the carrier *Enterprise*, the battleship *Missouri* and two destroyers were hit. The following day a further 140 kamikazes were launched as Operation Kikusi 2. Flying with the attackers was a strong fighter escort, the kamikazes gaining their first success against three destroyers, which were sunk. Damage was caused to the *Essex* and the battleships *Tennessee* and *Idaho*, while another twenty-two smaller vessels were also damaged, although many of the attackers were shot down by the defending fighters. Two days later another kamikaze attack damaged the battleship *New York* and four smaller vessels. TF.58 and its four carrier groups continued their operations around Okinawa during 15 and 16 April. These missions involved fighter sweeps over Kyushu, followed by bombing raids on the same area. Over the next ten days the carrier groups continued a rolling assault on the island, with a minimum of two groups being in operation at any one time. These rolling sorties were disrupted on 16 April when the Japanese launched Operation Kikusi 3 with 126 aircraft, followed by a further forty-nine; they hit the carrier USS *Intrepid*, the battleship USS *Missouri* and a destroyer. The *Intrepid* suffered severe fire damage to the hangar deck and the flight deck, which saw the carrier withdrawn from the battle for major repair work. With the *Intrepid* withdrawn, the remaining carriers were redistributed, and so TG.58.2 was disbanded, leaving TG.58.1, 58.3 and 58.4.

While much of TF.58 was concentrating on Okinawa, an amphibious group commanded by Rear Admiral Reifsnider would land the 77th Infantry Division on the small island of Ie Shima. Although the defenders resisted strongly, they were defeated, and so the 77th was quickly redeployed to Okinawa. While the 77th waited its chance, the TF.58 carrier groups would undertake attacks on the Japanese Divisions defending the Shuri defensive line on Okinawa. Over the period 18/19 April, over 650 missions were flown against these positions. Assisting in the breaking of this line were the battleships *Texas*, *Arkansas*, *Colorado*, *Idaho*, *New Mexico* and *New York*, which laid down an intensive barrage, assisted by six cruisers and eight destroyers. By 23 April the Japanese had pulled back from this first line of defence after suffering heavy losses. Assisting the main fleet in destroying the Japanese strongholds was TG.52.1, which included the escort carriers *Suwanee*, *Sangamon*, *Chenango* and *Santee*, whose assigned task was to attack the Ryuku Islands and northern Formosa, after which they would switch their attention to the Olin, Diato and Shima Island group to the east of Okinawa.

With TG.58.2 no longer in action, only TG.58.3 and 58.4 continued their rolling attacks over Okinawa, relieving each other for refuelling. As for TG.58.1, it had returned to Ulithi for a period of rest and recuperation, arriving there on 28 April and remaining until 8 May. TG.52.1.3, operating off Sakishima-Gunto, was also relieved by TG.52.1.1, whose carriers were the *Makin Island*, *Fanshaw Bay*, *Lunga Point* and *Salamaua*. While the carrier groups were being reshuffled, the Japanese were still relying on the kamikaze attacks to get them out of trouble, and so on 28 April Operation Kikusui 4 was launched, utilising more than 120 aircraft. Although none of the capital ships were damaged, seventeen smaller vessels were put out of action.

TF.58 resumed operations against Okinawa between 3 and 29 May. Initially the assigned carrier groups were TG.58.3, with the carriers *Essex*, *Bunker Hill*, *Shangri-La* and *Bataan*, and TG.58.4, with the carriers *Yorktown*, *Intrepid*, *Enterprise* and *Langley*. Other carriers in the area were assigned to the 5th Fleet Supply Train, including the *Attu*, *Admiralty Islands*, *Bougainville* and *Windham Bay*, while air support was provided by the escort carriers *Shamrock Bay* and *Makassar Strait*, with thirty-five destroyers looking after the entire group. Departing Ulithi on 8 May, TG.58.1, with the carriers *Hornet*, *Bennington*, *Randolph*, *Belleau Wood* and *San Jacinto*, arrived two days later to relieve TG.58.4, which in turn sailed for Ulithi. Unfortunately for the USS *Enterprise*,

Fire crews spray vulnerable aircraft aboard the light carrier USS Belleau Wood after it had suffered a kamikaze strike. (US Navy/NARA via Dennis R. Jenkins)

it had to remain with TF.58, as it was the only carrier configured specially for night operations.

A large kamikaze attack on 11 May caused serious damage to the carrier *Bunker Hill*, one aircraft striking the after flight deck, where the parked aircraft created such an intense fire that it buckled the after lift, while the other crashed near the island, causing extensive fires throughout the ship. After much bravery by the crew, the fires were brought under control and the *Bunker Hill* was withdrawn from action, being escorted across the Pacific to be repaired. The loss of life was extensive, with 392 being killed and a further 264 being wounded. The repairs lasted until July, although the carrier would see no further service during the war. Those vessels that could be restored quickly were repaired by specialist vessels situated in the Kerama Roads, which enabled the task force to maintain its operational strength.

Towards the end of May TF.58 would concentrate on the greatest menace, the kamikaze airfields. Raids launched on 24 May were concentrated on the airfields at Kyushu, during which many aircraft were destroyed on the ground, while a flight of Ohka bombers were destroyed just as they were preparing to take off from Kanoya. TF.58 was also starting to send smaller units to attack lesser but important targets, and so on 17 May TU.12.5.3, commanded by Rear Admiral C.A.F. Sprague, was ordered to attack the Japanese-held islands of Taroa and Maloelap in the Marshalls group. To that end the carrier USS *Ticonderoga* with an escort of three destroyers launched aerial attacks against their designated targets without loss.

Over 27/28 May Admiral Spruance handed over command of the 5th Fleet to Admiral Halsey, the command being renamed the 3rd Fleet, and at the same time Vice-Admiral McCain replaced Vice-Admiral Mitscher, and so TF.58 became TF.38. This was intended to rest the senior commanders before they re-entered the fray at a later date. TF.38 continued the task started by TF.58, the aerial assault on Okinawa. Admiral Halsey had raised his flag on the '*Mighty Mo*', while Vice-Admiral McCain had raised his on the Essex-class carrier USS *Shangri La*. As before, two carrier groups alternated in providing aerial defence over the fleet, plus attack aircraft when needed. As TG.38.2 had departed to Leyte for rest and repairs, the other two, TG.38.1 and TG.38.4, remained available. TG.38.1 had remained off Okinawa to support the fleet while TG.38.4 made a further attack on the kamikaze airfields on Kyushu over 2/3 June, using the carriers *Shangri La*, *Ticonderoga*, *Yorktown*, *Langley* and *Independence*, the missions being carried out with minimal losses. TG.38.1 was not so lucky, as a storm building up near the Philippines hit the ships of the task force on 5 June, after confused reporting had unfortunately failed to confirm the direction of the storm. All of the ships in this formation suffered damage to a greater or lesser extent, the worst being the cruiser USS *Pittsburgh*, which lost 100 feet of its bows. TG.38.4 was luckier, being able to retire to the north, although the *Missouri* suffered some light damage.

Once the storm had passed, the remaining ships undertook a refuel on 6 June before resuming operations the following day. TG.38.1 launched missions over Okinawa, with the new carrier USS *Bon Homme Richard* entering the fray instead of the *Bennington*, which had suffered some damage during the earlier storm. After leaving the combat zone, this Essex-class carrier

With the destroyers USS Charles S. Perry and Wilkes-Barre alongside, providing support, the crew of the USS Bunker Hill fight the fires caused by a kamikaze hit. (US Navy/NARA via Dennis R. Jenkins)

Now experiencing quieter times, the flight deck of the USS Essex has a full complement of Vought F4Us undergoing maintenance. (US Navy/NARA via Dennis R. Jenkins)

would be withdrawn for repairs. At the completion of the Okinawa raids TG.38.1 launched an attack on Olin Adit Shima on 9 June, using napalm bombs. Assisting the aerial attack was a bombardment laid down by the battlecruisers *Alaska* and *Guam* and their five destroyer escorts. At the conclusion of these raids the entire TF.38 departed to its new forward operating base at Leyte, arriving on 13 June after three months of continuous operations.

Over 21/22 June the ground fighting on Okinawa came to an end with the suicides of the Japanese commander, Lieutenant-General Ushijama, Commander 32nd Army, and his Chief of Staff Major-General Ho. During the fighting more than 130,000 Japanese soldiers and 42,000 civilians were killed, while nearly 11,000 were captured. On the American side the US Army lost more than 7,500, with more than 31,000 wounded, while the US Navy suffered nearly 5,000 dead and a similar number wounded. Ship losses for the US Navy totalled thirty-six sunk and 368 damaged. Aircraft losses were 763 for the US forces, while Japanese losses were nearly 8,000.

After a short period in Leyte, TF.38 would depart on 1 July, its primary task being to mount aerial attacks on the Japanese home islands. Only three carrier

170

Another swarm of Grumman F6F Hellcats assigned to VF-1 aboard the USS Yorktown are prepared for another sortie. (US Navy/NARA via Dennis R. Jenkins)

task groups were available, the first being TG.38.1, under the command of Rear Admiral T.L. Sprague. The ships in this group included the carriers *Bennington, Lexington, Hancock, Belleau Wood* and *San Jacinto*, the battleships *Indiana, Massachusetts* and *Alabama*, plus five cruisers and eighteen destroyers. The second group, TG.38.3, commanded by Rear Admiral Bogan, consisted of the carriers *Ticonderoga, Randolph, Essex, Monterey* and *Bataan,* with the battleships *South Dakota* and *North Carolina,* and five cruisers and seventeen destroyers. The final group was TG.38.4, commanded by Rear Admiral Radford, in whose force were the carriers *Yorktown, Shangri La, Bon Homme Richard, Independence* and *Cowpens,* while the assigned battleships were the *Iowa, Missouri* and *Wisconsin,* with five cruisers and nineteen destroyers. After a pre-strike replenishment over 7/8 July, the carrier groups launched over 1,000 missions to attack the airfields around Tokyo on 10 July. A refuelling break took place on 12 July, although the attacks scheduled for the following day were cancelled due to bad weather. A further attack was launched on 14 July, involving over 1,300 sorties, the targets being in the Honshu and Hokkaido areas, together with shipping traffic in the Tsugaru Strait. During

Captured during a more peaceful moment, the fighters of VF-1 are prepared for their next mission aboard the USS Yorktown. (US Navy/NARA via Dennis R. Jenkins)

the attacks on shipping, six naval ships and thirty-seven merchant vessels were sunk and a further forty-one ships were damaged. A further raid took place on 17/18 July, using a combined force of USN and RN carriers. The fighter suppression force completely negated the Japanese air defences and the anti-aircraft guns. This allowed the bombers from the USS *Yorktown* to attack the battleship *Nagato* and put it out of action, while a further three ships were sunk and a further five were damaged. While the aircraft carriers were undertaking their raids, the major naval units were shelling targets around Tokyo and other areas, this being followed up by further aerial attacks on 19 July, when aircraft from TF.38 badly damaged the new IJN carriers *Amagi* and *Katsuragi* and the battleship *Haruna*. The entire task force withdrew out to sea on 19 July due to the threat of an incoming typhoon.

While TF.38 was attacking the Japanese home islands, TF.95, commanded by Vice-Admiral Oldendorf, was operating in the vicinity of Okinawa, providing radar pickets to counter sorties being mounted by enemy aircraft and ships. The first major operation by this force took place over 26–28 July against Japanese forces in the Yangtse estuary off Shanghai. Within this task

172

A VF-8 Grumman F6F Hellcat is cleared for take-off from the USS Intrepid by the deck crew. Note the lack of tail insignia that would be applied during a lull in operations. (US Navy/NARA via Dennis R. Jenkins)

force were the battlecruisers *Alaska* and *Guam*, the battleships *Nevada*, *Tennessee* and *California*, the escort carriers *Makin Island*, *Lunga Point* and *Cape Gloucester*, and four cruisers and eighteen destroyers. A further raid between 1 and 7 August was mounted against shipping in the East China Sea and against targets in the Tinghai region.

While major operations against Japan and Germany continued, the Potsdam conference, Terminal, involving President Truman, Josef Stalin and Winston Churchill took place. Not only did the leaders discuss the future of Germany and the further prosecution of the war against Japan, but the upshot of this meeting was the issuing of a declaration on 27 July requiring Japan to surrender unconditionally. However, the Japanese government decided to ignore this request, and so President Truman authorised the dropping of the first atomic bomb on Japan.

While the Allied leaders were at Potsdam, the US Navy was carrying out

The fate of many a Japanese Navy aircraft carrier close to the end of the war: the stricken Amagi lies heeled right over after being hit by American bombers while docked at Kure. (US Navy/NARA via Dennis R. Jenkins)

raids on the few remaining enemy strongholds in the Pacific outside Japan. Many of these were carried out by ships returning for active service with TF.38. The first target was the Wake Island garrison, which was attacked by the carrier USS *Wasp* on 18 July as it was proceeding in company with four cruisers and seven destroyers to the Pacific war zone. All these vessels joined TF.38 on 22 July. This initial raid was followed by another on 1 August by the USS *Cabot*, while the USS *Intrepid* did the same on 8 August.

To support the US Navy attacks against China and Japan, one of the largest fleet trains was assembled as Task Group 30.8 commanded by Rear Admiral Beatty aboard the command cruiser USS *Detroit*, this being supported by the escort carriers *Chenango*, *Thetis Bay*, *Hollandia*, *Roi*, *Munda* and *Gilbert Islands*, plus fifteen tankers, five ammunition ships and four supply freighters. During the period between the end of July and the end of the second week in August this group dispensed 60,000 tons of fuel oil, a similar amount of aviation fuel, over 6,000 tons of ammunition, nearly 2,000 tons of supplies, ninety-nine replacement aircraft and 412 replacement personnel to both TF.38 and TF.37 of the Royal Navy.

Much of the supply material dispensed by TG.30.8 was utilised against targets around the Inland Sea. The first raids were launched against the harbours at Kobe and Kure. During the 1,700+ sorties launched on 24 July, the carrier aircraft sank the IJN carrier *Amagi* and a cruiser, while three battleships were badly damaged, as were the carriers *Katsuragi*, *Ryuho* and *Hosho*. Further damage was caused to six destroyers and five other naval vessels, while fifteen merchant vessels were also sunk. After this attack the Allied forces refuelled from TG.30.8, resuming their raids on 28 July. These finished off many of the ships previously damaged, and a further three vessels were sunk. Kobe was the next target for the Allies on 30 July, when ten vessels were sunk and a further eight were damaged. On 1 August the combined task forces withdrew for refuelling, this break lasting for seven days.

Although TF.38 had withdrawn for refuelling, TG.95.2 was in the East China Sea to undertake anti-shipping strikes off Shanghai. The primary force consisted of the battlecruisers *Alaska* and *Guam*, plus four cruisers and nine destroyers, while the covering force was provided by TG.95.3, with three battleships, three escort carriers, two cruisers and nine destroyers. TG.38 was back in action on 9 August in company with TG.37 of the Royal Navy, and the first targets for all four groups were northern Honshu and Hokkaido, where 251 Japanese aircraft were destroyed. A further carrier raid took place the following day against the airfields and railways of northern Honshu, and other aircraft sank fifteen ships and damaged a further three. A replenishment break took place over 11/12 August for both task forces, this being followed by further attacks against airfields in the Tokyo area, during which 254 Japanese aircraft were destroyed on the ground and a further eighteen were destroyed in the air.

On 6 August 1945 the Boeing B-29 Superfortress 'Enola Gay', commanded by Colonel Paul Tibbets, assigned to the 509th Composite Group of the XXth AAF, dropped the first usable atom bomb 'Little Boy' on Hiroshima, resulting in widespread devastation of the city and causing over 92,000 deaths and

The battleship Haruna sits sunk up to its gunnels at Kure after being hit by American bombers. Although the vessel was incapable of putting to sea, enough worked for the ship to be used as an anti-aircraft platform. (US Navy/NARA via Dennis R. Jenkins)

37,500 injured from the population. A second weapon, 'Fat Man', was dropped by the B-29 'Bockscar', commanded by Major Sweeney USAAF, on 9 August on the city of Nagasaki. This bomb caused the deaths of at least 40,000 persons, with another 60,000 injured. The final death toll, including those caused by radioactive fall-out and radiation, would approach 200,000. While the use of such weapons has always raised controversy, the American decision to use such bombs was approved by the President and the Joint Chiefs of Staff as a rapid way of ending a war that would have probably caused greater Japanese casualties had the Allies been forced to invade or bomb the Japanese into a surrender posture. Also, by this time the IJN was either sunk or so badly damaged as to be ineffective, while the Army losses and the inability to mount effective aerial attacks had rendered the Japanese forces almost useless. At long last the Japanese would accept the terms of the Potsdam declaration. In response the Allies would appoint General of the Army Douglas MacArthur to accept the surrender and to oversee the subsequent occupation of Japan. Although the official war on Japan was declared over on 15 August, TF.38 still mounted a last carrier strike against the Tokyo area, meeting heavy opposition in the process. A second strike planned for that afternoon was later cancelled. Two days after the surrender, General Prince Higashikuni was named as the new Prime Minister of Japan.

Although the main Japanese forces had surrendered, their forces in China remained active until 19 August before officially surrendering. Two days later Captain Grow USN accepted the surrender of Japanese forces on Mille Atoll in the Marshall Islands. Meanwhile, in Japan, TF.38 was fully occupied in supplying aerial patrols over the home islands, their purpose being to control shipping, road and rail movements, and where possible locate any prisoner-of-war camps. The first aircraft to land on Japanese soil touched down at Atsugi on 28 August, the airfield being declared safe two days later, and so General MacArthur arrived to assume his new role. On 27 August the US 3rd

The USS Missouri steams towards Tokyo Bay in company with the biggest naval fleet ever assembled, prior to accepting the Japanese surrender. (US Navy/NARA via Dennis R. Jenkins)

With its deck lined by interested personnel, the Japanese surrender is signed in accordance with the Potsdam Directive. (US Navy/NARA via Dennis R. Jenkins)

Fleet under the command of Admiral Halsey sailed into Sagami Bay off Tokyo. This was a massive force, which comprised twenty-three fleet and escort carriers, twenty-four battleships, twenty-five cruisers, over a hundred destroyers and numerous other vessels. Further Japanese surrenders took place at the end of August, including Truk, the Marcus Islands and Ominato on the northern tip of Honshu. The formal surrender of all Japanese forces was signed aboard the USS *Missouri*, *'The Mighty Mo'*, on 2 September. The signatories were the foreign affairs minister Mamoru Shigemitsu for Japan, and General Richard K. Sutherland US Army for the Allies.

Further surrenders followed: on 2 September the forces on the Palau Islands officially downed their weapons, being followed by the Carolines and the Marianas on 4 September, while the remaining forces would finally acknowledge the official cease-fire by the end of October. The official occupation of Japan, Operation Blacklist, began on 2 September, being fully in place by 22 October. With the cessation of hostilities there was a need to return the American servicemen and women to the United States, and so Operation Magic Carpet was activated. Prior to this starting, a priority return sailing was initiated using TF.11 commanded by Vice-Admiral Sherman, utilising the battleships *New Mexico*, *Idaho*, *Mississippi* and *North Carolina*, plus the carriers

The USS Tarawa was one of the last of the Essex class to be commissioned. Seen on its flight deck are the Curtiss Helldivers of VB-4, complete with immediate post-war markings. (US Navy/NARA via Dennis R. Jenkins)

Monterey and *Bataan*, supplemented by a dozen destroyers. The vessels involved in Magic Carpet were designated TG.16.12, under the command of Rear Admiral Kendall, and originally consisted of eight escort carriers, although this soon expanded to a total of 369 ships, which included six battleships, eleven fleet carriers, forty-six escort carriers and twelve hospital ships. By March 1946 over one million personnel had been returned home by ship, while further troops had been flown home. The largest single quota of personnel carried by a single vessel was that of the carrier USS *Saratoga*, which managed to ship over 29,000 servicemen home. Although most of the US forces would return home, a sufficient number would remain on Japanese soil to administer the surrender. The ending of the war in the Pacific would also see great changes applied to the US Navy, which was at its greatest strength by the end of the war.

CHAPTER SEVEN

Police Action in Korea

I n a similar manner to the other Allied nations, the United States' armed
forces would undergo a period of serious contraction after 1945. The Axis
nations, on the other hand, had little left to disperse, as the German and
Japanese fleets were almost destroyed, while the Italian Navy was destined to
be divided between the victors and scrapped.

As for the US Navy, it too would see a serious contraction of its strength,
not only in vessels, but in manpower as well. With the massive reduction of
the latter, due to most being 'hostilities only' personnel, there were not
enough sea and air crews to maintain such a large carrier fleet, nor was there
a perceived need for it in the immediate future, although the attitude and
expansion plans of the Soviet Union, an erstwhile ally, were giving rise to
concern.

Of the remaining hardware, the elderly USS *Saratoga* was deemed life
expired after its war exertions, and the carrier was also struggling to cope
with the larger aircraft entering service. As this was before the days of the
memorial and preservation societies, the *Saratoga* was expended as a target at
Bikini Atoll atomic bomb test on 25 July 1946. Thus was lost the chance to
preserve one of the early steps in American naval aviation. Of the Yorktown
class, only the USS *Enterprise* had survived the war. At close of play the
Enterprise was fully equipped with the latest radar sets, including the CXAM-
1, SC-2, SP and fire-control set Mk 4. Other modifications had included the
lengthening of the flight deck and the fitment of hull bulges to improve
protection and improve stability. As with all such vessels subject to kamikaze
attacks, the edge of the flight deck fairly bristled with weaponry. The
Enterprise had been in the dockyard at the end of the war after a kamikaze hit
had blown the forward lift completely out of alignment. Although fully
repaired and redesignated as an anti-submarine carrier, *CVS-6*, the *Enterprise*
would not re-enter service, being placed in the reserve. The carrier entered the
New York Naval Shipyard on 18 January 1946 for deactivation, being fully

decommissioned on 17 February 1947. In 1946 the *Enterprise* had been scheduled for handing over to the state of New York as a permanent memorial. However, this plan was suspended in 1949. Although further attempts were made at preserving the ship, fund-raising efforts were unsuccessful, and so the '*Big E*' was sold in July 1958 to the Lipsett Corporation of New York City for scrapping at Kearny, New Jersey.

The *Independence* class of light carriers, based on the hulls of Cleveland-class cruisers, would have mixed fortunes after the war. Of the nine vessels commissioned, eight had survived their Pacific experiences, and those destined for post-war operational service were seen purely as fighter carriers, as they were considered too small for the larger types. The intended aircraft complement was forty-eight Grumman F8F Bearcats, although none of the class ever put to sea with this configuration. The USS *Independence* would be used as a peripheral target at Bikini, after which the carrier was formally decommissioned in August 1946. Over the following five years the *Independence* was used as a weapons trials ship before being sunk as a target in February 1951. The *Cowpens* was formally deactivated in January 1947, being redesignated as an auxiliary aircraft transport, *AVT-1*, in May 1959, although it was removed from the Navy List in November, being sold for scrap two years later. The *Monterey* was one of the few Independence class to see significant post-war service. Decommissioned in February 1947, the carrier was reactivated in September 1950 for use as a training carrier by NAS Pensacola in support of Korea operations. After five years in this role the *Monterey* entered the reserve, being redesignated *AVT-2* in 1959. The carrier remained swinging at anchor at Philadelphia until sold for scrapping in 1971. It would be the USS *Langley* that would have an extended second career. Having been decommissioned in January 1947, after completing a refit the

The final single-engined fighter that Grumman delivered to the US Navy was the F8F Bearcat. (US Navy/NARA via Dennis R. Jenkins)

carrier was loaned to the French Navy in January 1951 as the *Lafayette*. The *Langley* returned to the United States in 1963, being sold immediately for scrap. The USS *Cabot* would also have a second career with another navy – in this case Spain. Having been decommissioned in February 1947, the *Cabot* was returned to service in October 1948 for training duties, this continuing until 1955 in support of Korea operations. Withdrawn after this period, the carrier was reclassified as *AVT-3* in May 1959, remaining in the reserve until lent to Spain in August 1967 as the *Dedalo*. The Spanish Navy would purchase the carrier outright in 1972, the vessel remaining in service until withdrawn in 1988. The *Bataan* was also placed in reserve in 1947, but would be reactivated in mid-1950 for Korean war duties, the only one of this class to take an active part in this conflict. Withdrawn again in 1954, the vessel was reclassified as *AVT-4* in May 1959, although it was struck off the Navy List in September, being sold for scrap in 1960. The *San Jacinto* would see no post-war service, being completely deactivated in January 1947. Although redesignated as *AVT-5* in 1959, the carrier was struck from the Navy List in early 1970, being sold for scrap that same year.

It was the escort, or jeep, carriers that disappeared from the service of the US Navy very quickly at the war's end. The Sangamon class saw the name ship scrapped in 1948, while the *Suwannee*, *Chenango* and *Santee* were placed in reserve in 1946. All three were reclassified as CVHE for helicopter operations in 1955, although they were removed from the Navy List in 1959, being sold for scrap the following year. Of the eleven Bogue class, only the USS *Block Island* had been lost during war service, while the others had mixed fortunes. Most of the class were placed in reserve by the end of 1946, being redesignated as helicopter escort carriers, CVHE, in 1955, although most were scrapped in 1960, having seen no further usage. Carriers known to have suffered this fate included the *Bogue*, *Copahee*, *Nassau*, *Altamaha*, *Barnes*, *Breton* and *Prince William*. Of the others, the USS *Card* also entered the reserve in 1946, although the ship was reactivated in 1958 as an aircraft transport, this being followed by service in a similar role during the Vietnam War. During this period the *Card* struck a mine in Saigon Harbour in May 1964. The vessel was raised and repaired, returning to the reserve afterwards, although it was struck from the Navy List in 1970 and sold for scrap. The USS *Core* was also another carrier resurrected for transport use by the Maritime Sea Transportation Service in July 1958, although it is highly unlikely that the carrier was used in this role, as it was sold for scrap in 1970. The USS *Breton* also entered the reserve in 1946 before being recommissioned again by the MSTS in 1958. After returning to the reserve, the carrier was sold for scrapping in 1970. As with the rest of the Bogue class, the USS *Croatan* entered the reserve in 1946. The carrier was reactivated in June 1958 and assigned to MSTS in a non-commissioned status, being manned by a civilian crew. In August 1963 the *Croatan* was used to transport twenty-three F-104 Starfighters on delivery to the Royal Norwegian Air Force. In October 1964 the vessel served as an experimental ship under NASA control until May 1965. The purpose of the NASA deployment was to launch Nike-Cajun and Nike-Apache sounding rockets, these being carried on launchers each side of the deck elevator. The rest of the flight deck was covered by trailers holding telemetry and guidance equipment. The *Croatan* was struck from the Navy List in September 1970 and sold for scrap in 1971.

One of the largest classes of escort carriers was the Casablanca class, which consisted of fifty vessels. Of this total five were sunk in action, these being the *Liscombe Bay, St. Lo, Gambier Bay, Bismark Bay* and *Ommaney Bay*. Of the others, the *Wake Island, Solomons, Kalinin Bay, Kitkun Bay, Makin Island, Salamaua, Admiralty Islands, Attu* and *Roi* were all withdrawn from use at the end of the war, being sold for scrap the following year. The remaining vessels were placed in reserve as CVHE for helicopter duties in 1958, although most were struck from the Navy List from 1959 onwards, the last going in 1966. A handful did find other uses, however. The *Corregidor* was taken over by the MSTS for Korean War transport duties, although the carrier's career ended in 1958, and it was finally decommissioned in 1960. The *Thetis Bay* had a much more adventurous post-war career, as it was converted to be the first amphibious assault ship in the US Navy. By now designated CVHA, the *Thetis Bay* was recommissioned in July 1956, being deployed with both the Atlantic and Pacific fleets. The experience gained from the *Thetis Bay* led to the development of the Iwo Jima and Tarawa class of assault vessels. The USS *Thetis Bay* was finally struck from the Navy List and scrapped in 1966. The *Makassar Strait* also had a post-war career. However, it was destined to be used as a target for Tartar and Terrier missiles to see how well they performed as ship-to-ship weapons. Eventually this mistreatment caused the rather ragged carrier to sink in 1962.

The final escort carrier class was the Commencement Bay class, consisting of nineteen ships. Few of these carriers entered the reserve for any length of time as most had post-war careers. Of those that did retire most were re-designated as helicopter escort carriers in 1955, the ships involved being the class name ship, the *Cape Gloucester, Vella Gulf, Puget Sound, Bairoko, Rabaul, Palau* and *Tinian*. Others of the class were employed as anti-submarine carriers, due to the fleet carriers being heavily employed in the Korean War. Carriers employed in this role included the *Kula Gulf, Salerno Bay, Siboney, Rendova, Badeong Strait, Sicily, Point Cruz* and *Mindoro*. The *Badeong Strait* had been utilised as the development ship for the remainder of the class in the ASW role, although all of these vessels had been retired by 1955. It was the USS *Gilbert Islands* that had the most varied career of the class. Although placed in reserve after the war, the carrier was recommissioned in 1951 for transport duties during the Korean War before retiring again in 1955. After six years awaiting disposal, the carrier was chosen for conversion to become a Major Communications Relay Ship, *AGMR-1*, being recommissioned in March 1964 as the USS *Annapolis*. The newly renamed ship remained in service until finally withdrawn at the end of 1969, having served from 1965. The *Gilbert Islands/Annapolis* was finally removed from the Navy List in

October 1976. In contrast, the *Kula Gulf*, after its period as an ASW vessel, returned to the reserve, although it would return to sea for use a transport during the Vietnam War under MSTS auspices. The *Kula Bay* was removed from the Navy List in September 1970. The USS *Rendova* also had a post-war career, being used in the training, transport and ASW role before being sold for scrap in 1971. The *Point Cruz* was also a busy ship, for not only was it used in the ASW role during the Korean War, but it was reactivated during the Vietnam conflict for use in the transport role. After this final wartime adventure, the carrier was again placed in the reserve, being sold for scrap in 1970.

The retirement of the venerable *Saratoga* and the decommissioning of the greater part of the escort carrier fleet left the US Navy with the twenty-four ships of the Essex class. The name ship of the class had been commissioned in December 1942, while the last ship, the USS *Philippine Sea*, joined the fleet in May 1946. Two further ships of this class had also been laid down, these being the USS *Reprisal* laid down at the New York Navy Yard in July 1944, while the other was the USS *Iwo Jima*, laid down in January 1945 at the Philadelphia Navy Yard. As the former had been partly completed, it was used as a target after the war, while the barely started latter vessel was broken up on the slips. A further five units designated as the enlarged Essex class were cancelled before construction began.

In the immediate post-war period the entire Essex class was subject to a series of modifications that enabled them to operate the heavier piston aircraft already coming into service and to cope with the jet-powered machines that were on the horizon. Known as SCB-27A, the programme started in 1947 and ended in 1955. The SCB-27 modernisation was extensive, and required at least two years to complete for each vessel. To handle the much heavier, faster aircraft of the early jet era, the original lightweight flight deck support structure was significantly reinforced, enabling it to support aircraft weighing up to 52,000 lb. To complement the reinforced flight deck, stronger elevators, much more powerful catapults, and new Mk 5 arresting gear was installed. The aft elevator was relocated from its original position in the centre of the flight deck to the port deck edge. On the armament side the original four twin 5-inch gun mounts were removed, completely clearing the flight deck of guns. The replacement 5-inch gun battery consisted of eight weapons, two being carried on each quarter of the flight deck. Also added were twin 3-inch gun mounts that replaced the original 40 mm guns, these offering much greater effectiveness through the use of proximity fused ammunition.

The island was completely redesigned, being increased in height, although it was shorter overall due to the removal of its gun mounts. In addition the boiler uptakes were rebuilt and angled aft to accommodate a single radar and communications mast atop the island. To better protect aircrews, their ready rooms were moved from the original gallery deck to below the armoured hangar deck, this being complemented by a large escalator on the starboard side amidships to move flight crews up to the flight deck. Internally the aviation fuel capacity was increased by fifty per cent to 300,000 US gallons, while

The McDonnell Aircraft Company would provide the US Navy with one of its earliest jet fighters – the F2H Banshee. (US Navy/NARA via Dennis R. Jenkins)

its pumping pressure was increased to 50 US gallons per minute. Given the problems experienced by the carriers of TF.38 during the war, the ships' fire-fighting capabilities were enhanced through the addition of two emergency fire and splinter bulkheads in the hangar deck, the instillation of a fog/foam fire-fighting system, improved water curtains and a cupro-nickel fire main. Also given a much-needed improvement was the electrical generating power system, while weapons stowage and handling facilities were also improved. All of these modifications added considerable weight to each vessel in the class, so that displacement increased by some twenty per cent. Blisters were fitted to the hull sides to compensate for the weight, this widening the water-line beam by eight to ten feet. These changes also meant that the carriers also sat lower in the water, which in turn reduced the top speed to 31 knots.

The prototype for the SCB-27A modification programme was the USS *Oriskany*, which was still incomplete at the end of the war while a decision was made about the depth of work that would be undertaken. The *Oriskany* entered the New York Navy Yard in August 1947, being returned to service in September 1950. The class ship USS *Essex* was decommissioned in January 1947, remaining in reserve until moved to the shipyard at Puget Sound in September 1948, finally emerging in September 1951 for recommissioning. The carrier's new air wing comprised McDonnell F2H Banshees, Grumman F8F Bearcats and Douglas AD Skyraiders. The third vessel to enter the programme was the *Wasp* which entered the New York Yard in May 1949 from the reserve, with work being completed in September 1951. The *Kearsarge* had remained in active service until entering the Puget Sound Yard in February 1950, being ready for recommissioning two years later. The *Lake*

Champlain was another newly completed carrier that entered the reserve quickly after the war in March 1946. Norfolk Navy Yard would be the venue for this ship's modernisation, this beginning in August 1950, being ready for commissioning again in September 1952. The next vessel put through the conversion process was the USS *Bennington*, which had undertaken a period of war service in the Pacific. The carrier was withdrawn to the Norfolk Navy Yard and to the reserve in November 1946, entering that dockyard in December 1950 for SCB-27A modifications. This work was completed by November 1952, when the carrier was recommissioned. Another veteran of the Pacific campaign was the *Yorktown*, which entered the reserve in January 1947. Four years later the carrier entered the Puget Sound Yard, being ready for recommissioning in February 1953. The USS *Randolph* was also a Pacific veteran, although it would remain in the training role until being placed in reserve in June 1947. The *Randolph* entered Newport News Yard in June 1951, the modification programme being completed in July 1953. Following the *Randolph* into the conversion programme was the USS *Hornet*, which was placed in reserve in January 1947 before entering the New York Yard in July 1951, returning to service in September 1953. The *Hancock* would enter Puget Sound Yard in December 1951, having been in reserve in May 1947. Unlike the earlier carriers, the *Hancock* was subject to the SBC-27C modification programme, which introduced Type C11 steam-powered catapults, a British innovation, jet blast deflectors, deck cooling, a fuel-blending system, an emergency barrier and storage and handling for nuclear weapons. The fuel-blending system would enable the carrier to operate both piston and jet-powered aircraft.

The extended modifications further increased the aircraft carrier's beam

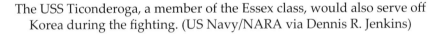

The USS Ticonderoga, a member of the Essex class, would also serve off Korea during the fighting. (US Navy/NARA via Dennis R. Jenkins)

After Korea had ended, the US Navy carriers and the aircraft carried were updated. This is the USS Saratoga, complete with all modifications, while the flight deck has McDonnell Demons, Vought Crusaders and Douglas Skyraiders sitting on it. (US Navy/NARA via Dennis R. Jenkins)

and weight. As these modifications were more extensive, the *Hancock* was not -ecommissioned until February 1954. The *Intrepid* was also subject to the SBC-27C programme, having been in the reserve since 1947. The carrier entered the Newport News Yard in April 1952, being recommissioned in June 1954. In a similar manner to the other vessels of the class, the USS *Ticonderoga* was placed in reserve in January 1947 before entering the New York Yard in April 1952 for SBC-27C modifications. These were completed in September 1954, the carrier being recommissioned soon afterwards. The final three vessels to undergo modification were the *Shangri La*, *Lexington* and *Bon Homme Richard*. Unlike the earlier Essex carriers, these ships were further modified under programme SBC-125. These changes were even more radical as they included an angled flight deck, another British innovation, a hurricane weather bow that improved the weather security of the ship, and also a space for an auxiliary bridge and steering position. The *Shangri La* entered Puget Sound Yard in October 1952, where it underwent the combined SBC-27C and SBC-125 modifications, which kept the carrier out of service until January 1955. The *Lexington* would enter the same dockyard a year later, although its conversion was completed by August 1955. Mare Island Yard was the location for the *Bon Homme Richard* modification, which started in May 1953, being completed by September 1955. It was the USS *Antietam* that was entered straight into the SBC-125 modernisation programme instead of being subject to any of the earlier SBC programmes. The *Antietam* had been commissioned too late to take part in Pacific operations although it would spend some time in the Far East after hostilities had ended. Unlike its sister vessels, the *Antietam* was not placed in reserve until June 1949, although its time laid up

186

Deck tractors scurry around the deck of the USS Valley Forge. Once relocated, the F4U Corsairs will be fuelled and armed before their next missions. (US Navy/NARA via Dennis R. Jenkins)

was short, as the vessel resumed active service in January 1951 for Korean War service. This was completed in April 1952, the carrier entering the New York Yard some five months later. Utilised very much as the prototype for the SBC-125 angled deck, the carrier received few of the other modifications, and so its 10.5-degree offset deck was the only indication of its partly modified state. The *Antietam* was recommissioned in April 1953, being subject to much trials work to prove the angled deck. Although the *Antietam* was utilised in front-line operations, the carrier was relegated to the training role in 1957, remaining as such until struck from the Navy List in May 1963. After ten years in the reserve fleet the carrier was sold for scrapping in 1973.

But not all of the Essex class underwent the upgrade process. This batch included the *Hancock*, which entered the reserve in 1947; although it was reclassified during this period the carrier never re-entered service, being taken off the Navy List in 1966. The *Bunker Hill* would suffer a similar post-war career, although a period with the Naval Electronics Laboratory in San Diego delayed its scrapping until 1973. In contrast, the USS *Boxer* had a second career, remaining in constant service throughout the 1940s and 1950s. Eventually no longer able to operate modern aircraft, the *Boxer* would be reclassified as an amphibious assault ship, LPH-4, for use by the USMC, for which purpose a range of helicopters was carried. The *Boxer* was finally removed from the Navy List in December 1969, going for breaking two years later. The USS *Princeton* was another of the class to be converted for amphibious operations, being redesignated as *LPH-5* in May 1959. Prior to that the ship had operated in the Far East between 1945 and 1949. At the conclusion of this commission the *Princeton* was placed in reserve. However, this was short, as the carrier was recommissioned in 1950 for Korean War operations, these continuing until 1953, when the ship was laid up for conversion to ASW standard. A change of role to helicopter carrier followed, the *Princeton* remaining as such until 1962, when the vessel was entered into the Fleet Requirements And Modification Programme, FRAM II, also known as SBC-144. This programme saw the installation of an SQS-23 bow-mounted sonar, installation of a stem hawse pipe and bow anchor and modifications to the combat information centre. The *Princeton* resumed operational service from 1964 off Vietnam, which came to an end in 1968 when the carrier entered the reserve. The USS *Princeton* was struck off the Navy List in January 1970, being sold for scrap in 1973.

The USS *Tarawa* was commissioned in December 1945, too late to take part in Pacific operations. The role found for the *Tarawa* was to act as a training carrier, a role it fulfilled until October 1948. By June 1949 the carrier was in reserve, being reactivated in February 1951, initially as a training carrier, although the ship was later used in the attack role. The *Tarawa* underwent conversion to ASW standard during the first half of 1955, resuming its anti-submarine duties soon afterwards. In May 1960 the *Tarawa* was placed in reserve, being redesignated as an aircraft transport, *AVT-12*, soon afterwards. Never to sail again, the *Tarawa* was struck off the Navy List in January 1967, going for scrap the following year. The USS *Valley Forge* was the last Essex carrier to be launched in November 1945, being commissioned for service in November 1946. The *Valley Forge* was the first carrier to operate off Korea, from June 1950. Four tours of duty followed, although there was a gap between April and December 1952 when the *Valley Forge* was in the Puget Sound Yard for a much-needed refit, which resulted in the ship being reclas-

The NAA AJ Savage was originally delivered for nuclear weapons, but at a later date the remaining aircraft were converted to tankers for aerial refuelling. (US Navy/NARA via Dennis R. Jenkins)

One of the most usual aircraft operated by the US Navy was the Vought F7U Cutlass. It took a lot of development for the type to become a viable proposition. This F7U-3 is pictured undertaking trials aboard the USS Hancock. (US Navy/NARA via Dennis R. Jenkins)

sified as an attack carrier. Although the *Valley Forge* spent some time operating as an ASW carrier, she did not enter the FRAM II- SBC-144 programme until 1964, although by 1965 she was operating helicopters as *LPH-8* off the coast of Vietnam. The *Valley Forge* was withdrawn and decommissioned in January 1970, being sold for scrap soon afterwards. The final ship of the Essex class was the USS *Philippine Sea*, which was commissioned in May 1946. War service off Korea started in 1950 and continued until the cease-fire in July 1953. In 1955 the *Philippine Sea* was reclassified as an ASW carrier, although she was placed in reserve during 1958. The *Philippine Sea* was struck from the Navy List in 1969, being sold for breaking up soon afterwards.

Even as the last of the Essex-class carriers was completing, a further three ships were being built – the Midway class of carriers. The decision to build these vessels had been as a result of the performance of the British carriers in the Far East, which had shaken off hits by 500 lb and 1,000 lb bombs, in contrast to their American contemporaries, which had suffered losses or extensive damage when struck by weapons of the same size. Originally it was decided by the Navy Board that they would be built within the lapsed limitations of the Washington Treaty, although eventually common sense prevailed and a better ship resulted. The need to incorporate extensive armour on the flight deck and the aircraft hangars meant that these were the biggest carriers built to date, with an overall length of 968 feet and a flight deck that was 113 feet across. The increased size of the class saw an increase in the number of aircraft carried, so that the air wing on paper could consist of a mix of seventy-three Grumman F6F Hellcats and Vought F4U Corsairs, together with sixty-four Curtiss SB2C Helldivers. To service the hungry beasts, the aircraft fuel bunkerage was increased to 350,000 US gallons, while the increased aircraft complement saw an increase in aircrew that brought the total ship's crew close to 4,000 personnel. Much of the hull design and propulsion was based on the cancelled class of Montana battleships, and so the machinery was placed *en echelon*, while the compartments were subdivided as much as possible in the machinery spaces to reduce the possible areas of flooding. The armoured flight deck was equipped with two hydraulic catapults forward and three lifts, two inset in the main deck, with the third mounted on the port side. Although extensive armament was specified, it is highly unlikely that any of the class was ever fully equipped. Originally the class was to have numbered six vessels. However, the end of the war saw the last three cancelled. The name ship of the class, the USS *Midway*, was constructed at the Newport News Yard, the carrier being commissioned in September 1945. The *Midway* was followed down the slips by the third vessel, the USS *Coral Sea*, which was commissioned in October 1947. The second ship of the class, the USS *Franklin D. Roosevelt*, was built at the New York Naval Yard and commissioned in October 1945.

Not long after the Midway class had been launched, they were back in the hands of the shipyards for strengthening of the flight decks, so that the North American AJ Savage bomber could be operated. The opportunity was also taken to rearrange the armament slightly. Added to the ship's arsenal at the same time was the Chance Vought Regulus I missile. The SSM-N-8A Regulus was the weapon deployed by the Navy from 1955 to 1964. Ten aircraft carriers were configured to carry and launch Regulus missiles, although only six ever actually launched one. The USS *Princeton* (CV-37) did not deploy operationally with the missile. However, it did conduct the first launch of a Regulus from a warship, while the USS *Saratoga* (CVA-60) also did not deploy this weapon but was involved in two demonstration launches. The USS *Franklin D. Roosevelt* (CVA-42) and the USS *Lexington* (CV-16) each conducted one test launch. During a deployment, the USS *Randolph* (CV-15) deployed to the Mediterranean carrying three Regulus missiles, while the USS *Hancock* (CV-19) deployed to the Western Pacific with four missiles in 1955. The *Lexington*, *Hancock*, *Shangri-La* (CV-38) and USS *Ticonderoga* (CV-14) were involved in the development of the Regulus Assault Mission (RAM) concept. RAM converted the Regulus cruise missiles into an unmanned aerial vehicle, UAV, so that they could be launched from cruisers or submarines, and once

Photographed prior to modernisation is the USS Franklin D. Roosevelt, a member of the Midway class. None of this class of carriers would undertake operations during the Korean War. (US Navy/NARA via Dennis R. Jenkins)

in flight, guided to their targets by carrier-based pilots using remote-control equipment.

A further modification programme was instituted during the 1950s when all three vessels underwent SCB-110 modernisation, this adding angled decks, three C11 steam catapults, mirror landing systems, and other modifications that would allow them to operate the forthcoming heavier naval jets. The flight deck lifts were also reconfigured, the aft deck lift was removed and re-located to the starboard side and the fore deck was considerably enlarged to handle larger aircraft. In addition the original open bow was replaced by a hurricane bow that sealed the area off from foul weather. The island was also extended to improve accommodation, while the ships' masts were altered: that of the *Roosevelt*, and later the *Coral Sea*, was a tapered pole, while that of the *Midway* was a lattice assembly. Mounted on these masts were the scanners for the latest suite of electronics, including the SPS-12, SPS-8A and SC-2 on the *Roosevelt*, while the *Midway* sported the SPS-43, SPS-12 and SPS-8A. All of these replaced the wartime and immediate post-war systems fitted initially. The internal aircraft fuel capacity was also increased, although to allow for all of these modifications much of the hull armour was removed, while the defensive armament was also reduced. Even with these weight reduction measures in place, the *Roosevelt* now displaced 51,000 tons standard and 63,400 tons deep load, the *Midway* being of a similar displacement.

The *Coral Sea* was also subject to modernisation, although this did not take place until November 1957. This programme was designated SCB-110A and was a far more extensive upgrade than that applied to the other two vessels. As well as the angled deck and hurricane bow, the *Coral Sea* had completely

191

rearranged lifts, as the forward deck lift was deleted completely, being relocated on the starboard deck edge forward of the island. Another deck edge lift was located on the port side, far aft, to completely clear the flight deck. This change meant that *Coral Sea* had no centre-line lifts, two being to starboard with the other to port. As in the other ships of the class, three C11 steam catapults replaced the original hydraulic units, two mounted on the bow and the third on the forward edge of the landing deck. To cope with the increasing weight of naval aircraft, the arrester gear was upgraded to Mk 7 standard. To restore the carrier's stability, bulges were added to the hull, although to compensate for this extra weight the hull armour was removed. The island was also modified, while the pole mast carried the scanners for the SPS-12, SPS-37 and SPS-8A radars. In common with the other two ships, further weight saving was needed to compensate, and so much of the defensive armament was removed. All of these periods in dock for modernisation meant that the Midway class missed the Korean War.

Only two other carrier vessels entered service in the immediate post-war period, these being two light carriers that were loosely based on the preceding Independence class. The hull was based on that of the Baltimore-class cruisers, upon which was mounted a hangar deck, above which was the flight deck, stressed to accommodate aircraft weighing up to nine tons. This deck was longer and wider than that of the Independence class, having a wider section aft to allow for easier aircraft movement. Two lifts were fitted, one each fore and aft, although they were more widely spaced than those of the earlier Independences. Two catapults were fitted at the bow end, these being staggered instead of the diverging ones in previous escort carrier designs. Forward of the island was a heavy-duty crane that could be used for the transfer of stores. It was also capable of dipping into the forward lift area. The island design was borrowed from the Commencement Bay class, having a

The USS Wright was the second vessel of the Saipan class. They were an attempt to improve upon the earlier Independence class. (US Navy/NARA via Dennis R. Jenkins)

heavy mast above, while a second mast was located aft of the island. Mounted on these masts were the initial radar fit scanners, which included the SP and SK-2 fitted to the *Saipan*, and the SR-2 installed on the USS *Wright*. Both vessels were fitted with Mk 29 fire-control radar sets, while the projected air group was intended to be twelve Grumman Avengers plus two full squadrons of fighters, either Grumman F6F Hellcats or Chance Vought F4U Corsairs.

Only two ships of the Saipan class were ordered, the name ship and the USS *Wright*. The former was commissioned in July 1946, while the latter was accepted in February 1947. After the initial shake-down cruise, the *Saipan* undertook eight months of pilot training, later joining the Operational Development Force based at Norfolk, Virginia, in December 1947. The purpose of this force was to gain experience in operating jet aircraft from aircraft carriers. In May 1948 the *Saipan* undertook the first operational deployment of jet aircraft, in this case the McDonnell FH-1 Phantom. This deployment ended in the early 1950s as the *Saipan* was redeployed for training duties, although the carrier was placed in the reserve in October 1957. In May 1959 the *Saipan* was redesignated as an aircraft transport, remaining as such until 1963, when it was slated for conversion to a command ship, being designated *CC-3*. By 1966 the vessel had left the Alabama Dry Dock and Shipbuilding Company at Mobile, and was ready for service, although by this time it had been redesignated as the AGMR-2 USS *Arlington*. The greater majority of the conversion work was hidden from sight, and so the only visible signs were the high aerials mounted along the flight deck. The *Arlington* undertook communication and relay duties during the Vietnam

The USS Saipan was the class leader of this small class of carriers. Both would eventually have another role in the field of communications. (US Navy/NARA via Dennis R. Jenkins)

conflict, being deactivated in 1967 and sold for scrap three years later. The USS *Wright* followed a similar operating pattern to the *Saipan* during its early years, being mainly engaged in training pilots. In June 1952 the carrier was reconfigured for ASW duties operating with hunter killer forces in the Atlantic, although she returned to training duties soon afterwards. In May 1955 the *Wright* was assigned to TG.7.3, which was tasked with undertaking nuclear tests in the Pacific under the codename Operation Wigwam. The *Wright* was decommissioned into the reserve in March 1956 at Puget Sound. As with the *Saipan*, the carrier was redesignated as an aircraft transport in May 1959, although it was moved into Puget Sound Dockyard in March 1962 for conversion to command ship status.

Redesignated CC-2, the conversion included extensive alterations to enable the ship to function as a fully equipped mobile command post for top-echelon commands and their staff that would enable them to act on the strategic direction of area or world-wide military operations. Facilities were built into the ship for global communications and rapid, automatic exchange, processing, storage and the display of command data. A portion of the former hangar deck space was utilised for special-command spaces and the extensive electronics equipment needed, while a major portion of the flight deck was utilised for the mounting of specially designed communications antenna arrays. In addition, facilities were provided to enable the vessel to operate three helicopters. In its new guise, the *Wright* was recommissioned in May 1963 and undertook duties across the world. The ship remained in commission until deactivated in May 1970, although it remained on the Navy List until December 1977, being sold for scrap in 1980.

While the US Navy was trying to retain its two ocean carrier fleets plus the manpower and aircraft to operate them, changes were taking place half a world away that would bring the carrier forces to the fore once again. In a move that would have been noticed by the United States government in quieter times, the leadership of Russia officially declared war on Japan on 9 August 1945, close to the war's end, even though America and Russia had signed an agreement to that effect earlier that year. What the rest of the Allies had failed to notice was that the Russian influence had spread across Eastern Europe, courtesy of the Soviet invasion of Germany. It would be this startling spread of communism, a great theory but ruined by people, that would alarm the nations of the West. By 10 August the Red Army had occupied the northern part of the Korean peninsula, and on 26 August halted at the 38th Parallel for three weeks to await the arrival of US forces from the south. Even as the Russians were moving into their positions, the Americans were having doubts that the Soviets would honour their part of the Joint Commission agreement, the American-sponsored Korean occupation agreement. The dividing line across Korea had been decided in July when two of the American Commission officers, Colonel Dean Rusk and Colonel Charles H. Bonesteel III, had split the peninsula at the 38th Parallel after concluding that the US Korean Zone of Occupation had to have a minimum of two ports, and that the capital of Korea should be in the area of responsibility of the American forces.

At the Potsdam Conference held during July and August 1945, the Allies had decided to divide Korea, without consulting the Korean people, in contravention of the Cairo Conference, which had stated that Korea would become a free and independent country, free from outside control. On 8 September 1945, Lieutenant-General John R. Hodge arrived in Inchon to accept the surrender of Japanese forces south of the 38th Parallel. Appointed as military governor, General Hodge controlled South Korea via the United States Army Military Government in Korea between 1945 and 1948. As governor, General Hodge established control by restoring to power the key Japanese colonial administrators and their Korean and police collaborators, as the USAMGIK refused to recognise the provisional government of the short-lived People's Republic of Korea (PRK), since he suspected it was a communist organisation. These policies contradicted the notion of Korean sovereignty, and so they provoked civil insurrections and guerrilla warfare.

From December 1945 Korea was administered by a Joint American and Russian Commission, as had been agreed at the 1945 Moscow Conference, although the Koreans were excluded from these talks. The commission decided that the country would become independent after a five-year trusteeship. This news was not received well by the population, which openly revolted. In the south of the country some protested, while others armed themselves with weapons liberated from the Japanese occupation forces. In order to take the sting out of these actions, the USAMGIK banned strikes on 8 December 1945, this being followed by the outlawing of the PRK Revolutionary Government and the PRK People's Committees four days later. Continued unrest saw a strike by railway workers in Pusan on 23 September 1946, this being followed by civil disorder that spread throughout the country. On 1 October 1946, Korean police shot three students in the Daegu Uprising, and as a result of this action protesters made a counter-attack, during which thirty-eight policemen were killed. This was followed on 3 October when approximately 10,000 protesters attacked the Yeongcheon police station, killing three policemen and injuring a further forty. Elsewhere in Korea some twenty landlords and pro-Japanese South Korean officials were killed, in the light of which the USAMGIK was left with no option but to declare martial law.

In response to all this civil unrest, the Representative Democratic Council, led by the nationalist Syngman Rhee, would make clear its opposition to the Soviet-American trusteeship of Korea, rightly arguing that after thirty-five years of Japanese colonial rule most Koreans opposed further foreign occupation. To stop the country descending into a civil war, the USAMGIK decided to scrap the five-year trusteeship agreed upon in Moscow, and to invoke the 31 March 1948 United Nations election deadline that was intended to achieve an anti-communist civil government in the American Zone of Occupation. The proposed national general elections were first opposed and

195

then boycotted by the Russians, who insisted that the Americans should honour the trusteeship agreed to during the Moscow Conference. The resultant anti-communist South Korean government would issue a national political constitution on 17 July 1948, elect a president, the American-educated Syngman Rhee, three days later, and establish the Republic of South Korea on 15 August 1948. In the Russian Korean Zone of Occupation, the USSR established a communist North Korean government led by Kim Il-Sung. In reply, President Rhee's regime expelled all communists from southern national politics. As nationalists, albeit of different hues, both Syngman Rhee and Kim Il-Sung were intent upon reunifying Korea under their own preferred political mantle.

As they were better armed, courtesy of the USSR, the North Koreans could and did escalate the continual border skirmishes and raids, and then looked to invade South Korea with proper provocation. During this period the American government assumed that all communists globally were controlled or directly influenced by Moscow, and so the US portrayed the border infractions in Korea as Soviet inspired. American troops were withdrawn from Korea in 1949, leaving behind an ill-equipped South Korean army. The Soviet Union had already left Korea in 1948, although its sponsored regime was well equipped. Under the guise of rebuffing a South Korean provocation raid, the North Korean Army (KPA) crossed the 38th Parallel behind an intensive artillery barrage on Sunday 25 June 1950. The KPA stated that the Republic of Korea Army (ROKA) troops had crossed the border first, and that they would arrest and execute Rhee. Both Korean armies had continually harassed each other with skirmishes, and each had continually mounted raids across the 38th Parallel border. The United Nations Security Council immediately condemned the North Korean invasion of the Republic of South Korea, issuing UN Resolution 82, which called for an immediate withdrawal. The USSR had boycotted the UN Security Council meetings since January 1950, protesting that the Republic of China, Taiwan, and not the People's Republic of China, had a permanent seat on the Council. In response, on 27 June, President Truman ordered American air and sea forces to assist the South Korean regime.

After debating Korea, the Security Council published Resolution 83 on 27 June 1950, recommending that member states provide military assistance to the Republic of Korea. On 4 July the Soviet Deputy Foreign Minister accused the Americans of starting armed intervention on behalf of the South Koreans. The Russians challenged the legitimacy of external intervention for several reasons, in that the ROK Army intelligence upon which Resolution 83 was based was based on US Intelligence, that North Korea was not invited as a sitting temporary member of the UN, which violated UN Charter Article 32, and that the Korean conflict was beyond the United Nations Charter remit, as the initial north–south border fighting was classed as civil war. The North Korean Army had launched the liberation war with a comprehensive air and land invasion utilising 231,000 soldiers, who captured their scheduled objectives and territory, among them Kaesong, Chuncheon, Uijeongbu, and Ongjin. Their forces included more than 200 Soviet T-34 tanks, over 150 Yak fighters, 110 IL-2 Stormovik attack aircraft, 200 artillery weapons and thirty-five reconnaissance aircraft. In addition to the invasion force, the North Korean KPA had retained 114 fighters, a further seventy-eight bombers, 105 T-34 tanks and some 30,000 soldiers in reserve in North Korea. In contrast, the ROK Army defenders were unprepared, having 98,000 soldiers, no tanks, and twenty-two aircraft, comprising twelve liaison types and ten North American AT-6 Texan trainers.

Although there were no large foreign military garrisons in Korea when the invasion started, there were large American garrisons and air forces in Japan. Within days of the invasion, large numbers of ROK Army soldiers were either retreating southwards or were defecting *en masse* to the north to join the KPA. However, despite the rapid post-1945 Allied demobilisations, there were still substantial US forces stationed in Japan under the command of General Douglas MacArthur that could be made ready to fight the North Koreans. On Saturday 24 June 1950, the US Secretary of State, Dean Acheson, informed President Harry S. Truman by telephone that the North Koreans had invaded South Korea. Truman and Acheson discussed their response with senior Defense Department officials, who agreed that the United States was obliged to repel military aggression and to stem the onward flow of communism. President Truman announced that America would counter this aggression and support the efforts of the United Nations Security Council to terminate this attack. In Congress the Joint Chiefs of Staff Chairman, General Omar Bradley, warned against appeasement, saying that Korea was the place to stop the expansion of communism. Following much discussion in August 1950, the President and the Secretary of State obtained the consent of Congress to appropriate $12 billion to cover the military expenses of the Korean police action.

In line with Secretary of State Acheson's recommendation, President Truman ordered General MacArthur to transfer armaments to the Army of the Republic of Korea, while giving air cover to the evacuation of US nationals. The President disagreed with his advisers recommending unilateral American bombing of the North Korean forces. However, he did order the US 7th Fleet to protect Taiwan, whose Nationalist government had asked to fight in Korea. The Americans denied the Nationalist Chinese request to join the fray lest it provoke a Communist Chinese retaliation. In a move that was almost certain to upset the Navy, the Joint Chiefs ordered that the US 7th Fleet be placed under the direct control of General Douglas MacArthur on 29 June 1950. This was in direct contrast to the situation in the Second World War when both Admiral Ernest J. King, the Commander-in-Chief US Fleet, and Admiral Chester W. Nimitz the Commander-in-Chief Pacific Areas, had refused point-blank to hand over any assets to General MacArthur's direct control, as both Admirals thought that the Army viewed the aircraft carriers and their crews as expendable. This command decision almost never

A Grumman F9F Panther of VF-71 flies over Task Force 77 in 1952. (US Navy/NARA via Dennis R. Jenkins)

happened, as General MacArthur had departed from his headquarters in Japan to fly to South Korea to assess the situation in the country personally. As the General's transport was on approach to the airfield at Suwon, twenty miles south of Seoul, it was attacked by a flight of North Korean Yak-9 fighters. Fortunately there was a combat air patrol of NAA P-51 Mustangs in the vicinity, their intervention saving the inbound transport aircraft.

The USS *Valley Forge* was the first American carrier deployed to the Far East for exercises, having departed the west coast on 1 May 1950. The carrier was anchored in Hong Kong harbour for a visit by 25 June, when the news was received that North Korean forces had crossed the 38th Parallel into South Korea's territory. Ordered to depart Hong Kong the next day, the carrier steamed south to Subic Bay in the Philippines, where she was provisioned and refuelled, and then she set course for Korea as part of Task Force 77. On board the carrier were the Grumman F9F Panthers of VF-51 and 52, the Vought F4U Corsairs of VF-53 and 54, Douglas AD-4 Skyraiders of VA-55, Vought F4U-5Ns of VC-3 for night-fighter duties, Douglas AD-3W Skyraiders of VC-11 for airborne early warning coverage, and a small detachment of helicopters for air-sea rescue duties.

The first carrier air strike of the Korean conflict was launched from the *Valley Forge* on 3 July 1950 in support of the South Korean troops who, under equipped as they were, battled desperately against the tide of Communist troops and tanks. In concert with aircraft from HMS *Triumph*, waves of Douglas AD Skyraiders and Vought F4U Corsairs attacked the North Korean airfield at Pyongyang, south-west of Seoul, while Grumman F9F-2 Panthers flew fighter cover. Tons of bombs from the attacking American aircraft hit hangars, fuel storage dumps, parked aircraft and railway marshalling yards.

While the attack aircraft were hitting the ground targets, a pair of escorting Grumman Panthers from VF-51 flown by Lieutenant (jg) Plog and Ensign Brown downed two Yak-9s and damaged another. In spite of the attempts by United Nations forces led by America and Britain to stop the steady flow of Communist infantry and armour, the North Korean forces steadily pushed the defending South Koreans back into a defensive perimeter around Pusan. After this initial strike the Douglas Skyraiders from the *Valley Forge* attacked and destroyed the North Korean oil refinery at Wonsan. Six days later a reconnaissance flight from the *Valley Forge* reported that a large force of North Korean troops was massing for a further push into South Korea. In order to counter this, since such a move would completely overwhelm the remaining South Korean forces, the 7th Fleet and the aircraft of TF.77 were tasked to use all means necessary to destroy these forces.

After these opening attacks, the commanders of the USAF forces and their Navy counterparts held a conference to determine their depth of co-operation. The deal thrashed out saw the US Navy maintaining direct control of its assets when taking part in Navy-sponsored attacks, although when operating in the zone of USAF responsibility the Navy's air assets came under Air Force control so that strikes could be better co-ordinated.

On 19 July the *Valley Forge* launched another strike mission, although only piston-powered machines were used. At the completion of these sorties the carrier was placed on Condition 1 alert in the face of the incoming Typhoon Bill that was due to hit the ships of the 7th Fleet later that day, although 7th Fleet Command ordered the ships to pull back to the Sea of Japan, where they remained until 21 July. On the following day the *Valley Forge* restarted

A scene of frenzied activity aboard the USS Boxer as armourers move bombs towards the F4Us on the flight deck. (US Navy/NARA via Dennis R. Jenkins)

operations, launching a combat group consisting of Douglas AD Skyraiders and Vought F4U Corsairs in support of ground forces, while the carrier's jet aircraft were tasked to attack targets north of Seoul. Missions were launched during both the morning and afternoon while the *Valley Forge* cruised about a hundred miles off the Korean coast. During the period of the combat operations a standing patrol of four F4U Corsairs was maintained, while a single AEW Skyraider and a single AD attack Skyraider maintained an anti-submarine patrol. At the conclusion of these missions the *Valley Forge* withdrew for refuelling and restoring near Danjo-Gunto before the carrier and her escorts returned to Okinawa, Japan, for rearming. Unlike the previous conflict in the Pacific, the US Navy did not operate a large fleet train for carrier support.

While the *Valley Forge* was involved in attacking the enemy, another carrier from the Essex class, the USS *Boxer*, was undertaking another important task – that of aircraft transport. Arriving at Yokosuka on 21 July, the handling teams unloaded 145 P-51 Mustangs for USAF and ROK use, six L-5 liaison aircraft and nineteen naval aircraft. Also on board were over 1,000 passengers

With its wings folded, a Vought F4U Corsair aboard the USS Philippine Sea is ready for its next mission. In front of this aircraft an armourer pushes some more bombs on a cart to the aircraft behind. (US Navy/NARA via Dennis R. Jenkins)

During the Korean War the port at Sasebo was a crowded place. In this view can be seen HMS Unicorn, behind which is the USS Valley Forge. (US Navy/NARA via Dennis R. Jenkins)

destined to join various units in theatre. During the crossing from Alameda, California, to Japan the USS *Boxer* set a trans-Pacific record for such a journey, of eight days and sixteen hours. After unloading her cargo, the *Boxer* departed Japan for the return trip to the United States, as no air group was available for operational use, although this would change at a later date.

The *Valley Forge* group departed Japan on 4 August, undertaking exercises with Douglas JD Invaders supplied by UTRON 7, after which the carrier and her escorts arrived off the Korean coast the following day. By this time the

USS *Philippine Sea*, of which more later, had joined the 7th Fleet carrier force, so that two carriers were available to support the efforts of the UN-sponsored forces. The *Valley Forge* aircraft were deployed in support of ground forces operating in south-eastern Korea, while those from the *Philippine Sea* were tasked with destroying targets in the south-west. At the completion of these missions both carrier groups withdrew to the Yellow Sea to conduct attacks against targets on the west coast over the following two days. By 10 August both carrier groups had withdrawn for refuelling, returning to the Yellow Sea two days later. Over the next two days the carrier air groups conducted operations along the west coast above the 38th Parallel before withdrawing to Sasebo on 14 August for refuelling and rearming. This break was short, as both groups were back on station off the east coast in the Sea of Japan, launching air strikes against targets and troop concentrations in central Korea. Only a few of these were completed, as the 5th Air Force, USAF, put in an emergency request for naval air assistance to support the evacuation of the ROK 3rd Division from Yondok when this force was in danger of being overrun. At the completion of this mission the carrier groups moved further north to undertake strikes against targets north of the 42nd Parallel, withdrawing south on completion. A refuel took place on 18 August before the carriers moved round to the west coast to undertake attacks against targets on 20 August, these being located north of the 38th Parallel. At the conclusion of these operations the carrier groups again withdrew to Sasebo.

The break in Sasebo was slightly longer this time, the task force not departing until 25 August. As before, both carriers were deployed under the aegis of Operations Order 10-50. The following day the carriers were cruising off the east coast of Korea, where strikes were launched in support of ground forces, while other aircraft were flown against hard targets such as railways and armour in the east of the country. At the completion of these missions the carrier groups steamed northwards, where they would be in a position to launch missions on 27 August 1950 against designated targets in the Wonsan–Chongjin area. After the air groups had returned, the carriers turned south, refuelling *en route* before entering the Yellow Sea in the night hours of 28 August. As the North Korean forces were again pushing south, strikes were launched by both carriers against enemy forces operating near Seoul and Inchon. The following day the carriers, still cruising in the same location, dispatched aircraft to attack targets in the vicinity of Chinampo–Pongyeng. The beginning of September saw further strikes carried out against targets in the same region, although there was a rapid switch of targets at midday as emergency orders were received from Commander Navy Forces Far East (ComNavFE), to switch all missions to support the 25th Division of the 8th Army, which was under pressure from the North Korean forces. These sorties started in the early afternoon and would continue until dusk. The carrier groups remained in the area overnight, restarting support missions against specific targets and continuing throughout the day. The carriers withdrew at dusk for refuelling on 3 September, although this was curtailed in early after-

Jockeying for position aboard the USS Philippine Sea are these Vought F4U Corsairs of VF-113. Once airborne these aircraft will provide support for UN forces. (US Navy/NARA via Dennis R. Jenkins)

noon after an emergency request from Headquarters 8th Army. The task groups were in a position to begin operations in late afternoon against targets in south-east Korea. The following day the carrier groups were off the west coast, although these were quickly curtailed after yet another request from the 8th Army, which was then annulled by ComNavFE. On 5 September the carrier group was on its way to Sasebo as the weather forecast for the next few days was not conducive to air operations.

Six days later TF.77 with its two carrier groups departed Sasebo and headed towards the area of Inchon where the carriers' aircraft were prepared for the Korean D-Day on 15 September. These would be the landings at Inchon and Wolmi-Do. The air support element undertook attacks against hard and soft targets. Not only were short, close-support missions flown, some of the aircraft were sent on long-range, deep-support missions. Over the next six days the carriers flew missions every day, although on refuelling days only defensive flight operations were conducted. During this period, on 18 September, the carrier force was increased by the arrival of the carrier USS *Boxer* with Carrier Air Group Two aboard.

The arrival of the USS *Boxer* would allow the *Valley Forge* to withdraw for a much-needed refit at Puget Sound before she returned to the fray in November 1951. She departed Sasebo on 5 November, but the transit to Korea was delayed by heavy seas and high winds, and so strikes were not launched until the following day. The designated targets were located in the Manchurian border area, where strikes, close air support and jet fighter sweeps were undertaken. Three days later the task force was joined by the USS *Philippine Sea*. With two carriers available, the air groups were tasked with destroying the bridges across the Yula river on the border of Korea and

A typical winter scene aboard a US Navy carrier operating off Korea. It would be the weather over the land that would curtail operations, although any bad weather over the task force also had a detrimental effect. (US Navy/NARA via Dennis R. Jenkins)

Manchuria. The first target was the Changtion-ho-kou road bridge, which suffered some damage that was quickly repaired. A day spent refuelling on 10 November followed before the carrier returned to action. Again her designated targets were the bridges across the Yula, during which a span of the Sinuiju bridge was downed by aircraft from the *Valley Forge* and the newly arrived USS *Leyte*. A change of targets on 13 November saw both carriers launching strikes against military installations in the Hyosonjin area. After a quick refuel on 14 November both carriers were back in action the following day, undertaking close air support missions as the strike against the Sinuiju bridge were cancelled due to limited visibility. The bridge was finally attacked again on 18 November, and this was followed by a combined strike by aircraft from the USS *Leyte* and the *Philippine Sea*, which dropped the bridges at Hyosonjin. The *Valley Forge* would leave the combat zone on 19 November, proceeding to Yokosuka to destore prior to returning to the United States and Puget Sound for a much-needed refit.

The *Valley Forge* refit was quickly completed and the carrier returned to Yokosuka with Carrier Air Group 2 aboard. The units assigned to the CAG included VF-24, VF-63 and VF-64 flying Vought F4U Corsairs, VA-65 flying Douglas AD Skyraiders, VC-35 with AD4Q Skyraiders, VC-3 flying night-fighter Corsairs, VC-11 equipped with AEW Skyraiders, VC-61 flying reconnaissance Corsairs, and HU-1 flying Sikorsky HO3S Dragonfly helicopters for planeguard duties. Also aboard the carrier were eight helicopters that were launched off Itami, in Japan, for onward transition to the USMC unit VMO-6.

By 23 December 1950 the carrier launched close air support missions against targets near Hamhung which included troops on roads and villages, as these were advancing on UN forces that were awaiting evacuation. The carrier's aircraft were directed by US Army and USAF Forward Air Controllers (FACs). During these attacks the Vought F4U piloted by Ensign J.R. Brinkley was shot down, the pilot being lost in his blazing aircraft. Strikes were also carried out against Kolori, Tongdong, the Chosin Reservoir, Wangpung-ni, Songburi, Changhungni, Toejo and Oro-ri, during which fifty-six sorties were flown. By 28 December the Hamhung evacuation had been completed, and the carriers of TF.77 undertook close air support missions against North Korean troops while other aircraft were directed by FACs against specific targets in Kalchon, Papori, Kuun-ni, Chigyong-di, Hwachon and Songdongi, during which thirty-two sorties were flown. Further sorties for close air support were flown on 29 December, during which villages, troops and vehicles were attacked, a total of seventy-six missions being flown during this period. The following day twelve sorties were flown, with hits being made against troops, villages and a bridge, considerable damage being inflicted.

A refuel break took place on the last day of the year, with combat sorties restarting on 1 January 1951, when close air support and reconnaissance missions were undertaken. During the ensuing air strikes damage was inflicted on warehouses, buildings, trucks and bridges. Further close air support missions were undertaken over the following two days before the carriers joined up with TG.79.1 for refuelling, after which the *Valley Forge* resumed operations, launching attacks against targets in the Kosong area, during which heavy casualties were inflicted on the enemy. As bad weather stopped flying operations, the carrier departed from the combat zone to undertake refuelling throughout 7 January. The bad weather continued until 11 January, when close air support missions were undertaken against various ground targets at Kangnong, Suwon and Pyongyong-ni, during which various buildings and railway trucks were destroyed; this involved sixty missions in total. At the completion of this day's flying the task group joined up with TG.79.1 for refuelling.

Between 12 and 19 January over 250 sorties were flown, during which buildings, railway vehicles and marshalling yards and small coastal vessels were attacked and destroyed, after which the carrier and her escorts returned to Sasebo for refuelling and restoring. The *Valley Forge* remained in harbour until the end of the month, when she departed in company with the *Philippine Sea* and the rest of TF.77, arriving off the east coast of Korea the following day. As before, the carriers undertook attacks against the usual range of targets, these being augmented by night heckler sorties flown by the night-fighter Corsairs. During this period over 300 sorties were flown, although not without loss, as a Corsair launching from the *Valley Forge* ended up in the sea, the pilot not being found. The second casualty concerned another Corsair, which was lost the same day, 7 February 1951, when landing on the carrier,

The Douglas AD Skyraider played a significant part in the Korean War. This example was operated by VC-5. (US Navy/NARA via Dennis R. Jenkins)

although in this case the pilot was recovered by the ship's rescue helicopter. After this period of frenetic activity, the two carrier groups departed the area on 27 February and headed for Yokosuka for refuelling and other replenishments. On 11 March the carrier groups departed from Japan, being joined *en route* by the battleship USS *Missouri*. Three days later the carriers were back off the coast of Korea. As before, the carrier groups launched missions against a full range of targets, during which locomotives, bridges, vehicles, troop concentrations and vehicles on the roads were attacked and destroyed. During this period the carriers also added the role of early-morning hecklers to their list of missions, as well as that of bombardment spotting. During this period the carrier would lose two aircraft, although fortunately both pilots were rescued. After nearly 700 sorties the carrier groups returned to Yokosuka on 26 March, a day earlier than planned, as the weather had deteriorated below operating minima. In the operating report issued by the *Valley Forge* command staff, one of their main comments was that trying to operate five squadrons from an Essex-class carrier was extremely difficult, even when the complement was reduced to four units, as on its last cruise there was difficulty in coping with the aircraft and crews. The report then stated that the ideal number of squadrons would be three, with the remainder being made up of specialised flights.

The *Valley Forge* departed from Yokosuka and headed for Puget Sound Naval Yard, where she underwent a much-needed refit between April and November 1951. When the carrier departed San Diego she had aboard four complete squadrons and some specialist flights. The assigned flying units included VF-52 with Grumman F9F Panthers, VF-111 also with Panthers, VF-194 flying Douglas AD Skyraiders, and VF-653 with Vought F4U Corsairs. Also aboard were flights from VC-3 with night-fighter Corsairs, VC-11 with

AEW Skyraiders, VC-35 with night-operations Skyraiders, VC-61 flying reconnaissance Panthers, and HU-1 operating rescue helicopters.

Having arrived at Yokosuka at the beginning of December, the carrier underwent final preparations for Korean operations. These completed, the *Valley Forge* left port on 7 December, and in transit the air group undertook various combat exercises, during which two VF-653 Corsair pilots were killed when their aircraft collided. On 14 December the carrier air groups started their operations against targets on the north-eastern railway network in Korea. During these missions the air group had a Corsair and Skyraider divert to the airfield at K-18. Between 14 and 24 December the carrier groups undertook their usual range of attacks against shipping, building and troop concentrations among other targets, during which more than 300 sorties were mounted.

On Christmas Day the carrier group withdrew for refuelling and to celebrate the season, resuming full operations three days later, once the weather had cleared. On 28 December eighty-four sorties were launched, the primary targets being the railway network infrastructure and any traffic thereon. Losses during this early period of operations included an F9F whose engine flamed out on approach to the carrier, the pilot being recovered successfully. On 3 January 1952 a total of sixty-seven missions were launched, during which seventy-eight tonnes of bombs were dropped. During one of these attacks the Skyraider of Ensign Riemers was hit by anti-aircraft fire that caused severe damage to the aircraft's starboard wing. As the AD became harder to control, the pilot was left with no other option that to ditch in Songjin harbour, having flown over sixty miles to get there. After ditching, the pilot was rescued within eight minutes, suffering from shock and dampness. Inclement weather and refuelling kept the air group grounded until 6 January, when operations resumed against bridges, with over 140 missions being flown. Refuelling occupied 7 January, with operations resuming next day, and over the next three days missions were flown against numerous targets. In the eighty-one sorties flown two aircraft were lost, although one pilot was rescued.

Flight operations resumed on 12 January, having been delayed by rough weather, during which a Grumman F9F slid over the side after a severe roll. The missions launched on 12 January were in support of Operation Moonlight Sonata, during which the heckler aircraft took full advantage of the full moon to attack the railways. During this period seventy-six sorties were flown, and a number of locomotives and railway vehicles were completely destroyed. The Moonlight Sonata missions continued until 17 January before the *Valley Forge* returned to Japan for ten days' rest and recuperation. At the end of January she departed Yokosuka in company with the USS *Antietam* and *Essex* and the rest of TF.77. On 2 February air operations began, during which eighty sorties were flown. However, the air group did suffer some losses when two F4U Corsairs from VF-653 were lost at sea, although both pilots were recovered safely. The following day a further eighty-three sorties were

Undergoing a refuel from an oiler is the USS Essex, and behind the Essex is another of the class undertaking the same operation. (US Navy/NARA via Dennis R. Jenkins)

launched, during which a Skyraider of VF-194 was shot down, the pilot being rescued. Although there were a few losses, the missions were successful, with a great number of railway targets being completely destroyed. After a period refuelling, combat operations resumed on 14 January, although they were then curtailed until 17 January due to bad weather. Over the next two days attacks were undertaken against railway infrastructure and vehicles, troop concentrations and numerous buildings. These missions were conducted in concert with the USS *Philippine Sea*, and were deemed successful even though a Grumman F9F was lost. On 20 February the *Valley Forge* and the *Philippine Sea* were relieved by the *Essex* and *Antietam*, and headed towards Yokosuka.

The *Valley Forge* departed her Japanese rest stop on 3 March and headed towards the east coast of Korea in the vicinity of the 38th Parallel, where she joined up with the rest of TF.77, which already included the *Essex* and *Antietam*. The *Valley Forge* undertook her first air operations two days later, when two locomotives and other rolling stock were destroyed. Over the next two days similar missions were undertaken, during which much of the railway infrastructure was damaged. Overall 180 sorties were flown in these three days. On 8 March only a few sorties were flown due to bad weather, although the *Valley Forge* aircraft did mount thirty missions that garnered some success. A replenishment period followed, with operations resuming on 11 March. As before, the subsequent days were occupied with attacks against railways, although during these sorties some of the carrier's aircraft were damaged by anti-aircraft fire. Again the carrier withdrew from the zone for refuelling on 14 March before resuming operations the following day.

Railway infrastructure and rolling stock were the targets, although the aircrew were getting a bit annoyed about having to attack targets more than once, since the North Koreans inconveniently repaired them with commendable speed. During the next few days air operations were hampered by bad weather, but even so the railways were attacked again. Unfortunately for the *Valley Forge* pilots, the North Koreans were becoming aware of their interest in the railways, and so defensive anti-aircraft weapons abounded. These extra weapons caused damage to half a dozen aircraft, while two others were shot down, with one pilot being killed. By 29 March over 600 sorties had been completed, with the US Navy having the upper hand, as the railways were being hammered almost daily, with minimal damage and losses to the carriers. The final days of flying before departing for Yokosuka were undertaken on 31 March and 1 April, the *Valley Forge* leaving the area after flying and recovery was completed.

The carrier remained in port for nearly two weeks, departing on 14 April to rejoin TF.77, the other carriers in the force being the USS *Boxer* and *Philippine Sea*. Combat operations began on 17 April, when the Douglas Skyraider of Commander Crabill, Commander Air Group, was hit by anti-aircraft fire, the pilot ditching his aircraft, although he was successfully rescued. Further operations were carried out over the next three days, during which the Skyraider of Lieutenant Workman of VF-194 was struck by defensive fire. Although the pilot managed to bale out, his parachute failed to open properly and he was killed. Between 22 April and 15 May the *Valley Forge* air group continued its sorties against the Korean railways, although eight aircraft were lost and two pilots were killed. After the last of these losses, the *Valley Forge* departed for Yokosuka on 15 May, arriving there the following day.

The *Valley Forge* departed from Japan on 24 May, arriving on station off the east coast of Korea. This operational period was marred on the first day when the aircraft of Ensign Sterrett was shot down, although he managed to escape his doomed aircraft. A large rescue effort was mounted, during which two pilots lost their lives when their aircraft crashed into the surrounding hills. All of this effort was in vain, as Ensign Sterrett was not recovered. Combat operations were conducted as before against the railways, this spell lasting from 31 May to 10 June 1952, before the carrier withdrew for refuelling. She undertook a single day's operations before departing for Yokosuka on 12 June.

The *Valley Forge* returned to Puget Sound during June for a major refit, this being completed in December 1952. The carrier then returned to Japan, where she entered Yokosuka to prepare for further combat operations. The *Valley Forge* departed from Japan to join TF.77, where she joined up with the *Essex*, *Kearsarge* and *Oriskany*. On 2 January the *Valley Forge* began the operational part of her fourth Korean tour. The first attack wave was launched in late morning, with Lieutenant (jg) Kramer being the first to depart. Overall a total of seventy-two sorties were dispatched, with a range of targets being destroyed for no losses. The following day saw ninety-six missions being launched, the targets being power stations and any identified sub-stations. During this day's flying an F4U Corsair was forced to ditch after engine failure, while an F9F of VF-51 was forced to ditch after an engine exploded, but both pilots were recovered successfully. After a replenishment period the carrier air group resumed flying on 5 January, although bad weather curtailed operations over the following two days. When the weather cleared the *Valley Forge* aircraft resumed their attacks, this time the targets being along the North Korean front line, where they destroyed trenches, pill boxes and ammunition dumps. The following day followed a similar pattern, although flying started earlier as hecklers were launched against the front line. No flying was undertaken between 10 and 19 January as the task force was either refuelling or was unable to fly due to bad weather. Combat flying resumed on 20 January and continued until 22 January, after which the *Valley Forge* returned to Yokosuka.

Departing from Yokosuka on 8 February, the *Valley Forge* headed towards Korea to rejoin TF.77, where she joined the *Kearsarge, Philippine Sea* and *Oriskany*. Upon her arrival, Rear Admiral Soucek relieved Rear Admiral Hickey as TF.77 commander. Once the *Valley Forge* had arrived, the entire force refuelled on 11 February, resuming combat operations the following day. The carrier launched eighty-four sorties, during which the air group destroyed four lorries and caused extensive damage to a range of buildings and various items of railway rolling stock. While the propeller aircraft were destroying various scheduled targets, the F9Fs of VF-51 were undertaking armed reconnaissance sorties that allowed them some freedom to roam, during which they destroyed at least seven troop shelters and cratered some roads. The following day's operations were hampered by bad weather, although the early-morning heckler flights did manage to depart. Fortunately the weather was better on 14 February, and so the hecklers departed to cause early-morning mayhem, being followed by the propeller strike force. These two groups of aircraft struck at the usual range of road traffic, troops and buildings, while the jet flights concentrated on the railways. Over the next three weeks the *Valley Forge* and the other carriers of TF.77 continued their assaults on their usual range of targets before the ship departed the zone on 15 March, heading for Sasebo, although this was only a short stop, since the *Valley Forge* had been ordered to proceed to Hong Kong, where she arrived on 18 March for a visit. The *Valley Forge* was back at Yokosuka by 20 March, rejoining TF.77 two days later, where she was in company with the USS *Oriskany*.

Combat operations would resume on 23 March, when in the early hours of the morning the heckler flights were launched, hitting targets at Sinpo, Kowon and Tanchon, where buildings, lorries and railway stock were attacked and destroyed. The propeller strike force launched around dawn to undertake missions in support of IX and X Army Corps, some of which were within yards of the American front line. The jet fighters were tasked to hit a supply area at Pukchong, and then a truck park at Hamhung. Altogether the air wing flew 118 sorties during the day. The following day presented a similar pattern to the previous one, after which the task force withdrew for refuelling. Operations resumed the following day, most of which was in support of the two army corps. Air operations over 28 and 29 April were reduced due to bad weather, and then a refuel break followed.

The opening day of May continued in much the same vein as the previous month, although they would be hampered again by bad weather on 11 May, after which there was a refuel break. Although TF.77 had returned to active duty the following day, bad weather again hampered operations, so that only 14 May was available for attacks, these being similar to those carried out before. At the conclusion of operations the *Valley Forge* departed Korea for Yokosuka, arriving there on 17 May. She returned to Korea for her final dose of combat on 27 May, when she joined the USS *Boxer* and *Philippine Sea*. Combat operations resumed in the early hours of 2 June when the hecklers were launched. The following propeller and jet forces supported the I, IX and X Army Corps and the II Corps ROK. Over the following three days the air group undertook a similar range of missions. However, on 6 June it was time for the *Valley Forge* to return to the United States. The carrier departed Korean waters on 7 June, heading for Yokosuka, although *en route* medals and other commendations were presented to the ship's personnel by Vice-Admiral Clark, Commander of the 7th Fleet. At the completion of this ceremony most of the ship's aircraft were transferred to the USS *Boxer*. During the transit to Japan, Typhoon Judy was forecast to arrive across the normal transit route, and so the carrier was forced to divert to miss it. On 9 June the carrier launched the remainder of her aircraft to join those at NAS Atsugi, and she reached port later that day. After destoring, the USS *Valley Forge* headed for America, where she would later be converted for the anti-submarine role.

CHAPTER EIGHT

Further Korean Carrier Operations

Whenver the Korean War started, the US Navy carriers were mainly equipped with piston-powered aircraft, these being the Vought F4U Corsair, soon to leave service, and the Douglas AD Skyraider, which was destined to have a long and illustrious career. Prior to pure jet aircraft entering service with the US Navy, the service experimented with a mixed-powerplant aircraft. The manufacturer of this most unusual aircraft was the Ryan Corporation, its product being designated the FR-1 Fireball. In appearance the Fireball resembled a small fighter mounted on a tricycle

The Ryan FR-1 Fireball was a mixed-power aircraft that had a piston engine in the nose and a jet engine in the tail. It was obvious that the Navy was utilising the type for trials purposes, as few were purchased. This example was operated by VF-66, based at North Island in 1945. (US Navy/NARA via Dennis R. Jenkins)

The Grumman F9F-8P Panther became the primary reconnaissance aircraft for the Navy before its place was taken by the Vought RF-8 Crusader. (John Ryan Collection)

undercarriage. The primary powerplant was a Wright piston engine mounted in the nose, while mounted in the tail was a General Electric turbojet rated at 1,600 lb st. The first production aircraft were delivered to VF-66 at San Diego, this unit being formed specifically for this purpose. This squadron undertook the initial carrier qualifications, although it would be decommissioned in

After the F9F series of fighters, Grumman produced the F11F Tiger, the prototype of which is seen here. (US Navy/NARA via Dennis R. Jenkins)

213

The Douglas F4D Skyray was assigned to the Navy squadrons during the 1960s, its primary role being that of all-weather fighter. The machine was allocated to VFAW-3 when photographed. (Terry Jones Collection)

October. The Fireballs were then transferred to VF-41, which undertook sea-going trials aboard the USS *Wake Island*, *Bairoko* and *Badeong Strait*. But after nearly two years of service, the Ryan FR-1 Fireballs were withdrawn. Although the type was successful as far as the concept went, it became obvious that the mixed-powerplant aircraft was not really capable of further development. However, the jet engine was starting to make an impact on the Navy, and would eventually result in the extant vessels and those built in the future being configured to operate jet aircraft from the outset. It was the Grumman Corporation that was the first supplier of jet fighters to the Navy, having already delivered a range of piston fighters and attack aircraft to the same service. The first type from Grumman was the F9F Panther, the proto-type of which had flown in November 1947. The aircraft that was delivered was a single-engined, straight-winged fighter armed with four 20 mm cannon plus pylons under the wings for a range of weaponry and fuel tanks to supplement those mounted on the wingtips. First deliveries began in May 1949 to VF-51, and eventually a total of 1,092 fighters were delivered, including a short run of reconnaissance aircraft. The straight-winged model was followed by a swept-wing version – the F9F Cougar. The prototype made its maiden flight in September 1951, while the first operational unit, VF-32, received its first examples in 1952. Eventually a total of 774 examples, including reconnaissance models, were constructed. Grumman ramped up the specifications of its fighters when the F11F Tiger was ordered by the US Navy in April 1953, although deliveries did not begin until 1955.

The Douglas Aircraft Company entered the jet fighter market with the F4D Skyray in January 1951, when the prototype first flew. As with most jet aircraft of the period, the Skyray took some time to enter service, the first not joining the Navy until April 1956, the first recipient being VC-3. When production ended a total of 420 machines had been delivered.

214

These McDonnell F3H Demons were assigned to VF-31 when pictured. The Demon suffered from engine problems, although the design did lead to the F-4 Phantom II, a much better aircraft. (US Navy/NARA via Dennis R. Jenkins)

It was the appearance of the McDonnell, later McDonnell Douglas, Aircraft Corporation in the Navy's roll of suppliers that caused some surprise, as it was better known for supplying the Air Force with aircraft. The reason for choosing McDonnell was that the major suppliers were fully occupied in manufacturing programmes for the Navy. Another reason for choosing such a company was that such a young and inexperienced team would not be so restricted by previous programmes. This team's first product was the FD/FH Phantom, which entered service in July 1947. Many of these aircraft were used by the USMC, although the type's service life was short, as better and more powerful aircraft were already preparing to leave the drawing-boards. Following on from the Phantom came the F2H Banshee, which bore a strong resemblance to its older sibling. First deliveries began in March 1949, with VF-171 being the recipient. The earlier models were mainly used in the day-fighter role, and a total of 436 were delivered, these including night-fighters and reconnaissance versions. Following on from these early models, a further 400 were constructed, these having a nose-mounted search radar and extra internal fuel. A complete change in the McDonnell design ethic appeared with the F3H Demon. Gone were the two engines and straight wings of the earlier McDonnell machines, and in their place came a single engine, sharply swept back flying surfaces, a belly full of cannon and the capability to carry and launch a variety of air-to-air missiles. While the type suffered from problems with its Allison engine, the F3H Demon was an important stepping-stone towards that doyen of naval fighters, the McDonnell F-4 Phantom II.

Another major USAAF aircraft supplier that entered the US Navy lexicon for a short period was North American. Better known for the B-25 Mitchell

The North American FJ-4 Fury was the primary fighter for the US Navy during the late 1950s and early 1960s. (Terry Jones Collection)

One of the most usual aircraft operated by the US Navy was the Vought F7U Cutlass. It took a lot of development for the type to become a viable proposition. This F7U-3 is pictured undertaking trials aboard the USS Hancock. (US Navy/NARA via Dennis R. Jenkins)

After their stint in the Pacific, the Grumman Avenger was used in the carrier onboard delivery role. Here a COD Avenger prepares to depart from an unknown carrier. (US Navy/NARA via Dennis R. Jenkins)

and P-51 Mustang, North American was awarded a contract for a jet fighter that would eventually satisfy the needs of both the USAF and the US Navy. The aircraft for the US Navy was the FJ-1 Fury, which was a straight-winged, single-engined fighter. While it was a somewhat unprepossessing aircraft, its performance was adequate enough to enter service in 1948 with VF-5A, later VF-51. These first Furies only lasted in front-line service for fourteen months before being reassigned to the Naval Reserve Units. The follow-up to the straight-winged Fury was a far more advanced design, which divided into two separate programmes – the F-86 for the USAF and the FJ-2/4 Fury. The initial contract was issued in February 1951, the resultant aircraft having folding wings, an AN/APG-30 radar, four nose-mounted cannon and a wider-track undercarriage. The first model was delivered in 1953, with all aircraft being delivered to the USMC. The following versions, FJ-3 and FJ-4, would be the models delivered for naval service, the FJ-3 being delivered from September 1953, while the FJ-4 entered service in February 1955.

It was Chance Vought Aircraft Inc. that provided one of the most unusual jet aircraft to enter US Navy service. The basis of this aircraft was research gained from Germany after the end of the war. The result was the F7U Cutlass, which featured a sweep of 38 degrees, to the rear of which were elevons that controlled pitch and roll. The resultant aircraft had a high rate of climb and a high top speed, allied to which were outer wing panels that could be folded for stowage. The first production machine flew in March 1950, with four units eventually being equipped, these being VF-81, VF-83, VF-122 and VF-124. The initial model, the dash 1, had numerous stability problems, which

217

were ironed out in later versions, and these also had provision for launching guided missiles. Production ended in December 1955, while service use ended a couple of years later.

The aircraft of choice for carrier operations over Korea was the Grumman F9F Panther, which was not only reliable, but could carry a reasonable amount of external weaponry. They were already deployed aboard the *Valley Forge*, and the next carrier to deploy them was the USS *Princeton*, which was pulled out of reserve in July 1950 and prepared for combat service. The *Princeton* arrived in Yokosuka at the beginning of December, having spent the intervening period bringing the mostly reserve crew up to operational standard, and departed for Korea in the middle of the month. This first adventure only lasted a couple of days, the first sorties being launched in the early hours of 21 December. The selected aircraft types were a single F4U Corsair and a Douglas AD Skyraider, both being dispatched on heckler raids. They were successful, hitting targets at Chakto-ri and Hongwon, with trucks being destroyed and a building napalmed. The next mission was launched a few hours later, utilising a pair of Skyraiders, both of which visited the same region and attacked road and rail traffic. Six aircraft were launched after breakfast, and they too visited the same area, hitting buildings and rail and road traffic. Lunchtime saw a further ten aircraft, of which two were Grumman Panthers, the others being a pair of Corsairs and the remainder Skyraiders. Targets hit and destroyed included a pair of ox-drawn carts, a favourite method of moving weapons and ammunition, a fuel dump was hit with napalm and the ADs concentrated on hitting buildings and the airfield at Yonpo. Once the Skyraiders had departed Yonpo, the airfield was attacked again by Grumman Panthers and F4U Corsairs, which caused further destruction. Two smaller raids followed in the evening, each involving a pair of Skyraiders that continued the work carried out earlier that day. On 22 December the early-morning hecklers consisted of a single AD and a single F4U. As before, the raiders returned to the previous day's area, attacking anything they could find, using rockets, bombs and napalm. The next group of raids included two Grumman Panthers and a mix of Corsairs and Skyraiders, which attacked the usual range of targets; a troop concentration was also hit. The next wave of aircraft was launched in mid-morning and was a mix as before, with each flight concentrating on applying pressure to the North Korean forces by attacking mainly communications targets. The mid-afternoon strike concentrated their efforts on the Hamhung area, where a command post was destroyed, as were other buildings suspected of housing military personnel. The final sortie for the day was dispatched in late afternoon and consisted of a pair of F4U Corsairs, which were directed to attack railway and road traffic. After both aircraft had returned to the *Princeton*, she withdrew to Yokosuka for replenishment and restoring.

The *Princeton* departed from Japan on 29 December, arriving in theatre on 1 January 1951 and launching the first strike, eight F4Us and six ADs, at breakfast time. Arriving at the zone attacked on the previous visit, the carrier's

The USS *Ticonderoga* was assigned to ASW duties when photographed, here Grumman S-2 Trackers from the carrier provide a flypast.

US Navy/NARA via Dennis R Jenkins

CVA-62 USS *Independence* was assigned to the Atlantic fleet when photographed, note the forward section of the landing deck lowered to act as a hangar side lift.

US Navy/NARA via Dennis R Jenkins

The pilot of an MDD F-4S Phantom II of VF-161 kicks in the afterburners as it launches from the waist catapult of the USS *Midway*.

US Navy/NARA via Dennis R Jenkins

Grumman provided the carrier onboard delivery aircraft to the US Navy for many years. The original type was the C-1 Trader although this was replaced by the far more capable C-2 Greyhound as seen here.

US Navy/NARA via Dennis R Jenkins

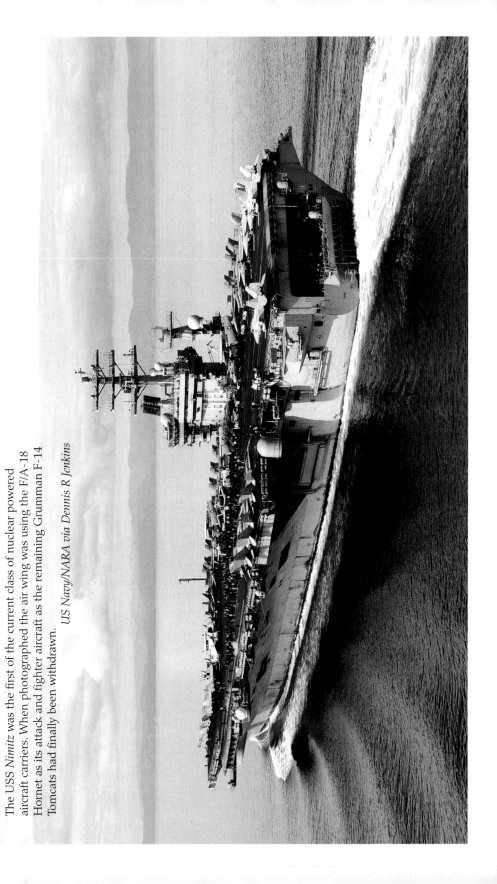

The USS *Nimitz* was the first of the current class of nuclear powered aircraft carriers. When photographed the air wing was using the F/A-18 Hornet as its attack and fighter aircraft as the remaining Grumman F-14 Tomcats had finally been withdrawn.

US Navy/NARA via Dennis R Jenkins

With the retirements of the Crusader and Vigilante the navy was reliant of RF-4B Phantoms of the USMC for reconnaissance purposes. Here an RF-4B of VMFP-3 prepares to launch from the USS *Midway*.

US Navy/NARA via Dennis R Jenkins

With its bomb racks clean the A-6E prepares to depart from the USS *Nimitz*. The centreline pylon carries a refuelling pod to supplement the air wings KA-6D Intruder tankers.

US Navy/NARA via Dennis R Jenkins

Seen tied up its home base of Maryport, Florida, is the USS *Saratoga* complete with F-14 Tomcats, A-7 Corsairs, A-6 Intruders, S-3 Vikings, SH-3 Seakings, E-2 Hawkeyes and a solitary EKA-3B Skywarrior.

US Navy/NARA via Dennis R Jenkins

The crew of the USS *America* celebrate the 75th year of US Naval aviation in a graphic manner.

US Navy/NARA via Dennis R Jenkins

A Grumman F-14D Tomcat of VF-213 Black Lions turns towards its home carrier, the nuclear powered USS *Theodore Roosevelt*. After a period of austerity the aircraft of the US Navy began to sport some colour as shown here.

US Navy/NARA via Dennis R Jenkins

Currently awaiting its fate is the USS *John F Kennedy*, CVA-67, that was decommissioned in 2007.
Seen in happier days the JFK has a full range of modern aircraft aboard as it cruises in the Atlantic.
US Navy/NARA via Dennis R Jenkins

An LTV A-7E Corsair of VA-56 aboard the USS *Midway* taxies towards the catapult, in the
background are a range of F-4 Phantoms sporting air defence weapons fits.
US Navy/NARA via Dennis R Jenkins

Electronic support is a vital part of naval tactical warfare as it can be used to jam enemy radars. Originally the EA-3B Skyraider was utilised in this role being replaced later by the EA-6A converted from standard Intruders. This is an EA-6B Prowler operating from the USS *Enterprise,* this model has now been replaced by specially configured Boeing Hornets.

US Navy/NARA via Dennis R Jenkins

Pictured while en route to the Arabian Gulf is the USS *Dwight D Eisenhower* with its air wing on deck. Waiting to launch are an EA-6B Prowler and an E-2C Hawkeye on the bow catapults while the waist catapult has an F/A-18 Hornet waiting to go while others form a queue.

US Navy/NARA via Dennis R Jenkins

With its flight deck quiet the USS *Carl Vinson* heads towards its station in the Indian Ocean prior to launching combat sorties against Taliban forces fighting in Afghanistan.

US Navy/NARA via Dennis R Jenkins

In 1992 the USS *Ranger* hosted a pair of B-25 Mitchell's that were launched to commemorate the fiftieth anniversary of the Doolittle Raid

US Navy/NARA via Dennis R Jenkins

CVN-71 USS *Theodore Roosevelt* is seen here cruising in the Arabian Gulf as part of Southern Watch and Enduring Freedom. This carrier had also taken part in Operation Desert Storm in 1991.

US Navy/NARA via Dennis R Jenkins

The USS *Abraham Lincoln* would take part in Operation Iraqi Freedom, the toppling of Saddam Hussein. After taking part in Enduring Freedom the carrier entered Puget Sound for maintenance which was completed in 2010.

US Navy/NARA via Dennis R Jenkins

The current general fleet fighter is the F/A-18 Hornet. This aircraft is assigned to VFA-32 and is configured as a tanker as it sports a centreline refuelling pod plus fuel tanks on all four underwing pylons.

US Navy/NARA via Dennis R Jenkins

This F-14D of VF-213 is seen here operating in Bombcat mode complete with bombs on the under fuselage mounts plus the LANTIRN guidance pod under the right hand glove pylon. At the time the aircraft was operating from the USS *Theodore Roosevelt*.

US Navy/NARA via Dennis R Jenkins

The Lockheed S-3 Viking undertook numerous role aboard the carriers of the US Navy. Originally delivered for the ASW role the aircraft later undertook electronic warfare duties and as tankers as shown here.

US Navy/NARA via Dennis R Jenkins

This overhead view is of Task Force 155 underway to the Arabian Gulf to take part in Operation Desert Storm.

US Navy/NARA via Dennis R Jenkins

The nuclear powered aircraft carrier USS *George Washington* is currently home ported in Japan, the only one of its class to be based outside of the United States.

US Navy/NARA via Dennis R Jenkins

A sight to cheer up any commander and to dismay any enemy, three nuclear carriers with the USS *Ronald Reagan* closest to the camera head towards their next tour of duty.

US Navy/NARA via Dennis R Jenkins

CVN-74 USS *John C Stennis* was named after the Senator and strong supporter of the US Navy. The *Stennis* was commissioned December 1995.

US Navy/NARA via Dennis R Jenkins

Named after President Harry S Truman CVN-75 that was commissioned in July 1998. Note the Seahawk anti submarine helicopter on approach.

US Navy/NARA via Dennis R Jenkins

This rear end shot of the USS *Ronald Reagan* reveals the enormous size of the latest US Navy aircraft carriers, something that dry dimensions cannot portray.

US Navy/NARA via Dennis R Jenkins

The final member of the Nimitz class of aircraft carrier is the CVN-77 USS *George HW Bush* seen here undertaking its sea trials.

US Navy/NARA via Dennis R Jenkins

aircraft came under the control of the Mosquito FAC, who directed the aircraft to attack numerous troop concentrations and emplacements, using bombs, rockets and napalm bombs. Another large strike mission was launched in mid-morning, consisting of seven ADs and five F4Us, and yet again they came under the control of the Mosquito FAC, being targeted against a train parked in a tunnel. This was attacked with bombs and napalm, the former being skip-bombed into the tunnel mouths. The final mission for the day was dispatched in the early afternoon, and consisted of four each of F4Us and Skyraiders. This mission concentrated upon destroying buildings that were either occupied or could be used by the enemy. There was no early heckler mission launched on 2 January, the first sortie consisting of six F4Us. Their targets were a pair of bridges, which they only damaged, but more success was gained against a warehouse and other buildings that were completely destroyed. A further six F4Us and an equal number of ADs were launched soon afterwards, and again a range of buildings and vehicles were destroyed. The midday mission consisted of ten Corsairs and six ADs, their targets being military vehicles pointed out by the Mosquito FAC, together with some ammunition oxcarts that exploded satisfactorily.

The pattern for 3 January was similar to that of the preceding day, although the first mission was directed at the village of Hoeyang, where the four F4Us and four Skyraiders concentrated upon destroying three command posts and any military material in the vicinity. A much larger sortie was dispatched at midday, and consisted of two groups of Corsairs, five and seven respectively, plus a flight of four Skyraiders. The latter initially attacked troops and vehicles in the operational area, after which they moved on to bombing the town of Pongsuwon, leaving many buildings burning. The larger group of F4Us, meanwhile, were ordered by the Mosquito FAC codenamed Cottonseed to attack troop concentrations and their military vehicles. As this flight departed the combat area, they destroyed one last target, a radio antenna. The smaller flight of F4Us meanwhile concentrated upon buildings and troop concentrations, being guided by Mosquito FAC Tumbleweed. At the conclusion of these raids the *Princeton* withdrew from the area to undertake refuelling.

After refuelling, the *Princeton* returned to the operations zone, resuming flying in the early morning of 5 January. A total of twelve Corsairs and three Skyraiders were dispatched and undertook attacks on troop concentrations, which were successful, as was the follow-up on the buildings they had been occupying. A further attack was launched at midday consisting of ten F4Us and four Skyraiders, concentrating upon the targets from the previous attack, and further casualties were inflicted on the North Korean forces, using a full range of weaponry.

The *Princeton* withdrew from the area and set sail for Sasebo for restoring and refuelling, arriving there on 7 January. She remained in port until 18 January, joining up with TF.77 the following day, and combining with the USS *Philippine Sea*, *Valley Forge* and *Leyte*. All four carriers were operating off the east coast of Korea and were tasked with providing close support to Allied troops where requested and interdiction against enemy forces where needed. As before, the carriers launched hecklers to keep the enemy on their toes, and these were followed up by a full range of sorties to suppress any enemy troop movements. While the strike force was attacking enemy forces on the ground, the anti-submarine Skyraiders were ensuring that no enemy submarines were in the area. After the day's attacks had been completed, photo-reconnaissance flights were undertaken by Grumman F9F-2P aircraft to assess the damage. Over the following fifteen days the carriers of TF.77 undertook a full range of missions against enemy forces before withdrawing for refuelling on 8 February 1951.

Although the *Princeton* and her consorts returned to the east coast of Korea the following day, the weather was not good enough for general flying, although a special mission was launched to attack the railway tunnels near Sinpo. Two Corsairs and four ADs were launched, and the tunnels were attacked using rockets, bombs and napalm. Although the damage inside was undetermined, the railway tracks were destroyed. The following day the weather had cleared, and so the *Princeton* was able to launch a full attack, which comprised twenty-two Corsairs, eleven Skyraiders and four F9Fs. These sorties covered close support, deep penetration attacks and strikes on bridges and buildings determined to be housing enemy forces. A similar mission was launched the following and saw the air groups supporting forces around Seoul and attacks further afield against targets near Wonsan, Hamhung and the Choshin reservoir. The *Princeton* spent the next day refuelling and restoring at sea before setting out for Yokosuka, where she arrived on 15 February.

On 23 February the *Princeton* departed Japan and rejoined TF.77, joining up with the *Philippine Sea* and the *Valley Forge*. Three days later the carrier groups launched a massive attack on enemy concentrations at Pyongchang and down towards Seoul. These attacks destroyed numerous vehicles, troop concentrations and buildings. These strikes were followed up by jet reconnaissance flights to determine the extent of the strikes. The following attack was launched although the cloud density meant that bombing was radar guided. The following day saw a much larger force dispatched, concentrating on the usual range of targets. Over the next two weeks the *Princeton* air group undertook a similar range of missions, with short breaks for refuelling, before departing the area on 4 April and arriving at Yokosuka two days later.

After ten days in port, the *Princeton* set sail from Japan, arriving off the coast of Korea, where it joined up with TF.77 and the *Boxer* and *Philippine Sea*. The carrier joined up with the task force just in time to participate in that afternoon's strikes against enemy forces in the Hamhung area. The following day, 19 April, saw limited operations as the weather was inclement, although it cleared the following day. This was fortuitous, as the UN ground forces were being heavily attacked and required close air support to deter the enemy forces. The *Princeton* launched twelve F9Fs, twenty-six Skyraiders and forty-two Corsairs. Using the full range of available weaponry, the aircraft, under the command of a forward air controller, mounted attack after attack on the enemy positions. Such was the intensity of flying that stocks of some items began to run low, resulting in the dropping of a kitchen sink attached to one of the few bombs still available. A similar quantity of aircraft was launched the following day, undertaking similar missions as before, while those of 22 April saw an even greater number of aircraft being launched, as the North Korean forces were pushing the UN forces hard.

The *Princeton* departed the combat zone after the aircraft had returned, although this absence was cut short because the carrier had to return to the area when her aircraft were desperately needed to counter a Communist attack that had just been launched. Virtually the whole air wing was launched, over eighty aircraft, to provide close air support for the UN troops. However, the air strikes, though effective, were not enough to halt the Communist advance. The following day, 25 April, saw another maximum effort launched, although this time the purpose was to protect the UN forces that were withdrawing in good order. Over the following seven days the carrier continued to launch maximum efforts although she suffered her first loss on 6 May when the F9F being flown by Ensign Sullivan of VF-191 was hit by anti-aircraft fire, which caused the engine to explode, killing the pilot. The air group suffered another loss four days later when the F9F of Ensign Brewer was also struck by anti-aircraft fire, which caused his aircraft to explode. After a two-day break due to inclement weather, operations resumed, the air group continuing to launch maximum efforts in support of retreating UN troops. A further three days of intensive flying saw the *Princeton* attacking the usual troop concentrations before departing for Yokosuka.

A flight of Vought F4U Corsairs from VF-884 overfly their home carrier, the USS Boxer. (US Navy/NARA via Dennis R. Jenkins)

While *en route* to Yokosuka the *Princeton* was recalled in order to provide the maximum amount of aircraft from TF.77. A full air strike was launched, although two losses were incurred, these being Commander Merrick, the air group commander, whose Skyraider was hit by anti-aircraft fire, and Lieutenant Hawkins of VF-871, whose F4U was also struck by anti-aircraft fire. The *Princeton* launched its last sorties for the period on 19 May, after which she departed Korea and headed for Yokosuka, arriving there on 22 May. The *Princeton* rejoined TF.77 at the end of the month, combining with the USS *Boxer* and *Bon Homme Richard*, and resuming operations on 2 June, launching thirty-two aircraft to undertake the usual range of missions. The following day saw ninety-four aircraft launched, as close air support was required along the central front. A similar pattern followed over the next two days, during which a pilot, Ensign Randolph, was killed when his F9F hit the round-down of the flight deck while landing. After refuelling the *Princeton* continued combat operations during the next three days,. However, the air group suffered another loss when the AD-4Q of the air group commander was seen to crash near Kunsong: both Commander Stapler, CAG-19, and AT1 Blazevic were killed. After searching for CAG-19 the air wing resumed flying operations on 11 June, continuing to support UN troops and attack FAC selected targets, although these came at a cost, including Lieutenant (jg) Harris of VA-55, whose Skyraider crashed during a strafing run. At the conclusion of this period the *Princeton* departed for Yokosuka, arriving there on 3 July.

After nine days of rest and recuperation, the USS *Princeton* departed Japan under the aegis of Operation Order 22-51, which outlined the carrier's mission

With its destroyer escort turning in concert, the USS Bon Homme Richard moves into position to launch its aircraft. The air wing on this vessel operated F4U Corsairs, Douglas Skyraiders and Grumman Panthers. (US Navy/NARA via Dennis R. Jenkins)

Airborne early warning had started to play a significant part in the Pacific campaign, the favoured mount being the Grumman Avenger. During the Korean War and after it would be the Douglas Skyraider. Here an aircraft from VC-11 taxies up the deck of the USS Boxer. (US Navy/NARA via Dennis R. Jenkins)

for this period. This included close air support, interdiction, reconnaissance and bombing missions in support of UN forces. By 14 July the *Princeton* had arrived off Korea, where she linked up with the *Boxer* and *Bon Homme Richard* and the remainder of TF.77. Over the following twenty-eight days the *Princeton* conducted air operations in concert with the other two carriers in support of the operations order, although yet again the air group incurred losses. The first loss occurred on 16 July when the F4U piloted by Lieutenant Martin of VF-871 crashed during a napalm run. VF-871 lost a further pilot, Ensign Moody, who was shot down by anti-aircraft fire that set his F4U ablaze. The other Corsair unit aboard the *Princeton*, VF-821, lost a pilot, Lieutenant (jg) Ray, whose aircraft crashed soon after take-off. The final casualty occurred on 9 August when VF-821 suffered the loss of Lieutenant (jg) Hughes, whose Corsair was also hit by defensive fire. This deployment ended on 11 August, and the carrier arrived in Japan the following day.

The *Princeton* departed Japan and headed for the United States for a much-needed refit. After returning to Japan, she later rejoined TF.77 and the *Boxer* and *Philippine Sea* on 30 April 1952. Air operations resumed for real on 1 May, and continued until 16 May, when the *Princeton* returned to Yokosuka. She returned to the east coast of Korea on 4 June. As in the previous deployment, the air group suffered some losses, the first being Lieutenant Tennyson, whose AD-4 was hit by anti-aircraft fire during a bombing run on a railway line on 4 June. The next loss, on 12 June, concerned another VA-195 pilot, Lieutenant Jackson, another victim of ground fire. Yet again the pilot had

A stream of Douglas Skyraiders proceed to the catapults on the USS Bon Homme Richard. Once airborne, the aircraft will undertake attacks in support of UN forces. (US Navy/NARA via Dennis R. Jenkins)

been undertaking a bombing run on a railway line. On 14 June the *Princeton* lost her first jet when the F9F of Lieutenant (jg) Cross of VF-191 was hit by anti-aircraft fire during a railway bombing run. As this was a period of maximum launches, the number of losses was commensurate with the number of sorties flown. This operational period ended on 26 June, the carrier arriving in Yokosuka two days later.

The *Princeton* resumed operations on 6 July in company with the *Boxer*, *Philippine Sea*, *Bon Homme Richard*, the *Philippine Sea* being replaced by the *Essex* part-way through the deployment. Flying operations began on 7 July and continued until 3 August, the carrier departing for Japan the following day. During this deployment the *Princeton*'s air group undertook more than 1,100 sorties, although three pilots were killed in action. The carrier returned to Korea on 18 August. Flying operations resumed on 22 August when almost the entire air group was launched against targets in the Changp-yong-ni on the Korean west coast, where the F9Fs engaged MiG 15s without suffering any losses. Much of the flying scheduled for the remainder of August was cancelled due to adverse weather conditions. The following month was not much better, as the weather deteriorated again, but even so some 1,000 sorties were flown before the carrier departed for Japan on 20 September. By 4 October the *Princeton* was back on station, linking up with the carriers *Essex*, *Bon Homme Richard* and *Kearsarge*. During this deployment the carrier groups encountered numerous MiG 15s over the Wonsan area. Most of the sorties

Refuelling at sea was an important part of the process of keeping the fleet close to the area of operations. Here the USS Lake Champlain is fuelled by an oiler, as is an escorting destroyer. (US Navy/NARA via Dennis R. Jenkins)

during this period were close air support missions in support of UN forces. Over 700 missions were undertaken, during which two pilots were killed. The *Princeton* departed Korea on 16 October, arriving in Japan two days later.

The *Princeton* departed Japan for another refit before returning to the Korean theatre in March 1953. The carrier rejoined TF.77 on 9 March, linking up with the *Valley Forge* and the *Philippine Sea*. Combat operations resumed on 14 March and continued until 31 March. During this period the carrier flew more than 1,000 sorties, undertaking mainly close air missions in support of UN ground forces. Fortunately losses were light, being one pilot killed and one wounded. At the conclusion of this deployment the *Princeton* returned to Yokosuka, arriving there on 3 April. After ten days in port she was back in the combat zone, rejoining TF.77 and the other carriers on station, these being the *Oriskany*, *Valley Forge*, *Philippine Sea* and *Boxer*. All five carriers were heavily involved with close air support missions in support of UN forces. These began on 17 April and ended on 14 May, with more than 1,500 missions being flown. Given the number of sorties flown it is surprising that only seven pilots were lost operationally. The *Princeton* returned to Sasebo on 16 May, although by 19 May the carrier was in Hong Kong for a visit.

The *Princeton* rejoined TF.77 on 11 June, where she linked up with the carriers *Lake Champlain*, *Philippine Sea* and *Boxer*. Combat flying resumed on 12 June, the deployment lasting until 1 August. Again the mission tally was high, passing 1,500 during the period, and only three pilots were killed. The *Princeton* arrived at Yokosuka on 3 August.

After eleven days in port the *Princeton* departed Japan, arriving on station to join TF.77 two days later. The other carriers already with the task force were the *Boxer*, *Kearsarge* and *Lake Champlain*. Combat operations began on 18 August and lasted until 1 September, although three days were lost due to bad weather. The USS *Princeton* departed for Yokosuka on 2 September, arriving there the following day.

Caught just at the point of touchdown is this Douglas AD Skyraider of VA-35 assigned to the USS Leyte. (US Navy/NARA via Dennis R. Jenkins)

One of the carriers that had a short deployment was the Essex-class vessel USS *Leyte* that was deployed to Korea in October 1950. The *Leyte* departed from Sasebo on 5 November in company with the USS *Missouri* and *Valley Forge*, arriving off the west coast of Korea the following day. From 6 to 8 November the *Leyte* undertook 220 sorties against railway vehicles, and close air support missions to cover UN forces. After a day spent refuelling, she returned to the west coast to link up with the *Philippine Sea* and *Valley Forge*, and all three carriers conducted operations against enemy forces in the Chongjin and Namsan-ni areas, during which the *Leyte* launched 102 sorties. Further sorties were carried out in the same region the following day, although this time the targets were railway orientated. Refuelling took place on 13 December, the carrier rejoining TF.77 the following day. It was the Myongchong and Kapsan areas that were the focus of the *Leyte* air group. As before, the air group flew missions in support of UN forces before withdrawing for refuelling.

Upon returning to the west coast, the *Leyte* air group resumed air support operations during which, on 18 November, a VF-31 Grumman Panther shot down a MiG 15 and damaged another. The *Leyte* entered a cycle of two days' combat followed by a refuelling day, although some days were lost due to bad weather, which included severe snowstorms. The *Leyte*, in company with her fellow carriers, launched a maximum effort in support of UN forces on 30 November, this continuing for a further four days before she withdrew for refuelling. Normal missions resumed on 6 December and continued for the next five days. On 12 December the carrier resumed missions after a refuel break, continuing her task against targets in the Wonsan and the Fusen reservior area against Red Chinese troops. Close air support missions continued until 24 December, the *Leyte* departing Korea on Christmas Day, heading for Sasebo.

Another carrier that was an early Korean arrival was the USS *Boxer*, which arrived in Japan at the beginning of September 1950. After refuelling and taking on extra stores the *Boxer*, with Air Group 2 aboard, left Sasebo on 14 September, joining TF.77 the following day. The mission for the task force during this period was to continue the already established air supremacy missions, isolate enemy forces in the Inchon area and provide close air support during the Inchon landings that began in the early morning of 15 September with a US Marine assault on the island of Wolmi-do, where the shocked and dazed North Korean troops were completely overwhelmed, this being the result of three days of continuous air and sea bombardment. During this period the *Boxer* was running with one engine shut down and locked off as the main reduction gearbox had failed, which reduced the carrier's top speed to 26 knots, although 28 knots could be achieved for short periods. The *Boxer* completed this deployment on 2 October, and entered Yokosuka dock-yard for repairs to number four engine. She departed Yokosuka on 11 October, joining TF.77 three days later, bringing the number of carriers available to three, as the *Philippine Sea* and *Valley Forge* were already on station. During this deployment TF.77 undertook missions against the Wonsan harbour area in preparation for a landing, for which purpose countermining, reconnaissance, gunfire spotting and attack sorties were to be flown. The landing against Wonsan began on 20 October, the harbour and its environs being declared safe five days later. During this period the air wing suffered no losses, and so it was a relatively happy ship that arrived at Yokosuka on 25 October. The *Boxer* returned to America to have the attendant problem of number four propeller shaft dealt with, having completed the previous deployment on three engines, with number four propeller removed to reduce drag and vibration.

At the completion of repairs the *Boxer* undertook work-up exercises around Hawaii before departing from Pearl Harbor for a direct transit to Korea and TF.77, arriving on station on 26 March 1951. Having taken part in the Wonsan and Inchon support missions, the air group aboard the *Boxer* found its priorities changed as the mission brief was now to include close- and long-range air support, interdiction, reconnaissance and air bombardment. The *Boxer* stayed on station until 19 April, during which period the air group undertook air strikes on targets as specified by command orders or at the request of Mosquito FACs. During this period at least two pilots were lost, both aircraft being brought down by anti-aircraft fire.

After nine days in port the USS *Boxer* departed Japan on 30 April to rejoin TF.77 off the Korean coast, arriving on station on 2 May. The other carriers on station during this period were the *Philippine Sea* and the *Princeton*. During the period 3 May to 3 June the *Boxer* air group, in concert with the other carriers, undertook the full range of assigned sorties. On 6 May a small celebration was

In good weather the Douglas Skyraiders of VA-115 aboard the USS Philippine Sea are armed up for their next mission. (US Navy/NARA via Dennis R. Jenkins)

held to commemorate the 41,000th landing aboard the *Boxer*. While much of this deployment was uneventful, some days' flying were lost in June due to inclement weather, although the air wing managed to launch 1,495 propeller and 404 jet sorties respectively. Some losses were incurred during this period, as North Korean anti-aircraft batteries had increased in number. The first loss occurred on 7 May when the AD-4 Skyraider piloted by Lieutenant (jg) Robbins assigned to VA-702 was shot down during a close air support mission. The next loss was that of an F4U Corsair of VF-884, the pilot, Lieutenant (jg) Dragastin, being killed on impact. Another VF-884 Corsair was lost on 18 May, the pilot, Lieutenant-Commander Carmichael, dying of his injuries soon after rescue. The USS *Boxer* departed the combat zone on 2 June, arriving at Yokosuka two days later. While in port the opportunity was taken to carry out major repairs to the jet blast deflectors, catapults, deck planking and the engines.

When the *Boxer* departed Japan on 15 June 1951, Air Group 2 had been replaced by Air Group 101, the two days' transit time being used to bring the new air group up to operational standard. The mission briefing was the same as that of the earlier deployment, although protection and support of UN troops was given a higher priority than previously. The carrier rendezvoused with TF.77 on 17 June, launching its first sorties soon after arrival. This deployment continued until 15 July, although by this time the amount of close air support work was leading to a significant increase in fatal casualties. The first occurred on 20 June when the Corsair of Lieutenant (jg) Shaeffer crashed into the sea three miles south of Songjin after the aircraft had been badly damaged by ground fire. Two days later an AD-2 Skyraider piloted by Lieutenant Arrivee was seen to crash in flames while strafing a ground target. A luckier pilot was Ensign Nelson, whose badly damaged F4U-5NL was abandoned over Wonsan Bay, the pilot being rescued by helicopter a few minutes later. A further three aircraft were lost during this period, although the crews were rescued. The *Boxer* departed TF.77 on 15 July, arriving at Yokosuka two days later.

The *Boxer* was back on station by 28 July, linking up with the *Princeton*, the other TF.77 carrier. Combat operations began immediately after arrival and continued until 22 August except for breaks for a refuelling and bad weather, which included a diversion to the north on 20 August to avoid the attentions of Typhoon Marge. Losses to enemy fire during this period were nil. However, Lieutenant (jg) Rines of VF-721 was killed after launching when the engine of his F4U failed. At the conclusion of this operational period the *Boxer* departed for Yokosuka once flying had ceased on 22 August, the carrier arriving in port two days later.

On 5 September the *Boxer* returned to the fray, having departed Japan some two days earlier. Upon arrival the carrier linked up with the USS *Essex*, also part of TF.77. Operations began the following day and continued until 3 October. During this period the usual range of targets were attacked, while on 16 September the resident air group had to make room for some guests, as many aircraft from the USS *Essex* were diverted to the *Boxer* due to an F2H missing all the arrester wires and the crash barrier, and ploughing into the aircraft sitting on forward deck park. As many were fuelled and armed, the resulting conflagration stopped flying while the fire was suppressed. This meant that the *Boxer* received a total of six jet aircraft that remained on board overnight. These six aircraft were later factored into the next flying programme of the *Essex*, and so they launched the following morning to join up with the remainder of the *Essex* strike wave, as the carrier had been declared fit to continue, although the starboard catapult was temporarily out of action. The first loss of this cruise happened on 17 September when the F4U of Lieutenant Pederson, assigned to VF-884, was shot down during a close air support sortie. The wingman's aircraft was also hit during this attack, although the pilot managed to make an emergency landing at K-18, an emergency landing strip. At the conclusion of flying on 3 October, the *Boxer* departed Korean waters to return to the United States, calling at Yokosuka *en route*.

After a much-needed refit the USS *Boxer* returned to Japan, arriving at Yokosuka in March 1952, having collected Air Group 2 from Hawaii on the

A VA-65 Douglas Skyraider taxies down the deck of the Philippine Sea after returning home. Of note are the exhaust stains down the side of the fuselage. (US Navy/NARA via Dennis R. Jenkins)

way. The *Boxer* departed Japan on 29 March, having spent the intervening period working up to an operational standard. Two days later the carrier joined TF.77, where it linked up with the *Philippine Sea* and *Valley Forge*. Combat operations began soon after arrival that same day and continued until the end of April. The mission for the TF.77 carriers was as before, to strike at the enemy as directed and to cause as much disruption and destruction as possible. However, such operational intensity was not without casualties the first occurring on 18 April when the AD Skyraider piloted by Lieutenant-Commander Neel of VA-65 was seen to crash after the port wing root failed, apparently due to enemy fire. This accident was the event that would spur concerned pilots to press for armour plate to be fitted to the AD, which would allow it to survive such wounds and bring its crew to safety. Fortunately no other aircrew were lost during this period, and so the carrier was able to depart Korean waters on 30 April, arriving at Yokosuka on 2 May.

The rest period concluded on 12 May when the *Boxer*, in company with the *Philippine Sea*, departed Japan and headed towards Korea to undertake further operations against Communist Chinese and North Korean forces. Both carriers and their escorting destroyers rendezvoused with TF.77 on 14 May, although combat operations did not resume until the following day. During the period 15 to 26 May, over 250 sorties were launched, the air group suffering only one loss, that of Lieutenant (jg) Kordefleski, whose Corsair was shot down while he was undertaking a rescue support mission. The *Boxer* departed Korean waters after she ceased flying on 26 May, setting course for Yokosuka, where she tied up two days later.

On 9 June 1952 the *Boxer* again departed Yokosuka for Korea, where she joined up with TF.77 on 11 June. As this was to be a period of maximum effort, three other carriers were already on station when the *Boxer* arrived, these being the *Princeton, Philippine Sea* and *Bon Homme Richard*. Standard air operations were conducted over the three days before the force was refuelled. Maximum effort attacks began on 16 June and saw over 200 aircraft launched from the four carriers against targets in the Kowon area of North Korea. The following day saw a similar assault against targets in the Hungham area, but it was not achieved without casualties as three aircraft and pilots were lost. Two were AD Skyraiders from VA-65, which were hit by anti-aircraft fire, the pilots, Lieutenant (jg) Rowe and Ensign Faler, being killed. The third aircraft was an F4U of VF-63 piloted by Lieutenant (jg) De Masters, which was observed going down with a wing missing; while a trailing parachute was observed on the ground, the pilot was never observed. On 23 June another maximum effort was launched by the carrier air group, again with over 200 aircraft dispatched to their targets of hydroelectric facilities in North Korea. Fortunately, despite a strong defence by the enemy, no aircraft were lost, although the F4U piloted by Lieutenant-Commander Miller of VF-63 was hit by defensive fire while attacking the Koysen hydroelectric plant. Although the aircraft was badly damaged and had a tendency to flame when fuel touched hot metal, the pilot managed to go 'feet wet', ditching his fighter just south of Tanchon, from where he was picked up by a rescue helicopter. Group-strength strikes were launched over the following four days, this being followed by a refuelling day and a two further days' down time due to bad weather. Full air operations resumed on 2 July and continued until 5 July, although the combat record was saddened by the loss of Lieutenant Griffith of CAG-2 staff, who was flying an F9F on a photo escort mission over Wonsan. The carrier refuelled on 6 July, after which it departed Korea for Yokosuka in company with the USS *Philippine Sea*, arriving in port two days later.

The next deployment for the *Boxer* was a short one that lasted from 21 to 24 July. The carrier had departed from Yokosuka on 21 July, taking station off Japan. The purpose of this short deployment was to provide simulated attacks against the bases on the Japanese islands, with strikes being launched against Tachikawa, Yokota, Atsugi, Misawa and Chitose bases over the next three days. All of these simulated attacks were deemed successful, as the defending forces failed to intercept the attackers until the aircraft were departing the targets. At the conclusion of this exercise the carrier returned to Yokosuka, where it remained until 1 August.

On that day the carrier departed on its fateful deployment, joining up with TF.77 and the USS *Essex* three days later. Operations began on 5 August when 106 sorties were launched against a range of pre-determined targets. These sorties were conducted without loss. The following day saw the launch of eight sorties, when there was an outbreak of fire in the hangar deck that quickly developed into a raging inferno. It immediately set off the fuel in one aircraft, and this spread rapidly to the others in the hangar. Also on the deck were aircraft fully armed for the next missions, and so bombs, rockets and cannon shells were set off, further increasing the danger to the ship and its crew. The captain and his officers were faced with the choice of launching the remaining aircraft to clear the deck or to taxi the aircraft forward, dump the ammunition and slow the ship, and then concentrate upon fighting the fire. The latter was the chosen course of action. Initial reports had indicated that only the port side of the hangar was afire, although the entire hangar was confirmed as being enveloped within minutes. This being the case, the only way to fight the fire was through No. 2 elevator, which was in the raised position. In order to present the fire-fighting crews with a better chance, the decision was made to turn the carrier to starboard. Even so, the fire crews faced a dangerous task, as ammunition was still exploding, and this was re-inforced by the explosion of a 500 lb bomb that sprayed shrapnel across the hangar. The change in the carrier's direction also allowed more than sixty crewmen who had been trapped to jump over the side, being quickly rescued by the attending destroyers. Although the fire crews were battling valiantly, the smoke pall that enveloped the ship and the tenacity of the fires led the captain to contemplate abandoning ship. Praise was later heaped on the engineering team who kept the engines running, which in turn allowed the ship to be handled in support of the fire teams' efforts. While the fire crews continued their battles below deck, on the flight deck handling parties began to remove any ammunition from aircraft and ready lockers and off the deck, heaving all of it into the sea, thereby reducing the chances of further explosions. The ammunition clearance teams having done their bit, they turned their attentions to fighting the fires in other parts of the ship. After more than four hours the crisis was declared over, and so the task of sorting out the ship and assessing the chances of making it combat ready began. Given the severity and spread of the fire, it was fortunate that casualties were so light – eight killed, one missing, one critically injured, one severely burned and a further seventy suffering from smoke inhalation effects.

With the fires out the crew then set about repairing the ship and preparing the *Boxer* to resume flying operations, although eighteen aircraft were either destroyed or badly damaged, while much of the available ammunition had been heaved over the side. While higher command praised the efforts of the crew, it was decided to return the *Boxer* to Yokosuka for further assessment and repairs as needed. As the carrier departed Korean waters the commander of TF.77 sent this signal to the *Boxer*: 'My admiration for you and your fine crew is greater than ever. Performance was magnificent.' On 8 August the carrier departed TF.77 and headed towards Japan, arriving in port on 11 August. In dock an inspection of the ship's structure revealed many buckled frames and bulkheads, while the flight deck itself was peppered with access holes cut to allow access to the fire below. While on the face of it the damage would keep the carrier off the line, it was estimated that with minimal repairs the *Boxer* could resume operations.

Repair work kept the carrier in Japan for a few extra days while emergency

The USS Princeton also undertook operations off Korea. Here a range of Skyraiders, already armed, are lashed to the deck before being dispatched on their next missions. (US Navy/NARA via Dennis R. Jenkins)

repairs were effected. On 23 August the repaired *Boxer* departed Yokosuka, joining TF.77 three days later. Operations commenced on 27 August, the targets being in the region of Wonsan, being followed by strikes on the Choson area on the following day. Also aboard for this final deployment was GMU-90, with its selection of F6F-5(K) Hellcat drones and a pair of AD-2(Q) drone controllers. Their deployment required that a pair of Skyraiders were left on shore. The first use of these drones took place on 28 August when a single drone was launched under the control of the command aircraft. Further drone launches were undertaken on 29 August, 1 September and 2 September. After these launches the *Boxer* departed Korean waters for the last time on 4 September, arriving in Japan two days later. During the transit the carrier's excess aircraft were flown off to Atsugi. After a rest period in Japan the *Boxer* returned to the United States to await full repairs.

One of the longest-serving carriers in Korean waters was the USS *Philippine Sea*, the last of the Essex class. Having arrived in Japan in late July, the *Philippine Sea* departed Okinawa for Korean waters on 4 August, arriving in theatre the following day. Also in TF.77 was the carrier *Valley Forge*. Sorties were launched soon after arrival and were aimed at providing close support for UN forces, although these were not completely successful as the operation suffered from overloaded communications and problems in utilising the carriers' aircraft. This resulted in many running short of fuel before they could undertake an attack. Up to 14 August further sorties were launched to provide close support for UN forces, although the only time the system worked correctly was on 11 August, resulting in complete destruction of

233

enemy forces. At the conclusion of that day's flying the *Philippine Sea* returned to Sasebo for rest and restoring. The rest period was short, as the carrier departed from Japan the following day to return to Korean waters. This combat period lasted until 18 August, the carrier operating off both coasts during this period. The *Philippine Sea* returned to Sasebo for rest and restoring, and remained there for four days. She then resumed combat operations in support of UN forces. However, by this time most of the communications and scheduling problems had been dealt with, so that many of the attacks were successful. The carrier departed Korea on 5 September, arriving in Sasebo the following day.

A break for a short refit followed before the *Philippine Sea* returned to Japan to undertake further service. This resumed on 23 November, and her air group was fully involved in driving back a combined North Korean/Chinese force pushing hard down the peninsula. From this date until 7 December 1950 the carrier's air group continued to support the withdrawing UN troops. During this period Air Group 11 supported the US Marines in repulsing the Communist forces all the way to Hungnam. At the conclusion of this operational period the carrier departed for Yokosuka for rest and recuperation.

The *Philippine Sea* resumed operations on 4 April 1951 in company with the *Boxer* and *Princeton*. Combat flying resumed the following day and consisted of close air support and interdiction of enemy supply routes until 8 April, after which the group refuelled. The carrier resumed flying on 11 April, remaining on station for the following two days. A refuel period occupied the group over 14/15 April before it returned to Korean waters the following day. Combat operations continued between 16 April and 3 May before the carrier returned to Yokosuka. Between 4 and 16 May she remained in port before rejoining TF.77 on 17 May. During this period the carrier launched maximum

Deck crew struggle across the deck of the USS Essex as the blizzard continues to blow. As flying is cancelled, the aircraft are lashed down and have their covers secured to keep the snow out. (US Navy/NARA via Dennis R. Jenkins)

The USS Essex would be the only carrier to operate the McDonnell F2H Banshee operationally over Korea. Here one comes up on the elevator while a helicopter of HU-1 takes off in the background. (US Navy/NARA via Dennis R. Jenkins)

air strikes in order to repulse the Communist offensive, after which she returned to Japan. At the conclusion of this deployment the *Philippine Sea* returned to the United States, entering the dock at San Francisco for a much-needed refit. After working up and cruising off the western American coast, the *Philippine Sea* redeployed to the Korean theatre. The carrier undertook combat operations against the Sui-Ho dam and took part in a combined operation against Pyongyang. The carrier returned to San Diego in August 1952, rejoining TF.77 in December with Air Group 9 aboard. As before, operations were conducted in support of UN forces, after which the *Philippine Sea* returned to America.

The class-name ship, the USS *Essex*, also served off Korea for much of the war, arriving there in early August 1951. On 22 August the *Essex* joined TF.77 off the west coast of Korea in company with the USS *Boxer* and the *Bon Homme Richard*. Combat operations began on 23 August, and unfortunately the air wing lost its first aircraft, an F4U piloted by Lieutenant (jg) Franz, whose aircraft crashed near Wonsan harbour. Combat operations continued over the

VA-75 was one of the Skyraider squadrons aboard the USS Bon Homme Richard during the Korean conflict. Here one of the unit's aircraft, well loaded with bombs, awaits its turn to depart. (US Navy/NARA via Dennis R. Jenkins)

next two days without major incident before the *Essex* withdrew for refuelling. Operations resumed on 29 August and continued until 19 September. Losses during this period included Lieutenant (jg) Smith and ATAN Black, who were killed when their AD-4 burst into flames and crashed after take-off on 26 August. The next loss was Lieutenant Sistrunk in an F4U that was shot down on 3 September, while on the same day the F9F of Ensign Armstrong was also lost. The following day was no better, as two F9Fs were lost and their pilots, Lieutenant (jg) Bramwell and Lieutenant (jg) Ashford, were killed. Four days later the Skyraider piloted by Lieutenant (jg) Parse was shot down during a bombing run. The *Essex* was one of the few carriers to deploy the McDonnell F2H Phantom operationally, and it was one of these that wreaked havoc on the flight deck of the *Essex* on 16 September. On a second landing attempt Lieutenant (jg) Keller missed the arrester wires, bounced over the barrier and crash-landed into the aircraft parked on the forward deck, destroying a pair of F2Hs and two F9Fs. Three personnel were killed, four were declared missing, and a further sixteen were injured. Once the fire had been contained, and the wreckage and injured removed, the *Essex* was declared fit for further operations. After flying was completed on 19 September, a more sober carrier and its crew departed for Japan, arriving at Yokosuka two days later.

After a period of rest and recuperation and the replacement of crew and

Douglas AD Skyraiders of VA-728 sit on the bow catapults on the USS Antietam, while others of the same squadron wait behind for their turn to launch. (US Navy/NARA via Dennis R. Jenkins)

aircraft, the *Essex* put to sea on 1 October, joining up with TF.77 on 3 October. Air operations continued until the end of the month except for those days lost to refuelling and bad weather. The second day of operations saw the loss of Lieutenant (jg) Teague, whose AD-4 was hit by anti-aircraft fire, subsequently crashing. Another loss occurred on 16 October when an F2H piloted by Lieutenant-Commander Oxley was hit by ground fire, and the aircraft was later seen to crash and explode. Eight days later one of the *Essex* F4Us piloted by Ensign Bateman was shot down by enemy ground fire. After the final combat operations had been flown, the *Essex* departed Korean waters on 30 October, arriving in port the following day.

The USS *Essex* rejoined TF.77 on 14 November, linking up with the other carrier on station, the USS *Bon Homme Richard*. Combat operations occupied the *Essex* air wing until 12 December, and included attacks on targets mainly over North Korea, during which two pilots were killed, while another four required rescuing by rescue helicopters and ships. At the completion of this deployment the *Essex* departed Korean waters on 12 December, arriving at Yokosuka two days later. The *Essex* departed Japan on Boxing Day 1951, arriving off Korea on 28 December to join TF.77. Air operations resumed on 28 December and continued until they were interrupted on 3 January 1952. The cause of this interruption was a 20 mm cannon whose breech-block lock failed and allowed the air supply to fire off a single round that in turn hit an F9F on the flight deck. The Grumman fighter then exploded, injuring five personnel. On the flying side five pilots, including a USAF exchange pilot, were lost to enemy action, while a similar number required rescuing. At the conclusion of flying on 31 January the carrier prepared to leave Korea on 1 February 1952, arriving at Yokosuka two days later.

On 18 February the *Essex* departed Japan to rejoin TF.77, where it linked up with the carriers *Valley Forge, Antietam* and *Philippine Sea*. The *Essex* carried out its support operations from 21 February to 5 March, during which two pilots were killed and another required rescuing. The *Essex* returned to its Japanese home port on 7 March, transferring some of its spare aircraft to the *Valley Forge*, while the remainder were flown to the Atsugi pool. The *Essex* departed Japan on 11 March and headed for San Diego for a much-needed refit, calling at Pearl Harbor *en route*.

The *Essex*'s refit was completed in June 1952, with the carrier returning to Japan in early July. On 29 July she departed Yokosuka to rejoin TF.77, arriving on station on 1 August. Combat operations began that same day and continued until 2 September against targets in North Korea, and some were flown in support of UN troops. Losses were slight during this period, and so the carrier was able to depart Korean waters on 4 September with a full complement aboard. The *Essex* was later deployed to the China Sea as part of the Peace Patrol before returning to Puget Sound for refitting in mid-1955.

As well as the five long-serving Essex carriers, another six undertook tours

A batsman guides a Sikorsky helicopter from HU-1 aboard the aircraft carrier USS Boxer. The helicopter proved invaluable during this and following conflicts. (US Navy/NARA via Dennis R. Jenkins)

in Korean waters for short periods. The first of these was the USS *Leyte*, which commenced combat operations over Korea on 10 October 1950, the aircraft being supplied by Air Group 3. Missions covered the usual spectrum and included support for the Wonsan and Songjin invasions. The *Leyte* completed its operations on 29 October, arriving in Sasebo two days later. She returned to combat on 7 November, joining TF.77 and the *Valley Forge*. As before, the air group undertook the usual range of missions in support of UN forces, including a maximum effort on 30 November against enemy forces in the Chonjin reservoir area. This maximum effort flying continued until 24 December, after which the *Leyte* departed for Sasebo, where she arrived two days later. The carrier returned to action on 7 January 1951, resuming her role within TF.77 in company with the *Philippine Sea*, *Princeton* and *Valley Forge*. Combat operations were delayed until 13 January due to bad weather, and the carrier remained on station until 19 January. During this period over 400 sorties were flown, after which the *Leyte* departed for Sasebo on 19 January, staying there for a short period before returning to America.

The USS *Bon Homme Richard* had been recalled to action in January 1950 for use off Korea. The carrier's first deployment began on 30 May, the assigned aircraft being Air Group 102. Within its make-up the air group consisted of VF-781 and VC-61 flying versions of the Grumman F9F, VF-783 and VF-874, plus VC-3 flying F4U Corsairs, VA-923 and VC-11 and VC-35 operating versions of the Skyraider, and HU-1 with rescue helicopters. The carrier launched its first missions that same day, and continued to generate sorties until 17 June, when she arrived in Sasebo on 16 June for rest and recuperation. The *Bon Homme Richard* departed Japan at the end of June, returning to TF.77 the following day. Combat operations resumed that same day and continued until 28 July, the carrier returning to Sasebo and thence to America for a refit soon afterwards. The *Bon Homme Richard* returned to Korean combat in May 1952, this lasting until December. Aboard the carrier was Air Group 7, which comprised VF-71 and VF-72 flying F9Fs, VF-74 operating F4U Corsairs, VA-75 with Skyraiders, plus VC-4, VC-12, VC-33, VC-66 and HU-1 flying Corsairs, Skyraiders for the other three VC units and helicopters for rescue purposes. At the conclusion of this deployment the carrier returned to America for refitting and conversion.

In October 1951 the USS *Antietam* was deployed to Korea for war service. Aboard was Air Group 15, which comprised VF-713 operating Corsairs, VF-831 and VF-837 flying F9Fs, VA-728 with Skyraiders, and VC-3, VC-11, VC-35, VC-61 and HU-1 flying the same types as aboard the *Bon Homme Richard*. The *Antietam* began operations with TF.77 on 11 October, continuing these until 16 November and returning to Yokosuka two days later. The *Antietam* returned to Korean waters on 18 January 1952, resuming its combat operations the same day. These continued until 2 February when the carrier returned to Japan, where it remained until departing for the United States soon afterwards.

The USS *Kearsarge* was an unusual ship in that it had undergone SCB-27A modifications before undertaking its Korean tour. During its short deployment the *Kearsarge* operated in company with the *Bon Homme Richard* and *Princeton*. On 14 September 1952 the *Kearsarge* departed from Yokosuka and headed to the east coast of Korea, where it joined up with TF.77 on 16 September. The *Kearsarge* deployment continued until 18 October, when the carrier departed for Yokosuka, arriving there two days later. She resumed operations with TF.77 at the end of the month, remaining on operations until March 1953, when she returned to her home port of San Diego.

The USS *Oriskany* was another short-term participant in Korean operations, having departed San Diego on 15 September 1952 and arrived at Yokosuka on 17 October with Air Group 102 aboard. The carrier joined Task Force 77 off the Korean Coast on 31 October, beginning combat operations the following day. The air group aircraft attacked their targets with bombs and rockets, also strafing enemy supply lines and co-ordinating bombing missions and surface bombardments along the coast. The carrier's air group pilots also downed two Soviet-built MiG 15 jets and damaged a third on 18 November. Strikes continued until 11 February before the *Oriskany* returned to Yokosuka for rest and recuperation. Departing Japan, the *Oriskany* returned to combat on 1 March 1953, remaining in action until 29 March before making a short port call at Hong Kong, after which the carrier resumed its air strike duties on 8 April. The *Oriskany* departed the Korean coast on 22 April, returning to Yokosuka for a short period and departing for San Diego on 2 May, arriving there on 18 May before returning to San Diego. She departed San Francisco on 14 September to enforce the uneasy truce in Korea, arriving at Yokosuka on 15 October. From Korea the carrier cruised the Sea of Japan before she returned to San Diego on 22 April 1954.

The location for the F4Us of VMA-332 is the escort carrier USS Point Cruz, this being one of the USMC escort carriers utilised during the Korean War. (US Navy/NARA via Dennis R. Jenkins)

The USS *Lake Champlain* was another carrier that had undergone SCB-27A modifications being recommissioned again in September 1952. After her shakedown cruise the carrier arrived at Yokosuka on 9 June 1953. Combat operations began on 13 June as part of TF.77, and she remained on station until 27 June when she retired to Japan, arriving at Yokosuka on 29 June. After carrying out some secondary peacekeeping missions, the *Lake Champlain* returned to her home port of Maryport in December.

Only one of the Independence class of light carriers was involved in the Korean war, this being the USS *Bataan*. A veteran of the Pacific campaign, the *Bataan* was prepared for war service again in early 1950. She was recommissioned on 13 May 1950 at Philadelphia. In July the carrier entered San Diego, being loaded with USAF cargo and personnel and departing for Japan soon afterwards. Upon returning to the United States, the *Bataan* embarked a USMC fighter-bomber group comprising VMA-212 and VMA-312, both flying F4U Corsairs. The carrier also had a detachment of HU-1 helicopters for planeguard and rescue duties. The *Bataan* headed for the Far East, arriving in Japan on 16 November. After working up, the carrier arrived in Korean waters on 15 December, where she undertook missions in concert with TF.77. By the end of December the *Bataan* had arrived at Sasebo for a period of rest and recuperation. Departing Sasebo on 1 January 1951, she was initially ordered to join up with TF.77. However, the orders were changed *en route*, and so the carrier was diverted to the west coast of Korea to join TG.96.8. Between 3 and 8 January she undertook close air support duties on behalf of UN forces before departing for Sasebo, arriving there on 9 January.

The *Bataan* departed Sasebo on 15 January to link up with TG.95.1, replacing the Royal Navy carrier HMS *Theseus* under the command of Vice-Admiral Andrews RN. With TG.95.1 the *Bataan* launched continuous sorties against North Korean forces throughout daylight hours. Except for 21 January the carrier launched sorties over the period 17–25 January, during which period the USMC fighter-bomber squadrons lost two aircraft and pilots to enemy ground fire. At the conclusion of flying, the *Bataan* departed Korean waters and headed for Sasebo, arriving there on 26 January, having handed over support duties to HMS *Theseus*.

The *Bataan* left Sasebo on 3 February, arriving off the Korean coast on the following day, where it replaced the Royal Navy carrier. As before, she undertook duties in support of UN forces before departing for Japan on 13 February, having been replaced by the *Theseus.*

Ten days later the US Navy carrier had relieved its British counterpart, remaining on station until 4 March. By the following day the carrier was off Pusan, where she swapped VMF-212 for VMF-312 before heading to Sasebo, arriving there on 7 March. After a six-day break, the *Bataan* returned to the fray, relieving the *Theseus* and remaining on station until departing for Yokosuka on 22 March. The *Bataan* departed Yokosuka on 30 March, returning to the west coast of Korea to replace the *Theseus*. The *Bataan* remained with the task group until 6 April before returning to Japan. She continued her turn and turn about with the *Theseus* before departing Japan and heading for the Bremerton Naval Yard, arriving there on 9 July 1951 for a much-needed refit. The *Bataan* was ready for service again in November, departing for Yokosuka in January 1952. Upon arrival the carrier was involved in working-up exercises before departing for Korean waters and arriving off the west coast on 29 April. Combat operations were carried out by VMF-312 Corsairs against Communist targets in support of UN forces. The *Bataan* remained on station until 10 May, when, after recovering her final aircraft, the carrier headed for Sasebo, having been relieved by HMS *Ocean*.

The *Bataan* returned to the west coast on 19 May, remaining there until relieved by the *Ocean* on 28 May, the American vessel returning to Sasebo for her scheduled break. The *Bataan* relieved HMS *Ocean* on 5 June, continuing her role of supporting UN forces, using the Corsairs of VMF-312 to prosecute her mission. Ten days later the *Bataan* was replaced by the *Ocean*, the American carrier returning to Sasebo. Combat operations resumed on 24 June, with the *Bataan* replacing the *Ocean* as the west-coast carrier. The carrier remained on station until relieved by the British carrier on 3 July, and she arrived in Japan the following day. On 21 July the *Bataan* had again relieved the *Ocean* as part of TG.95.11, launching her Corsairs against the usual range of targets. This deployment ended on 23 July 1952, the *Bataan* departing soon afterwards for Bremerton, where she arrived on 11 August to await refitting.

The *Bataan* was back at Sasebo by the beginning of March 1953, with VMF-312 and its Corsairs aboard. The carrier departed her Japanese base on 6 March, heading for the west coast of Korea, where she replaced the Royal Navy carrier HMS *Ocean*. The *Bataan* remained on station for the next ten days before returning to Sasebo. After a period of rest and recuperation the carrier returned to the west coast on 11 April, remaining on station until relieved by her British counterpart on 19 April. The *Bataan*'s last deployment was under-

The USS Block Island was one of the carriers that used units from the USMC to provide the strike force. (US Navy/NARA via Dennis R. Jenkins)

The USS Cabot would also operate USMC F4U Corsairs while engaged in combat operations over Korea. (US Navy/NARA via Dennis R. Jenkins)

taken between 27 April and 6 May, after which the carrier returned to San Diego to await further usage.

While the majority of US Navy air operations were carried out by the Essex-class carriers and the single Independence-class light carrier, technically a US Marine Corps vessel, some use was made of the large escort carrier fleet held in reserve. Only five CVE carriers were used, and all came from the Commencement Bay class. The first of the class to deploy was the USS *Sicily*, which arrived in Kobe to collect the USMC unit VMF-323 and its twenty-three Corsairs. After working up the air group, the carrier put into Sasebo for a refuel and restoring, departing on 13 June 1951 to join up with TG.95.1 on the west coast of Korea. Combat operations continued until 22 June until she was replaced by HMS *Glory*. After a break in Sasebo, the *Sicily* returned to Korea on 1 July, resuming combat operations in support of UN forces. Nine days later the carrier had been replaced by the *Glory* and returned to Sasebo. The break for the *Sicily* ended after ten days, when the carrier returned to the Korean west coast on 19 July. This stint lasted ten days, much of it in concert with the *Glory*, as a maximum effort was needed to repel a North Korean and Chinese attack. After this effort the *Sicily* departed the war zone on 29 July, returning as ever to Sasebo. She resumed her combat operations on 4 August, remaining on station until relieved by HMS *Glory* on 14 August. By 25 August the *Sicily* was back on station, resuming her attacks on designated targets. This deployment was completed on 1 September, when she returned to Japan. The carrier remained in port slightly longer than usual, and so she did not replace the *Glory* until 9 September. Operations off the west coast continued until 16 September 1951. The *Sicily* undertook two further tours off the Korean west coast, these taking place between 4 and 13 September and 6 and 16 October 1952. At the conclusion of the Korean conflict the USS *Sicily* returned to the Far East, where she helped support the shaky Korean truce. This deployment lasted from 14 July 1953 to 25 February 1954.

One of the shortest deployments was that of the USS *Rendova*, which lasted from 25 September to 6 December 1951. During this period the carrier had VMF-212 and its Corsairs aboard. During this period the *Rendova* swapped

The USS Essex continued in service after the Korean War. This view of the carrier clearly shows the locations of the forward elevator and the deck-edge elevator to the fore of the landing deck. (US Navy/NARA via Dennis R. Jenkins)

over with the Australian carrier HMAS *Sydney*. At the conclusion of this deployment the *Rendova* was replaced by the USS *Badeong Strait* and headed for San Diego.

The USS *Badeong Strait* undertook Korean combat tours during the period 29 July 1950 to 23 January 1951, 2 October 1951 to 14 February 1952, and 6 October 1952 to 11 February 1953. During these periods the carrier embarked USMC units, the first being VMF-212, followed by VMF-312, as part of Task Group 95.11. At the conclusion of her war service the carrier underwent conversion for anti-submarine duties. Another escort carrier with a reasonably long Korean war service was the USS *Bairoko*. The *Bairoko* was recommissioned on 12 September 1950, undertaking three deployments to Korean waters from 14 November 1950 to 15 August 1951, 1 December 1951 to 9 June 1952 and February to August 1953, supporting UN forces. The embarked USMC unit was VMF-312 and its Corsairs. In a similar manner to the other escort carriers deployed to Korea, the *Bairoko* was part of Task Group 95.11. On 9 May 1951 the carrier had five men killed and thirteen injured by an explosion and flash fire in Japanese waters. From the early part of 1951 the *Bairoko* was reworked as an anti-submarine carrier and remained as such until the end of hostilities. The shortest deployment of all concerned the USS *Santa Cruz*, which lasted from 26 August to 29 October 1953. This carrier had no air group assigned, being used as a platform to land an Indian peacekeeping force under the aegis of Operation Platform in the Korean demilitarised zone. This brought an end to the US Navy's active deployment in the Korean conflict.

Vietnam –
A Long-Drawn-Out Affair

When the Korean conflict ended on 27 July 1953, the American Administration was fairly sure that it would not be involved in another conflict for a few years. But by 24 April 1954, this situation had changed completely, as it was asked to help out the French forces embattled at Dien Bien Phu, a position that they had been in since 13 March. The proposed intervention was codenamed Operation Vatour. This saw the heavy bombers of Strategic Air Command being escorted by fighters launched from carriers of the 7th Fleet cruising in the Gulf of Tonkin. To add spice to the plan, the Joint Chiefs of Staff had proposed the use of three tactical nuclear weapons to emphasise their seriousness to the North Vietnamese. But the plan was not implemented, as the French capitulated by 3 May. The surrender was followed by the signing of the Geneva Accords that divided the country at the 17th Parallel.

The 7th Fleet was called into action again on 4 September after a Chinese bombardment of the Quemoy Islands near Formosa. The 7th Fleet dispatched three carriers from Manila to defend the Nationalist Chinese stronghold. This move confirmed the pledge made by President Truman, later affirmed by President Eisenhower, that the United States would use its forces to defend Formosa. By 16 October the number of carriers in the Formosa Strait had been increased to four, at which time Secretary of State Dulles warned China that American forces in the Pacific would be used if needed. The Chinese response was to send a force of a hundred aircraft to attack the Nationalist-held Tachen Islands north of Taiwan on 10 January 1955. The Americans responded to this attack by transferring the USS *Midway* to the Pacific, where she joined up with Task Force 77. Already on station were the carriers *Yorktown*, *Kearsarge* and *Princeton*, and all four provided air cover for the evacuation of the islands, which involved the removal of 18,000 civilians and 20,000 military personnel.

The USS Midway was assigned to Yankee Station in the Tonkin Gulf on numerous occasions, and took part in various operations, including Iron Hand missions against SAM sites. (US Navy/NARA via Dennis R. Jenkins)

The China–Taiwan crisis flared up again on 23 August 1958 when Communist forces started to bombard the islands of Matsu and Quemoy. The President authorised the 7th Fleet to provide support for the garrison at Quemoy, and so six carriers were placed on station and remained there until the crisis cooled again in December.

The US Navy found itself involved in the Middle East in July 1958 when President Camille Chamoun of the Lebanon requested help from the Americans. The help that was forthcoming were the carriers of the 6th Fleet, the *Essex*, *Saratoga* and *Wasp*, while land support was supplied by the US Marine Corps. This show of strength allowed the American negotiators to bring the civil war to an end and allow an election to be held. At the same time that the Americans landed in the Lebanon they were reinforced by British troops who were flown into Jordan, as that country was also under the threat of civil war.

It was South-East Asia that would become the biggest thorn in the side of the Americans. In September 1951 President Truman authorised the setting up of the Military Assistance Advisory Group in Vietnam to supervise the use of the $10 million of US military aid that had been supplied to the French forces engaged in fighting the Vietnamese Communists. However, the French commanders were more concerned in re-establishing themselves as a colonial power. But as events proved, the French approach could not contain the Communist forces, and their decision to fully accept American help was too late.

After the division of Vietnam and the withdrawal of the French there was a conference in Washington DC on 5 December 1955 that decided that all future American aid would be directly supplied to the forces of South

The flight deck of the USS Saratoga has a standard air wing aboard for the 1960s, consisting of F3H Demons, F-8 Crusaders, A-3 Skywarriors, E-1 Tracer and the HUP-1 Retriever for rescue purposes. (US Navy/NARA via Dennis R. Jenkins)

Vietnam. The first commander of the MAAG was Lieutenant-General O'Daniel, whose command consisted of a few personnel. However, this had grown to 740 troops by June 1956, as the Americans had to fill the void left by the departure of the remaining French forces, who departed under the Geneva Accords. Over the next few years South Vietnam was stressed by internal political fighting. This, coupled with President Diem's reluctance to allow the MAAG to work with Vietnamese Army units in case they gained influence and control, resulted in a weakened ARVN. This state of affairs saw the North Vietnamese mounting strong incursions below the 17th Parallel from 1961. When John F. Kennedy was elected President in 1961 he promised to increase American assistance to Vietnam in exchange for better co-oper-ation by the Vietnamese President. During the period 1961–4 the number of MAAG advisors in Vietnam increased from 746 to 3,400, at which point the organisation was renamed Military Assistance Command – Vietnam (MACV). The first commander of this unit was Lieutenant-General Harkins.

To provide further support for MACV and the South Vietnamese Army, ARVN, President Kennedy authorised the US Navy to deploy aircraft carriers and escorts to the Gulf of Tonkin. By this time the carriers of the US Navy were the most modern in the world, and the American force was the largest at sea, numbering over twenty-five vessels. Some of these were purely anti-submarine vessels, although the majority were classified as attack carriers, including the first nuclear-powered vessel, the USS *Enterprise*. The first carrier to deploy was the USS *Bon Homme Richard*, which joined the resurrected Task Force 77 in February 1964 with CVW-19 aboard. Within the air wing were VF-191 and VF-194 flying models of the Vought F-8 Crusader, VA-192 and VA-195 with Douglas A-4s, and VA-196 flying Douglas Skyraiders, while flights were supplied by VAH-4, Douglas A-3 Skywarriors, VFP-63, Vought

RF-8s, VAW-11, E-1B, and HU-1, Kaman Seasprites. During this deployment, which lasted until November, the carrier lost only one aircraft, a Vought F-8, due an accident. It was during this period that the Gulf of Tonkin incident occurred on 2 August. The vessel involved was the destroyer USS *Maddox*, engaged in Operation DeSoto, an intelligence-gathering exercise, that was patrolling in international waters in the Gulf of Tonkin. Also known as Operation Plan 34A, this had begun in February 1964 and was intended to deter North Vietnamese waterborne incursions into the south. Three North Vietnamese gun boats attacked the *Maddox* at high speed, although no damage was caused to the American ship.

In response, the USS *Ticonderoga*, which had arrived on Yankee Station on 11 May 1964, launched four F-8s of VF-51 to intercept the attack boats, one of which was sunk. Once the fighters had returned to the carrier, the *Maddox* resumed its patrol, although by now it had been reinforced by the USS *Turner Joy*. Over the night 4/5 August both destroyers reported that they were scanning an incoming attack on radar. In support of the destroyers the *Ticonderoga* launched a further fighter patrol, although the pilots reported that the seas near the destroyers were clear. Although the detected attack failed to materialise, this further provocation allowed President Johnson to authorise Operation Pierce Arrow, a limited strike on military facilities in North Vietnam. Pierce Arrow involved a force of sixty-four aircraft drawn from the carriers *Ticonderoga* and *Constellation*, the latter having arrived on Yankee Station on 11 June 1964. The air strike force hit the torpedo boat bases at Hon Gai, Loc Chao, Quang Khe and Ben Thuy and the oil storage facility at Vinh. Only two aircraft were lost, both from the *Constellation*. The first was a Douglas A-1H Skyraider, part of a group of ten aircraft, that was hit during a

Airborne early warning became the province of the Grumman E-1 Tracer that replaced the Douglas Skyraiders previously used in the role.
(US Navy/NARA via Dennis R. Jenkins)

The USS Ticonderoga was used in both the ASW and attack roles during the Vietnam War. Here flights from the ASW units, Grumman S-2 Trackers, fly past their nautical home base. (US Navy/NARA via Dennis R. Jenkins)

dive-bomb attack and was seen to hit the ground without a parachute being oberved. The second concerned the pilot of a Douglas A-4 that was hit by anti-aircraft fire, although in this case the pilot managed to escape, becoming a prisoner of war – an experience he managed to survive. Altogether the *Constellation* launched ten Skyraiders, eight A-4s and two F-4 Phantoms in one wave, while the second wave consisted of five Skyhawks, four A-1s and three F-4s. The *Ticonderoga* launched a total of thirty-four aircraft, of which eight were F-8 Crusaders. As a result of the *Maddox* attacks the US Congress passed the Gulf of Tonkin Resolution on 10 August, which handed over much of the control of the forthcoming conflict to the President. This allowed the Joint Chiefs of Staff to increase the number of carriers available on Yankee Station. Therefore by August the carriers on station included the *Bon Homme Richard*, *Ticonderoga*, *Constellation* and *Kearsarge*, which arrived on 11 August, and the USS *Ranger*, which arrived on 17 August. Throughout the remainder of 1964 the US Navy carriers undertook routine patrols, and so none of their aircraft were lost to enemy action, although fourteen were lost due to accidents. By the close of the year the *Bon Homme Richard* had sailed for Japan for rest and recuperation, and she was soon followed by the *Ticonderoga* and *Kearsarge*. Remaining on station were the *Constellation*, *Ranger* and *Hancock*, which had joined TF.77 in mid-November.

It was 7 February 1965 before the US Navy was back in action again. The original plan had been to involve the carriers from 2 December 1964 in accordance with the intentions previously expressed by President Johnson. However, an attack by the Viet Cong on US facilities in Saigon on 24 December was followed by assaults on Pleiku and Camp Holloway. Both of these attacks saw President Johnson authorise Operation Flaming Dart 1, an attack on targets within North Vietnam. The carriers involved were the *Coral*

Sea, which came on station on 23 January, and the *Hancock* and *Ranger*. The targets allocated to the carriers were Dong Hoi and Vit Thu Li. The air strike was led by Commander Sells, Commander Air Group 21 from the *Hancock*. However, his force was depleted from the outset when the thirty-four aircraft dispatched from the *Ranger* had to abort due to incoming monsoon weather. The twenty-nine aircraft from the *Hancock* and the twenty *Coral Sea* aircraft did get airborne, and concentrated their efforts on attacking the barracks and port facilities at Dong Hoi. Due to cloud cover the attack was conducted below 700 feet in rain and poor visibility. Given these poor conditions it is lucky that only one aircraft was lost, the pilot being killed. Lieutenant Dickson of VA-155 had been a section leader and his aircraft had been hit by anti-aircraft fire *en route* to the target. Even though there were some problems with the Skyhawk's handling, the pilot continued his run in to the target even though his aircraft was seen to be burning. Dickson successfully dropped his Snakeye bombs on target. With the weapons cleared, the pilot ejected from his blazing aircraft, but unfortunately his parachute failed to open and he was killed.

The Flaming Dart attack on North Vietnam on 7 February failed to have the desired effect, as Viet Cong forces attacked the American base at Qui Nhon on 10 February, causing serious casualties. The following day President Johnson authorised Flaming Dart II. Three carriers were involved, these being the *Coral Sea*, *Hancock* and *Ranger*, which between them launched ninety-nine aircraft against the NVA barracks at Chanh Hoa, close to Dong Hoi. As before, the weather was poor, rain being coupled with low visibility, during which the *Coral Sea* force lost two aircraft, with one pilot being captured. The first aircraft lost was the Vought F-8D from VF-154 piloted by Lieutenant-Commander Shumaker. It was suspected that his aircraft had been hit by debris from the rockets fired against an anti-aircraft position, and these had struck the rear of the fighter, causing the afterburner to explode and resulted in serious damage to the hydraulic system. With the aircraft becoming uncontrollable, the pilot ejected at low level, the aircraft crashed into the sea, and Shumaker, having ejected at low level, suffered serious back injuries. After eight years in various prison camps, Shumaker would resume his flying career after release. The other aircraft was a Douglas A-4C of VA-153 piloted by Lieutenant Majors. The pilot had dropped his CBU-24 bombs onto his designated target and had climbed his aircraft to height and headed towards the sea. However, during the flight the engine suffered a catastrophic failure that left the pilot with no option but to eject. Majors was quickly recovered from the sea by a USAF rescue helicopter that arrived within minutes. Post-strike assessment of the attack on Chanh Hoa revealed that twenty-three of the seventy-six buildings within the camp boundaries had been damaged or destroyed, although the losses incurred were seen as rather high for this kind of raid.

Although Flaming Dart II had been more successful than the previous effort, the NVA failed to take any notice of the attacks. In response to the continued Viet Cong attacks, President Johnson authorised the USAF and the US Navy to undertake a programme of graduated attacks against North Vietnam, This was named Operation Rolling Thunder, which started on 2 March 1965 and continued until October 1968. The carriers involved in the opening rounds of this campaign were the *Coral Sea*, *Hancock* and *Ranger*, these being replaced during 1965 by the *Yorktown*, *Midway*, *Oriskany*, *Bon Homme Richard*, *Independence* and *Bennington*. While the USAF undertook the initial strikes, the US Navy launched its first assault on 15 March. The Navy had been allocated targets to the east of Hanoi and close to the coast. The first target was the ammunition dump near Phu Qui, with no aircraft being destroyed during the attack, although an A-1H Skyraider of VA-95 from the USS *Ranger* was lost when it flew into the sea, killing the pilot.

The second carrier Rolling Thunder mission was launched on 26 March, utilising seventy aircraft, of which three were lost. The chosen targets were radar installations that were suspected of warning the North Vietnamese air defence system of incoming raids. The chosen sites were located at Bach Long Vi, Cap Mui Ron, Ha Tinh and Vinh Son. The first-named site was on a small island that was strategically located in the Gulf of Tonkin, seventy miles south of Haiphong, being located between the Red River mouth and the Chinese island of Hainan. On this raid three aircraft were lost. Two were from the USS *Hancock*, one being an A-1H Skyraider of VA-215, and the other an A-4E Skyhawk from VA-212. Both pilots survived the experience of ejecting and were successfully rescued. The final loss was of an F-8D from VA-154 on the USS *Coral Sea*, and the pilot of this aircraft was also rescued successfully. Three days later the carriers of TF.77 launched another attack against Bach Long Vi. The planning for this attack had been undertaken in Washington and was one of the worst features of the early Rolling Thunder campaign, as the planners insisted on attacking targets until they were destroyed or losses were too high. In response, the NVA commanders soon recognised this repetitive behaviour, and quickly reinforced the anti-aircraft weaponry at these targets. The result of this third attack was another three lost aircraft, two of which were squadron commanders from the USS *Coral Sea*. Seventy aircraft were launched for this attack, including six Douglas A-3B Skywarrior bombers of VAH-2. The first aircraft lost was that of Commander Harris, commanding officer of VA-155 from the *Coral Sea*, although he was quickly picked up from the sea after ejecting from his ailing Skyhawk. The second squadron commander from the *Coral Sea* to be shot down was Commander Donnelly of VF-154, whose Crusader was damaged during his first attack run, and again the pilot managed to escape, being rescued soon afterwards. The third loss was that of Lieutenant-Commander Hume of VA-154, whose Crusader was damaged during an attack run. The pilot headed his damaged fighter towards Da Nang, although it was seen to dive towards the sea. The canopy was seen to clear the airframe, but no further escape action was undertaken, and so the pilot was recorded as killed in action.

On 31 March the *Coral Sea* and the *Hancock* continued their war against the

NVA radar system, and this time it was the sites at Vinh Son and Cap Mui Ron that gained the attentions of the ninety navy aircraft. During this attack the *Coral Sea* lost an A-1H Skyraider of VA-215, the pilot being killed. The *Coral Sea* lost another Skyraider from VA-215 the following day, although this time the target was the Triple A sites along the Ho Chi Minh trail, this being the main arms conduit between North and South Vietnam via Laos.

When not engaged in specific missions the carriers launched armed reconnaissance sorties on a seek-and-destroy basis. One such mission was dispatched from the *Coral Sea* on 7 April consisting of a flight of A-4C Skyhawks from VA-153. During this patrol one of the Skyhawks was shot down while attacking a Triple A site near Dong Cao. It was the *Ranger* that suffered the next loss, on 9 April, when a flight of F-4 Phantoms was launched to relieve a similar patrol flying in the northern sector of the Gulf of Tonkin. *En route* the two replacement Phantoms were intercepted by a flight of four MiG 17s wearing the markings of the Chinese People's Liberation Army. While preparing to deal with the incoming fighters, the F-4 crews broadcast their predicament. The actual combat took place at altitude near the island of Hainan. During the entanglement one of the Phantoms was shot down, although the crew managed to down one of the MiG 17s before crashing.

During the remainder of April the carriers continued to launch armed reconnaissance missions. However, on 8 May TF.77 was briefed to attack the VNAF airfield at Vinh. The carrier *Midway* launched this attack, during which the strike force lost an F-8 Crusader to ground fire – a problem that was increasing on a weekly basis. The *Midway* launched another strike package against the airfield and city of Vinh on 27 May, and yet again the defending ground fire took its toll when the commanding officer of VF-111 was shot down attacking a Triple A site. Vinh continued to be the *Midway*'s bugbear, as the carrier lost an RF-8 Crusader on 1 June while undertaking a reconnaissance mission on 1 June.

With its wing pylons hung with bombs, a Grumman A-6 Intruder from the USS Enterprise heads towards a target in Vietnam. The start of the Intruder's service in Vietnam was marred by problems with the navigation systems, and premature bomb explosions that damaged the airframe. (US Navy/NARA via Dennis R. Jenkins)

Also on 1 June, the USS *Independence* arrived in the South China Sea to join TF.77, bringing with her a new aircraft to the conflict, the Grumman A-6A Intruder. A two-seat attack aircraft, the Intruder was capable of toting a heavy bomb load and delivering it accurately when the Digital Integrated Attack and Navigation Equipment (DIANE) was working correctly. The *Independence*, normally allocated to the Atlantic Fleet, finally joined TF.77 on 27 June, beginning operations soon afterwards. The first A-6 was lost on 14 July when a bomb failed to clear its ejector and exploded on the pylon, badly damaging the starboard engine and causing disruption to the hydraulics, and eventual failure of the port engine, leaving the crew with no option but to eject. On 18 July the *Independence* A-6 Intruders mounted an attack on Ham Rong harbour near the Dragons Jaw bridge at Thanh Hoa. During an attack run one of the Intruders was hit by Triple A, leaving the crew with no option but to eject, and they became prisoners for the next eight years. The *Independence* suffered a third Intruder loss on 24 July when another VA-75 aircraft suffered a premature bomb explosion, although in this case the crew survived their ejections and were rescued later. The Intruder was also garnering a reputation as a bit of a lemon due to the unreliability of the attack avionics, whose reliability was rated at thirty-five per cent. Fortunately the A-6 would eventually have all its problems solved and would have a proud career with the Navy.

In August the US Navy aircraft encountered SA-2 surface-to-air missiles (SAMs), when an A-4 Skyhawk was shot down near Thanh Hoa. The following day the US Navy began its own SAM suppression campaign, aimed at destroying the sites before they were completed. In support of this policy the first Iron Hand mission was launched from the *Coral Sea* on 12 August. At this time none of the US forces had the means to detect and destroy SAM sites, and so each one had to be detected using low-level armed reconnaissance, a very risky business. This was illustrated when an A-4E of VA-155 was shot down by Triple A while searching unsuccessfully for the star-shaped sites. Fortunately the remaining seventy-five aircraft from the *Midway* and *Coral Sea* returned home safely. The following day, on what became known as 'Black Friday', the *Coral Sea* and *Midway* launched further strikes. During these attacks two Skyhawks and an RF-8 Crusader were shot down, but fortunately two of the pilots survived.

The *Independence* mounted another major strike on 20 September on the bridge at Dao Nung that carried the railway from Hanoi into China, which was a vital link for the NVA war effort, as supplies for North Vietnam arrived by this route. This target was also the deepest penetration raid in North Vietnam to date by the Navy. Fortunately only one aircraft was lost on this mission, this being an A-4E of VA-72, and the pilot survived the experience to fly again. It was the turn of the *Coral Sea* to lose an aircraft while undertaking an Iron Hand mission in support of an attack mission on the Lien Qui barracks. The SAM suppression mission was undertaken by a flight of A-4 Skyhawks from VA-155. During an attack on one of these sites the aircraft of

Lieutenant-Commander Moore was hit in the engine. Although the A-4 managed to keep going, it was obvious that the failing engine and associated fuel leaks would soon see it downed. Fortunately an KA-3B tanker was in the area and refuelled the Skyhawk, which got the pilot close to an SAR destroyer, and after ejection the pilot was quickly recovered, while the bantam bomber crashed into the sea. The *Independence* suffered another run of casualties on 17 October when three Phantoms were lost. The carrier launched an Alpha Strike against the Thai Nguyen road bridge due north of Hanoi. Altogether fifteen aircraft were launched to strike the target, and the losses occurred to and from the bridge, two coming from VF-84 and the other from VF-41. The run of bad luck that had dogged the *Independence* continued when another Phantom from VF-84 was lost on 26 October while attacking the radar site at Bach Long Vi, which was replaced every time the Navy knocked it out.

The threat of SAMs was becoming such a worry to all of the air forces that the USAF and the Navy decided to co-operate on missions to destroy the sites. On the last day of October a detachment of A-4E Skyhawks from VA-164 was deployed to the USAF base at Korat, Thailand, to act as pathfinders for the based F-105 Thunderchiefs which were briefed to destroy the targets when found. The A-4 and the Thunderchiefs were launched to suppress these sites as a large force of USAF and USN aircraft attacked the bridge at Kep. Unfortunately for the A-4 pilot, he was shot down while dropping his marker bombs. A further attack on SAM sites was made on 7 November by aircraft of VA-163 from the *Oriskany*. The target was a new base at Nam Dinh, against which the carrier launched its Skyhawks. During the raid one of the attacking aircraft was damaged, but fortunately the limping A-4 managed to get its pilot over the sea, where he ejected, being rescued soon after.

The *Oriskany* and the *Bon Homme Richard* launched a strike against the Hai Duong bridge on 17 November. As this bridge had been attacked before, the NVA had increased the Triple A around the target, this increase having its benefits when four aircraft were shot down in the space of thirty minutes, three from the *Oriskany* and one from the *Bon Homme Richard*. Of the pilots, two were killed, while the others managed to survive, being rescued later. The *Bon Homme Richard* attacked another bridge on 18 November, the target being the Phong Bai bridge north of Vinh. This saw only one aircraft being lost, despite heavy defensive fire. After Phong Bai, the *Oriskany* air wing turned its attention to the Phuong Dinh bridge close to Thanh Hoa on 28 November when two F-8 Crusaders were lost; one pilot was rescued while the other became a prisoner.

The first day of December saw the air wing of the USS *Ticonderoga* lose its first aircraft in combat. This was a remarkable record, as the carrier had undertaken two tours on Yankee Station totalling eighty-six days. The target for the carrier's air wing was the bridge at Hai Duong, which had been attacked previously and had since been reinforced by the NVA. Therefore, as the strike wing attacked, the Triple A opened up with a vengeance that resulted in the loss of an A-4 and pilot from VA-144. December saw the combat debut of the nuclear-powered carrier USS *Enterprise*, which had arrived in the South China Sea in late November. The carrier had arrived at her combat location, Dixie Station, on 2 December, starting her missions soon afterwards. One of the first sorties was undertaken by VF-92, a pair of whose Phantoms were dispatched to support troops in action near An Loc, not far from the Cambodian border. During a bombing run one of the Mk 82 bombs dropped from one of the F-4s exploded upon release, causing extensive damage that caused the crew to eject, but fortunately both survived and were rescued soon afterwards. The *Enterprise* lost a further pair of aircraft on 22 December during an attack on the Uong Bi power station. Over a hundred aircraft had been launched by the '*Big E*', *Kitty Hawk* and *Ticonderoga*, and the attack was successful as the power station was extensively damaged, taking some time to repair, even though two A-4s from VA-36 and VA-76 were shot down.

Two days later on Christmas Eve President Johnson announced a halt to the bombing of North Vietnam under the impression that it was having a significant effect upon the North Vietnamese and would force Ho Chi Minh to negotiate a peace settlement. The carriers *Oriskany* (27 April to 6 December 1965), *Bon Homme Richard* (12 May 1965 to 4 Jan 1966), *Independence* (5 June to 21 November 1965), *Bennington* (29 July to 9 September 1965), *Hornet* (11 October 1965 to 8 February 1966), *Ticonderoga* (25 October 1965 to 7 May 1966), *Kitty Hawk* (15 November 1965 to 6 June 1966), *Enterprise* (21 November 1965 to 14 June 1966) and *Hancock* (6 December 1965 to 21 July 1966) had all served on Dixie and Yankee stations.

Although there was a bombing halt to operations over North Vietnam, the same did not apply to the south of the country, and so the Navy carrier air

An F-4 Phantom of VF-96 aboard the USS Independence lets loose a salvo of Zuni rockets against a target in North Vietnam. (US Navy/NARA via Dennis R. Jenkins)

wings concentrated their efforts there. The two carriers involved were the *Enterprise* and the *Ticonderoga*, both operating in the Steel Tiger area of Laos. These attacks continued until the end of January, when the bombing ban over the north was lifted. Reconnaissance efforts were stepped up from the beginning of February to observe any changes in the Navy target areas. This was not without cost, as on 3 February an RA-5C Vigilante assigned to RVAH-13 from the *Kitty Hawk* was hit by Triple A as it crossed the coast near the island of Hon Me. As the Vigilante reached the coast the aircraft started to malfunction, the hydraulics failing completely and leaving the crew with no other option but to eject. As they departed their stricken machine it exploded, and unfortunately only one of the crew survived to become a prisoner for the remainder of the war. Following on from the reconnaissance missions, the *Ticonderoga* began launching air strikes against targets in the Vinh–Thanh Hoa area. As before, the NVA had reinforced its Triple A in the area, and so these missions resulted in losses for VA-56 and VA-144. By 18 February Washington had decided to extend the bombing range for the carriers further up the country. It was the USS *Enterprise* and the *Kitty Hawk* that undertook the first missions to targets seventy miles north of Hanoi. Some of the Enterprise aircraft, F-4s from VF-92, were allocated as escorts to a Lockheed EC-121 Big Look aircraft that was being used to monitor SA-2 SAM launches. Somewhere along the line the system possibly failed, as one of the escorting Phantoms was hit by one such missile, which destroyed the aircraft, although one of the crew survived.

For a short period the US Navy tried various camouflage schemes on its aircraft. Here a Douglas Skyraider of VA-115 in a tatty coat of green paint taxies down the flight deck with a load of bombs under the wings. (US Navy/NARA via Dennis R. Jenkins)

With its forward lift in the down position, waiting to receive aircraft from the hangar of the USS Constellation. Soon the flight deck will be full of armed aircraft waiting to head towards Vietnam. (US Navy/NARA via Dennis R. Jenkins)

Rolling Thunder missions occupied the latter part of March, with targets being located in the Vinh area. Missions were launched from the *Enterprise* from 17 March onwards, although not without losses, as the SA-2 SAMs began to make their presence strongly felt when VA-36, VA-94 and VA-144 all lost aircraft to the missile menace. April 1966 continued in the same vein, although it was the *Hancock* and *Ticonderoga* that were operating on Yankee Station, attacking targets in the Thanh Hoa area. Again strong defences and SAMs took their toll, the exception being a KA-3B that was shot down by Chinese MiG 21s while passing the Luichow Peninsula while *en route* to the *Kitty Hawk*. The *Kitty Hawk* had another bad day on 17 April when it lost an A-6A of VA-85, an A-1H of VA-115 and a VA-113 Skyhawk. Over the next few days both the *Kitty Hawk* and the *Ticonderoga* lost aircraft in the Vinh area as the Triple A and SAM defences were further increased. During one of these missions on 27 April an A-6A of VA-85 from the *Kitty Hawk* was hit by a single rifle round that struck the pilot, Lieutenant Westerman. As the pilot was slipping in and out of consciousness the navigator managed to fly the aircraft to reach the sea, where the pilot was ejected. The navigator, Lieutenant (jg) Westin, flew the aircraft for a few more miles before he too ejected. Recovered quickly by the rescue services, he directed the helicopter to his pilot's position. Going down on the hoist, Westin stayed with his pilot in the shark-infested sea while another rescue helicopter was called. Both aircrew were then picked up, and Westin was awarded the Navy Cross for bravery.

Vinh was again the target area for the Navy carriers when the *Hancock* and *Ranger* undertook these missions in the first week of May. The *Hancock* air wing had a really bad time during this month, as it lost six aircraft during strike missions. Not every mission saw aircraft shot down, however, and on

12 June the US Navy scored its first aerial victory when Commander Marr of VF-111, flying from the USS *Hancock*, shot down a MiG 19 over North Vietnam using a Sidewinder missile. During June both the *Hancock* and the *Ticonderoga* continued to fly missions against targets in North Vietnam. However, the spread of SAM sites across the country increased the chances of aircraft being lost, a situation that was causing dismay to both the USAF and the US Navy, which were desperately trying to develop systems to counter this threat.

When the *Enterprise* came off the line it was replaced by the USS *Constellation*, which had arrived in the South China Sea on 29 May, moving to Yankee Station on 14 June. The '*Connie*' began combat missions almost immediately, with losses to gunfire and missiles starting on Day One. Petrol, oil and lubricant (POL) sites continued to be a favourite for the carrier air wings, with the *Constellation* picking up the first missions while the *Hancock* concentrated upon bridges. July 1966 also saw the deployment of the first dedicated Wild Weasel anti-SAM aircraft. The first effort was based on the two-seat F-100 Super Sabre, although it was decided that the two-seat Thunderchief would make a better platform, and so the F-105G became the main missile-site killer for the remainder of the conflict.

Yankee Station saw the arrival of the USS *Oriskany* on 12 July, this being the carrier's second tour of duty. During this period the carrier stayed on active duty for eighty-seven days, during which it lost sixteen aircraft in action. Also on the line was the USS *Ranger*, which was tasked with undertaking anti-SAM attacks against sites near the Red River, although the first such mission on 15 July saw at least one of the attacking A-4Es shot down by the very missiles they were sent to attack. The *Oriskany* launched her first major strike of the tour on 23 July against a primary POL dump near Vinh, which was effective, although one aircraft from VA-163 was hit by ground fire. This was Commander Foster, the commanding officer of VA-163, who managed to reach the rescue area before ejecting. Although the commander lost part of his right arm, it was replaced by a prosthetic one that allowed him to return to duty. Iron Hand was the focus of the *Oriskany* during the latter part of July, although this time the A-4s were carrying a mix of bombs and Shrike anti-radar missiles. Although they had some success, the air wing still lost aircraft to SAMs. On the last day of the month the USS *Franklin D. Roosevelt*, another carrier normally assigned to the Atlantic Fleet, joined TF.77, where it replaced the USS *Ranger*.

To help ease the burden on the Pacific Fleet strike carriers, the Essex-class carrier USS *Intrepid* entered the war at the beginning of August. Having served for a few years as an anti-submarine carrier, she replaced her ASW wing with CVW-10, which was purely an attack wing, consisting of two squadrons of A-4 Skyhawks and a similar number of A-1 Skyraider units. The *Intrepid* lost her first aircraft on 7 August soon after arrival. Over the next few days the carriers on station, the *Constellation*, *Oriskany* and *Franklin D. Roosevelt*, mounted strikes against sampans near Haiphong, attacks on Vinh

The Grumman Tracker was used for a variety of tasks, including delivering items to aircraft carriers, although this task was normally carried out by another Tracker derivative, the C-1A Trader. (US Navy/NARA via Dennis R. Jenkins)

and targets in the Thanh Hoa, continuing these until the end of the month. It was the *Oriskany* that started off the month badly when a flight of F-8E Crusaders from VF-111 were bounced by MiG 17s near Ninh Bin on 5 September. In the ensuing dogfight a Crusader piloted by a USAF exchange officer was shot down, the pilot being captured. On 12 September the USS *Coral Sea* returned to Yankee Station for her second tour of duty, and lost her first aircraft two days later due to a SAM hit that blew the aircraft to pieces, killing the pilot. The *Coral Sea* had a run of bad luck over the next few days, when the air wing lost four Phantoms, some of these courtesy of SA-2 missiles.

The *Coral Sea* came off station at the beginning of October for a few days' rest and recuperation at Subic Bay in the Philippines before returning to the fray a few days later. The run of bad luck that had dogged the *Coral Sea* during September continued during October. Within the first ten days of the month the air wing lost four aircraft, one of which was an F-4B Phantom of VF-154 that had been assigned to anti-aircraft suppression duties while aircraft from all of the carriers undertook a major strike against the railway bridge at Phu Ly, thirty miles south of Hanoi. Over the next two weeks both the *Constellation* and the *Franklin D. Roosevelt* continued their attacks on various targets in North Vietnam, with railway bridges being a favourite, even though they were heavily defended and caused losses to the air wings of both carriers. During two of these strikes the *Constellation* lost three aircraft and four aircrew, a heavy price to pay.

November saw the carriers on Yankee Station launching aircraft on SAM site strikes and armed reconnaissance missions. Skyhawks were preferred for the former while Phantoms undertook the latter. By the middle of the month the monsoon rains had arrived at full strength, and so many missions were scrubbed, while some were aborted *en route*. As the landing of aircraft with live bombs onto carriers was not allowed, the normal practice was to either jettison the load in level flight or to practise a loft manoeuvre. Some missions did go ahead, however, one being an Iron Hand launched from the *Ticonderoga* on 23 November, the carrier having returned to Yankee Station ten days earlier to undertake its third tour of duty. During this mission the commanding officer of VA-192 had his A-4E shot down, but the pilot survived, being rescued soon afterwards. December saw further SAM hits on naval aircraft, the first two being a pair of A-4 Skyhawks of VA-172 from the *Franklin D. Roosevelt*. This section had been ordered to undertake a night armed reconnaissance near Phuc Nhac, and both were shot down by SAMs. The *Ticonderoga* also lost a pair of Skyhawks on 13 December during an Iron Hand mission near the Xuan Mai bridge, both of these also falling to SA-2s. As the year drew to a close, the *Franklin D. Roosevelt* completed her only tour of duty on 27 December.

The ceasefire ended on 2 January 1967, this being marked by the USAF launching one of the largest strikes against the SAM sites around the Red River area. In order for this to succeed, Operation Bolo was also launched. This saw a large force of USAF Phantoms taking on many of the NVA MiG 21s in air-to-air combat over Hanoi, shooting down seven of them, which left the NVA with only nine serviceable fighters. The carriers on Yankee Station resumed their air war on 4 January when the *Coral Sea* launched a strike against a vital road bridge at Thu Diem near Haiphong. Ten days later the *Enterprise* dispatched a night combat mission over Laos, although this was very unsuccessful as the aircraft collided *en route*, with one pilot being killed.

Further changes to the carriers on Yankee Station took place on 5 February when the USS *Hancock* arrived to undertake its third combat tour. Unlike the two previous occasions, the carrier had Air Wing 5 aboard instead of its usual

The Douglas A-3 Skywarrior was originally delivered to the Navy as a bomber, although they later became tankers and electronic warfare aircraft. This example, still a bomber, was assigned to VAH-9. (John Ryan Collection)

With examples of its air wing on the flight deck, the USS Bon Homme
Richard heads towards its launch point on Yankee Station. (US Navy/NARA
via Dennis R. Jenkins)

unit, Air Wing 21. During February combat missions were mounted by the
Enterprise, *Hancock* and *Ticonderoga*, but none of these were carried out without
loss, as all the air wings lost aircraft to both SAMs and Triple A. March saw
another role added to those already practised by the Navy. Originally the
Pentagon was very wary of mining ports and rivers due to the risk of sinking a
foreign-registered vessel, even though these were blatantly bringing in military
supplies to North Vietnam. An even greater risk was that of sinking a Soviet
Bloc ship, as this would bring the superpowers into a face-to-face confrontation,
with all the attendant risks. Although it was not until 1972 that the ports such
as Haiphong were mined, the rivers were not seen as exempt. And so the
Pentagon war planners gave their consent to this course of action. One of the
first missions was undertaken on 8 March by a Douglas A-3 Skywarrior from
VAH-4 aboard the USS *Kitty Hawk*. This was the second such mission, as the
first had been flown on 26 February by seven A-6As from VA-65, which mined
the estuaries of the Song Ca and Song Giang rivers. The A-3B was ordered to
mine the estuary of the Kien Giang river during the night of 8 February, but the
bomber went off radar as it approached the coast near Dong Hoi, and it was
suspected that the aircraft had been shot down by Triple A.

Iron Hand missions still exercised the carrier air wings, and so on 11 March
the *Ticonderoga* sent a strike to a suspected SAM site near Hanoi. As the
Skyhawks of VA-192 reached the site they discovered that it was a storage
location where missile components were assembled, the completed units
being moved to the actual SAM sites when needed. Although not a primary

The catapults on the USS Ranger are occupied by a pair of Douglas A-4 Skyhawks, with others of the breed lining up behind. (US Navy/NARA via Dennis R. Jenkins)

target, any interruption in the supply of missiles would be welcomed, and so the Skyhawks began their attack. Although the raid was measured as a success, it was not without loss, as the squadron lost a very experienced pilot to a SAM, although fortunately he survived, becoming a prisoner until 1973. Further reinforcements arrived on Yankee Station when the USS *Bon Homme Richard* returned to the Gulf of Tonkin on 26 February for her third tour of duty. One of the earliest missions undertaken by this carrier was an Operation Sea Dragon patrol along the coasts and rivers of Vietnam, the intention being to stop the use of small vessels to move supplies from north to south for the NVA.

Although much of April was concerned with normal patrols and missions, this all changed on 24 April when permission was finally given to attack the MiG bases at Kep and Hoa Lac airfields. The *Kitty Hawk* dispatched a large strike force to attack these bases. However, the NVA decided to launch its own aircraft in an effort to destroy the bomb carriers. It was the job of the Phantom escorts to keep the MiGs away. During the ensuing dogfight an F-4 crewed by Lieutenant Wisely and Lieutenant (jg) Anderson shot down a MiG 17. As the *Kitty Hawk* strike force was engaging with the NVA fighters, aircraft from the *Bon Homme Richard* were attacking the railway yard at Hon Gay, using eight Skyhawks to carry the bombs while being escorted by F-8 Crusaders, one of which was unfortunately lost. On 26 April the *Ticonderoga* undertook a raid on a POL site near Haiphong. During this raid one of the A-4s from VA-192 was engaged in an Iron Hand suppression mission. Piloted

The largest reconnaissance aircraft carried aboard aircraft carriers was the NAA- Rockwell RA-5C Vigilante, converted from the earlier nuclear bomber. This example was assigned to RVAH-5 aboard the USS America. (US Navy/NARA via Dennis R. Jenkins)

by Lieutenant-Commander Estocin, the Skyhawk was in a position to fire at a SAM launcher. However, an approaching missile exploded close to the A-4, causing extensive damage to the aircraft's systems. The pilot managed to regain control even though flames were streaming from the rear of the aircraft. Escorted by an F-8 Crusader, the Skyhawk limped towards the coast. Just as the coast was reached the A-4 rolled over and crashed into the sea, killing the pilot. As a result of the pilot's action and dedication to duty, he was awarded the Medal of Honor posthumously.

May saw a continuation of attacks on the usual range of targets, although those that took place on 19 May were from the carriers *Enterprise*, *Bon Homme Richard* and *Kitty Hawk*. The first Alpha strike was aimed at the Vin Dien vehicle and missile transport park. As this date was also the birthday of Ho Chi Minh, the defences seemed to be even more ferocious than usual. This was the target for the *Enterprise* air wing, after which those launched by the *Bon Homme Richard* and *Kitty Hawk* took over as each air wing completed its task. The *Bon Homme Richard* also featured in the raid launched against the Hanoi thermal power plant and the Van Dien transport depot on 21 May, although while the raid was fairly successful one of the escorting F-8s was shot down, the pilot being safely recovered.

June saw the resumption of raids against the Hanoi thermal plant and the Van Dien vehicle depot on 10 June. The defences were again aggressive, bringing down an A-4 and F-8 from the *Enterprise* and *Bon Homme Richard* respectively. June closed with a raid launched by the *Intrepid* against the thermal power plant on the Song Ca river. As this was a vital target it was heavily defended, but even so the Skyhawks of VA-15 rolled into the attack,

263

With bombs on the outboard wing pylons, this LTV A-7A Corsair II of VA-146 is guided to the catapults aboard the USS Constellation. (US Navy/NARA via Dennis R. Jenkins)

one being lost in the process. On 14 July the USS *Oriskany* returned to the Gulf of Tonkin for her third tour of duty. During this first month of deployment the carrier was unfortunate enough to lose ten aircraft in combat. Three of these occurred on 18 July when Skyhawks from VA-164 were shot down during a raid on the Co Trai road and rail bridge, two pilots being recovered, while the last would die when a prisoner. It was the *Forrestal* that suffered the greatest tragedy, on 29 July. During the morning, as aircraft were being launched, an uncommanded voltage leak launched a Zuni rocket from an F-4 Phantom. The stray rocket hit a parked Skyhawk, which immediately burst into flame and exploded, scattering flaming debris far and wide. The resultant conflagration saw eleven A-4s, seven F-4s and four RA-5C Vigilantes destroyed. Major structural damage was caused to the armoured deck and hangar below, while the losses to personnel were horrendous, consisting of 134 killed and sixty-two suffering various degrees of injury. Given the extent of the damage and loss, it was obvious that the *Forrestal* could not continue, and so she was withdrawn and returned to the United States for a full refit.

The *Oriskany* also continued her run of bad luck during August, losing her first aircraft on 4 August when an A-4 was shot down during a raid on Luc Nong POL depot. The *Constellation* also had a bad day on 21 August when the air wing lost three A-6 Intruders from VA-196 while attacking the Duc Noi railway yards. Unfortunately only three of the six aircrew survived, becoming prisoners.

Haiphong was the primary target on the last two days of August 1967. The intention of this campaign was to isolate the city port from the rest of North

A Douglas A-1 Skyraider from VA-145 from the USS Intrepid taxies past the revetments at Da Nang air base in South Vietnam during the Vietnam War. (US Navy/NARA via Dennis R. Jenkins)

Vietnam, as this was the primary port of entry for weapons and supplies, and direct action was forbidden. The first day of attacks had concentrated upon the roads and some of the railway bridges. It was the turn of the *Oriskany* to launch a ten-strong Skyhawk package against the railway bridge at Vat Cach Thuong. The aircraft came from VA-163 and VA-164, and were unfortunate to run into a hail of SAMs and Triple A that would chop three of the A-4s out of the sky, leaving one pilot dead and the other two in captivity until 1973. Haiphong and its transport links continued to be the focus of attention for September, although as the attacks continued the NVA increased the defensive ring. As could be expected, such an improvement made the entire area a dangerous place to be, as Lieutenant-Commander Hawkins found out on 18 September. Flying a VA-34 Skyhawk as part of a formation of six aircraft, the pilot was bracketed by a pair of SAMs that exploded just below the aircraft. Fortunately it remained flyable, even though the radio, oxygen and ailerons were inoperable. Careful flying saw the A-4 come within sight of the coast before the pilot was forced to eject, being picked up by a Navy SAR helicopter. October followed a similar pattern to the previous month, with Haiphong being the centre of attention. However, other missions were flown in support of these attacks, concentrating upon the Fan Song radars used as part of the SAM air defence network. While these missions, part of the Iron Hand programme, were vital to protect normal sorties, they too were dangerous, as the NVA was determined to protect this most vital part of the defence chain.

Beginning on 22 October, the *Oriskany* launched a series of attacks on the Haiphong railway yard. The primary unit involved was VA-163, which lost two aircraft and a pilot over the three days of attacks. While the *Oriskany* was attacking Haiphong, the air wing from the *Coral Sea* was concentrating upon the major air base at Phuc Yen, having already pounded the base at Kep. As

The aftermath of the fire aboard the nuclear-powered carrier USS Enterprise on 14 January 1969, with the destroyer USS Rogers alongside, helping to damp down the fires. (US Navy/NARA via Dennis R. Jenkins)

both were major bases they were heavily defended, and so both raids lost aircraft to SAMs. A further attack was mounted by VA-163 from the *Oriskany* on 25 October against the air base at Phuc Yen. As the Skyhawks and escorts approached the airfield, a wall of cannon shells rose to meet them, interspersed with SAMs, one of which cut one of the A-4s out of the sky, killing the pilot. The following day both the *Oriskany* and the *Coral Sea* attacked the air base, and as before, aircraft from both carriers were lost to a hail of Triple A and SAMs. November saw the *Coral Sea* air wing switch from its previous mission to Rolling Thunder attacks, its target being the Hai Duong railway bridge, during which the attacking Phantoms were met by a swarm of SAMs that brought down one of the attackers.

On 3 December the carrier USS *Ranger* returned to active duty in the Gulf of Tonkin, beginning its combat tour thirteen days later. The *Ranger* also introduced another new aircraft to the South-East Asia conflict. This was the LTV A-7A Corsair II that had been developed to replace the Douglas A-4. Bearing a strong resemblance to the F-8 Crusader, the A-7 could carry a maximum bomb load of 15,000 lb, all being managed by a combined weapons and navigation avionics system. The A-7 made its combat debut on 22 December, during which one of them was shot down. The *Ranger* had dispatched a flight of A-7s to undertake an Iron Hand mission against a Firecan Triple A control radar located south-west of Haiphong. As the A-7 flight approached the target a SAM Fan Song radar painted the aircraft, this being followed by the launch of three SA-2s, one of which badly damaged one of the A-7s so that the pilot was forced to eject.

As the start of 1968 rolled round, it would prove to be a successful year for the NVA and the Viet Cong, with the Tet Offensive, the fall of Khe Sanh and the cessation of the Rolling Thunder programme. For the US Navy the hunt for SAMs continued, with Iron Hand missions being launched from the *Kitty Hawk* on 3 January. The target of VA-112's A-4 flight was a SAM site near the Kien An road bridge south of Haiphong. During the approach the SAM radars locked onto the flight, with three SA-2s being launched, one of which downed a Skyhawk, with the pilot becoming a prisoner. The *Oriskany* continued to lose aircraft, with two A-4s being lost during the remainder of January. The NVA and Viet Cong launched the Tet Offensive against the major US bases in South Vietnam over the night 30/31 January. While the US Navy was not directly involved, the knock-on effect showed the vulnerability of the American bases, this being exacerbated by further Viet Cong attacks.

For TF.77 February and March continued much as usual, although in a change of policy the Grumman A-6 Intruders were being used more for night attacks, as diligent work by the avionics manufacturers and carrier engineers had finally ironed out the bugs in the DIANE system. For the A-6 community it meant that they were the only attack aircraft operating over North Vietnam during this period, so that this was the only type suffering losses. In fact it was the middle of April before the carrier aircraft in general began to attack North Vietnam again. By this time a new version of the Skyhawk had begun to equip the attack units. This was the A-4F, which featured an improved avionics package mounted in a dorsal hump. Many of the missions carried out during late April and May were undertaken at dusk and at night, and so resulted in few losses.

In June 1968 the USS *America* joined TF.77, having arrived in the combat zone in mid-May. Aboard this carrier was a new Phantom version, the F-4J. A

Toting a load of bombs on its centre-line pylon, this Douglas A-4 Skyhawk is guided towards the catapults aboard the USS Enterprise prior to attacking targets in North Vietnam. (US Navy/NARA via Dennis R. Jenkins)

This head-on view of the USS Saratoga shows another strike and fighter package preparing to launch against targets in North Vietnam. (US Navy/NARA via Dennis R. Jenkins)

development of the earlier F-4B, the J model featured more powerful engines, improved avionics, strengthened undercarriage and modified wings and tailplane to permit better manoeuvring. Combat missions undertaken during June and July saw both the A-7A and the F-4J feature more heavily in both day and night attacks, with attendant losses to both types. Joining the A-7A family was the USS *Constellation*, which returned to active duty on 28 June for its fourth war cruise. In common with the *America*, the '*Connie*'s' A-7A fleet was used for a mix of day and night missions, leaving the purely day missions in the hands of the Skyhawks, which encompassed the A-4B, A-4C, A-4E and A-4F models.

August saw the introduction of the A-6B version of the Intruder aboard the *Constellation*. This was a modified version of the basic A-6 that was optimised for the Iron Hand mission. Its primary weapon for this task was the huge AGM-78 Standard ARM missile with extra avionics to match. One of the first A-6B missions was launched on 28 August against a known SAM site north-west of Vinh, during which one A-6B was shot down, this being the last of this version to be lost in the war. September saw a continuation of the standard mission packages, together with those aimed at suppressing the SAM menace. The A-7s of the *Constellation* continued Iron Hand missions during October, as the type had proved an excellent platform for the mission using Shrike missiles. October was also the month when the Rolling Thunder missions ceased on the last day of the month, as public opinion in the United States and the failure of the attacks to bring the North Vietnamese to the negotiating table meant that

Awaiting clearance to launch is this Vought F-8 Crusader aboard the USS Saratoga. Behind the fighter are various other fighter and strike packages, all destined for targets in Vietnam. (US Navy/NARA via Dennis R. Jenkins)

they were not having the desired effect. Not aiding the military were the restrictions placed on it by the politicians, which hampered mission planning. With the cessation of the Rolling Thunder campaign, the carriers in the Gulf of Tonkin turned their attentions to the Ho Chi Minh trail, the campaign being codenamed Operation Steel Tiger, confined to an area of Laos. The change of emphasis saw a reduction in the number of aircraft lost, this being confined to two A-6As from VA-196 aboard the USS *Constellation* during December.

When 1969 opened, Yankee Station hosted the *Intrepid*, close to the end of its tour, the *Hancock*, also nearly tourex, *Coral Sea, Hornet, Ranger, Kitty Hawk* and *Ticonderoga*. As the emphasis was on operations in Laos, the loss to the carrier wings was limited to a single A-4 Skyhawk assigned to VA-216 aboard the USS *Coral Sea*. Fortunately the pilot was rescued. January proved unlucky for the *Enterprise*. On the morning of 14 January a MK 32 Zuni rocket loaded on a parked F-4 Phantom exploded due to being overheated by an aircraft start unit mounted to a towing tractor. The resultant explosion set off fires and further explosions across the flight deck. The fires were brought under control fairly quickly. However, the cost was twenty-seven killed and an additional 314 personnel suffering injuries. The fire destroyed fifteen aircraft, and the resulting damage to the ship's structure required the *Enterprise* to put in for repairs, primarily to the flight deck armour plating. By early March 1969 repairs to the vessel were undertaken at Pearl Harbor, Hawaii, after which the ship proceeded on her deployment to Vietnam and the Tonkin Gulf.

After a quiet January, the following month saw the *Coral Sea* suffering quite

The McDonnell F-4 Phantom was the primary fighter-bomber for a long period. Here four aircraft from VF-84 aboard the USS Independence pose for the camera. (US Navy/NARA via Dennis R. Jenkins)

a few losses. The first occurred on the night of 14 February when a pair of Skyhawks on support duty for an A-6A Intruder operating near Ban Kate on the Ho Chi Minh trail were shot down. While the Intruder was using its radar to search for ground targets, some well-hidden Triple A opened up, delivering strong bursts towards the A-4s. One aircraft crashed almost immediately, while the pilot of the other managed to go 'feet wet' before ejecting, being rescued soon afterwards. Four days later the USS *Ticonderoga* entered the Gulf of Tonkin, rejoining TF.77 soon afterwards, with operations resuming on 4 March. With the *Ticonderoga* on station it was the turn of the *Coral Sea* to depart for a break, which it did on 29 March, heading towards Alameda. April was a quiet month in comparison to others, as the carriers concentrated upon the Ho Chi Minh trail. April also saw the creation of Task Force 71 in response to the North Koreans shooting down a Lockheed EC-121 Warning Star aircraft that had been transiting the Sea of Japan. TF.71 comprised the carriers *Enterprise*, *Ticonderoga*, *Ranger* and *Hornet* plus the battleship *New Jersey*, being escorted by three cruisers and twenty-two destroyers, all commanded by Rear Admiral Cagle. The task force was authorised on 14 April and remained on station for ten days before the situation cooled down. Once this task was completed, the ships of TF.71 returned to the Gulf of Tonkin to resume duties with TF.77.

May, June and July were also relatively quiet months for the carriers on Yankee Station, as losses were kept to a minimum while target strikes were rated as a success overall. The remainder of the year was also fairly quiet, although the problems with the A-7 TF33 engine resulted in a handful of aircraft being lost.

Although there was a slight slackening of attacks over the Christmas and New Year period, combat flying resumed on 2 January 1970. The originator of this mission was VA-196 from the USS *Ranger*, which dispatched a pair of aircraft to attack a POL dump near the Mu Gia pass in response to a USAF FAC request. Unfortunately one of the Intruders was lost when its ordnance blew up just after release, killing both crewmen. The *Ranger* lost another aircraft on 6 February during a Steel Tiger mission, the aircraft being hit by Triple A. Fortunately the crew managed to eject safely, being rescued later by a USAF helicopter. Steel Tiger also claimed other aircraft during the remainder of February and March, with the *Coral Sea* and *Hancock* suffering losses. April also saw the *Constellation* losing A-7As from VA-97, both on Steel Tiger sorties. Adding to the *Constellation*'s problems were the A-7s that were lost due to engine failures, at least two aircraft crashing due to this fault.

On 12 April the USS *Shangri La* arrived on the line to undertake her only tour of duty off Vietnam. Prior to this deployment she had been employed in the anti-submarine role. The *Shangri La*, in a similar manner to the *Intrepid*, was employed as an attack carrier, and so she only had Skyraiders and Skyhawks aboard. The carrier lost only one aircraft in combat during this cruise – an A-4C of VA-172 that was shot down while attacking a target at Ban Talan, with the pilot being killed. The middle of May saw the return of the USS *America* to TF.77, the ship resuming combat missions on 26 May. During the remainder of 1970 the carriers on Dixie and Yankee Stations continued their attacks on the Ho Chi Minh trail, although the number of missions were considerably reduced. At the end of the year President Nixon signed the

With its unique wingtip airbrakes deployed, an A-6 Intruder prepares to touch down on the carrier USS John F. Kennedy. By this time the fuselage airbrakes had been locked in the closed position, as they were found not to be needed. (US Navy/NARA via Dennis R. Jenkins)

repeal of the Tonkin Gulf Resolution that had introduced United States forces into Vietnam.

1971 saw the start of the withdrawal of US forces from Vietnam, but even so the carriers *Hancock*, *Kitty Hawk* and *Ranger* continued to launch attacks against targets along the Ho Chi Minh trail. On 10 March the carriers *Kitty Hawk* and *Ranger* launched 233 sorties over North Vietnam, a record for a single day of combat. It was 13 March before the Navy lost an aircraft in combat, this being an A-7E assigned to VA-113 aboard the *Ranger*. The aircraft had been launched on a Steel Tiger strike against traffic using a road near the A Shua valley, during which it was hit by Triple A that caused extensive damage to the airframe. Although the pilot escaped, he was later declared as missing in action.

May saw the return of the USS *Midway* to the Gulf of Tonkin after an absence of six years while she underwent extensive modernisation. The *Midway* returned to Yankee Station in June, beginning missions almost immediately. Soon after the *Midway* resumed her combat career it was joined by the *Oriskany*, which had returned to South-East Asia from Alameda on 16 June for her sixth operational cruise. When the *Midway* returned to combat she brought another new aircraft with it, the Grumman KA-6D Intruder tanker. The KA-6D was fitted with a hose-drogue unit in the rear fuselage and was capable of transferring up to 12,000 lb of fuel during one sortie. But while the *Midway* was bringing a new aircraft to the Navy, the service was also saying goodbye to an old stalwart, the Douglas AD Skyraider, which was formally retired on 7 July 1971. The USS *Enterprise* returned to South-East Asia on 16 July for her fifth war cruise, resuming combat missions soon afterwards. At the end of 1971 the Navy had the carriers USS *Constellation*, *Coral Sea*, *Enterprise*, *Hancock*, *Kitty Hawk*, *Midway* and *Oriskany*.

In order to provide electronic warfare support, Grumman came up with the idea of using redundant A-6 Intruders as a basis for a new aircraft. The first type developed for the role was designated the EA-6A, which featured a fintip aerial package, with further equipment being carried in underwing pods and on the leading edges of the pylons. This example was operated by VAQ-33, the fleet electronic support unit. (US Navy/NARA via Dennis R. Jenkins)

Awaiting clearance to launch is this Vought F-8 Crusader aboard the USS Saratoga. Behind the fighter are various other fighter and strike packages, all destined for targets in Vietnam. (US Navy/NARA via Dennis R. Jenkins)

The year 1972 was the last full year of US Navy combat action. During this period the carrier air wings concentrated upon targets in both North Vietnam and along the Ho Chi Minh trail. Their operational emphasis changed on 30 March when the NVA and Viet Cong launched their Easter offensive against South Vietnam, as they perceived quite rightly that the South Vietnamese forces were weak and rife with corruption, and were ripe for conquering. The Communist forces undertook three major thrusts into the south, meeting little real opposition on the way. In fact, such was their progress that the NVA was close to taking the capital, Saigon. In response, President Nixon authorised a massive increase in air power, which for the US Navy meant that the number of carriers immediately available on Yankee Station increased to six. While much of the invasion force consisted of tanks and their support vehicles, some of those in the convoys were SAM carriers and launchers. These missiles wreaked havoc among the Navy aircraft, downing A-7s from the *Kitty Hawk* and *Coral Sea.* Further losses were suffered by the *Kitty Hawk* and *Coral Sea* as the strike-back continued, with one aircraft, an F-4B from the *Coral Sea*, lost in combat with a pair of MiG 21s on 27 April. The Iron Hand campaign was also stepped up in a desperate attempt to suppress the missile menace, although some losses were taken by the attacking aircraft.

In order to stop the NVA incursion into South Vietnam, and force the North Vietnam government to the negotiating table, President Nixon authorised the JCS to undertake Operation Linebacker I. Much of the heavy bombing was undertaken by the Boeing B-52s of Strategic Air Command.

The aircraft that would replace the F-4 Phantom would be the Grumman F-14 Tomcat, an example of which is seen here aboard the USS America. (John Ryan Collection)

Linebacker I started on 10 May and continued until 23 October. The US Navy part of the operation was known as Pocket Moon, which utilised the Grumman A-6s and A-7 Corsairs from the *Coral Sea* air wing to drop mines in the waterways leading to Haiphong harbour, as well as those at Cam Pha, Hon Gay, Vinh and Thanh Hoa. On 10 May the *Coral Sea, Constellation* and *Kitty Hawk* launched a ninety-strong strike package against targets around Haiphong. During the period when North Vietnam was not being attacked, the NVA had increased the numbers of fighters available significantly, although to counter this threat the Navy had put in place the Top Gun programme. In concert with the Linebacker I missions, the carriers also restarted the armed reconnaissance missions over North Vietnam, although with the increase in SAMs the casualties also increased. Attacks were also restarted on targets in North Vietnam that had been struck before, including the Nam Dinh thermal power plant and the railway yard at Thieu Giuong.

The carrier force was increased on 18 May when the Atlantic Fleet carrier USS *Saratoga* arrived on 18 May for its only operational tour. The *Saratoga* undertook a full range of missions, suffering its first losses within a week of starting sorties on 7 June, a total of four being shot down. Combat losses continued to afflict the carriers during July and August, although in return the air wings did manage to destroy their targets. September saw the carriers lose a lot of aircraft to SAMs, with seventeen being shot down, the aircraft coming from the *America, Hancock, Midway, Oriskany* and *Saratoga*. October and November followed a similar pattern to the two previous months, with aircraft being lost on Iron Hand and Linebacker missions – a total of thirteen being downed. Linebacker II started on 18 December, the primary target being Hanoi. Much of the effort was delivered by the Boeing B-52 force, although the carriers did their bit by attacking other targets in an effort to spread the NVA air defence forces thinner. Both Iron Hand and strike missions were launched, as were mining missions against the harbours.

On 3 January 1973 the North Vietnamese agreed to resume peace talks in Paris in exchange for a halt on the bombing above the 20th Parallel. Nine days later an F-4 Phantom from the *Midway* air wing shot down a MiG 21 over North Vietnam, this being the last US aviator kill in the war. The *Midway* was the carrier that claimed the first shoot-down in the war in June 1965. While the negotiations in Paris continued, the US Navy carriers continued their missions over Vietnam, with the *Midway* bearing the brunt of the losses. The ceasefire came into effect on 29 January, although the carriers continued to fly missions against targets in Cambodia and Laos, the vessels involved being the *Constellation, Enterprise, Oriskany* and *Ranger*. With the ceasefire in place, the carriers on Yankee and Dixie Stations slowly returned to their normal duties, the last vessel to leave being the USS *Hancock*, which came off the line on 23 December 1973. South Vietnam finally fell to the forces of North Vietnam in April 1975.

While much of the carrier fleet was employed on Vietnam combat duties, other vessels were engaged in more peaceful duties. One of the most unusual missions involved the nuclear-powered carrier USS *Enterprise*, the nuclear cruiser *Long Beach* and the nuclear frigate *Bainbridge*, all three departing Norfolk, Virginia, on 3 October 1964. Designated Operation Sea Orbit, the cruise lasted sixty-four days, the vessels visiting numerous ports *en route*. During the cruise the vessels took on no supplies of any kind. Recovery of returning space capsules and their crews also kept the US Navy occupied. The first saw the *Intrepid* recovering the astronauts from the Gemini capsule 'Molly Brown' on 23 March 1965. It was the turn of the USS *Wasp* to recover astronauts, this being the crew of Gemini 4, who were picked up on 4 June 1965. The next recovery mission involved the *Lake Champlain*, which collected the Gemini V astronauts on 21 August. On 4 December Gemini 7 was launched, undertaking a fourteen-day mission before being recovered by the *Wasp*, which also brought home the crew of Gemini 6, which splashed down on 15 December.

The year 1966 saw the start of the Saturn series of space launches, the first capsule being recovered by the USS *Boxer* on 22 February, although this had been an unmanned launch. The *Independence* was utilised for the operation of a completely different flying-machine. This was the Hawker Siddeley XV-6A, which undertook ship handling trials from 11 to 18 May and eventually led to the adoption of the Harrier by the USMC. The *Bennington* was also involved in V/STOL trials, although this was an American-built aircraft, the XC-142A, that was trialled aboard the carrier during the middle of May.

The replacement for the C-1A Trader was another Grumman product, the C-2A Greyhound, a derivative of the E-2 Hawkeye. (US Navy/NARA via Dennis R. Jenkins)

The Saturn rocket series occupied the US Navy again on 25 August, when the carrier *Hornet* recovered the capsule from the second unmanned shot. Having undertaken V/STOL trials with the XC-142A, the *Bennington* was used to recover the unmanned Apollo 4 capsule near Hawaii on 9 November 1967.

In 1968 the manned Apollo 7 was launched on 11 October, and the capsule and its crew were safely recovered on 22 October by the USS *Essex* near Bermuda. It was the turn of the *Yorktown* to become involved with the Apollo programme when it was the recovery ship for Apollo 8. Having been launched on 21 December, the spacecraft orbited the moon before returning to earth on 27 December. Apollo 9 undertook its flight during the first week of March 1969, being recovered by the *Guadalcanal*. The Apollo programme continued to accelerate, with the crew of Apollo 10 being collected by the USS *Princeton* on 26 May. The next mission was undertaken in November when the rescue ship, the *Hornet*, collected the crew of Apollo 12. The next mission was the unlucky Apollo 13 that managed to struggle back to earth after a catastrophic failure in flight. The crew were very glad to see the helicopters from the *Iwo Jima* on 11 April 1970.

The US Navy was deactivating many of its older vessels in 1970, including the USS *Shangri La*, the orders for this being announced on 17 September, bringing the total of ships retired since January 1969 to 286 vessels. Outside the Vietnam conflict, activity by the remaining aircraft carriers was much reduced, being confined to just one spacecraft recovery. This was the capsule of Apollo 15, whose crew made the first moon landing, returning to earth on 7 August 1971, the recovery carrier being the USS *Oriskany*. The *Ticonderoga* had the honour of collecting the crew of Apollo 16 when they returned home on 27 April 1972. They too had landed on the moon to undertake observations. The *Ticonderoga* was also the recovery ship for Apollo 17, which splashed down in the Pacific on 19 December after yet another successful moon landing. This was the last Apollo mission, as the remainder were cancelled. In 1973 the US Navy carriers resumed their spacecraft collection duties, although these space flights were in support of the Spacelab programme. The *Ticonderoga* was the first carrier to become involved in recovery work, picking up an all-Navy crew and their capsule on 22 June 1973 after splashing down in the Pacific.

Although Vietnam had fallen to Communist forces in April 1975, the Cambodian Khmer Rouge was becoming a nuisance to shipping in international waters. This came to a head on 12 May when the freighter *Mayaguez* was seized after being attacked by a Cambodian gun boat. After attempting to negotiate the release of the vessel and its crew, the USS *Coral Sea* launched its air wing to carry out suppressive attacks against Cambodian air and naval assets while the crew were rescued from an off-shore island. The *Mayaguez* was recovered by a boarding party from the USS *Harold E. Holt*. During this operation eighteen US military personnel were killed, with a further fifty being injured.

As the 1970s came to a close, many of the stalwarts of the carrier force were withdrawn. The main class to bear the brunt of the withdrawals was the Essex class, the name ship being decommissioned in mid-1970, the *Intrepid* following in March 1974. The *Hornet* left service in June 1970 and was placed in reserve, while the *Franklin* went in October 1973, with the *Antietam* and *Ticonderoga*. The *Randolph* had been decommissioned in February 1969. The *Wasp* left service in June 1972, while the *Hancock* and *Oriskany* remained in commission until January 1976. The *Shangri La* was deactivated in July 1971, and the *Kearsarge* and *Princeton* had gone by February 1970. The longest-serving member of the class was the USS *Lexington*, which remained in service until November 1991, having served as a training carrier for twenty-two years. The last pair of Essex carriers, the *Valley Forge* and *Philippine Sea*, were retired in 1970 and 1969 respectively. Of the Midway class, the name ship and the *Coral Sea* remained in service, while the *Franklin D. Roosevelt* had gone by 1977. The two vessels of the Saipan light carrier class were withdrawn by 1970 after use as communications ships.

Of the newer carriers, the entire Forrestal class, the *Forrestal*, *Saratoga*, *Ranger* and *Independence*, remained in service, as did the entire Improved Forrestal class, the *Kitty Hawk*, *Constellation*, *America* and *John F. Kennedy*. Nuclear-powered aircraft carriers in the shape of the first example to enter service, the *Enterprise*, continued in service, and this was joined by the Nimitz class, which consisted of the class name vessel, together with the *Dwight D. Eisenhower*, *Carl Vinson* and *Theodore Roosevelt*. This group of carriers would be the backbone of the fleet for the remainder of the twentieth century, which would include war in the Middle East.

CHAPTER TEN

From Desert Storm to
the Future

When the first day of 1980 dawned, the US Navy had retired its last few Essex carriers and was using its super carriers for force projection on behalf of American interests around the globe. The nuclear-powered carrier was also becoming more prevalent: the *Enterprise* had already been in service for nearly twenty years, and it was joined by the four vessels of the Nimitz class, these being followed by a further six of the class, although these had been improved over the original design. The name ship undertook its first deployment to the Indian Ocean in January 1980, bringing the total number of carriers in this area to three, as the *Kitty Hawk* and *Midway* were already on station. All three ships transited into the Arabian Sea later that month. The *Nimitz* remained in the Arabian Sea to take its part in Operation Eagle Claw, the rescue of the American hostages from the Embassy in Iran, who were ultimately held captive for 444 days. The *Nimitz* provided the launching pad for the eight Sikorsky RH-53D Sea Stallion helicopters provided by the Navy. The helicopters were reduced by two when they were forced to land due to a sandstorm. Of the remaining six, one had flown in using its back-up hydraulic system, while another and a C-130 were destroyed when they collided during refuelling, killing three marines and five USAF personnel. As the mission had descended into a shambles, the remaining personnel were ordered to destroy any equipment that could not be removed and return to safer soil.

While the *Nimitz* was undertaking its Arabian Sea operation, the Indian Ocean was still seeing US carrier groups arriving and departing, and in April the *Coral Sea* battle group was replaced by that of the *Constellation*. The 'Connie' was joined by the *Dwight D. Eisenhower* group that was nominally replacing the *Nimitz* group. June saw the start of a recurring problem for the Navy when it was reported that the USS *John F. Kennedy* was unable to put to

With its deck clear of the assigned air wing, the USS John F. Kennedy is under assault by numerous helicopters undertaking vertical replenishment of spares and supplies. (US Navy/NARA via Dennis R. Jenkins)

sea due to the shortage of skilled manpower, which meant that the carrier was declared not fit for combat. The *John F. Kennedy* finally departed from Norfolk, Virginia, after borrowing fifty petty officers seconded from other ships. As the end of September approached, the *Saratoga* put into the Philidelphia Naval Yard to begin its service life extension program (SLEP), which cost $526 million and took twenty-eight months to complete. The program saw the hull reworked, while the main propulsion, auxiliary machinery, electrics and pipework were replaced where needed. The radar and communications systems were upgraded, a similar process being applied to the aircraft recovery and launching systems. The SLEP was intended to add a further fifteen years' life to each carrier it was applied to.

The year 1981 saw the Reagan administration increasing the overall defence budget, which from the point of view of the Navy would see an increase in the new-build programme, while it was proposed to reactivate the carrier USS *Oriskany* and the battleships *Iowa* and *New Jersey* were also brought back on strength. It was the *Nimitz* that gained the headlines again in August 1981. On the morning of 19 August a pair of VF-41 'Black Aces' F-14A Tomcats were flying combat air patrol to cover aircraft engaged in a missile exercise. An E-2B Hawkeye from VAW-124 made radar contact with two Sukhoi Su-22 Fitters which had departed Okba Ben Nafi airbase near Tripoli and were heading towards the US Navy fighters. The two F-14s were ordered to intercept the Libyan fighters. Only a few seconds before crossing, one of the Libyan aircraft fired an AA-2 Atoll missile in the direction of the F-14s, although this missed. The two Su-22s then flew past the Americans and tried to escape. The Tomcats evaded the Libyan aircraft and were cleared to return fire, as this was self-defence after the initiation of hostile action. The F-14s

Grumman Intruders and Prowlers dominate this scene aboard the USS
Ranger. Seen here are EA-6B Prowlers, A-6E Intruders and KA-6D tankers.
(US Navy/NARA via Dennis R. Jenkins)

turned hard to port and placed themselves behind the Libyan aircraft. The
American fighters fired AIM-9L Sidewinders, each Tomcat claiming a kill.
Both Libyan pilots were seen to eject, although one parachute failed to open.

Less than an hour later, while the Libyans were conducting a search-and-
rescue operation for their downed pilots, two fully armed MiG 25s entered the
airspace over the Gulf and headed towards the *Nimitz* at Mach 1.5, conducting
a mock attack in the direction of the carrier.

Two VF-41 Tomcats and one VF-84 Tomcat headed towards the Libyans,
who then retraced their track back to base. Even as the Tomcats turned home
they were required to retrace their steps, as the Libyan MiG 25s headed
towards the US carriers once more. After being tracked by the fighters' radars
the MiGs finally departed for home. One more Libyan fighter formation
ventured into the Gulf later that day, heading towards the carrier, although
they turned for home without attempting to engage with the Americans.

The Nimitz-class carrier USS *Carl Vinson* was commissioned on 13 March
1982, the carrier's first commander being Captain Martin USN. On 30 June the
US Navy finally said goodbye to the final version of the Crusader still in operational use – the RF-8G. The disestablishment of the final unit, VFP-63, left the
Navy without a dedicated reconnaissance aircraft, although detachments of
RF-4B Phantoms would be provided by the USMC. During 1983 the carriers
found themselves operating in various parts of the world, the *Ranger*, for
example, being stationed off Nicaragua in response to the flow of Soviet
weaponry into that country. In August the situation in the Lebanon began to
deteriorate when, on 29 August, Lebanese terrorists began attacks on various
USMC positions around Beirut. In response the US government sent the USS
Dwight D. Eisenhower, which launched F-14 Tomcats carrying tactical airborne

reconnaissance pod system (TARPS) pods to scan the area. During these over-flights the F-14s were fired on by Triple A and surface-to-air missiles, although no aircraft were damaged. On 4 December the carriers *Independence* and *John F. Kennedy* launched an air strike consisting of twelve A-7E Corsair IIs and sixteen A-6E Intruders against gun and missile positions located in the hills near Beirut, their mission being to suppress the actions of these locations. During the attack one Intruder was shot down, with the pilot being killed and the navigator being taken prisoner, although he was released later. An A-7E was also shot down, although the pilot was rescued safely, while another from the 'Indie' was damaged but did manage to return to base.

As well as operations off Nicaragua and Lebanon, the US Navy found itself engaged in Operation Urgent Fury, the invasion of Grenada. The situation had deteriorated under the Communist government, and the welfare of many foreign nationals was threatened. The naval support force for this operation included the USS *Independence* and *America.* This overwhelming force landed on 25 October, completing the suppression of enemy forces within thirty-six hours. In contrast to 1983, the following year was fairly quiet for the carrier fleet, although the USS *Kitty Hawk* did manage to collide with a nuclear-powered Victor SSN submarine that had surfaced directly in front of the carrier. Although both vessels were damaged, the *Kitty Hawk* reached port from the Sea of Japan unaided, while the submarine had to remain on the surface, being escorted home to Vladivostok by a Russian cruiser.

On 7 October 1985 four Palestinian terrorists seized the Italian cruise ship *Achille Lauro* in the eastern Mediterranean. They demanded the release of fifty of their comrades held in Israel. During the period that the ship was held, the terrorists shot a disabled American Jew, throwing the body overboard. On 9 October, after intensive negotiations, the terrorists left the ship, entering temporary sanctuary at the Al Maza airbase while the cruise ship entered Port Said. The following day the terrorists left Egypt in an Egyptair Boeing 737, which was intercepted by four F-14 Tomcats from the USS *Saratoga* that was

The USS America plus destroyer escort transits the Suez Canal en route to the Arabian Sea to take part in Operation Desert Storm. (US Navy/NARA via Dennis R. Jenkins)

A MiG 23 of the Libyan Air Force heads towards the American carriers cruising in the Indian Ocean. (US Navy/NARA via Dennis R. Jenkins)

cruising in the Mediterranean. The fighter forced the airliner to land at the joint Italian–US base at Sigonella, where the terrorists were arrested by the Italian police. The *Saratoga* then proceeded to the Gulf of Sidra, where it linked up with the *Coral Sea* on 24 January 1986, both vessels undertaking Operation Attain Document, which was intended to demonstrate the freedom of the seas near Libya. This first exercise ended seven days later, while a second phase, Attain Document II, ran from 10 to 15 February. In response to the American show of force, the Libyans launched SA-5 surface-to-air missiles at aircraft flying from the *Coral Sea* on 24 March. These first two missiles missed, as did the later four launched for the same purpose. The Libyans also sent a Combattante II missile craft towards the task force. This was countered by a pair of A-6E Intruders from the USS *America* that launched Harpoon missiles at the craft, badly damaging it. That evening a flight of A-7Es from the *Saratoga* attacked high speed onto radiation missiles, HARMs, against radars supporting the SA-5 missiles. This was followed by an A-6E attack on a Nanuchka-class missile ship, damaging the vessel with its Rockeye cluster bombs. A further attack was thwarted when the missile ship took cover along-side a neutral merchant ship, and the *Nanuchka* eventually sneaked away under the cover of darkness to Benghazi. A further attack was undertaken against radar sites based at Surt, using HARM missiles. The American attacks were later known as Operation Prairie Fire. The following day, A-6E Intruders from both carriers attacked another Nanuchka missile vessel, leaving it dead in the water. The vessel was subsequently abandoned by its crew.

In order to emphasise American displeasure with the behaviour of the Libyan government, the Americans decided to launch Operation El Dorado Canyon. Launched on 15 April, the attack force was centred around eighteen F-111Es launched from Britain, while the carriers' aircraft were used to provide electronic jamming, defence suppression and their own attacks on bases near Tripoli. The mission was deemed a success with only one aircraft being lost, an F-111E that crashed *en route*, both crewmen being killed. While the conventional carriers were attacking the Libyans, another Nimitz-class carrier was commissioning. This was the USS *Theodore Roosevelt*, which joined the US Navy on 25 October 1986, the first commander being Captain Parcells USN.

During 1987 American forces became heavily involved in the Gulf as the Iraqi and Iranian forces continued their war. The continued fighting between these two nations had an impact on shipping in the area, with both protagonists firing at neutral shipping. On 14 April the US Navy frigate USS *Samuel B. Roberts* struck a mine in the Persian Gulf, which left the ship badly damaged. Four days later aircraft from the carrier *Enterprise* cruising in the Gulf of Oman attacked Iranian vessels and installations. During these attacks three vessels were sunk and another was badly damaged.

In 1989 the USS *John F. Kennedy* found itself engaging Libyan aircraft again when on 4 January a pair of missile-armed MiG 23s approached the carrier. The intercepting F-14s fired at the incoming MiGs, both of which were downed. Also in 1989, the commissioning of a further member of the Nimitz-class vessel, the USS *Abraham Lincoln*, took place. She joined the fleet on 11 November, the carrier's first commander being Captain Hayden USN. Three days later a momentous event took place when the Berlin Wall was dismantled, being completed by 21 November. This signalled the collapse of the Warsaw Pact and the determination of Western politicians to cash in on the 'Peace Dividend'. This would later be seen as misguided, as the disappearance of Russia as a world power saw much smaller countries engaging in military adventures against their neighbours, a situation that would normally have been held in check by the Cold War antagonists. Even as the politicians were trying to shrink their armed forces, these conflicts were requiring the West to spread its forces in order to protect its interests.

Although the inconclusive Iran–Iraq War finally ended in August 1988, the leader of Iraq, Saddam Hussein, was still intent on throwing his weight around. On 2 April 1990 Iraq Radio issued a statement that declared that, 'Those who are threatening us with nuclear bombs, we warn them that we will hit them with the binary weapons in our possession. I also say that if Israel dares to hit even one piece of steel on any industrial site we will make the fire consume half of Israel.' Having threatened the one country that had already attacked Iraq successfully when the Israeli Air Force bombed the nascent nuclear reactor in 1981, the Iraqi Dictator decided to move over 100,000 troops and their equipment to the Kuwaiti border on 24 July. The Iraqis had taken this move as they were convinced that the Kuwaitis had been stealing Iraqi oil, using illegal drilling practices. In response to this move, all US forces in the Persian Gulf area were placed on high alert.

In the early hours of 2 August 1990 the Iraqi forces massed on the Kuwaiti border swept across, meeting little resistance from the far smaller Kuwaiti armed forces. Unable to resist the invasion, the Emir of Kuwait and his family fled to the safety of Saudi Arabia. Four days after the invasion, the UN Security Council passed Resolution 661, which ordered a global embargo

A pair of A-7 Corsairs from VA-82 aboard the USS Nimitz fly past the carrier while on a training mission. The last battle for the A-7 would be Desert Storm. (US Navy/NARA via Dennis R. Jenkins)

on trade with Iraq and the seizure of the country's assets overseas. On 7 August President George Bush ordered the movement of aircraft, troops and naval vessels into the Gulf and onto the border between Saudi Arabia and Kuwait. Such a move was deemed neccesary as Saddam Hussein had a serious grievance against the Saudi Royal Family. During the conflict with Iran, the Iraqi government had borrowed millions of dollars from Saudi Arabia, which quite rightly requested that the loans be repaid. However, Saddam Hussein had other ideas, and he stated that as his country had lost many soldiers fighting the Iranian Shia regime, Iraq should not repay these loans because these sacrifices had protected Saudi Arabia from invasion. After the invasion of Kuwait and the financial spat with Saudi Arabia, the latter country was seriously worried about Iraq attacking Saudi Arabia, as its oil fields were in an area with a mainly Shia population.

Later known as Operation Desert Shield, the response by the US Navy was to dispatch two carrier battle groups to the area on 7 August. King Fahd of Saudi Arabia had requested the presence of the troops and aircraft, as both the King and President Bush were extremely worried about Iraq gaining control of the majority of the world's oil supply. The first carrier into the region was the USS *Independence*, which arrived in the Gulf of Oman on 8 August, the purpose of this deployment being to blockade the Indian Ocean. Aboard the *Independence* was Carrier Wing 14, consisting of two F-14 Tomcat squadrons,

Pictured from overhead is Task Force 155, the main carrier force in the Arabian Sea. (US Navy/NARA via Dennis R. Jenkins)

VF21 and VF-154, a single squadron of Grumman A-6Es and KA-6Ds, VA-196, a detachment of Grumman EA-6B Prowlers with VAQ-139, VAW-113 with Grumman E-2C Hawkeyes, VS-37 with Lockheed S-3A Vikings, HS-8 with Sikorsky SH-3 Sea Kings, and a detachment of Grumman C-2As from VRC-50 for carrier onboard delivery (COD). As the 'Indie' was taking up its blockade position, the USS *Eisenhower* was transiting the Suez Canal *en route* to the Red Sea, where it could intercept any traffic heading for the Jordanian port of Aqaba. Aboard the *Eisenhower* was Carrier Wing 7, which comprised two squadrons of F-14 Tomcats, VF-142 and VF-143, two squadrons of MDD, later Boeing, F/A-18 Hornets with VFA-131 and VF-136, VF-34 flying Grumman A-6Es/KA-6D Intruders, VAW-121 with Grumman E-2Cs, VAQ-140 flying Grumman EA-6Bs, VS-31 operating the Lockheed S-3A Vikings, and HS-5 with the Sikorsky SH-3 Sea Kings.

Also *en route* to the area was the USS *Saratoga*, which had sailed from Maryport with Carrier Wing 17 aboard on 7 August, arriving in the Red Sea on 22 August. The wing comprised VF-74 and VF-103 flying F-14 Tomcats, VFA-81 and VFA-83 with F/A-18 Hornets, VA-35 operating A-6Es and KA-6Ds, VAQ-132 flying EA-6Bs, VAW-125 flying E-2C Hawkeyes, VS-30 with S-3A Vikings, and HS-3 flying Sea Kings. The next carrier to be dispatched was the *John F. Kennedy*, which departed its home port on 15 August with Carrier Wing 3 aboard, consisting of VF-14 and VF-32 flying Tomcats, VA-75 operating Grumman A-6Es and KA-6Ds, while VA-46 and VA-72 were taking the LTV A-7E Corsair II on their last war cruise. Also aboard the '*JFK*' was VAQ-130 with the EA-6B Prowler, VAW-126 flying E-2C Hawkeyes, and VS-22 operating S-3A Vikings in the anti-submarine role, while HS-7 was flying the SH-3 Sea King. When all four carriers were in position they brought to bear the striking power of over 300 aircraft, a formidable force that become larger as time passed and the crisis deepened.

As the Allied forces were gathering, Saddam Hussein broadcast over

Baghdad radio that the annexation of Kuwait was needed to redress the flawed regional borders that had been drawn up by colonial powers and had left a corrupt minority in charge of some of the Arab world's richest territory. In response, the UN Security Council passed Resolution 662 on 9 August, which declared the annexation of Kuwait null and void. The following day, in Cairo, twelve of the twenty-one members of the Arab League voted to honour the United Nations' embargo of Iraq while also pledging to supply forces to the Saudi defence force. They also agreed that the Saudi invitation to the Americans was valid. In a desperate measure to stave off the forthcoming storm, Saddam Hussein brokered a peace plan that would see Iraq pull out of Kuwait in exchange for Israel withdrawing from the occupied territories on the West Bank and Gaza, coupled with Syria's withdrawal from the Lebanon. On 17 August the Iraqi regime angered the world by declaring that all Westeners still in Iraq and Kuwait would be used as human shields at civil and military installations in an effort to stop attacks against these locations. The UN Security Council passed Resolution 664, which demanded that all Western hostages held by the regime should be released immediately. It took until 6 December for this to be complied with.

The pressure being exerted by the rest of the world was increased further on 9 September when President Bush and President Gorbachev met in Helsinki, Finland, both declaring unconditional support for the United Nations' sanctions against Iraq. On 12 January 1991 the US Congress voted to allow the President to use military force if needed to end the Gulf crisis. In support of this decision, the carriers *Ranger* and *Midway* arrived in the Persian Gulf. Aboard the *Ranger* was Carrier Air Wing 2, which comprised VF-1 and VF-2 flying Grumman F-14 Tomcats, VA-143 and VA-155 operating A-6Es

A USMC RF-4B Phantom taxies along the deck of the USS Midway. The Marine Phantoms provided a reconnaissance capability to the fleet until the F-14 TARPS pod was available. (US Navy/NARA via Dennis R. Jenkins)

and KA-6Ds, VAQ-131 flying EA-6Bs, VAW-116 with E-2Cs, VS-38 with S-3A Vikings, and HS-14 with Sea Kings. The *Midway* deployed with an entirely F/A-18 Hornet fighter-bomber force that included VFA-151, VFA-192 and VFA-195. Also aboard were VA-115 and VA-185 flying Grumman A-6Es and KA-6Ds, the latter in the tanker role, while VAQ-136 operated EA-6Bs. The other units were VAW-115 flying E-2Cs and HS-12 operating SH-3 Sea Kings. Following on from the *Ranger* and *Midway* came the *Theodore Roosevelt*, which arrived in the Red Sea on 14 January, being followed the next day by the USS *America*. Aboard the *Theodore Roosevelt* was Carrier Air Wing 8, which consisted of VF-41 and VF-84 with Grumman Tomcats, VFA-15 and VFA-87 flying F/A-18 Hornets, VA-36 and VA-65 operating A-6Es and KA-6Ds, VAW-124 with E-2C Hawkeyes, and VAQ-141 flying Grumman EA-6B Prowlers, while VS-24 flew S-3A Vikings and HS-9 provided the Sea Kings. The USS *America* deployed with Carrier Air Wing 3 aboard this comprising of VF-33 and VF-102 with F-14s, VFA-82 and VFA-86 with F/A-18 Hornets, VA-85 flying A-6E and KA-6D tankers, VAQ-137 with Prowlers, VAW-123 with Hawkeyes, VS-32 with Vikings and HS-11 providing Sea Kings.

On 16 January 1991 the first move of what would become Operation Desert Storm began when a wave of Boeing B-52s departed from Barksdale AFB to begin their more than eleven-hour journey to Iraq. That evening a White House spokesman declared that the liberation of Kuwait had begun. Desert Storm officially began in the early hours of 17 January with a strike against the main Iraqi defence radars, which were rendered useless. With this hole opened, the Coalition air forces began to stream through, being accompanied by waves of Tomahawk cruise missiles aimed at major Iraqi facilities that needed precision attacks to limit collateral damage.

The carriers available for this attack were the *Independence, Dwight D. Eisenhower, Saratoga, John F. Kennedy, Midway, Ranger, America* and *Theodore*

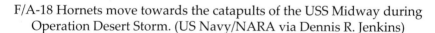

F/A-18 Hornets move towards the catapults of the USS Midway during Operation Desert Storm. (US Navy/NARA via Dennis R. Jenkins)

An A-6E Intruder from the USS Saratoga undertakes a training mission during Operation Desert Shield, the build-up phase of the Gulf War. (US Navy/NARA via Dennis R. Jenkins)

Roosevelt. These carriers launched strike packages of Grumman A-6E Intruders, F/A-18 Hornets, F-14 Tomcats and EA-6B Prowlers, the latter having begun its role before the others entered the war zone, as its jamming capability was much needed. A new weapon also made its debut in this conflict, this being the AGM-84E SLAM, a pair of which were launched from an A-6E against a hydroelectric plant. The missiles were guided by an A-7E that put the first on target and the second straight through the hole created by the first. The first combat success was scored by F/A-18 Hornets from the USS *Saratoga*. *En route* to their target and still toting their bombs, the fighters were guided onto a pair of incoming MiG 21s that the Hornets shot down using AIM-9 Sidewinders and AIM-7 Sparrows before continuing onwards to bomb their targets. During these opening rounds the Iraqis fired al-Hussein, modified Scud-B missiles, towards Israel and Saudi Arabia. When Desert Storm started, Allied forces in the region numbered almost 700,000. Saddam Hussein proclaimed that this was the start of the 'Mother of all Battles', but after a month of aerial bombardment the situation changed to the 'Mother of all Surrenders'. By 24 February over 10,000 Iraqi troops had surrendered.

In the first seven days of the air offensive, over 12,000 sorties were flown, with the Allied High Command stating that the sortie rate was on target even with the delays caused by bad weather. On Day 8 over 3,000 sorties were launched, many of which were aimed at power stations and oil-refining capability, as well as the chemical plants scattered throughout the country. At the end of the seventh day of attacks the Iraqi Air Force had been rendered useless, with many aircraft fleeing to the country's erstwhile enemy, Iran. Phase 2 missions were concentrated upon targets within Kuwait, while Phase 3 concentrated upon destroying Iraqi ground units in Kuwait prior to the ground invasion. Phase 4 involved all the Allied air forces supporting the Allied ground forces as they rolled over the Kuwaiti border. During Phases 1 and 2 it became obvious to the carrier crews that the Iraqi Air Force had no stomach for a fight. Every time that incoming enemy fighters were detected, they turned away as the Navy fighters turned to intercept, and this pattern was repeated throughout this early period of the war until the Iraqi aircraft were grounded for good.

While the combat pilots were hitting targets and chasing the Iraqi Air Force, the Grumman E-2C Hawkeyes from the carriers were operating in conjunction with the other AWACS aircraft in theatre to provide airborne early warning and much-needed air traffic control facilities for inbound and outbound strike packages and the tankers assigned to each mission. The Lockheed S-3B Vikings were also busy undertaking patrol and reconnaissance missions around the Gulf, during which a high-speed attack vessel was detected by the cruiser USS *Valley Forge*. The Viking detected the enemy ship using its infra-red detection system, locked onto it with its radar, and then dropped bombs on it, the vessel sinking almost immediately. The Navy also used its Intruders and Hornets to strike against the ships of the Iraqi Navy using Harpoon missiles and Skipper and Rockeye bombs to sink missile gunboats, minesweepers, patrol craft and other smaller vessels. Also struck by the same aircraft were Silkworm anti-ship missile sites and hovercraft, all of which were successfully destroyed.

Desert Storm also marked the debut of the newest aircraft in the Navy's inventory, these being Grumman F-14+, the F/A-18C and the F/A-18D night-attack aircraft. The F/A-18 Hornets flew over 4,400 sorties during the conflict, while the Navy's A-6 Intruders undertook more than 4,000 missions. On the last full day of the conflict the carriers flew over 600 missions, which continued to reduce the capabilities of the Iraqi forces as they fled Kuwait. The main strike happened on the road from Kuwait city to Basra, where the fleeing convoy had its ends topped and tailed by A-10 Thunderbolts, the trapped vehicles in between being destroyed by wave after wave of attackers.

The land war commenced on 27 February under a protective umbrella of air power. This not only ensured that the Iraqis had no idea what the Allies were up to but allowed them to continue striking targets of opportunity that resulted in mass surrenders by Iraqi troops who had already been pounded for days by air and sea power. The Iraqis were unaware that the Allies had secretly moved two entire divisions of the US Army, supported by British and French divisions, far to the west in one of the largest and swiftest battlefield troop movements in history. This impressive end run by more than 250,000 soldiers spread over several hundred miles quickly moved deep into Iraqi territory from the Saudi border, slipping behind the Iraqi forces to deliver a fatal flanking manoeuvre that not only cut off all avenues of retreat north and west of Kuwait, but also fulfilled Chairman of the Joint Chiefs of Staff, General Colin Powell's prediction that the Coalition was going to destroy the Iraqi Army. During these attacks the A-6 Intruders from the carriers and the USMC continued to pound Iraqi positions, their attacks being augmented by Boeing B-52s that were bombing Saddam's élite guard units into

The USS Enterprise will be the first nuclear carrier to be replaced when the first Gerald R. Ford class becomes available. (US Navy/NARA via Dennis R. Jenkins)

submission. At 08.00 hours on 28 February 1991, Allied operations were suspended as the Iraqi forces had sued for peace. The success of Desert Storm was based on tactics developed during the Second World War – first gain control of the air, then attack your enemy with massive air, ground and naval strikes in order to destroy facilities and troops; then continue to destabilise and demoralise the remaining forces. Once these objectives had been completed, the final ground push could then take place.

The Iraqi government continued to cause problems for the Allies, especially in the north and south sectors of the country, these being codenamed Provide Comfort and Southern Watch respectively. Although Iraq was banned from placing troops and equipment and flying into these two protected zones, they continued to push the Allies to the limit. Operations Provide Comfort and Provide Comfort II were undertaken to protect both these zones. The Allied Coalition finally lost patience with Iraq in the closing days of 1992 as Saddam placed SAM sites along the 32nd and 36th Parallels and the remaining Iraqi Air Force fighters penetrated into the no-fly zones. The fighter incursion saw MiGs entering the zone and engaging patrolling USAF fighters,. However, the obvious lack of combat skills that the Iraqi pilots had soon saw one of them shot down, with no loss to the Americans. Even after this loss the Iraqis continued to push the Coalition. In response the *Kitty Hawk* was diverted from Operation Restore Hope, arriving in the Persian Gulf on 12 January 1992. With the carrier in place, over a hundred aircraft were launched to attack various targets thought to be part of the defence network. The bombing continued, with short stops due to inclement weather, until 29 January, when Iraq called a ceasefire as a goodwill gesture for the inauguration of President Clinton.

Eventually the Allies had finally had enough of Saddam's antics, deciding to invade the country and topple the leader from power. Not only were the

290

Cruising in calm waters, the USS Constellation would end its career after taking part in Operation Iraqi Freedom, the carrier retiring in 2003. (US Navy/NARA via Dennis R. Jenkins)

provocations of a military nature, but the continued blocking of the UN Weapons Inspectors in checking for nuclear, biological and chemical weapons and facilities, known as weapons of mass destruction, was very trying. The UN inspectors had finally had enough and decided to withdraw. Unfortunately the premise behind this invasion was shaky, to say the least, and has led to numerous enquiries within the Allied nations.

On 11 September 2001 al Qaeda flew hijacked airliners into the twin towers in New York and the Pentagon, not only shocking the world but shaking America to its roots. In response President George W. Bush declared a 'War on Terror' focusing on Afghanistan as the primary home of al Qaeda. This saw a temporary halt in the bombing raids on Iraq, which had been increasing in intensity during the previous two years, as the battle groups under the control of the Fifth Fleet turned their attentions to attacking Afghanistan. To that end the carriers redeployed to the Arabian Sea and the Indian Ocean, the ships involved being the *Enterprise, Carl Vinson, Theodore Roosevelt* and *George Washington*. The missions launched by the carriers, using F/A-18 Hornets, lasted between eight and ten hours. In conjunction with forces provided by the Allies, the Americans pushed into the country, finally defeating the Taliban regime in early 2002.

While the Allies were concentrating upon Afghanistan, the Iraqi regime had been moving SAMs and Triple A into the restricted zones. Although Allied air power, mainly British, continued strikes against these sites, not enough air power was available to keep them suppressed for long. The US Navy returned to the Gulf in September 2002, and when the USS *George Washington* arrived she restarted missions almost immediately against air defence sites in the south of Iraq. The *George Washington* was replaced by the *Abraham Lincoln* in

The F-14 would have another role from Desert Storm onwards, that of Bombcat. On the centre-line pylons are a pair of LGBs being carried by an aircraft from VF-32. (US Navy/NARA via Dennis R. Jenkins)

October, the latter continuing her predecessor's tasks. The *Abraham Lincoln* was replaced by the *Constellation* in December, this being the twenty-first and last operational deployment by the the *'Connie'* in her forty-one years of service. On 19 March 2003 the Allies launched Operation Iraqi Freedom, destined to destroy and discover any weapons of mass destruction and to topple the regime of Saddam Hussein. The initial attacks were conducted using cruise missiles, a pair of F-117 stealth fighters and ECM jamming from US Navy EA-6B Prowlers. On Day 2 the air campaign stepped up in intensity as hundreds of aircraft attacked sites throughout the country. The strength of the Allied forces saw the country virtually under Allied control by Day 26. The carriers involved in this operation included the *Kitty Hawk, Abraham Lincoln, Nimitz* and *Theodore Roosevelt*, whose primary attack aircraft was the F/A-18 Hornet, while F-14 Tomcats provided combat air patrols, although some were later upgraded to 'Bombcat' standard, having had a bomb-carrying capability added. It was Day 14, 2 April 2003, before a Navy attack aircraft was lost, this being an F/A-18 Hornet from the *Kitty Hawk*. Mopping-up continued for a few more weeks, although the lack of post-conflict planning saw insurgents and locally grown terrorists starting a campaign against the occupying Allied forces that continues at some level to this day.

After Desert Storm there was a fundamental change in world politics when a coup in Russia saw a change of leadership and direction in that country. On 24 August 1991, President Gorbachev resigned as General Secretary of the Communist Party of the USSR, and that effectively ended the seventy-four-year reign of the Communist Party. Eight days later the Soviet Congress of People's Deputies dissolved the Soviet Union, as the various satellite states were clamouring for their independence, and the possibility of fighting and the resultant civil war quite rightly worried the authorities.

En route to a target in Iraq is an A-6E Intruder of VA-65 from the USS Theodore Roosevelt, carrying a decent load of iron bombs. (US Navy/NARA via Dennis R. Jenkins)

Changes within the carrier fleet were also under way, with the last of the Essex-class carriers leaving service. This was the USS *Lexington*, which had served as a fleet air training carrier until decommissioning on 26 November 1991, and later became a floating museum at Corpus Christi, Texas. Another change saw the USS *Midway* replaced by the USS *Independence* as the forward ported carrier outside the United States. The '*Indie*' took over this task in August 1991, picking up Carrier Air Wing 5 from the *Midway* at Pearl Harbor *en route*. The *Midway* arrived in San Diego, where it currently resides as a museum, while the *Independence* continued to Yokosuka. New carriers were also coming into service, all being nuclear powered. By 1990 the Nimitz-class carriers *Carl Vinson*, *Theodore Roosevelt*, *Abraham Lincoln*, *George Washington*, *John C. Stennis* and *Harry S. Truman*, while the *Ronald Reagan* and the *George H.W. Bush* would be commissioned in the early years of the twenty-first century.

The primary AEW aircraft currently in service with the US Navy is the Grumman E-2 Hawkeye. This example belongs to VAW-112 aboard the USS John C. Stennis. (US Navy/NARA via Dennis R. Jenkins)

Sporting a mix of bombs and fuel tanks is this F/A-18 Hornet from VFA-113 aboard the USS Ronald Reagan. The F/A-18 series is now the primary combat aircraft for the USN and USMC. (US Navy/NARA via Dennis R. Jenkins)

On 4 May 1980 Marshal Tito, President of Yugoslavia and the man regarded as the bonding force for that disparate country, passed away. His death saw old racial tensions reappear as the country was rent by civil war, the highlight of which was the distasteful practice of 'racial cleansing'. By 1991 the country had completely broken apart, with fighting taking place between various factions. Two years later the United Nations and NATO finally decided to intervene by starting Operation Deny Flight, which not only gave the Allies control of the skies, but enabled them to provide close air support to UN troops should it be needed. The primary carrier deployed in support of Operation Deny Flight was the USS *Theodore Roosevelt*, which started its deployment in March 1993, remaining on station until September, and being joined by the USS *America*, which remained in theatre until February 1994. Both carriers' air wings undertook missions in co-ordination with 5 ATAF and NATO. The average sortie rate during this period was between thirty and forty per day. While Deny Flight was supposed to stop military flying by the countries that made up Yugoslavia, it was not unusual for reconnaissance flights to be shadowed by Serbian MiGs. The fighters flew both combat air patrols and close air support missions as required, while the A-6E Intruders were used for strike attacks. The EA-6B Prowlers of VAQ-137 frequently reported that the radars for the SA-6 Gainful surface-to-air missiles were noted tracking NATO aircraft as they undertook their sorties.

The next carrier on station in the Mediterranean was the USS *Saratoga*, which took up her mission in the Adriatic at the beginning of January 1994, the vessel remaining on station until June 1994. Entering the Adriatic on 1 February, the *Saratoga*, with Carrier Air Wing 17 aboard, launched the first of thousands of sorties in support of UN and NATO operations over Bosnia-Herzegovina. After forty-four consecutive sea duty days, the *Saratoga* visited

Now retired, the Grumman EA-6B Prowler was the primary electronic warfare aircraft for the Navy and the USMC before it was replaced by a version of the Hornet. (US Navy/NARA via Dennis R. Jenkins)

the northern Italian city of Trieste for rest and recuperation. The ship departed Trieste on 28 February 1994, returning to her station in the southern Adriatic again. The carrier remained on station until 10 March before departing for the eastern Mediterranean to take part of the world that was completed eight days later. After a period in Trieste, the *Saratoga* returned to the Adriatic for five more days of flying in support of Deny Flight and Provide Promise. Departing Groundhog Station on 7 April, the carrier transited the Straits of Messina between Sicily and the toe of southern Italy, for a port call at Naples, Italy, before returning to the Adriatic for the fourth time on 17 April. The *Saratoga* handed over to the USS *George Washington*, at the time the newest fleet carrier, in the first week of June. The *George Washington* continued the good work started by the *Saratoga* with Carrier Air Wing 7 being utilised in a similar manner to other deployments. The *George Washington* remained on station except for rest and recuperation periods until November 1994. By 1995 the carriers on station were the USS *Theordore Roosevelt* and the *America*, these taking part in Operation Deliberate Force in order to enforce the no-fly zone over Bosnia, this having been established as a result of the passing of United Nations Resolution 816, which stated that the UN safe areas had to remain safe from Bosnian Serb aggression. This was followed by Resolution 836, which was passed in September 1995, allowing the air forces in the area to use maximum force to stop the aggression.

Operation Allied Force, NATO, or Noble Anvil, USA, was the NATO military operation against the Federal Republic of Yugoslavia during the Kosovo War. These strikes lasted from 24 March to 11 June 1999. The purpose behind these missions was to totally destroy the forces and facilities available to President Milosevic. During these attacks, some of which were launched from the USS *Theodore Roosevelt*, with Carrier Air Wing 8 aboard, concentrated upon the airfields and the air defence network in Serbia, Kosovo and

Like the remainder of the current fleet, the USS Theodore Roosevelt is nuclear powered. The carrier undertook missions during Desert Storm, followed by stints with the task force dealing with Afghanistan and Iraq. (US Navy/NARA via Dennis R. Jenkins)

Montenegro, as well as power stations, the power grid, arms factories, and military and police barracks. Supporting many of the strikes were Grumman EA-6B Prowlers, originally those from the *Roosevelt* being utilised. However, such was their workload that other aircraft were diverted from other carriers and shore bases to take up the load. As the campaign continued, the number of aircraft and missions increased the weight of bombs dropped on various targets,and this quickly diminished the Serbs' ability to fight. While the Milosevic regime continued to shout defiance, it was obvious that its combat capability had been seriously reduced.

Operation Enduring Freedom has been the mainstay of US Navy carrier operations throughout the first decade of this century. During this period all of the current fleet of carriers have been involved save the newly commissioned USS *George H.W. Bush*. The *Nimitz*, with Carrier Air Wing 11 aboard, undertook deployments during the period September to November 2001 before returning to the United States for updating, followed by training exercises. The carrier returned to Enduring Freedom in March to November 2003, May to November 2005, April to September 2007 and January to June 2008, while its last tour was undertaken from July 2009 to March 2010. In common with all of the services carriers, short periods were spent supporting Allied troops operating against insurgents in Iraq as part of Operation Iraqi Freedom, as well as upgrade periods, exercises and goodwill visits to numerous ports, including some to the *Nimitz*'s home port of San Diego, California.

The USS *Dwight D. Eisenhower* was out of operation between 2001 and 2004 as it underwent the only refuelling it would ever need in its projected fifty-year life span. This involved replacing the nuclear rods in the reactor, during which period the staff at the Newport News Dockyard also overhauled the complete cooling system among other items. Having completed sea trials, the carrier resumed operations in October 2006 with Carrier Air Wing 7 aboard. Assigned to Enduring Freedom over Afghanistan, the carrier

With its deck festooned with F/A-18 Super Hornets, the USS Eisenhower launches a singleton off on another mission. (US Navy/NARA via Dennis R. Jenkins)

completed her deployment in May 2007. It was nearly two years before the vessel redeployed again for this duty, taking up her task in February 2009 and remaining on station until July. The USS *Carl Vinson* was involved in both Operation Southern Watch over Iraq and Enduring Freedom during its cruise, which started in July 2001 and ended in January 2002, the aircraft from Carrier Air Wing 11 providing the strike power. After a further cruise during much of 2003, the carrier returned to combat action in January 2005, taking part in Operation Iraqi Freedom during that period. By this time the vessel's aircraft came under the control of Carrier Air Wing 9, this air group having replaced the previous incumbents in 2003. The *Carl Vinson* returned to her home port of San Diego in July at the completion of this cruise. In November of that year the carrier was towed from Norfolk, Virginia, to the Northrop Grumman yard at Newport News, where it is currently undergoing a nuclear refuel and in-depth overhaul.

Operations Southern Watch and Enduring Freedom engaged the USS *Theodore Roosevelt* from September 2001 to March 2002, the vessel being deployed with Carrier Air Wing 1 embarked. At the completion of its cruise in the Mediterranean and Arabian Sea, the carrier returned to the United States, entering the Norfolk Naval Yard for a period of upgrading that was completed in October 2002. Cleared for sea duty once more, the carrier, with Carrier Air Wing 8 aboard, redeployed to both the Mediterrannean and the Arabian Sea in September 2005, taking part in Operations Enduring Freedom and Iraqi Freedom before returning to her home port of Norfolk, Virginia in March 2006. This cruise also marked the last combat deployment of the Grumman F-14 Tomcat, the type being withdrawn from service soon after-wards. After a period undergoing updating and maintenance, the carrier continued her part in both Iraqi Freedom and Enduring Freedom, beginning

The USS John C. Stennis was commissioned in 1995 and would be deployed on Southern Watch, followed by Enduring Freedom. (US Navy/NARA via Dennis R. Jenkins)

in September 2008. The carrier ended this deployment in April 2009, returning to the United States soon afterwards.

Named after one of the most famous Presidents in American history, the USS *Abraham Lincoln* was in Puget Sound Naval Yard for a six-month upgrade period in the first years of the new century. This was completed by July 2002, after which the vessel, with Carrier Air Wing 14 aboard, departed on her next cruise. This took in the Indian Ocean and the Arabian Sea as the carrier took part in Operations Northern Edge, Southern Watch, Enduring Freedom and Iraqi Freedom. The *Abraham Lincoln* was actually on her way home in January 2003 when the battle group was ordered to return to the Arabian Sea to take part in Iraqi Freedom. This delay meant that the carrier eventually returned to her home port of Everett, Washington, in May, having spent nine months at sea. A period in Puget Sound Naval Yard was completed in May 2004, the carrier collecting Carrier Air Wing 2 from San Diego *en route* to the Indian and Pacific Oceans, where she undertook numerous exercises before returning home in March 2005. After another exercise-filled cruise that took place between February and August 2006, the carrier entered Puget Sound Naval Yard for a further period of maintenance and upgrading. With this completed, the vessel departed for her next cruise, which took in the Indian Ocean and the Arabian Sea, and took part in Operations Enduring Freedom and Iraqi Freedom. This cruise drew to a close in October 2008, when the carrier returned to her home port. The *Abraham Lincoln* has since undergone a period of maintenance.

Named after the founding father of the United States, the USS *George Washington* is the fourth vessel to carry the name. Commissioned in 1992, this nuclear-powered carrier of the Nimitz class spent the year 2000 deployed to the Arabian Gulf before entering Portsmouth Naval Dockyard for a much-needed period of maintenance. After a working-up period the carrier found

The USS Harry S. Truman has taken part in Operations Enduring Freedom and Iraqi Freedom since commissioning in 1998. (US Navy/NARA via Dennis R. Jenkins)

herself deployed off New York, where she was tasked to provide local air defence after the terrorist attack on the World Trade Center twin towers. The carrier finally deployed to the Mediterranean and the Arabian Sea to take part in Enduring Freedom operations before entering Norfolk Naval Yard for a six-month period of upgrading. A further Enduring Freedom cruise took place between January and July 2004, this being followed by a further period in the Norfolk Dockyard. At the completion of this work the carrier undertook a Caribbean cruise that lasted from April to May 2006, after which the vessel re-entered the Norfolk yard for the modifications required for service in Japan. These were completed in August 2007, the carrier departing for Yokosuka in April 2008, where it became the permanent replacement for the USS *Midway*.

Named after a Secretary of the Navy, the USS *John C. Stennis* had commissioned in December 1995, and started the new century by relieving the USS *John F. Kennedy* for Southern Watch duties in January 2000, remaining on station until July that year. Departing from San Diego with Carrier Air Wing 9 aboard, ostensibly for Enduring Freedom operations, the carrier found her deployment delayed by two months as she was required to provide air defence for the west coast after the attacks on New York and Washington. The *John C. Stennis* finally took up her proper deployment position in November, remaining on station until May 2002. An upgrade programme kept her in dock from June 2002 to January 2003, the carrier returning to sea in February. After preparations for her next cruise, a support slot for Enduring Freedom, the carrier departed San Diego in May 2004, remaining on station until November. Upon returning to America, the *John C. Stennis* changed her home port from San Diego to Bremerton, Washington, from where she departed for further Enduring Freedom duties in January 2007, having undergone an extended maintenance and upgrade programme. The carrier returned to Bremerton in August 2007, entering the dockyard soon afterwards. The *John C. Stennis* returned to sea duty in January 2009 to undertake further Enduring Freedom operations before returning to Bremerton in July.

The USS Kitty Hawk was forward ported in Yokosuka, Japan, for much of its career before its retirement in May 2009. (US Navy/NARA via Dennis R. Jenkins)

Named after the thirty-third President of the United States, the USS *Harry S. Truman* was commissioned in July 1998. After an extended working-up period, the carrier was ready for her first deployment in November 2000, heading for the Mediterranean and the Arabian Gulf. By May 2001 she had returned to her Norfolk, Virginia, base. By December 2002 the *Harry S. Truman* was *en route* to the Indian Ocean and later the Arabian Sea to take part in Operations Enduring Freedom and Iraqi Freedom. The carrier had returned to Norfolk by May, entering the naval shipyard for a six-month maintenance period that was completed in February 2004. After the requisite work-up and training period, the carrier was ready for her next combat deployment, which began in October and lasted until April 2005. Most of 2006 was spent in the dockyard, the carrier undergoing a major update programme, and returning to the fleet in July 2007. After its shake-down cruise, the *Harry S. Truman* was ready for another deployment, which started in November 2007. During this period the aircraft carrier's Air Wing 3 took part in the battle for Basra that had been caused by the withdrawal of British Forces. The resultant vacuum had been filled by various factions, all causing a total breakdown in law and order. The Allies had already planned to attack the bases of the various factions in the middle of the year, but this was brought forward after pressure by the Iraqi Prime Minister, Nouri al-Maliki.The strike against the insurgents was a success, with the various factions being driven out of Basra. At the completion of this cruise, the carrier returned to Norfolk for a period of rest and recuperation. The *Harry S. Truman* returned to the fray in May 2009, remaining on station until August.

The USS *Ronald Reagan* was commissioned in July 2003, undertaking her first cruise in May 2004, when she sailed round Cape Horn *en route* to her new home port of San Diego in California. The carrier undertook her first Enduring Freedom cruise between January and July 2006, this being followed by a short cruise in the western Pacific to cover for the *Kitty Hawk*, which was undergoing a refit at the time. The next deployment for the *Ronald Reagan* began in May 2008, and lasted until November, the carrier taking part in operations on behalf of Enduring Freedom. With Carrier Air Wing 14 aboard, she departed from San Diego in May 2009, remaining on station until the beginning of 2010 before entering on a period of maintenance that is still ongoing.

The final carrier of the Nimitz class to be commissioned was the USS *George H.W. Bush*, which joined the fleet in January 2010. By the time this vessel was launched, she had changed significantly from the original Nimitz design, as lessons learned from operating others in the class were applied to the last of the class.

With the arrival of the *George H.W. Bush*, the US Navy was operating a completely nuclear-powered carrier fleet. Based in the Pacific are the carriers *Nimitz, Carl Vinson, Abraham Lincoln, John C. Stennis* and the *Ronald Reagan*, while the Atlantic Fleet can call on the *Theodore Roosevelt, Harry S. Truman, Enterprise, Dwight D. Eisenhower* and the newly available *George H.W. Bush*. While this gives the US Navy a two-ocean-carrier force, each carrier takes it in turn to undertake operations in support of Enduring Freedom, as well as operations in the Gulf when needed.

In 1997 the US Navy started the programme for the future-generation aircraft carrier programme that was known as the CVN (X) programme, although once the design had been firmed up the designation changed to CVN 21, an aircraft carrier for the twenty-first century. In January 2007 the US Navy announced that the new class would be called the Gerald R. Ford, or Ford, class. The first two ships, *Gerald R. Ford* (*CVN 78*) and the so far unnamed *CVN 79* will be commissioned in 2015 and 2019 respectively, with further ships of the class entering service at intervals of five years. A total of

Seen heading into port under the guidance of a tug is the nuclear-powered carrier USS Ronald Reagan. (US Navy/NARA via Dennis R. Jenkins)

This is an artist's concept of the Gerald R. Ford class of aircraft carrier, the first of which is due to enter service in 2015. (US Navy/NARA via Dennis R. Jenkins)

ten Ford-class carriers are planned, with construction continuing to 2058. The *Gerald R. Ford* will replace the USS *Enterprise*, which entered service in 1961 and will be approaching the end of its operational life by 2015. The total acquisition cost of the CVN 21 is expected to be $11.7 billion, although much of this covers design and development cost. The US Department of Defense awarded the Northrop Grumman Newport News Naval Yard in Virginia a $107.6 million contract in July 2003, this being followed by a $1.39 billion contract in May 2004 and $559 million to prepare for the carrier construction and to continue the design programme on the ship's propulsion system.

A $5.1 billion contract for the detailed design and construction was awarded to Newport News in September 2008, while the keel was scheduled to be laid in late 2009. Northrop Grumman was then awarded a contract for the planning and design of the second carrier, *CVN 79*, in November 2006. Construction of *CVN 79* is expected to begin in 2012. The Gerald R. Ford-class carriers will be of a similar displacement to their predecessor, the last of the Nimitz class, the USS *George H.W. Bush*, although it will require 500–900 fewer crew members. The manpower reduction was an additional key performance parameter added to the original operational requirements document for the CVN 21 programme. It is estimated that the new technologies will lead to a thirty per cent reduction in maintenance requirements, and further crew workload reduction will be achieved through higher levels of system automation. The other improvements in operational performance in comparison to the Nimitz class are increased sortie rates, at 160 a day, compared to 140, plus a weight and stability allowance over the fifty-year operational service life of the ship to cater for modifications and improvements, together with increased electrical power generation capability and distribution to sustain the ship's advanced technology systems.

The majority of American aircraft carriers since the 1960s have been constructed at Northrop Grumman Newport News. To cater for the new carrier contracts, Northrop Grumman has extended its design and ship-building capabilities by installing a new heavy plate workshop, a new 5,000-ton thick plate press, covered assembly facilities and a new 1,050-ton capacity crane. Northrop is also using an advanced suite of computer-aided design (CAD) tools for the CVN 21 programme, which includes the CATIA software suite for the simulation of the production process and a CAVE virtual environment package. The hull design is very similar to that of the current Nimitz-class carriers, and has the same number of decks. The island, however, is smaller, and has been moved further aft. The island has a composite-material mast mounted above it, with planar array radars, a volume search radar operating in the S band and a multi-function radar that operates in the X band. The mast also carries the stern-facing joint precision approach and landing system (JPALS) that utilises the local area differential global positioning system (GPS) for guidance rather than radar and the tradi-tional mirror system. In a change from previous practice, the flag bridge for the task force commander and his staff has been relocated to a lower deck in order to reduce the size of the island.

The ship's internal configuration and flight-deck designs have been altered, as the lower decks incorporate a flexible, rapidly reconfigurable layout covering different operational requirements, together with the instal-lation of new equipment in the command, planning and administration areas. The design requirement to build in weight and stability allowances will

Coming soon to a carrier near you, the Lockheed Martin F-35C that is destined to operate from the Nimitz- and Gerald R. Ford-class carriers. (US Navy/NARA via Dennis R. Jenkins)

accommodate the added weight of any new systems that might be installed over the fifty-year operational life of the ship. The removal of one aircraft elevator and the reduction in the number of hangar bays from three to two has contributed to a reduction in the weight of the new carrier.

For defensive purposes the carrier will be armed with the Raytheon-designed Evolved Sea Sparrow missile (ESSM), which is designed to defend against high-speed, highly manoeuvrable anti-ship missiles, while the close-in defensive weapons system is the rolling airframe missile (RAM) developed jointly by Raytheon and Ramsys GmbH.

Initially the new carrier will be capable of carrying an air wing of approximately ninety aircraft, including the F-35 joint strike fighter, F/A-18E/F Super Hornet, E-2D Advanced Hawkeye, EA-18G Super Hornet for electronic support, MH-60R/S helicopters and unmanned air vehicles and unmanned combat air vehicles. The design requirement for a higher basic sortie rate of 160 a day, with surges to a maximum of 220 sorties a day in times of crisis and intense air warfare activity, has led to some design changes to the flight deck. To increase the working area of the flight deck there are three rather than four deck-edge elevators, while deck extensions also increase the aircraft parking and preparation areas, as the aircraft maintenance points are located near the eighteen refuelling and rearming areas.

General Atomics Inc. has been awarded the contract to develop the electromagnetic aircraft launch system (EMALS), which uses a linear electromagnetic accelerator motor to launch aircraft. EMALS demonstrators have been tested at the Naval Air Systems Command (NASC) Lakehurst test centre in New Jersey. It is planned that EMALS, once cleared for service, will replace the current C-13 steam catapults used aboard the remaining Nimitz-class carriers. Should it prove successful, EMALS technology offers the potential benefits of finer aircraft acceleration control, which in turn leads to lower stresses to the aircraft and pilots and provides a slower launch speed for unmanned air vehicles, as well as catering for a wider range of wind-over-deck speeds required for the launch sequence. The contract for the development of an advanced turboelectric arrester gear has also been awarded to General Atomics. In operation, the electromagnetic motor applies control to the synthetic arrester cable to reduce both the maximum tensions in the cable and the peak load on the arrester hook and the aircraft's fuselage structure.

The flow of munitions to the aircraft parked on the flight deck has been redesigned to accommodate the required higher sortie rates. The ship carries stores of missiles and cannon rounds for fighter aircraft, bombs and air-to-surface missiles for the strike aircraft, and torpedoes and depth charges for anti-submarine warfare aircraft. To move these munitions the weapons elevators take the weapons from the magazines to the weapons-handling and weapons-assembly areas on the 02-level deck just below the flight deck, while express weapons elevators are installed between the handling and assembly areas and the flight deck. The two companies selected by Northrop Grumman to generate designs for the advanced weapons elevator are the Federal Equipment Company and Oldenburg Lakeshore Inc. The deployment of all-up rounds that are larger than traditional weapons requiring assembly will require double-height magazines and store rooms, which in turn will also affect the level of need for weapons-assembly facilities. The US Navy had also outlined a requirement for a minimum 150 per cent increase in the power generation capacity for the CVN 21 carrier, compared to the earlier Nimitz-class carriers, as the increased power capacity is needed for the four electromagnetic aircraft launchers and for possible future systems, such as directed-energy weapons that might become feasible during the carrier's lifespan. Raytheon Inc. was contracted in October 2008 to supply a version of the dual-band radar (DBR) originally developed for the Zumwalt-class destroyer for installation on the *Gerald R. Ford*, and this combines both X-band and S-band phased arrays. Northrop Grumman is also developing the advanced nuclear propulsion system around the A1B reactor and a zonal electrical power distribution system for the CVN 21. The A1B reactor designation stands for 'Aircraft carrier platform, First generation core, designed by Bechtel' the contracted designer. The arrival of the Gerald R. Ford class in service will provide America and the United States Navy with vessels that will help project United States foreign policy as the world's policeman.

The aircraft intended for the Gerald R. Ford class of carriers and the later Nimitz-class vessels is the Lockheed Martin F-35C carrier variant, which will have a larger folding wing and larger control surfaces for improved low-speed control than other versions. The aircraft also has stronger landing gear and an arrester hook to cope with the stresses of carrier landings. The larger wing area allows for decreased landing speed, increased range and payload, with twice the range on internal fuel compared with the F/A-18C Hornet, achieving much the same range as the heavier F/A-18E/F Super Hornet. The United States Navy will be the sole user of the carrier variant, with a projected purchase of 480 F-35Cs, replacing the earlier F/A-18A,B,C,D Hornets. On 27 June 2007 the F-35C carrier variant completed its air system critical design review (CDR), which allows for the first two functional prototype F-35Cs to be produced. The F-35C variant is expected to be available for service from 2014. The first production F-35C was rolled out on 29 July 2009. Coupled with the new carriers, the F-35C will present a formidable combination during much of the twenty-first century.

Primary Carrier Aircraft of the US Navy

Boeing F4B
Crew: one
Length: 20 ft 4 in (6.19 m)
Wingspan: 30 ft (9.14 m)
Height: 9 ft (2.74 m)
Loaded weight: 2,690 lb (1,220 kg)
Powerplant: 1 × Pratt & Whitney R-1340-17 Radial engine, 500 hp (373 kW)
Performance
   Maximum speed: 189 mph (304 km/h)
   Cruise speed: 160 mph (257 km/h)
   Range: 570 miles (917 km)
Armament
   Guns: Two 0.30-inch (7.62 mm) machine-guns or one 0.30-inch (7.62 mm)
      and one 0.50-inch (12.7 mm) machine-guns
   Bombs: 244 lb (111 kg) of bombs carried externally

Curtiss JN
Crew: two
Length: 27 ft 4 in (8.33 m)
Wingspan: 43 ft 7¾ in (13.3 m)
Height: 9 ft 10½ in (3.01 m)
Empty weight: 1,390 lb (630 kg)
Max take-off weight: 1,920 lb (871 kg)
Powerplant: 1 × Curtiss OX-5 inline piston, 90 hp (67 kW)
Performance
   Maximum speed: 75 mph (65 kn, 121 km/h)
   Cruise speed: 60 mph (52 kn, 97 km/h)
   Service ceiling: 6,500 ft (2,000 m)

The Curtiss Aircraft Company produced two versions of the Helldiver. This is the biplane version that had the SBC type designation. (US Navy/NARA via Dennis R. Jenkins)

Curtiss H-12/16

Crew: four
Length: 46 ft 6 in (14.18 m)
Wingspan: 92 ft 8½ in (28.26 m)
Height: 16 ft 6 in (5.03 m)
Empty weight: 7,293 lb (3,609 kg)
Gross weight: 10,650 lb (5,550 kg)
Powerplant: 2 × Rolls-Royce Eagle I, 275 hp (205 kW) each
Performance
   Maximum speed: 85 mph (137 km/h)
   Service ceiling: 10,800 ft (3,292 m)
   Rate of climb: 336 ft/min (1.7 m/s)
Armament
   4 × 0.303 in (7.7 mm) Lewis guns on flexible mounts
   4 × 100 lb (45 kg) or 2 × 230 lb (105 kg) bombs below the wings

Curtiss SBC Helldiver

Crew: two
Length: 28 ft 4 in (8.64 m)
Wingspan: 34 ft 0 in (10.36 m)
Height: 12 ft 7 in (3.84 m)
Empty weight: 4,841 lb (2,196 kg)
Loaded weight: 7,080 lb (3,211 kg)
Powerplant: 1 × Wright R-1820-34 Cyclone radial engine, 950 hp (709 kW)
Performance
   Maximum speed: 237 mph (206 kn, 381 km/h)
   Service ceiling: 27,300 ft (8,320 m)

Rate of climb: 1,630 ft/min (8.28 m/s)
Armament
   Guns: 1 × 0.30 in (7.62 mm) forward-firing M1919 Browning machine-gun,
     1 × 0.30 in (7.62 mm) flexible rearward-firing machine-gun
   Bombs: 1 × bomb of up to 1,000 lb (450 kg)

Curtiss SB2C Helldiver
Crew: two
Length: 36 ft 9 in (11.2 m)
Wingspan: 49 ft 9 in (15.2 m)
Height: 14 ft 9 in (4.5 m)
Empty weight: 10,114 lb (4,588 kg)
Loaded weight: 13,674 lb (6,202 kg)
Powerplant: 1 × Wright R-2600 Cyclone radial engine, 1,900 hp (1,400 kW)
Performance
   Maximum speed: 294 mph (473 km/h)
   Range: 1,200 miles (1,900 km)
   Service ceiling: 25,000 ft (7,600 m)
Armament
   Guns: 2 × 20 mm (0.79 in) cannon in the wings, 2 × 0.30 in (7.62 mm) M1919
     Browning machine-guns in the rear cockpit
   Bombs: in internal: 2,000 lb (900 kg) of bombs or 1 × Mark 13-2 torpedo
   Underwing hardpoints: 500 lb (225 kg) of bombs each

Douglas S/TBD Devastator
Crew: three
Length: 35 ft 0 in (10.67 m)
Wingspan: 50 ft 0 in (15.24 m)
Height: 15 ft 1 in (4.60 m)
Empty weight: 6,182 lb (2,804 kg)
Loaded weight: 9,862 lb (4,473 kg)

The Helldiver name would be used again by Curtiss, although this was
applied to a much more aggressive machine, the SB2C. Not only did
examples fight across the Pacific but numbers remained in front-line service
in the immediate post-war period. (US Navy/NARA via Dennis R. Jenkins)

One of the first attack types supplied by Douglas to the US Navy was the SBD/TBD Dauntless, capable of dispensing bombs and torpedoes. This is a pre-war aircraft assigned to VT-6 aboard the USS *Enterprise*. (US Navy/NARA via Dennis R. Jenkins)

Powerplant: 1 × Pratt & Whitney R-1830-64 Twin Wasp radial engine, 900 hp (671 kW)
Performance
    Maximum speed: 206 mph (331 km/h)
    Service ceiling: 19,700 ft (6,000 m)
    Rate of climb: 720 ft/min (3.7 m/s)
Armament
    1 × 0.30 in (7.62 mm) machine-gun forward-firing, or

The AD, Able Dog, Skyraider served in both Korea and Vietnam. Capable of carrying a great load of weaponry, the Spad, as it was also known, was one of the best piston-powered attack aircraft ever produced. (US Navy/NARA via Dennis R. Jenkins)

Douglas also manufactured the F4D Skyray fighter for the US Navy. Unlike contemporary fighters, this aircraft featured an ovoidal-shaped delta wing, with its combined flight controls mounted on the trailing edge. While it featured a cannon armament, the 'Ford' was also capable of carrying the Philco-Ford AIM-9 Sidewinder missile. (John Ryan Collection)

1 × 0.50 in (12.7 mm) machine-gun forward-firing
1 (later 2) × 0.30 in (7.62 mm) machine-gun in rear cockpit
1 × 1,000 lb (454 kg) bomb, or
1 × Mark XIII torpedo – 1,200 lb (544 kg)

Douglas AD Skyraider
Crew: one
Length: 38 ft 10 in (11.84 m)
Wingspan: 50 ft 0¼ in (15.25 m)
Height: 15 ft 8¼ in (4.78 m)
Empty weight: 11,968 lb (5,429 kg)
Loaded weight: 18,106 lb (8,213 kg)
Powerplant: 1 × Wright R-3350-26WA radial engine, 2,700 hp (2,000 kW)
Performance
   Maximum speed: 322 mph (280 kn, 518 km/h) at 18,000 ft (5,500 m)
   Cruise speed: 198 mph (172 kn, 319 km/h)
   Service ceiling: 28,500 ft (8,685 m)
   Rate of climb: 2,850 ft/min (14.5 m/s)
Armament
   Guns: 4 × 20 mm (0.79 in) M2 cannon
   Others: Up to 8,000 lb (3,600 kg) of ordnance on 15 external hardpoints
      including bombs, torpedoes, mine dispensers, unguided rockets, or gun
      pods

Douglas F4D Skyray
Crew: one
Length: 45 ft 3 in (10.21 m)
Wingspan: 33 ft 6 in (13.8 m)

The Douglas Company would also supply one of the largest carrier-borne aircraft ever taken to sea on a regular basis, the A-3 Skywarrior. Originally delivered as a nuclear-capable bomber, the type served in both the tanker and electronic warfare roles before retirement. (John Ryan Collection)

Height: 13 ft 0 in (3.96 m)
Empty weight: 16,024 lb (7,268 kg)
Loaded weight: 22,648 lb (10,273 kg)
Powerplant: 1 × Pratt & Whitney J57-P-8, -8A or -8B turbojet
  Dry thrust: 10,200 lbf (45 kN)
  Thrust with afterburner: 16,000 lbf (71 kN)
Performance
  Maximum speed: 722 mph (627 kn, 1,200 km/h)
  Service ceiling: 55,000 ft (17,000 m)
  Rate of climb: 18,300 ft/min (93.3 m/s)
Armament
  Guns: 4 × 20 mm (0.79 in) Mk 12-0 cannons, two (2) each just aft of wing
    leading edge, mid-wing, underside, with 65 rounds/gun
  Missiles: 2 × AIM-9 Sidewinder air-to-air missiles
  Bombs: 2 × 2,000 lb (907 kg) bombs

Douglas A-3 Skywarrior
Crew: three
Length: 76 ft 4 in (23.27 m)
Wingspan: 72 ft 6 in (22.1 m)
Height: 22 ft 9½ in (6.95 m)
Empty weight: 39,400 lb (17,900 kg)
Loaded weight: 70,000 lb (31,750 kg)
Powerplant: 2 × Pratt & Whitney J57-P-10 turbojet, 10,500 lbf (46.7 kN) each
Performance
  Maximum speed: 530 kn (610 mph, 980 km/h)
  Cruise speed: 450 kn (520 mph, 840 km/h)
  Service ceiling: 41,000 ft (12,500 m)

The Douglas A-4 Skyhawk, or Scooter, was one of the most capable attack aircraft ever built. Known as the Bantam Bomber, the A-4 was produced in many versions for the Navy and Marines. (John Ryan Collection)

Armament
    Guns: 2 × 20 mm (0.79 in) cannon in tail turret
    Bombs: 12,000 lb (5,443 kg) of free-fall bombs
        12 × 500 lb (227 kg) Mark 82 bombs or
        6 × 1,000 lb (454 kg) Mark 83 bombs or
        1,600 lb (726 kg) armour-piercing bombs or
        500 lb (227 kg) Mark 36 DST Destructor Mines or
        1,000 lb (454 kg) Mark 40 DST Destructor Mines or
        2,000 lb (907 kg) Mark 41 DST Destructor Mines or
        1 × Mark 15 free-fall nuclear weapon or
        1 × B43 free-fall nuclear weapon

Douglas A-4 Skyhawk
Crew: one (two in OA-4F, TA-4F, TA-4J)
Length: 40 ft 3 in (12.22 m)
Wingspan: 26 ft 6 in (8.38 m)
Height: 15 ft (4.57 m)
Empty weight: 10,450 lb (4,750 kg)
Loaded weight: 18,300 lb (8,318 kg)
Powerplant: 1 × Pratt & Whitney J52-P8A turbojet, 9,300 lbf (41 kN)
Performance
    Maximum speed: 585 kn (673 mph, 1,077 km/h)
    Range: 1,700 nmi (2,000 miles, 3,220 km)
    Service ceiling: 42,250 ft (12,880 m)

Grumman was associated with the US Navy for many years, being a primary supplier of aircraft. The F4F Wildcat was one of its first designs after its biplane period. Although quickly outclassed by the aircraft of other nations, it was a favourite aboard escort carriers employed on convoy duties. (NASA/ Dennis R. Jenkins)

Rate of climb: 8,440 ft/min (43 m/s)
Armament
    Guns: 2 × 20 mm (0.79 in) Colt Mk 12 cannon, 100 rounds/gun
    Hardpoints: 4 × underwing and 1 × under-fuselage pylon stations holding
       up to 9,900 lb (4,490 kg) of payload
    Rockets: 4 × LAU-10 rocket pods (each with 4 × 127 mm Mk 32 Zuni
       rockets)
    Missiles:
    Air-to-surface missiles:
       2 × AGM-12 Bullpup
       2 × AGM-45 Shrike anti-radiation missile
       2 × AGM-62 Walleye TV-guided glide bomb
       2 × AGM-65 Maverick
    Bombs:
       6 × Rockeye-II Mark 20 cluster bomb unit (CBU)
       6 × Rockeye Mark 7/APAM-59 CBU
       Mark 80 series of unguided bombs (including 3 kg and 14 kg practice
       bombs)
       B57 nuclear bomb
       B61 nuclear bomb

Grumman F3F

Crew: one
Length: 23 ft 2 in (7.06 m)
Wingspan: 32 ft 0 in (9.75 m)
Height: 9 ft 4 in (2.84 m)
Empty weight: 3,285 lb (1,490 kg)
Max take-off weight: 4,795 lb (2,175 kg)

Grumman also delivered one of the most capable attack aircraft of the Second World War – the Avenger. Although the type ended its combat career post-1945, many were converted for the carrier onboard delivery role for later service. (US Navy/NARA via Dennis R. Jenkins)

Powerplant: 1 × Wright R-1820-22 Cyclone 9-cylinder radial engine, 950 hp (710 kW)
Performance
  Maximum speed: 264 mph (229 kn, 425 km/h) at 15,250 ft (4,658 m)
  Cruise speed: 150 mph (130 kn, 240 km/h)
  Service ceiling: 33,200 ft (10,120 m)
  Rate of climb: 2,800 ft/min (14 m/s) at sea level
Armament
  Guns:
    1 × 0.30 in (7.62 mm) M1919 machine-gun, 500 rounds (left)
    1 × 0.50 in (12.7 mm) M2 machine-gun, 200 rounds (right)
  Bombs: 2 × 116 lb (52.6 kg) Mk IV bombs, one under each wing

Grumman F4F Wildcat
Crew: one
Length: 28 ft 9 in (8.76 m)
Wingspan: 38 ft (11.58 m)
Height: 11 ft 10 in (3.60 m)
Loaded weight: 7,000 lb (3,200 kg)
Powerplant: 1 × Pratt & Whitney R-1830-76 double-row radial engine, 1,200 hp (900 kW)
Performance
  Maximum speed: 331 mph (531 km/h)
  Service ceiling: 39,500 ft (12,000 m)

Rate of climb: 2,303 ft/min (11.7 m/s)
Armament
  Guns: 4 × 0.50 in (12.7 mm) M2 Browning machine-guns with 450 rounds
    per gun
  Bombs: 2 × 100 lb (45 kg) bombs and/or 2 × 58 gal (220 l) drop tanks

Grumman TBF/M Avenger
Crew: three
Length: 40 ft 11½ in (12.48 m)
Wingspan: 54 ft 2 in [18] (16.51 m)
Height: 15 ft 5 in (4.70 m)
Empty weight: 10,545 lb (4,783 kg)
Loaded weight: 17,893 lb (8,115 kg)
Powerplant: 1 × Wright R-2600-20 radial engine, 1,900 hp (1,420 kW)
Performance
  Maximum speed: 275 mph [19] (442 km/h)
  Service ceiling: 30,100 ft (9,170 m)
  Rate of climb: 2,060 ft/min (10.5 m/s)
Armament
  Guns:
    1 × 0.30 in (7.62 mm) nose-mounted M1919 Browning machine-gun or
    2 × 0.50 in (12.7 mm) wing-mounted M2 Browning machine-guns
    1 × 0.50 in (12.7 mm) dorsal-mounted M2 Browning machine-gun
    1 × 0.30 in (7.62 mm) ventral-mounted M1919 Browning machine-gun
  Bombs:
    up to 2,000 lb (907 kg) of bombs or
    1 × 2,000 lb (907 kg) Mark 13 torpedo

Grumman F6F Hellcat
Crew: one
Length: 33 ft 7 in (10.24 m)
Wingspan: 42 ft 10 in (13.06 m)
Height: 13 ft 1 in (3.99 m)
Empty weight: 9,238 lb (4,190 kg)
Loaded weight: 12,598 lb (5,714 kg)
Max take-off weight: 15,415 lb (6,990 kg)
Powerplant: 1 × Pratt & Whitney R-2800-10W Double Wasp two-row radial
  engine with a two-speed, two-stage supercharger, 2,000 hp (1,491
  kW[40])
Performance
  Maximum speed: 330 kn (380 mph, 610 km/h)
  Service ceiling: 37,300 ft (11,370 m)
  Rate of climb: 3,500 ft/min (17.8 m/s)

After the Wildcat, Grumman designed the much more capable F6F Hellcat, which was not only more heavily armed, but faster, and it had a longer range. (Rick Harding Collection)

Armament
> Guns:
>> 6 × 0.50 in (12.7 mm) M2 Browning machine-guns, with 400 rpg, F6F-3/F6F-5, or
>> 2 × 0.79 in (20 mm) cannon, with 225 rpg
>> 4 × 0.50 in (12.7 mm) Browning machine-guns with 400 rpg,F6F-5N.
> Rockets:
>> 6 × 5 in (127 mm) HVARs or
>> 2 × 11¾ in (298 mm) Tiny Tim unguided rockets
> Bombs: up to 4,000 lb (1,814 kg) full load, including:
> Bombs or torpedoes
>> 1 × 2,000 lb (907 kg) bomb or
>> 1 × Mk 13-3 torpedo

Grumman F8F Bearcat
Crew: one
Length: 28 ft 3 in (8.61 m)
Wingspan: 35 ft 10 in (10.92 m)
Height: 13 ft 9 in (4.21 m)
Empty weight: 7,070 lb (3,207 kg)
Loaded weight: 9,600 lb (4,354 kg)
Powerplant: 1 × Pratt & Whitney R-2800-34W Double Wasp two-row radial engine, 2,100 hp (1,567 kW)

Performance
   Maximum speed: 421 mph (366 kn, 678 km/h)
   Range: 1,105 miles (1,778 km)
   Service ceiling: 38,700 ft (11,796 m)
   Rate of climb: 4,570 ft/min (23.2 m/s)
Armament
   Guns: 4 × 0.50 in (12.7 mm) machine-guns or 4 × 20 mm M3 cannon F8F-
      1B)
   Rockets: 4 × 5 in (127 mm) unguided rockets
   Bombs: 1,000 lb (454 kg) bombs

Grumman AF Guardian
Crew: two
Length: 43 ft 4 in (13.21 m)
Wingspan: 60 ft 8 in (18.49 m)
Height: 16 ft 2 in (5.08 m)
Empty weight: 14,580 lb (6,613 kg)
Max take-off weight: 25,500 lb (11,567 kg)
Powerplant: 1 × Pratt & Whitney R-2800-48W 'Double Wasp' radial engine,
   2,400 hp (1,790 kW)
Performance
   Maximum speed: 317 mph (276 kn, 510 km/h)
   Service ceiling: 32,500 ft (9,900 m)
   Rate of climb: 1,850 ft/min (9.4 m/s)
Armament
   Rockets: 16 × 5 in (127 mm) unguided high-velocity aircraft rocket (HVAR)
      rockets
   Bombs: 4,000 lb (1,814 kg) of bombs, torpedoes, and depth charges

Grumman F9F Panther
Crew: one
Length: 37 ft 5 in (11.3 m)
Wingspan: 38 ft 0 in (11.6 m)
Height: 11 ft 4 in (3.8 m)
Empty weight: 9,303 lb (4,220 kg)
Loaded weight: 14,235 lb (6,456 kg)
Powerplant: 1 × Pratt & Whitney J42-P-6/P-8 turbojet, 5,950 lbf (26.5 kN) with
   water injection
Performance
   Maximum speed: 500 kn (575 mph, 925 km/h)
   Range: 1,300 miles (1,100 nmi, 2,100 km)
   Service ceiling: 44,600 ft (13,600 m)
Armament
   Guns: 4 × 20 mm (0.79 in) M2 cannon, 190 rpg
   Hardpoints: Underwing hardpoints and provisions to carry combinations of:

Rockets: 6 × 5 in (127 mm) rockets on underwing hardpoints
Bombs: 2,000 lb (907 kg) of bombs

Grumman F9F Cougar
Crew: one
Length: 42 ft 2 in (12.9 m)
Wingspan: 34 ft 6 in (10.5 m)
Height: 12 ft 3 in (3.7 m)
Empty weight: 11,866 lb (5,382 kg)
Loaded weight: 20,098 lb (9,116 kg)
Powerplant: 1 × Pratt & Whitney J48-P-8A turbojet, 8,500 lbf (38 kN) with
     water injection
Performance
   Maximum speed: 647 mph (1,041 km/h)
   Service ceiling: 42,000 ft (12,800 m)
   Rate of climb: 5,750 ft/min (29.2 m/s)
Armament
   Guns: 4 × 20 mm (0.79 in) M2 cannon, 190 rounds per gun
   Rockets: 6 × 5 in (127 mm) rockets
   Missiles: 4 × AIM-9 Sidewinder air-to-air missiles
   Bombs: 2 × 1,000 lb (454 kg) bombs

Grumman F11F Tiger
Crew: one
Length: 46 ft 11 in (14.3 m)
Wingspan: 31 ft 7½ in (9.6 m)
Height: 13 ft 3 in (4.0 m)

Grumman also provided the Navy with its first anti-submarine aircraft that
   combined both detection and attack in one airframe, this being the S-2
   Tracker. This particular machine was assigned to VS-33. (Trevor Jones
   Collection)

Empty weight: 13,810 lb (6,277 kg)
Loaded weight: 21,035 lb (9,561 kg)
Powerplant: 1 × Wright J65-W-18 turbojet
  Dry thrust: 7,400 lbf (32.9 kN)
  Thrust with afterburner: 10,500 lbf (46.7 kN)
Performance
  Maximum speed: Mach 1.1 (727 mph, 1,170 km/h) at 35,000 ft (11,000 m)
  Cruise speed: 577 mph (929 km/h)
  Service ceiling: 49,000 ft (14,900 m)
  Rate of climb: 16,300 ft/min (83 m/s)
Armament
  Guns: 4 × 20 mm (.79 in) Colt Mk 12 cannon, 125 rounds per gun
  Hardpoints: 4 and provisions to carry combinations of:
  Missiles: 4 × AIM-9 Sidewinders

Grumman S-2 Tracker
Crew: four
Length: 43 ft 6 in (13.26 m)
Wingspan: 72 ft 7 in (22.12 m)
Height: 17 ft 6 in (5.33 m)
Empty weight: 18,315 lb (8,310 kg)
Loaded weight: 23,435 lb (10,630 kg)
Powerplant: 2 × Wright R-1820-82WA radial engines, 1,525 hp (kW) each
Performance
  Maximum speed: 280 mph (450 km/h) at sea level
  Cruise speed: 150 mph (240 km/h)
  Service ceiling: 22,000 ft (6,700 m)
Armament
  2 × homing torpedoes (Mk 41, Mk 43, or Mk 34), depth charges (Mk 54), or
    mines in the bomb bay
  6 × underwing hardpoints for torpedoes, depth charges, or rockets

Grumman E-1 Tracer
Crew: four
Length: 42.25 ft (12.9 m)
Wingspan: 69.6 ft (21.2 m)
Height: 16.3 ft (4.9 m)
Empty weight: 18,750 lb (8,504 kg)
Loaded weight: 26,600 lb (12,065 kg)
Powerplant: 2 × Wright R-1820-82WA Cyclone 9-cylinder radial piston
    engine, 1,525 hp (1,137 kW) each
Performance
  Maximum speed: 287 mph (462 km/h)
  Service ceiling: 15,800 ft (4,800 m)
  Rate of climb: 1,120 ft/min (340 m/min)

Grumman E-2 Hawkeye
Crew: five
Length: 57 ft 7 in (17.56 m)
Wingspan: 80 ft 7 in (24.58 m)
Height: 18 ft 4 in (5.58 m)
Empty weight: 37,678 lb (17,090 kg)
Loaded weight: 55,000 lb (23,391 kg)
Powerplant: 2 × Allison T56-A-425 or -427 turboprop, 5100 shp (-427) (3,800 kW) each
Performance
  Maximum speed: 375 mph (604 km/h)
  Service ceiling: 30,800 ft (9,300 m)
  Rate of climb: 2,515 ft/min (13 m/s)

Grumman A-6 Intruder
Crew: two
Length: 54 ft 7 in (16.6 m)
Wingspan: 53 ft (16.2 m)
Height: 15 ft 7 in (4.75 m)
Empty weight: 25,630 lb (11,630 kg)
Max take-off weight: 60,626 lb (27,500 kg)
Powerplant: 2 × Pratt & Whitney J52-P8B turbojets, 9,300 lbf (41.4 kN) each
Performance
  Maximum speed: 563 kn (648 mph, 1,040 km/h)

Grumman also provided the Navy with its AEW aircraft. The first was based on the Avenger, the second was a modified version of the Tracker that became the E-1 Tracer, while the third, pictured here, was the E-2 Hawkeye, still in service. (US Navy/NARA via Dennis R. Jenkins)

Service ceiling: 40,600 ft (12,400 m)
Rate of climb: 7,620 ft/min (38.7 m/s)
Armament
Hardpoints: 4 × wing and 1 × fuselage with 18,000 lb (8,170 kg) load
Rockets:
2.75 in (70 mm) CRV7 rocket pod
5 in (127 mm) Zuni rocket pod
Air-to-ground missiles:
AGM-45 Shrike
AGM-62 Walleye
AGM-65 Maverick
AGM-84 Harpoon and
AGM-88 HARM
Bombs:
Mk 81 250 lb (113 kg) GP bombs
Mk 82 500 lb (241 kg) GP bombs
Mk 83 1,000 lb (454 kg) GP bombs
Mk-84 2,000 lb (907 kg) GP bombs
Mk-117 750 lb (340 kg) GP bombs
Mk-20 Rockeye II cluster bombs
CBU-89 GATOR mine cluster bombs
Mk 77 750 lb (340 kg) incendiary bombs
GBU-10 Paveway II laser-guided bombs
GBU-12 Paveway II laser-guided bombs
GBU-16 Paveway II laser-guided bombs
B61 nuclear bomb
B43 nuclear bomb

Grumman EA-6B Prowler
Crew: four
Length: 59 ft 10 in (17.7 m)

Once its avionics problems had been sorted out, the Grumman A-6 Intruder
served the US Navy throughout the Vietnam War, not finally retiring until
after Operation Desert Storm. (Trevor Jones Collection)

The F-14 Tomcat was the final fighter delivered by Grumman to the Navy. The F-14 featured swing wings, all-flying tailplanes and turbofan engines. It was also armed with the AIM-54 Phoenix missile, which had an extraordinary range. (US Navy/NARA via Dennis R. Jenkins)

Wingspan: 53 ft (15.9 m)
Height: 16 ft 8 in (4.9 m)
Empty weight: 31,160 lb (15,130 kg)
Max take-off weight: 61,500 lb (27,900 kg)
Powerplant: 2 × Pratt & Whitney J52-P408A turbojet, 10,400 lbf (46 kN) each
Performance
   Maximum speed: 566 kn (651 mph, 1,050 km/h)
   Cruise speed: 418 kn (481 mph, 774 km/h)
   Service ceiling: 37,600 ft (11,500 m)
Armament
   4 × AGM-88 HARM anti-radar missiles
   5 × ALQ-99 tactical jamming system (TJS) external pods

Grumman F-14 Tomcat
Crew: two
Length: 62 ft 9 in (19.1 m)
Wingspan:
Spread: 64 ft (19.55 m)
Swept: 38 ft (11.58 m)
Height: 16 ft (4.88 m)
Empty weight: 43,735 lb (19,838 kg)
Loaded weight: 61,000 lb (27,700 kg)
Powerplant: 2 × General Electric F110-GE-400 afterburning turbofans
   Dry thrust: 13,810 lbf (61.4 kN) each
   Thrust with afterburner: 27,800 lbf (124.7 kN) each
Performance
   Maximum speed: Mach 2.34 (1,544 mph, 2,485 km/h) at high altitude
   Service ceiling: 50,000 ft (15,200 m)
   Rate of climb: >45,000 ft/min (229 m/s)

Armament
  Guns: 1 × 20 mm (0.787 in) M61 Vulcan Gatling gun, with 675 rounds
  Hardpoints: 10 total: 6 × under-fuselage, 2 × under nacelles and 2 × on
    wing gloves with a capacity of 14,500 lb (6,600 kg) of ordnance and fuel
    tanks
  Missiles:
    Air-to-air missiles: AIM-54 Phoenix, AIM-7 Sparrow, AIM-9 Sidewinder
  Bombs:
    JDAM precision-guided munitions (PGMs)
    Paveway series of laser-guided bombs
    Mk 80 series of unguided iron bombs
    Mk 20 Rockeye II
  Others:
    LANTIRN targeting pod

Lockheed S-3 Viking
Crew: four
Length: 53 ft 4 in (16.26 m)
Wingspan: 68 ft 8 in (20.93 m)
Height: 22 ft 9 in (6.93 m)
Empty weight: 26,581 lb (12,057 kg)
Loaded weight: 38,192 lb (17,324 kg)
Powerplant: 2 × General Electric TF34-GE-2 turbofans, 9,275 lbf (41.26 kN)
    each
Performance
  Maximum speed: 493 mph (795 km/h) at sea level
  Cruise speed: 405 mph, 650 km/h
  Service ceiling: 40,900 ft (12,465 m)
  Rate of climb: 5,120 ft/min (26.0 m/s)
Armament
  Up to 4,900 lb (2,220 kg) on four internal and two external hardpoints,
    including:
    10 × 500 lb (227 kg) Mark 82 bombs
    2 × 1000 lb (454 kg) Mark 83 bombs
    2 × 2000 lb (908 kg) Mark 84 bombs
    6 × CBU-100 cluster bombs
    2 × Mark 50 torpedoes
    4 × Mark 46 torpedoes
    6 × mines or depth charges
    2 × B57 nuclear bombs
    2 × AGM-65E/F Maverick missiles
    2 × AGM-84D Harpoon missiles
    1 × AGM-84H/K SLAM-ER missile

Ling Temco Vought would deliver the A-7 Corsair II to the Navy. Based on the earlier Vought F-8 Crusader fighter, the A-7 was an attack aircraft capable of carrying a large range of weapons. (Trevor Jones Collection)

LTV A-7 Corsair II

Crew: one
Length: 46 ft 1½ in (14.06 m)
Wingspan: 38 ft 9 in (11.81 m)
Height: 16 ft 0¾ in (4.90 m)
Empty weight: 19,490 lb (8,840 kg)
Max take-off weight: 42,000 lb (19,050 kg)
Powerplant: 1 × Allison TF41-A-2 turbofan, 14,500 lbf (64.5 kN)
Performance
    Maximum speed: 698 mph (1,123 km/h) at sea level
Armament
    Guns: 1 × 20 mm (0.787 in) M61 Vulcan Gatling gun with 1,030 rounds
    Hardpoints: 6 × under-wing plus 2 × fuselage pylon stations for AIM-9
       Sidewinder
    Rockets:
       4 × LAU-10 rocket pods
    Missiles:
    Air-to-air missiles:
       2 × AIM-9 Sidewinders
    Air-to-surface missiles:
       2 × AGM-45 Shrike anti-radiation missiles, or
       2 × AGM-62 Walleye TV-guided glide bombs, or
       2 × AGM-65 Mavericks, or
       2 × AGM-88 HARMs, or
       2 × GBU-15 electro-optically guided glide bombs
    Bombs: Up to 30 × 500 lb (227 kg) Mk 82 bombs or any combination of the
       following:

Mk 80 series of unguided bombs (including 3 kg and 14 kg practice bombs)
Paveway series of laser-guided bombs

McDonnell FH Phantom
Crew: one
Length: 37 ft 3 in (11.35 m)
Wingspan: 40 ft 9 in; 16 ft 3 in with folded wings [8] (12.42 m/4.95 m)
Height: 14 ft 2 in (4.32 m)
Empty weight: 6,683 lb (3,031 kg)
Loaded weight: 10,035 lb (4,552 kg)
Powerplant: 2 × Westinghouse J30-WE-20 turbojets, 1,600 lbf (7.1 kN) each
Performance
   Maximum speed: 417 kn (479 mph, 771 km/h) at sea level
   Cruise speed: 216 kn (248 mph, 399 km/h)
   Service ceiling: 41,100 ft (12,525 m)
   Rate of climb: 4,230 ft/min (21.5 m/s)
Armament
   Guns: 4 × 0.50 in (12.7 mm) machine-guns

McDonnell F2H Banshee
Crew: one
Length: 48 ft 2 in (14.68 m)
Wingspan: 41 ft 9 in (12.73 m)
Height: 14 ft 6 in (4.42 m)
Empty weight: 13,183 lb (5,980 kg)
Loaded weight: 21,013 lb (9,531 kg)
Powerplant: 2 × Westinghouse J34-WE-34 turbojets, 3,250 lbf (14.5 kN) each
Performance
   Maximum speed: 580 mph (933 km/h) at sea level
   Cruise speed: 461 mph
   Service ceiling: 46,600 ft (14,205 m)
   Rate of climb: 6,000 ft/min (30 m/s) from sea level
Armament
   Guns: 4 × 20 mm (0.79 in) Colt Mk 16 cannon
   Rockets:
      8 × 60 lb high-explosive rockets, or
      6 × 500 lb bombs and 2 × 60 lb high-explosive rockets

McDonnell F3H Demon
Crew: one
Length: 59 ft 0 in (17.98 m)
Wingspan: 35 ft 4 in (10.77 m)
Height: 14 ft 7 in (4.45 m)
Empty weight: 21,287 lb (9,656 kg)

Possibly the most significant fighter of the twentieth century, the McDonnell F-4 Phantom II would eventually end up in service with many of the world's air forces. This example, an F-4B, was assigned to VF-151 aboard the USS Coral Sea. (Rick Harding Collection)

Loaded weight: 31,145 lb (14,127 kg)
Powerplant: 1 × Westinghouse J40-WE-22 turbojet, 14,400 lbf (64 kN)
Performance
Maximum speed: 716 mph (622 kn, 1,152 km/h)
Service ceiling: 42,650 ft (13,000 m)
Rate of climb: 14,350 ft/min (72.9 m/s)
Armament
Guns: 4 × 20 mm (0.79 in) Colt Mk 12 cannon, 150 rpg
Missiles: 4 × AIM-7 Sparrows or 2 × Sparrows and 2 × AIM-9 Sidewinders
Bombs: 6,000 lb (2,720 kg) of bombs

McDonnell F-4 Phantom II
Crew: two
Length: 58 ft 3¾ in (17.5 m)
Wingspan: 38 ft 4½ in (11.7 m)
Height: 16 ft 6 in (5.0 m)
Empty weight: 30,328 lb (13,757 kg)
Loaded weight: 41,500 lb (18,825 kg)
Powerplant: 2 × General Electric J79-GE-8B axial compressor turbojets, 17,000 lbf (79.4 kN) each
Performance
Maximum speed: Mach 2.23 (1,472 mph, 2,370 km/h) at 40,000 ft (12,190 m)
Cruise speed: 506 kn (585 mph, 940 km/h)
Service ceiling: 60,000 ft (18,300 m)
Rate of climb: 41,300 ft/min (210 m/s)
Armament
Up to 18,650 lb (8,480 kg) of weapons on 9 external hardpoints, including general-purpose bombs, cluster bombs, TV- and laser-guided bombs,

326

rocket air-to-ground missiles, anti-runway weapons, anti-ship missiles, targeting pods, reconnaissance pods, and nuclear weapons. Baggage pods and external fuel tanks may also be carried.

4 × AIM-7 Sparrows in fuselage recesses plus 4 × AIM-9 Sidewinders on wing pylons;

4 × AIM-9 Sidewinders

6 × AGM-65 Mavericks

4 × AGM-62 Walleyes

4 × AGM-45 Shrikes, AGM-88 HARMs, AGM-78 Standard ARMs

Martin T3M
Crew: three
Length: 41 ft 4 in (12.60 m)
Wingspan: 56 ft 7 in (17.25 m)
Height: 15 ft 1 in (4.60 m)
Empty weight: 5,814 lb (2,643 kg)
Loaded weight: 9,503 lb (4,320 kg)
Powerplant: 1 × Packard 3A-2500 liquid cooled V-12 engine, 770 hp (574 kW)
Performance
    Maximum speed: 109 mph (95 kn, 175 km/h)
    Service ceiling: 7,900 ft (2,400 m)
    Climb to 5,000 ft: 16.8 min
Armament
    1 × flexible mounted 0.3 in (7.62 mm) machine-gun in rear cockpit
    1 × torpedo or bombs under fuselage

North American AJ Savage
Crew: three
Length: 63 ft 1 in (19.2 m)
Wingspan: 71 ft 5 in (21.8 m)
Height: 20 ft 5 in (6.2 m)
Empty weight: 27,558 lb (12,500 kg)
Loaded weight: 47,000 lb (21,363 kg)
Powerplant:
    1 × Allison J33-A-1 turbojet, 4,600 lbf (20 kN)
    2 × Pratt & Whitney R-2800-44W radial engines, 2,400 hp (1,790 kW) each
Performance
    Maximum speed: 471 mph [4] (409 kn, 758 km/h)
    Range: 1,731 miles (1,505 nmi, 2,787 km)
    Service ceiling: 40,800 ft [5] (12,440 m)
    Rate of climb: 2,900 ft/min (14.7 m/s)
Armament
    Bombs: 12,000 lb (5,400 kg) conventional bombs, or 1 × nuclear bomb

North American, normally a USAF supplier, would deliver the FJ-3 Fury to the squadrons of the Navy; this aircraft was assigned to VF-145 when photographed. (Rick Harding Collection)

North American FJ Fury

Crew: one
Length: 36 ft 4 in (11.1 m)
Wingspan: 39 ft 1 in (11.9 m)
Height: 13 ft 11 in (4.2 m)
Empty weight: 13,210 lb (5,992 kg)
Loaded weight: 20,130 lb (9,130 kg)
Powerplant: 1 × Wright J65-W-16A turbojet, 7,700 lbf (34 kN)
Performance
  Maximum speed: 680 mph (1,090 km/h) at 35,000 ft (10,670 m)
  Service ceiling: 46,800 ft (14,300 m)
  Rate of climb: 7,660 ft/min (38.9 m/s)

In total contrast to the FJ-3 Fury, NAA/ Rockwell would develop the A-5A Vigilante for use in the nuclear delivery role at high speed. The Navy decided not to go ahead with this version, preferring instead to rework it as the RA-5C Vigilante reconnaissance platform. (US Navy/NARA via Dennis R. Jenkins)

Armament
  Guns: 4 × 20 mm (0.787 in) cannon
  Missiles: 4 × AIM-9 Sidewinder missiles
  Bombs: 3,000 lb (1,400 kg) of underwing ordnance, including missiles

North American A-5A Vigilante
Crew: two
Length: 76 ft 6 in (23.32 m)
Wingspan: 53 ft 0 in (16.16 m)
Height: 19 ft 4¾ in (5.91 m)
Empty weight: 32,714 lb (14,870 kg)
Loaded weight: 47,530 lb (21,605 kg)
Powerplant: 2 × General Electric J79-GE-8 afterburning turbojets
  Dry thrust: 10,900 lbf (48 kN) each
  Thrust with afterburner: 17,000 lbf (76 kN) each
Performance
  Maximum speed: Mach 2.0 (1,149 knots, 1,320 mph, 2,123 km/h) at 40,0000
    ft (12,200 m)
  Service ceiling: 52,100 ft (15,880 m)
  Rate of climb: 8,000 ft/min (40.6 m/s)
Armament
  Bombs:
    1 × Mk 27 nuclear bomb, B28 or B43 freefall nuclear bomb in internal
    weapons bay
    2 × B43, Mk 83, or Mk 84 bombs on two external hardpoints

Piasecki HUP Retriever
Crew: two
Length: 56 ft 11 in (17.35 m)
Rotor diameter: 35 ft 0 in (10.67 m)
Height: 12 ft 6 in (3.81 m)
Empty weight: 3,928 lb (1,782 kg)
Loaded weight: 5,750 lb (2,608 kg)
Powerplant: 1 × Continental R-975-46A radial, 550 hp (410 kW)
Performance
  Maximum speed: 105 mph (169 km/h)
  Service ceiling: 10,000 ft (3,048 m)
  Rate of climb: 100 ft/min (5.01 m/s)

Sikorsky HO3S
Length: 41 ft 2 in (12.5 m)
Rotor diameter: 48 ft (14.6 m)
Height: 12 ft 11 in (3.9 m)
Loaded weight: 4,815 lb (2,184 kg)

Performance
　　Maximum speed: 78 kn (90 mph, 145 km/h)
　　Service ceiling: 10,000 ft (3,000 m)

Sikorsky HO4S

Crew: two
Length: 62 ft 7 in (19.1 m)
Rotor diameter: 53 ft (16.16 m)
Height: 13 ft 4 in (4.07 m)
Empty weight: 4,795 lb (2,177 kg)
Loaded weight: 7,200 lb (3,266 kg)
Powerplant: 1 × Pratt & Whitney R-1340-57 radial engine, 600 hp (450 kW)
Performance
　　Maximum speed: 101 mph (163 km/h)
　　Service ceiling: 10,500 ft (3,200 m)
　　Rate of climb: 700 ft/min (213 m/min)

Sikorsky HSS-1 Seabat

Crew: two
Length: 56 ft 8½ in (17.28 m)
Rotor diameter: 56 ft 0 in (17.07 m)
Height: 15 ft 11 in (4.85 m)
Empty weight: 7,900 lb (3,583 kg)
Max take-off weight: 14,000 lb (6,350 kg)
Powerplant: 1 × Wright R-1820-84 radial engine, 1,525 hp (1,137 kW)
Performance
　　Maximum speed: 123 mph (107 kn, 198 km/h)
　　Range: 182 miles (293 km)

Sikorsky H-3 Sea King

Crew: four
Length: 54 ft 9 in (16.7 m)
Rotor diameter: 62 ft (19 m)
Height: 16 ft 10 in (5.13 m)
Empty weight: 11,865 lb (5,382 kg)
Loaded weight: 18,626 lb (8,449 kg)
Powerplant: 2 × General Electric T58-GE-10 turboshafts, 1,400 shp (kW) each
Performance
　　Maximum speed: 166 mph (267 km/h)
　　Service ceiling: 14,700 ft (4,481 m)
　　Rate of climb: 1,310–2,220 ft/min (400–670 m/min)
Armament
　　2 × Mk 46/44 anti-submarine torpedoes
　　Various sonobuoys and pyrotechnic devices
　　B-57 nuclear depth charge

By the mid-1920s the US Navy had started to buy aircraft in batches instead of the earlier mish-mash of types approach previously followed. One such aircraft was the Vought O2U-1 Corsair, a name that would be resurrected at a later date for a famous fighter. (NASA/Dennis R. Jenkins)

Vought VE-7
Crew: two
Length: 24 ft 5³/₈ in (7.45 m)
Wingspan: 34 ft 4 in (10.47 m)
Height: 8 ft 7½ in (2.63 m)
Empty weight: 1,392 lb (631 kg)
Loaded weight: 1,937 lb (879 kg)
Powerplant: 1 × Wright-Hispano E-3 two-bladed 8 ft 8 in (2.64 m) diameter
    propeller, 180 hp (134 kW)
Performance
  Maximum speed: 106 mph (171 km/h)
  Service ceiling: 15,000 ft (4,600 m)
  Rate of climb: 738 ft/min (225 m/min)

Vought O2U Corsair
Crew: two
Length: 27 ft 5½ in (8.37 m)
Wingspan: 36 ft (10.97 m)
Height: 11 ft 4 in (3.45 m)
Empty weight: 3,312 lb (1,502 kg)
Max take-off weight: 4,765 lb (2,161 kg)
Powerplant: 1 × Pratt & Whitney R-1690-42 Hornet radial, 600 hp (447 kW)
Performance
  Maximum speed: 167 mph (269 km/h) at sea level
  Service ceiling: 18,600 ft (5,670 m)

The Vought aircraft designers would develop one of the most significant fighters of the Second World War – the F4U Corsair. Having served through much of the Pacific campaign, the Corsair would have one last chance to shine over Korea. (US Navy/NARA via Dennis R. Jenkins)

Armament
  3 × 7.62 mm Browning machine-guns

Vought F4U Corsair
Crew: one
Length: 33 ft 8 in (10.2 m)
Wingspan: 41 ft 0 in (12.5 m)
Height: 14 ft 9 in (4.50 m)
Empty weight: 9,205 lb (4,174 kg)
Loaded weight: 14,669 lb (6,653 kg)
Powerplant: 1 × Pratt & Whitney R-2800-18W radial engine, 2,450 hp (1,827 kW)
Performance
  Maximum speed: 446 mph (388 kn, 718 km/h)
  Service ceiling: 41,500 ft (12,649 m)
  Rate of climb: 3,870 ft/min (19.7 m/s)
Armament
  Guns:
    6 × 0.50 in (12.7 mm) M2 Browning machine-guns, 400 rpg or
    4 × 0.79 in (20 mm) AN/M2 cannon
  Rockets: 8 × 5 in (12.7 cm) high-velocity aircraft rockets and/or
  Bombs: 4,000 lb (1,800 kg)

Vought F7U Cutlass
Crew: one
Length: 44 ft 3 in (13.49 m)

Wingspan: 38 ft 8 in (11.79 m)
Height: 14 ft 0 in (4.27 m)
Empty weight: 18,210 lb (8,260 kg)
Max take-off weight: 31,642 lb (14,353 kg)
Powerplant: 2 × Westinghouse J46-WE-8A turbojets, 4,600 lbf (20.46 kN) each
Performance
  Maximum speed: 680 mph (590 kn, 1,095 km/h)
  Range: 660 miles (570 nmi, 1,060 km)
  Service ceiling: 40,000 ft (12,000 m)
  Rate of climb: 13,000 ft/min (67 m/s)
Armament
  Guns: 4 × 0.79 in (20 mm) M3 cannon above inlet ducts, 180 rpg
  Hardpoints: 4 with a capacity of 5,500 lb (2,500 kg)
  Missiles: AIM-7 Sparrow air-to-air missiles

Vought F-8 Crusader
Crew: one
Length: 54 ft 3 in (16.53 m)
Wingspan: 35 ft 8 in (10.87 m)
Height: 15 ft 9 in (4.80 m)
Empty weight: 17,541 lb (7,956 kg)
Loaded weight: 29,000 lb (13,000 kg)
Powerplant: 1 × Pratt & Whitney J57-P-20A afterburning turbojet
  Dry thrust: 10,700 lbf (47.6 kN)
  Thrust with afterburner: 18,000 lbf (80.1 kN)
Performance
  Maximum speed: Mach 1.86 (1,225 mph, 1,975 km/h) at 36,000 ft (11,000 m)
  Service ceiling: 58,000 ft (17,700 m)
  Rate of climb: 31,950 ft/min (162.3 m/s)
Armament
  Guns: 4 × 0.79 in (20 mm) Colt Mk 12 cannon in lower fuselage, 125 rpg
  Hardpoints:
    2 × side-fuselage-mounted Y-pylons
    2 × underwing pylon stations holding up to 4,000 lb (2,000 kg) of
    payload
  Rockets:
    2 × LAU-10 rocket pods (each with 4 × 5 in (127 mm) Zuni rockets)
  Missiles:
    4 × AIM-9 Sidewinders

US Navy Aircraft Carriers

Langley Class
Displacement:
   11,500 long tons (11,700 t)
   13,000 tons
Length: 542.3 ft (165.3 m)
Beam: 65.3 ft (19.9 m)
Draught: 18 ft 11 in (5.77 m) (as *Langley*)
Installed power: 6,500 shp (4,800 kW)
Propulsion: General Electric turbo-electric drive
   3 × boilers, 2 × shafts
Speed: 15.5 kn (17.8 mph; 28.7 km/h)
Complement: 468 officers and men (as *Langley*)
Armament: 4 × 5 in (130 mm)/51 cal guns (as *Langley*)
Armour: none
Aircraft carried: 34

CV-1 USS *Langley*, later *AV-3*

Lexington Class
Displacement:
   49,000 long tons (50,000 t) (1940),
   50,000 long tons (51,000 t) (1942)
Length: 888 ft (271 m) (overall)
Beam: 105 ft 5¼ in (32.14 m) (waterline)
   106 ft (32.31 m) (overall)
Draught: 24.25 ft (7.39 m) (design)
Propulsion (design):
   16 × boilers at 300 psi (2.1 MPa)
   Geared turbines and electric drive
   4 × shafts

The USS Langley would be the first US Navy aircraft carrier, and would spend much of its earlier career undertaking development and proving trials. With the arrival of the purpose-built vessels, the Langley became an aircraft transport, being sunk by the Japanese in February 1942. (US Navy/NARA via Dennis R. Jenkins)

180,000 shp (130 MW); 209,710 hp (156.38 MW) reached in service

Speed: 33.25 kn (61.6 km/h) (design); 34.82 kn (64.49 km/h) kn reached in service

Range: 10,000 nmi (19,000 km) at 10 kn (19 km/h)

Complement: 2,122 officers and men

Sensors and processing systems: CXAM-1 RADAR

Armament (as built):
 4 × twin 8-inch (200 mm) 55 cal guns
 12 × single 5-inch (130 mm) guns

Armour:
 Belt: 5–7 in (130–180 mm)
 2 in (51 mm) protective 3rd deck
 3 in (76 mm) flat to 4.5 in (110 mm) over steering gear

Aircraft carried: 91

CV-2 USS *Lexington*, sunk 8 May 1942

CV-3 USS *Saratoga*, Bikini Atoll atomic bomb tests 25 July 1946

Ranger Class

Displacement:
 17,577 long tons (17,859 t) (full load)

Length: 730 ft (220 m) (waterline)

769 ft (234 m) (overall)
Beam: 80 ft (24 m) (waterline)
109 ft 5 in (33.35 m) (overall)
Draught: 22 ft 4.⁷/₈ in (6.833 m)
Installed power: 53,500 shp (39,900 kW)
Propulsion: 2 × steam turbines, 6 × boilers, 2 × shafts
Speed: 29.3 kn (33.7 mph; 54.3 km/h)
Range: 10,000 nmi (12,000 miles; 19,000 km) at 15 kn (17 mph; 28 km/h)
Complement: 216 officers and 2,245 enlisted men, including embarked air
    group
Sensors and processing systems: CXAM-1 RADAR
Armament:
    8 × 5 in (130 mm)/25 cal anti-aircraft guns
    40 × 0.50 in (13 mm) machine-guns
Armour:
    Belt: 2 in (5.1 cm)
    Bulkheads: 2 in (5.1 cm)
    Deck: 1 in (2.5 cm) (over steering gear)
Aircraft carried: 86 (maximum), 76 (normal)
Aviation facilities: 3 × elevators, 3 × catapults
            CV-4 USS Ranger, decommissioned 18 October 1946

Yorktown Class
Displacement (as built):
    19,800 long tons (20,100 t) light
    25,500 long tons (25,900 t) full load
Length (as built): 770 ft (230 m)

The USS Lexington was based on the hull of a battlecruiser that had been
suspended due to the restrictions of the Washington Treaty. The Lexington
was sunk by the Japanese in May 1942. (US Navy/NARA via Dennis R.
Jenkins)

The other member of the Lexington class was the Saratoga. Unlike its companion, the Saratoga survived the war, although it was used as a target during the Bikini atom bomb tests in 1946. (US Navy/NARA via Dennis R. Jenkins)v

824 ft 9 in (251.38 m) overall
Beam (as built): 83 ft 3 in (25.37 m) (waterline)
109 ft 6 in (33.38 m) (overall)
Draught: 25 ft 11½ in (7.912 m) (as built)
Propulsion: 9 × Babcock & Wilcox boilers, 4 × Parsons geared turbines, 4 × screws
Speed: 32.5 kn (37.4 mph; 60.2 km/h)
Range: 12,500 nmi (14,400 miles; 23,200 km) at 15 kn (17 mph; 28 km/h)
Complement: 2,217 officers and men (1941)
Sensors and processing systems: CXAM-1 RADAR from 1940
Armament:
(as built:)
8 × single 5 in/38 cal guns
4 × quad 1.1 in/75 cal guns
24 × 0.50 cal machine-guns
(after February 1942:)
8 × 5 in/38 cal
4 × quad 1.1 in/75 cal
30 × 20 mm Oerlikon cannon
Armour (as built):
2.5–4 in belt
60 lb protective decks
4 in bulkheads
4 in side and 3 in top round conning tower
4 in side over steering gear
Aircraft carried (as built): 90
CV-5 USS *Yorktown*, sunk 7 June 1942

CV-6 USS *Enterprise,* decommissioned 17 February 1947
CV-7 USS *Hornet,* sunk 27 October 1942

Wasp Class
Displacement: As built: 14,700 long tons (14,900 t) (standard)
   19,116 long tons (19,423 t) (full load)
Length: 688 ft (210 m) (w/l)
   741 ft 3 in (225.93 m) (o/a)
Beam: 80 ft 9 in (24.61 m) (waterline)
   109 ft (33 m) (overall)
Draught: 20 ft (6.1 m)
Installed power: 70,000 shp (52,000 kW)
Propulsion: 2 × Parsons steam turbines, 6 × boilers, 2 × shafts
Speed: 29.5 kn (33.9 mph; 54.6 km/h)
Range: 12,000 nmi (14,000 miles; 22,000 km)
Complement: 1,800 officers and men (peacetime), 2,167 (wartime)
Sensors and processing systems: CXAM-1 RADAR
Armament (as built):
   8 × 5 in (130 mm)/38 cal guns
   16 × 1.1 in (28 mm)/75 cal anti-aircraft guns
   24 × 0.50 in (13 mm) machine-guns
Armour (as built):
   60 lb (27 kg) STS conning tower
   3.5 in side and 22 ft 6 in (6.86 m) 50 lb deck over steering gear
Aircraft carried (as built): up to 76
               CV-7 USS *Wasp,* sunk 15 September 1942

Long Island Class
Displacement: 13,499 long tons (13,716 t)
Length: 492 ft (150 m)
Beam: 69 ft 6 in (21.18 m)
Draught: 25 ft 8 in (7.82 m)
Propulsion: 1 × diesel engine, 1 × shaft
Speed: 19.0 mph (30.6 km/h)
Complement: 970 officers and enlisted men
Armament:
   1 × 5 in (130 mm)/51 cal gun
   2 × 3 in (76 mm)/50 cal guns
Aircraft carried: 21
            CVE-1 USS *Long Island,* decommissioned March 1946

Charger Class
Displacement: 8,000 long tons (8,128 t)
Length: 492 ft (150 m)
Beam: 69 ft 6 in (21.18 m)

111 ft 2 in (33.88 m) extreme width
Draught: 26 ft 3 in (8.00 m)
Propulsion: 1 × diesel engine, 1 × shaft
Speed: 17 kn (31 km/h; 20 mph)
Complement: 856 officers and enlisted men
Armament:
    1 × 5 in (130 mm) gun
    2 × 3 in/50 cal guns
    10 × 20 mm guns
Aircraft carried: 30+

             CVE-30 USS *Charger*, decommissioned March 1946

Sangamon Class

Displacement: 11,400 long tons (11,600 t) standard, 24,275 long tons (24,665 t) full
Length: 553 ft (169 m)
Beam: 114 ft 3 in (34.82 m)
Draught: 32 ft 4 in (9.86 m)
Propulsion: 2 × steam turbines, 2 × shafts
Speed: 21 mph (33 km/h)
Complement: 830 officers and men
Sensors and processing systems: SG Radar
Armament:
    2 × 5 in (130 mm)/51 cal guns (2 × 1)
    8 × 40 mm anti-aircraft guns (4 × 2)
    12 × 20 mm anti-aircraft cannons (12 × 1)
Aircraft carried: 25

             CVE-26 USS *Sangamon*, decommissioned late 1945
             CVE-27 USS *Suwannee*, decommissioned 1946
             CVE-28 USS *Chenango*, decommissioned 1946
             CVE-29 USS *Santee*, decommissioned October 1946

Bogue Class

Displacement: 9,800 tons
Length: 495.7 ft (151.1 m)
Beam: 111.5 ft (34.0 m)
Draught: 26 ft (7.9 m)
Propulsion: 2 × steam turbines, 1 × shaft
Speed: 18 kn (33 km/h)
Complement: 890 officers and men
Armament: 2 × 5 in (127 mm) guns
Aircraft carried: 24

             CVE-9 USS *Bogue*, decommissioned 1946
             CVE-11 USS *Card*, decommissioned 1970
             CVE-12 USS *Copahee*, decommissioned 1946

The USS Bogue was the name ship of this class of escort carriers. The 'jeep' carrier was developed in a hurry to satisfy the need for extra carrier decks. (US Navy/NARA via Dennis R. Jenkins)

CVE-13 USS *Core*, decommissioned 1970
CVE-16 USS *Nassau*, decommissioned 1946
CVE-18 USS *Altamaha*, decommissioned 1946
CVE-20 USS *Barnes*, decommissioned 1946
CVE-21 USS *Block Island*, sunk May 1944
CVE-23 USS *Breton*, decommissioned 1970
CVE-25 USS *Croatan*, decommissioned 1970
CVE-31 USS *Prince William*, decommissioned 1960

Essex Short Hull Class
Displacement (as built):
   27,100 tons standard
   36,380 tons full load
Length (as built):
   820 ft (250 m) waterline
   872 ft (266 m) overall
Beam (as built):
   93 ft (28 m) waterline
   147 ft 6 in (45 m) overall
Draught (as built):
   28 ft 5 in (8.66 m) light
   34 ft 2 in (10.41 m) full load
Propulsion (as designed):
   8 × boilers, 4 × Westinghouse geared steam turbines, 4 × shafts
Speed: 33 kn (61 km/h)

The Essex class of carriers served the US Navy from the Second World War until the end of the Vietnam War. This is the USS Essex wearing its Pacific campaign camouflage. (US Navy/NARA via Dennis R. Jenkins)

Range: 20,000 nmi (37,000 km) at 15 kn (28 km/h)
Complement (as built): 2,600 officers and enlisted men
Armament (as built):
    4 × twin 5 in (127 mm) 38 cal guns
    4 × single 5 in (127 mm) 38 cal guns
    8 × quadruple 40 mm 56 cal guns
    46 × single 20 mm 78 cal guns
Armour (as built):
    2.5–4 in (60–100 mm) belt
    1.5 in (40 mm) hangar and protective decks
    4 in (100 mm) bulkheads
    1.5 in (40 mm) STS top and sides of pilot house
    2.5 in (60 mm) top of steering gear
Aircraft carried (as built): 90–100
CV-9 USS *Essex*, decommissioned 30 July 1969
CV-10 USS *Yorktown*, decommissioned 27 June 1970, preserved
CV-11 USS *Intrepid*, decommissioned 15 March 1974, preserved
CV-12 USS *Hornet*, decommissioned 26 June 1970, preserved
CV-13 USS *Franklin*, decommissioned 17 February 1947, scrapped
CV-16 USS *Lexington*, decommissioned 8 November 1991, preserved
CV-17 USS *Bunker Hill*, decommissioned November 1966, scrapped
CV-18 USS *Wasp*, decommissioned 1 July 1972, scrapped
CV-20 USS *Bennington*, decommissioned 15 January 1970, scrapped
CV-31 USS *Bon Homme Richard*, decommissioned July 1971, scrapped
After the SBC modification programmes the carriers were later designated
CVA (Attack)and CVS (Anti-Submarine)

After its period as an attack carrier, the Ticonderoga was reassigned to anti-submarine duties, along with other of the Essex class. (US Navy/NARA via Dennis R. Jenkins)

Essex Long Hull Class
Displacement (as built): 27,100 tons standard
Length (as built): 888 ft (271 m) overall
Beam (as built): 93 ft (28 m) waterline
Draught (as built): 28 ft 7 in (8.71 m) light
Propulsion (as designed):
   8 × boilers, 4 × Westinghouse geared steam turbines, 4 × shafts
Speed: 33 kn (61 km/h)
Complement: 3,448 officers and enlisted men
Armament (as built):
   4 × twin 5 in (127 mm)/38 cal guns

The Ticonderoga was a member of the Essex class. It is pictured here on Yankee Station during the Vietnam War. (US Navy/NARA via Dennis R. Jenkins)

The USS Princeton was also a member of the Essex class, and would be decommissioned in January 1970. (US Navy/NARA via Dennis R. Jenkins)

4 × single 5 in (127 mm)/38 cal guns
8 × quadruple Bofors 40 mm guns
46 × single Oerlikon 20 mm cannon
Armour (as built):
4 in (100 mm) belt
2.5 in (60 mm) hangar deck
1.5 in (40 mm) protectice decks
1.5 in (40 mm) conning tower
Aircraft carried: As built: 90–100

The USS Bon Homme Richard served during the Second World War, then Korea and Vietnam, before being decommissioned in July 1971. (US Navy/NARA via Dennis R. Jenkins)

With the crew forming the name of the carrier, the USS Leyte steams on its way to Korea as part of TF.77. The carrier would also serve in Vietnam before decommissioning. (US Navy/NARA via Dennis R. Jenkins)

CV-14 USS *Ticonderoga*, decommissioned 17 October 1973, scrapped
CV-15 USS *Randolph*, decommissioned 13 February 1969, scrapped
CV-19 USS *Hancock*, decommissioned 30 January 1970, scrapped
CV-21 USS *Boxer*, decommissioned 15 May 1959, scrapped
CV-32 USS *Leyte*, decommissioned December 1969, scrapped
CV-33 USS *Kearsarge*, decommissioned 15 February 1970, scrapped
CV-34 USS *Oriskany*, decommissioned 30 September 1976, sunk as reef 2006
CV-36 USS *Antietam*, decommissioned 1 May 1973, scrapped
CV-37 USS *Princeton*, decommissioned 30 January 1970, scrapped
CV-38 USS *Shangri-La*, decommissioned 30 July 1971, scrapped
CV-39 USS *Lake Champlain*, decommissioned 1 December 1969, scrapped
CV-40 USS *Tarawa*, decommissioned 1 June 1967, scrapped
CV-45 USS *Valley Forge*, decommissioned 15 January 1970, scrapped
CV-47 USS *Philippine Sea*, decommissioned 1 December 1969, scrapped
After the SBC modification programmes the carriers were later designated CVA (Attack) the CVS (Anti-Submarine)

Independence Class
Displacement: 10,662 tons standard,
   14,751 tons loaded
Length: 623 ft (190 m)
Beam: 71.5 ft (21.8 m) (waterline)
   109.2 ft (33.3 m) (extreme)
Draught: 24.3 ft (7.4 m)
Draught: 26 ft (7.9 m)
Propulsion: General Electric turbines, 4 shafts, 4 boilers

344

The USS Cabot was a member of the Independence class of light carriers. The Cabot would be decommissioned in 1947, being passed on to the Spanish navy. (US Navy/NARA via Dennis R. Jenkins)

Speed: 31 kn (57 km/h)
Range: 13,000 nmi (24,000 km) at 15 kn (28 km/h)
Complement: 1,569 officers and men
Armament: 26 × Bofors 40 mm guns
Aircraft carried: up to 30
CVL-22 USS *Independence*, decommissioned 28 August 1946, sunk 1951
CVL-23 USS *Princeton*, sunk 24 October 1944
CVL-24 USS *Belleau Wood*, decommissioned 31 January 1947, to French Navy
CVL-25 USS *Cowpens*, decommissioned 1 November 1959
CVL-26 USS *Monterey*, decommissioned 16 January 1956, scrapped
CVL-27 USS *Langley*, decommissioned February 1947
CVL-28 USS *Cabot*, decommissioned 11 February 1947, to Spain
CVL-29 USS *Bataan*, decommissioned 9 April 1954, scrapped
CVL-30 USS *San Jacinto*, decommissioned 1 March 1947, scrapped

Casablanca Class
Displacement: 7,800 tons (standard), 10,902 tons (full load)
Length: 512 ft 4 in (156.16 m) overall
Beam: 65 ft 3 in (19.89 m),
Extreme width: 108 ft 1 in (32.94 m)
Draught: 22 ft 6 in (6.86 m)
Propulsion: 2 × 5-cylinder reciprocating Skinner Unaflow engines, 4 × boilers,
    2 × shafts
Speed: 20 kn (37 km/h)
Range: 10,240 nmi (18,960 km)
Complement: 910–16 officers and men
Armament:

1 × 5 in (127 mm)/38 cal dual-purpose gun
16 × Bofors 40 mm guns (8 × 2)
20 × Oerlikon 20 mm cannons (20 × 1)
Aircraft carried: 28

CVE-55 USS *Casablanca*, decommissioned 10 June 1946, scrapped
CVE-56 USS *Liscombe Bay*, sunk 24 November 1943
CVE-57 USS *Anzio*, decommissioned 1 March 1959, scrapped
CVE-58 USS *Coregidor*, decommissioned 30 July 1946, scrapped
CVE-59 USS *Mission Bay*, decommissioned 1 September 1958, scrapped
CVE-60 USS *Guadalcanal*, decommissioned 27 May 1958, scrapped
CVE-61 USS *Manila Bay*, decommissioned 31 July 1946, scrapped
CVE-62 USS *Natoma Bay*, decommissioned 27 May 1958, scrapped
CVE-63 USS *St Lo*, sunk 25 October 1944
CVE-64 USS *Tripoli*, decommissioned 1 February 1959, scrapped
CVE-65 USS *Wake Island*, decommissioned 5 April 1946, scrapped
CVE-66 USS *White Plains*, decommissioned 1 July 1958, scrapped
CVE-67 USS *Solomons*, decommissioned 5 June 1946, scrapped
CVE-68 USS *Kalinin Bay*, decommissioned 15 May 1946, scrapped
CVE-69 USS *Kasaan Bay*, decommissioned 6 July 1946, scrapped
CVE-70 USS *Fanshawe Bay*, decommissioned 14 August 1946, scrapped
CVE-71 USS *Kitkun Bay*, decommissioned 19 April 1946, scrapped
CVE-72 USS *Tulagi*, decommissioned 30 April 1946, scrapped
CVE-73 USS *Gambier Bay*, decommissioned 27 November 1944, scrapped
CVE-74 USS *Nehanta Bay*, decommissioned 15 May 1946, scrapped
CVE-75 USS *Hoggatt Bay*, decommissioned 15 May 1946, scrapped
CVE-76 USS *Kadashan Bay*, decommissioned 14 June 1946, scrapped
CVE-77 USS *Marcus Island*, decommissioned 12 December 1946, scrapped
CVE-78 USS *Savo Island*, decommissioned 12 December 1946, scrapped
CVE-79 USS *Ommaney Bay*, sunk 4 January 1945
CVE-80 USS *Petrof Bay*, decommissioned 27 June 1958, scrapped
CVE-81 USS *Rudyerd Bay*, decommissioned 11 June 1946, scrapped
CVE-82 USS *Saginaw Bay*, decommissioned 19 June 1946, scrapped
CVE-83 USS *Sargent Bay*, decommissioned 23 June 1958, scrapped
CVE-84 USS *Shamrock Bay*, decommissioned 27 June 1958, scrapped
CVE-85 USS *Shipley Bay*, decommissioned 28 June 1946, scrapped
CVE-86 USS *Sitkoh Bay*, decommissioned 27 July 1954, scrapped
CVE-87 USS *Steamer Bay*, decommissioned 1 March 1959, scrapped
CVE-88 USS *Cape Esperance*, decommissioned 15 January 1959, scrapped
CVE-89 USS *Takanis Bay*, decommissioned 18 June 1946, scrapped
CVE-90 USS *Thetis Bay*, decommissioned 1 March 1964, scrapped
CVE-91 USS *Makassar Bay*, decommissioned 1 September 1958, scrapped
CVE-92 USS *Windham Bay*, decommissioned 1 January 1959, scrapped
CVE-93 USS *Makin Island*, decommissioned 19 April 1946, scrapped
CVE-94 USS *Lunga Bay*, decommissioned 24 October 1946, scrapped
CVE-95 USS *Bismarck Sea*, sunk 21 February 1945

CVE-96 USS *Salamaua*, decommissioned 21 May 1946, scrapped
CVE-97 USS *Hollandia*, decommissioned 1 April 1960, scrapped
CVE-98 USS *Kwajalein*, decommissioned 16 August 1946, scrapped
CVE-99 USS *Admiralty Islands*, decommissioned 8 May 1946, scrapped
CVE-100 USS *Bougainville*, decommissioned 3 November 1946, scrapped
CVE-101 USS *Matanikau*, decommissioned 11 October 1946, scrapped
CVE-102 USS *Attu*, decommissioned 8 June 1946, scrapped
CVE-103 USS *Roi*, decommissioned 21 May 1946, scrapped
CVE-104 USS *Munda*, decommissioned 1 September 1958, scrapped

Commencement Bay Class
Displacement: 10,900 long tons (11,100 t)
Length: 557 ft (170 m)
Beam: 75 ft (23 m)
Draught: 30 ft 6 in (9.30 m)
Propulsion: 2-shaft geared turbines,
Speed: 19 kn (22 mph; 35 km/h)
Complement: 1,066
Armament: 2 × 5 in (130 mm) guns (2 ×1)
36 × 40 mm AA guns
Aircraft carried: 34

CVE-105 USS *Commencement Bay*, decommissioned 30 November 1946, scrapped
CVE-106 USS *Block Island*, decommissioned 1 July 1959, scrapped
CVE-107 USS *Gilbert Islands*, became USS Annapolis AGMR-1 in 1963
CVE-108 USS *Kula Gulf*, decommissioned 6 October 1969, scrapped
CVE-109 USS *Cape Gloucester*, decommissioned 5 November 1946, scrapped
CVE-110 USS *Salerno Bay*, decommissioned 16 February 1954, scrapped
CVE-111 USS *Vella Gulf*, decommissioned 1 December 1970, scrapped
CVE-112 USS *Siboney*, decommissioned 1 June 1970, scrapped
CVE-113 USS *Puget Sound*, decommissioned 1 June 1960, scrapped
CVE-114 USS *Rendova*, decommissioned 1 April 1971, scrapped
CVE-115 USS *Bairoko*, decommissioned 18 February 1955, scrapped
CVE-116 USS *Badoeng Strait*, decommissioned 17 May 1957, scrapped
CVE-117 USS *Saidor*, decommissioned 1 December 1970, scrapped
CVE-118 USS *Sicily*, decommissioned 1 July 1960, scrapped
CVE-119 USS *Point Cruz*, decommissioned 15 September 1970, scrapped
CVE-120 USS *Mindoro*, decommissioned 1 December 1959, scrapped
CVE-121 USS *Rabaul*, decommissioned 1 September 1971, scrapped
CVE-122 USS *Palau*, decommissioned 15 June 1954, scrapped
CVE-123 USS *Tinian*, decommissioned 1 June 1970, scrapped

Midway Class
Displacement: 45,000 tons at commissioning
74,000 tons at decommissioning

Length: 972 ft (296 m)
Beam: 113 ft (34.4 m)
    136 ft (41.5 m); 238 ft (72.5 m) at flight deck after modernisation
Draught: 34.5 ft (10.5 m)
Propulsion: 12 × boilers, 4 × shafts
Speed: 33 kn (60 km/h)
Complement: 4,104 officers and men
Armament:
    (at commissioning:)
    18 × 5 in/54 cal Mk 16 guns
    84 × Bofors 40 mm guns
    68 × Oerlikon 20 mm cannon
    (at decommissioning:)
    2 × 8-cell Sea Sparrow launchers
    2 × Phalanx CIWS
Aircraft carried: 137 theoretical, 100 (WW2–Korea), 65 (Vietnam–retirement)
    CVB-41 USS *Midway*, decommissioned 11 April 1992, preserved
    CVB-42 USS *Franklin D. Roosevelt*, decommissioned 30 September 1977,
                                        scrapped
    CVB-43 USS *Coral Sea*, decommissioned 26 April 1990, scrapped

Saipan Class
Displacement: 14,500 tons
Length: 684 ft (208 m)
Beam: 76.8 ft (23.4 m) (waterline)
    115 ft (35.1 m) (overall)
Draught: 28 ft (8.5 m)
Propulsion: 4 × boilers, 4 × shafts
Speed: 33 kn

CV-61 USS Ranger was the third carrier of the Forrestal class of vessels, and would remain in commission until July 1993. (US Navy/NARA via Dennis R. Jenkins)

CVA-60 USS Saratoga would see active service during the Vietnam War, followed by service during Operation Desert Storm before withdrawal in 1994. (US Navy/NARA via Dennis R. Jenkins)

Complement: 1,721 officers and men
Armament: 40 × Bofors 40 mm guns
Aircraft carried: 50+ aircraft
        CVL-48 USS *Saipan*, decommissioned 14 January 1970, scrapped
        CVL-49 USS *Wright*, decommissioned 27 May 1970, scrapped

Forrestal Class

Displacement: 59,650 tons standard
    81,101 tons full load
Length: 990 ft (300 m) at waterline
    1,067 ft (325 m) overall
Beam: 129 ft 4 in (39.42 m);
    238 ft (72.5 m) extreme width
Draught: 37 ft (11 m)
Propulsion: Steam turbines, 4 shafts
Speed: 33 kn (61 km/h)
Complement: 552 officers, 4988 enlisted men
Armament:
    8 × 5 in/54 Mk 42 guns (removed)
    Mk 29 NATO Sea Sparrow
    Mk 15 Phalanx CIWS
Aircraft carried: 90
        CVA-59 USS *Forrestal*, decommissioned 11 September 1993
        CVA-60 USS *Saratoga*, decommissioned 20 August 1994
        CVA-61 USS *Ranger*, decommissioned 10 July 1993
        CVA-62 USS *Independence*, decommissioned 8 March 2004

The USS Kitty Hawk was the lead ship of the Kitty Hawk/Improved Forrestal class of carriers. The Kitty Hawk would remain operational until May 2009. (US Navy/NARA via Dennis R. Jenkins)

Kitty Hawk Class

Displacement: 61,351 long tons (62,335 t)
  81,985 long tons (83,301 t) full load
Length: 1,068.9 ft (325.8 m)
Beam: 282 ft (86 m) extreme
  130 ft (40 m) waterline
Draught: 40 ft (12 m)
Propulsion: Westinghouse geared steam turbines, 8 × steam boilers, 4 × shafts
Speed: 33 kn (61 km/h)
Complement: 5,624 officers and men
Armament:
  RIM-7 Sea Sparrow surface-to-air missiles
  2 × RIM-116 RAM
  2 × Phalanx CIWS automated anti-missile/aircraft defences
Aircraft carried: 85

CVA-63 USS *Kitty Hawk*, decommissioned 12 May 2009
CVA-64 USS *Constellation*, decommissioned 7 August 2003
CVA-66 USS *America*, decommissioned 9 August 1996, sunk
CVA-67 USS *John F. Kennedy*, decommissioned 23 March 2007

Enterprise Class
Displacement: 73,858 long tons (75,043 t) (standard)
  92,325 long tons (93,807 t) loaded
Length: 1,123 ft (342 m)[2]
Beam: 132.8 ft (40.5 m) (waterline)
  257.2 ft (78.4 m) (extreme)
Draught: 39 ft (12 m)
Propulsion: 8 × Westinghouse A2W nuclear reactors, four sets Westinghouse
  geared steam turbines, 4 × shafts
Speed: 33.6 kn (38.7 mph; 62.2 km/h)
Range: Essentially unlimited distance; 20 years
Complement: 5,828 (maximum)
Sensors and processing systems:
  AN/SPS-48 3D air search radar
  AN/SPS-49 2D air search radar
Electronic warfare and decoys:
  AN/SLQ-32
  Mk 36 SRBOC
Armament:
  2 × NATO Sea Sparrow launchers
  2 × 20 mm Phalanx CIWS mounts
  2 × RAM launchers
Armour: 8 in (20 cm) aluminum belt (equivalent to 4 in (10 cm))
Aircraft carried: up to 90
    CVN-65 USS *Enterprise*, Active Fleet

The USS Constellation would serve in both the Vietnam War and in the Arabian Gulf before decommissioning in August 2003. (US Navy/NARA via Dennis R. Jenkins)

Nimitz Class
Displacement: Approx. 101,000 long tons (103,000 t) full load
Length: 1,092 ft (332.8 m) (overall)
   1,040 ft (317.0 m) (waterline)
Beam: 252 ft (76.8 m) (overall)
   134 ft (40.8 m) (waterline)
Draught: Max navigational: 37 ft (11.3 m)
Limit: 41 ft (12.5 m)
Propulsion: 2 × Westinghouse A4W nuclear reactors, 4 × steam turbines, 4 × shafts
Speed: 31.5 kn (58.3 km/h)
Range: Essentially unlimited distance; 20 years
Complement:
   Ship's company: 3,200
   Air wing: 2,480
Sensors and processing systems:
   AN/SPS-48E 3-D air search radar
   AN/SPS-49(V)5 2-D air search radar
   AN/SPQ-9B target acquisition radar
   AN/SPN-46 air traffic control radars
   AN/SPN-43C air traffic control radar
   AN/SPN-41 landing aid radars
   4 × Mk 91 NSSM guidance systems
   4 × Mk 95 radars
Electronic warfare and decoys:
   SLQ-32A(V)4 countermeasures suite
   SLQ-25A Nixie torpedo countermeasures
Armament:
   2 × 21 cell Sea RAMs
   2 × Mk 29 Sea Sparrows
Aircraft: 89

CVN-68 USS *Nimitz*, Active Fleet
CVN-69 USS *Dwight D. Eisenhower*, Active Fleet
CVN-70 USS *Carl Vinson*, Active Fleet
CVN-71 USS *Theodore Roosevelt*, Active Fleet
CVN-72 USS *Abraham Lincoln*, Active Fleet
CVN-73 USS *George Washington*, Active Fleet
CVN-74 USS *John C. Stennis*, Active Fleet
CVN-75 USS *Harry S. Truman*, Active Fleet
CVN-76 USS *Ronald Reagan*, Active Fleet
CVN-77 USS *George H.W. Bush*, Active Fleet

Ford Class
Displacement: 100,000 long tons (approx. 101,600 metric tons or 112,000 short tons)

The USS Ronald Reagan was a late-build member of the nuclear-powered Nimitz class of vessels. (US Navy/NARA via Dennis R. Jenkins)

Length: 1,092 ft (333 m)
Beam: 134 ft (41 m)
Propulsion: 2 × A1B nuclear reactors
Speed: 30+ kn (34 mph; 56 km/h)
Complement: 4,660
Armament:
Surface-to-air missiles
Close-in weapons systems
Aircraft carried: more than 75
Aviation facilities: 1,092 × 256 ft (333 × 78 m) flight deck

CVN-78 USS *Gerald R. Ford*, under construction
CVN-79 Unnamed

Bibliography

Chesneau, Roger, Aircraft Carriers of the World: 1914 to the Present: an Illustrated Encyclopedia, Brockhampton Publishing, ISBN-13 9781860198755

Marolda, Edward J., The U.S. Navy in the Korean War, US Naval Institute Press, ISBN-13 9781591144878

Polmar, Norman, Chronology of the Cold War at Sea, 1945–1991, Naval Institute Press, ISBN-13 9781557506856

Rohwer, Jurgen, *Chronology of the War at Sea 1939–1945: The Naval History of World War Two*, Chatham Publishing, ISBN-13 9781861762573

Swanborough, Gordon, and Bowers, Peter M., *United States Navy Aircraft Since 1911*, Naval Institute Press, ISBN-13 9780870217920

Index

356